GEOFFREY GIULIANO is a top international biographer and authority on popular culture. His previous books include *The Beatles: A Celebration; John Lennon, My Brother* (written with Lennon's sister, Julia Baird); *Dark Horse: The Life and Art of George Harrison; The Beatles Album: Thirty Years of Music and Memorabilia; Rod Stewart: Vagabond Heart; Not Fade Away: The Rolling Stones Album: Thirty Years of Music and Memorabilia; The Illustrated Series; Paint It Black: The Murder of Brian Jones; The Lost Beatles Interviews; The Lost John Lennon Interviews;* and *Behind Blue Eyes: A Life of Pete Townshend.* Giuliano can be heard regularly on the Westwood One Radio Network. In addition, he has created a line of audio rocumentaries for Durkin Hayes Publishing as well as a series of biographical CD box sets and video documentaries on various popular musicians for Laserlight Digital. He is also a 25-year student of Vedic philosophy and culture, and an enthusiastic animal rights activist.

BRENDA GIULIANO is coauthor of *Not Fade Away: The Rolling Stones Collection; The Illustrated Series; The Lost Beatles Interviews;* and *The Lost John Lennon Interviews.*

Executive researcher DEBORAH LYNN BLACK is coauthor of several popular books, including *Gloria: The Autobiography of Gloria Hunniford,* as well as dozens of magazine articles in publications around the world. She has worked extensively with Giuliano on many past book projects.

Associate researcher, STEVEN GALBRAITH is a graduate of the State University of New York at Buffalo. In addition to writing, he composes and performs music. This is his second book with Geoffrey Giuliano.

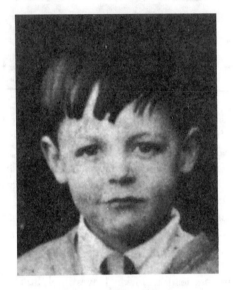

James Paul McCartney
circa 1946, aged four.

BLACKBIRD

THE LIFE AND TIMES OF

Paul McCartney

GEOFFREY GIULIANO

UPDATED EDITION

DA CAPO PRESS • NEW YORK

Library of Congress Cataloging-in-Publication Data

Giuliano, Geoffrey.
  Blackbird: the life and times of Paul McCartney / Geoffrey Giuliano.
—Updated ed.
    p.   cm.
  Includes bibliographical references and index.
  ISBN 0-306-80781-5 (alk. paper)
  1. McCartney, Paul. 2. Rock musicians—England—Biography. I. Title.
ML410.M115G58 1997
782.42166'092—dc21
[b]   97-21945
                                                                     CIP
                                                                      MN

Text design and pagination: Lynda Powell

First Da Capo Press edition 1997

This Da Capo Press paperback edition of *Blackbird* is an unabridged
republication of the edition first published in Toronto, Canada in 1991,
with the addition of a substantial new chapter, updated appendices,
and new photos. It is reprinted by arrangement with the author.

Published by Da Capo Press, Inc.
A Subsidiary of Plenum Publishing Corporation
233 Spring Street, New York, N.Y. 10013

JAI SRI GURU AND GAURANGA

Dedicated to the Supreme Lord, Sri Paramatma within the heart. To His Divine Grace A. C. Bhaktivedanta Swami Prabphupada for the knowledge and inspiration. To my family and friends for a lifetime of love. To Brenda for her patience and devotion. To my son Devin, because I still remember how hard it was to be a boy. And to my brother, Robert Noel Giuliano. God Speed.

—Om Tat Sat—

"A man without charity in his heart — what has he to do with music?"

— Confucius —

"I like peasant people. We're peasants too, from all corners of the globe, a gang of peasants who want to be in musical entertainment. This is the whole idea. It's like in medieval days. A few people just got together and made some music to make themselves happy, and then to make other people happy off it. And that's really all it is for me."

—Paul McCartney—

Contents

Blue Nights
A Foreword by Denny Laine

A piece of me, a piece of you,
A piece of both of us is gone, that's true.
I recall the leaves that fall and never leave a clue.
All the nights, all the nights are blue.

Something lost, nothing gained,
The pieces of the broken chain remain.
Unfree from memories of life I spent with you,
All the nights, all the nights are blue.

— From "Blue Nights" by Denny Laine —

As my old band, Denny and the Diplomats, ended our set at the Plaza Ballroom, Old Hill, Birmingham, on July 5, 1963, the clumsy revolving stage slowly turned, revealing the Beatles, Britain's number-one teen rave, touring the country on the strength of their smash single "From Me to You." I remember we all shared the same dressing room, and even though safely out of the line of fire from the fans the Beatles still studiously scrawled out their autographs on a huge pile of glossies plopped down in front of them by their trusty roadie, big Mal Evans, all the while cracking joke after joke.

Although not naturally envious, I must admit I was suitably impressed to try to become part of that world if I could. Ultimately, I guess the Moody Blues became my ticket to ride, and London the place where fate decreed we all would settle. As far as the Moodies and the Beatles well-known alliance is concerned, the old Ad Lib Club off Leicester Square became the place where we actually founded and expanded our now life-long friendships. It was also the same jolly watering hole in which we invented a heady, all-purpose elixir called scotch and Coke. Afterwards, we'd generally stumble out into the street and go for breakfast together at 5:00 a.m. It was quite a lovely, intolerable row!

Early on, quite frankly, the Moodies became rather more famous for our anything-goes get-togethers at our communal house in Roehampton than for our music. All the people of the day came along to meet their friendly rivals at our parties — Tom Jones, the Stones, Eric Burdon, and the Beatles, to name but a few. A lot of very important people in the business owe at least their initial introductions to that fine old house on Rowdean Crescent, and of course, plenty of great memories as well.

George became my first Beatle friend, and proudly we remain pals to this day. I often drove down to his house in Esher to spend the weekend with George and his girlfriend (later missus), the blonde and beautiful Pattie Boyd. We didn't really get up to too much of any great importance beyond sitting together in the garden, playing acoustic guitars and sipping George's signature red wine. Let's just say we hung out together at a time when hanging out was elevated almost to high art.

Around the same time, fellow Moodie Mike Pinder and I were over at John's house in Weybridge one evening to watch a film of the Beatles' Shea Stadium gig. I remember Julian was upstairs sleeping and Cynthia being the absolutely perfect hostess. On another occasion, after I had left the band, I recall sitting in somebody's flat in London with John when Pinder came rushing in on fire to play us an early acetate of the Moodies' *Days of Future Passed* LP. As majestic as that album obviously is, after about three or four times through both John and I were strongly hinting that too much of even a good thing was perhaps too much. Pinder, in his eternal enthusiasm, however, was lost to any such subtlety, and in the end we just about had to thump him to turn the bloody thing off.

As for the genesis of my relationship with Paul, I suppose that really started round the time the Moody Blues were invited to join the Beatles on one of their early British tours. An ambitious guy even then, Paul tried for ages to get me to record the song "Those Were the Days" (later an international mega-hit for Welsh songbird, Mary Hopkin). I'm sorry now I didn't take him up on the offer. From square one it was obvious we had a strong mutual respect going and always had a good laugh whenever we got together. While we were touring with the Beatles, Paul would invariably stand sidestage watching the Moodies close the first half of the show, rocking away quietly to our shaky white-boy blues. Years later when he rang up out of the blue one afternoon and invited me to join Wings, I was obviously pleased, but frankly, not all that surprised. Playing with Paul always seemed very natural for me, even if it was just busking together backstage in the dressing room. As they used to say so often in London music circles back then, the "vibe" was right.

As far as Wings is concerned, I think we managed quite a lot of very respectable work overall, and we certainly had some wicked fun. Working so closely with Paul in the studio was both exhilarating and challenging. Overcoming our first admittedly uncertain experiences on the road, by the time the 1976 Wings Over America tour rolled around we were razor-sharp and rock-steady. All in all, being an integral part of such a well-oiled and pampered machine as Wings was an experience I will never forget. Not a bad way to spend the better part of one's youth either!

Nowadays it seems Paul and I actually don't talk all that much anymore, but I still love the guy. Like anyone else, Paul is at times capable of being outrageous, funny, normal, brilliant, happy, sad, loving and, at the same time, occasionally as tough as nails, which of course is what helps to make him the musical giant he is — just the right blend of humanness, whimsy, and genius.

Unfortunately, a few years back, while living in Spain, I fell in with some fairly shady journalists who interviewed me extensively for a proposed biography and then bounced back to Britain and hacked away at the transcripts until they had what they felt were the makings of a first-rate gutter-press exposé. After it was flogged off to the highest bidder without so much as a word to old muggins here, the next thing the whole world thinks is McCartney and I are bitter enemies. As far as I'm concerned, though, Paul and I are still friends, maybe even brothers, but definitely a great team musically. I know that. Deep down Paul does too. So what else really matters?

I've known and worked with Geoffrey Giuliano for some time now and, like everything else the frantic, magic man puts his hand to, *Blackbird* hits home with a truth and authenticity seldom found in today's raunchy rock biographies. And it couldn't have been written by a more congenial geezer. Giuliano shares a covenant not only with Paul McCartney's music but also with the man and his message. Cheers, Geoff!

As for the rest of you lot, if you really want to get to know the real Macca, then read on. You won't readily find a more carefully crafted and compelling portrait.

Denny Laine
New Year's Day, 1990
Washburn House
Lockport, New York

Preface
Through the Looking Glass

To attempt to portray accurately via paper and ink the life of anyone is at best a risky business, at worst a grave insult to the mystical powers of heaven and earth from which we spring. With this, my fifth Beatles-related work, I can warrant the reader at least a reasonably well-researched fling in the general direction of one of Liverpool's most famous sons.

The Beatles were like a great stone thrown into the water. While the immediate, explosive splash may well have subsided, the far-ranging ripples of their great, inspired work certainly haven't. And despite Paul's commercial ups and downs of recent years, to the educated listener his music still has the power to entertain and enlighten in a way far beyond the scope of most of today's so-called current artists.

He composes, one is told, like a man possessed, his quicksilver intellect at any given moment teeming with more ideas than any ten albums might comfortably contain. That he sometimes has trouble editing down this embarrassment of riches to only the very best his musical muse delivers is certainly understandable.

That he is a master of his milieu is unquestioned. After all, even if McCartney were unable to ever again spin out another magical melody, his position in the rock 'n' roll pantheon is already assured. One of popular music's most sensibly down-to-earth demi-gods, nevertheless, McCartney is still a man of great mystery, perhaps the most affable enigma ever to grace the music business. Interviewed at astonishing length over and over about literally everything he has ever thought, felt, or done, McCartney triumphs as the crown prince of serious-sounding double talk. Ask him what he thinks about apartheid or Thatcher's Britain, and he will answer frankly with convincing logic and straightforward honesty. Try to uncover what really makes the man tick over, however, and he will look you straight in the eye, talk for fifteen minutes without pause, and, just as effortlessly as Dickens' Artful Dodger, bamboozle the pants off you.

Of course Paul McCartney, as always, speaks most eloquently through his by-now phenomenally eclectic body of music. That he chooses to continue working at all after having done so much is a measure of his discipline and dedication. "So, what is there left for you to do?" a reporter asked him after he had been presented with the Guinness Book of Records award in 1977 as the bestselling composer of all time. "Whatever there was to begin with," McCartney replied. "I'm not interested in resting on my laurels."

For James Paul McCartney, pushing the limits has become a way of life.

Geoffrey Giuliano
August 1991
On board the *Vrinda Rani*
Hudson River
Hyde Park, New York

Acknowledgments

I wish to thank my editor, Glen Ellis, and project production manager, Clive Powell, for their faith, professionalism and care, and the countless hours.

I would also like to thank the following for their kind assistance and encouragement: James Adams; Raymond and Mozelle Black; Carol Bonnett; Larry Brown; Stefano Castino; Pat Cherry; Matt Conley; Sriman Balabadra Dasa; Fisher's Newsroom (Albion); Kate Forster; Andrea Gallagher Ellis; Chauncey Gardner; Brenda Giuliano; Sesa, Devin, Avalon, and India Giuliano; Lenore Gray; Tim Hailstone; Richie Havens; Heidi Jo Hines; Laine Hines; House of Guitars (Rochester); ISKCON Toronto; Carla Johnson; Joseph and Myrna Juliana; Alcides Antino King, Esq.; Bill King; Denny Laine; Jo Jo Laine; Leif Leavesley; Donald Lehr; William Linehan Autographs; Constance Lofton; Don Loney; David L. MacIntyre; His Divine Grace B. H. Mangal Maharaj; Mark Studios; Doctor Marty; McGraw-Hill Ryerson; Judy McGuire; Melanie; Hayley Mills; MGA (Toronto); Kevin Mulroy; NAL/Dutton; Nigel Newton; The Nolan/Lehr Group; Boston Kane Paris Peter Phillip O'Donahue; John Otto; Wilder Penfield III; Jane Price and Summer; Dimo Safari; Rajeswar Singh; Timothy Smith; Wendell Smith; Lydia Smith; Vivian Stanshall; Brandon Stickney; Dennis Toll and family; Pamela and Holly Toenniessen; Pete Townshend; Anthony Violanti; Bill Wilbur; and Ronald Zuker.

I used to worry a lot about death when I was a kid. Now the fear of it means less and less to me. You know, when we were all the rage, we all used round-the-clock bodyguards because we genuinely feared for our lives. Now that we've been disbanded for so long it's a great relief that the terror has finally disappeared from our lives.

— John Lennon, 1980 —

We, ourselves, were each other's best friends. There were moments we touched each other's soul.

—Paul McCartney, 1988 —

1

Brief December

The Murder of John Lennon

A lone, in the dimly lit bedroom she had shared with John Lennon for the previous seven years, Yoko Ono walked soundlessly across the plush white carpet to a large mahogany bureau at the far end of the room. There, carefully turning through the pages of John's old, oversized address book, she stopped, finally, at an entry scrawled haphazardly across the journal's tatty inside back cover. Picking up the telephone she wondered if the number would still be any good. So much time had passed. So many heartaches. And now, the cruelest blow of all.

"Hello." It was a child's voice, faraway, on the other end of the wobbly transatlantic line.

"Who's calling, please?"

"Oh, hi." She struggled to find her normal speaking voice. "Is your daddy at home? It's Yoko."

A few, muffled, anxious moments later, Paul McCartney picked up the line.

"Yoko?" he said, his voice already full of surprise and obvious concern. "What's the matter?"

"It's John." She replied, attempting to control herself. "He's dead. Someone shot him. Can you believe it?"

A world away, standing in the cluttered kitchen of his tiny circular farmhouse in rural Sussex, McCartney looked helplessly towards his wife, Linda, who, minutes before had been busily preparing breakfast for her two youngest children.

"I don't know what to say," he finally answered. "Why? It can't be." And then simply, "No. . . my God."

Two hours later, just after noon on Tuesday, December 9, 1980, McCartney emerged from his home enroute to a Wings recording session at George Martin's AIR Studios in London, commenting only briefly to reporters assembled outside that he was far too shocked and upset to properly "take it in" at the moment and that John was a great man who would be remembered for his unique contributions to art, music, and peace. With that he drove off with Linda in their silver Volvo station wagon, silently lost in his thoughts for the two-hour-plus drive to London.

His current musical collaborator, Denny Laine, was also shaken by the news. He had arrived early for the session and was quietly remembering his rowdy Moody Blues days hanging out with Lennon when Paul and Linda arrived. McCartney put a call through to Yoko in New York. In the course of their conversation she told him just how fond her husband had been of him despite the many verbal barbs the often caustic Lennon had unleashed upon his former partner in recent years concerning their tempestuous, twenty-four-year relationship. Underneath it all, she said, John had been secretly proud of McCartney's astounding solo success, and had often remarked that, as an amateur talent scout, he really hadn't done too badly in discovering someone of Paul's superlative abilities. Besides, the occasionally crusty Lennon would argue, it's one thing for families to row, quite another to allow anyone else to have a go. To John's mind, anyway, said Yoko, he and McCartney had always remained brothers. Brawling brothers maybe, but family nonetheless.

Although he appreciated her kind words, especially considering the horrific pain she was herself experiencing, McCartney wasn't easily comforted and sought some measure of solace in his work in the studio. Session musician Paddy Mahoney was on board that afternoon and recalls what he perceived to be a get-on-with-the-job attitude among McCartney and the rest of Wings. "There was a kind of unspoken sadness," he later commented, "like when you lose an old soccer mate. It was subtle and there wasn't any crying or moping about. I don't think it had really sunk in yet."

Outside, the parasitic media were swarming all over each other, frantically trying to capture every drop of emotion they could squeeze out of their unwilling and very vulnerable prey. No Beatle or close family member was immune to their unwelcome scrutiny. With no confirmed sightings of McCartney for several hours straight, the circling British tabloid vultures began ritually feeding off themselves, rushing to phone boxes to call in reports of some of their colleagues' over-zealous efforts to get a peak at his private pain by scaling the wrought-iron fire escape system that clung to the exterior of the four-storey-high private studios. Wisely taking no chances with McCartney's personal safety, his office in Soho Square retained an elite corps of specially trained anti-terrorist bodyguards to help ease back the rapidly swelling crowds, attracted by all the fuss outside AIR and by the creeping awareness that Lennon's death was very much history in the making, one final blaze of publicity in a career filled with wild and outrageous acts.

Going through the motions of another rocking workday up at AIR, McCartney wasn't really fooling anybody, least of all Denny Laine, who at the time was perhaps his closest and most trusted friend. Laine remembers:

The really strange thing was that I went to work that morning somehow knowing Paul would ultimately show up — despite what had happened. Of course, from the point of view of his Liverpool upbringing, the best way to deal with something like that is to keep right on doing what you'd normally do. It helps to take your mind off it — being with friends, I suppose, even though it did occur to me that he might have just as easily rung up and cancelled the session. I remember the first thing he said to me was, "I just don't know what to think." He was obviously physically shaken, and even at the best of times wasn't really too articulate when it came to expressing how he felt about things. After one of the takes Paul and I were just hanging out, leaning up against AIR's huge floor-to-ceiling windows over-looking Oxford Circus, when I happened to notice this dark green truck going by that said LENNON FURNISHINGS or some-thing like that. "Oh God, look at that," I said, and he just sort of broke down, you know? "I'll tell you one thing, man," he said, "I'll never fall out with *anyone* again in my life for that amount of time and face the possibility of them dying before I get a chance to square it with them."

After that I never consciously mentioned anything about it. If he wanted to talk about it he did, and if he didn't, well, he didn't. Everybody in the world was very hurt by John's death, but especially Paul McCartney.

Making his way to the car following the seven-hour session, McCartney was momentarily cornered by the now deadline-frantic media who later quoted him as saying he hoped that everyone would "rally round Yoko." When pressed by one particularly aggressive microphone to comment on how he felt about Lennon's assassination, he grimaced slightly and, hanging precariously on the edge of tears, tossed off, "It's a drag, man," as he dove into the back of the waiting car. They were four words he would live to regret.

Within twenty-four hours headlines around the world pro-claimed the lie that McCartney had remained callously un-moved by his former partner's death, and when questioned, actually came off as being quite flip and even casual about the tragedy. For those who don't yet know it, however, nothing could be further from the truth. Denny Laine recalls: "I don't really understand what it was the media thought they'd got on him, I mean, it *was* a drag! What else do you say? What do you do, write a bloody book there and then? He might have burst into tears had he gone on, who knows? Of course the real fuckin' drag was having to face some asshole sticking a mike in your face, harassing you for a quote at a time like that. Of course it happens every day on the telly — 'Excuse me Mrs. Blootch, you've just lost your entire family to an escaped loony with a chainsaw. What's running through your mind?' I mean *really*, you tell me who's being callous? The public's 'right to know' doesn't give anyone license to badger people."

In part, to try to quell the uproar set spinning by this avalanche of nasty publicity, McCartney attempted to set the record straight once and for all by issuing the following "official" statement to the world's press:

> I have hidden myself in my work today. But it keeps flashing into my mind. I feel shattered, angry, and very sad. It's just ridiculous. He was pretty rude about me sometimes, but I secretly admired him for it, and I always managed to stay in touch with him. There was no question that we weren't friends — I really loved the guy. I think that what has happened will in years to come make people realize that John was an international statesman. He often looked a loony to many people. He made enemies, but he was fantastic. He was a warm man who cared a lot and with the record "Give Peace a Chance" he helped stop the Vietnam War. He made a lot of sense.

If this heartfelt statement wasn't enough to curb the media's demand for atonement, McCartney later dedicated an entire issue of MPL's (McCartney Productions Limited) fan club publication, Club Sandwich, to Lennon's memory. It included a beautiful full-color portfolio of Linda's touching photographs of him. There was also, of course, McCartney's soulful panegyric to Lennon, "Here Today," on his masterful, *Tug of War* album of 1982, as well as the appearance of the McCartneys and Denny Laine on George Harrison's tuneful tribute "All Those Years Ago."

For McCartney the specter of untimely death was nothing new. Throughout his turbulent life he has had to endure the unnatural passing of not only his mother, Mary, but also Beatles bassist Stuart Sutcliffe, Brian Epstein, Wings guitarist Jimmy McCulloch, as well as his close friend, Keith Moon. Although deeply moved, he was generally quite stoic. Ironically, it took the tragic death of a stranger to emotionally uncork the naturally reserved McCartney and force him to begin to come to terms with the tenuous nature of his own life journey. It occurred in October of 1980 in the tiny village of Tenterden, in Kent. Wings had been rehearsing in a manor house rented from prominent London publisher Martin Miller when they heard the terrible sounds of a car crash outside the main gates. Laine recalls: "Apparently, this young Japanese *au pair* girl who worked for the Millers was taking their infant daughter, Cara, for a walk in her pram when this supposedly drunken driver tried to overtake another car and knocked them both down. The baby flew up into the air and landed unhurt by a hedgerow, but the poor *au pair* was very badly injured."

Dashing outside, McCartney and Laine instructed Wings' road manager Trevor Jones to get the van and drive the little girl and her hysterical mother to a nearby hospital while they did what they could for the semi-conscious young woman until the summoned medical help arrived.

> I was actually the first to reach her, but Paul dove right in and started nursing her, trying to do what he could. I mean he certainly wasn't frightened of blood. It was obvious to both of us she had suffered very severe internal injuries and that unless there was some kind of miracle she probably wouldn't make it. I remember there was blood pouring out of her ears, and her eyes were rolled way back in her head. It was just terrible.

To make matters worse, being so far out in the countryside the ambulance took well over an hour to wind its way through the area's twisting, largely unmarked, lanes. McCartney, however, never moved an inch, all the while sitting there by the side of the road, cradling her head in his lap. Laine reflects: "Paul was just saying things like, 'It'll be alright, luv, don't worry,' but we were getting no response. At one point he glanced over at me and slowly shook his head. He knew. We both knew. Still, he just sat there stroking her long black hair, talking and sometimes even singing softly as she lay there dying."

That evening, in an East Sussex hospital, twenty-one-year-old Hisako Kawahara died of her injuries. Out of respect for the privacy of the Kawahara and Miller families, McCartney ordered his London office to enforce a tight media ban on his assistance.

"I'm a bit of a cover-up," McCartney commented in October of 1986. "There are many people like me in the world who don't find it easy to have public grief. But that was one of the things that brought John and I very close together. We used to talk about it, being sixteen or seventeen. We actually used to know how people felt when they said, 'How's your mother?' and we'd say, 'Well, she's dead.' We almost had a sort of joke; we'd have to say, 'It's alright, don't worry.' We'd both lost our mothers. It was never really spoken about much; no-one really spoke about anything real. There was a famous expression: 'Don't get real on me, man.'"

Perhaps the most telling tale as regards McCartney's inability to either exhibit real emotion or open up to those around him has to do with his father's passing. Denny remembers:

We were in Paris. Wings had just done a great show so we were all in pretty high spirits. Afterwards we shuffled down to this press conference where we met up with our old pal David Cassidy. I remember Paul was struggling to answer all these typically mundane questions from the media while David did his best to crack us all up, making faces and stuff just behind the camera. Eventually this one guy pipes up and asks Paul if either of his parents are still living, to which he offhandedly replies simply, "No."

At that point Laine just about fell off his chair. The tight-lipped McCartney had never so much as mentioned a word to anyone about his father's death, which both surprised and hurt the sensitive Laine. "Over the years I'd become pretty close to old Jim," he confides, "and I was pretty upset that Paul had never bothered to let me know what was up. You see, Paul is very publicly shy in some ways but unfortunately, he's also quite privately shy as well. What can I say? It was just his personality."

The death of John Lennon put an abrupt and unhappy end to speculation about a possible Beatles reunion. The band had almost magically metamorphosed over the years from the black-leather-clad Cavern Club rockers to the four cheeky lads with the daring hairdos and collarless jackets first seen by most North Americans on Ed Sullivan's "really big shoe" in the winter of 1964. Over the next three years they further evolved into the introspective, psychedelic lords of London, resplendent in neo-Edwardian finery, purveyors of eerie otherworldly love songs from the edge of the galaxy. In their final incarnation, as the thirtyish Picassos of recorded sound, they had become a musical collective of such staggeringly successful proportions as to eventually collapse under the weight of their own shared fame.

Finally, even the longstanding brotherly bond was strained to the limit and beyond, disintegrating amidst salvos of accusation. "It's a simple fact," said Lennon of McCartney. "He can't get his own way so he's causing havoc."

McCartney, in particular, seemed to come out of it all feeling dejected and depressed. Photographs from that period depict a downcast Paul, hands dug deep into his pockets, burly beard, big, sad eyes, and slow, round-shouldered gait. Never mind the breezy let's-look-to-the-future banter he was giving out to the media, the body language alone was undeniable. "My overwhelming feeling was I was of no use anymore, my usefulness was gone," McCartney told interviewer Bernard Goldberg in 1990. "What do I do now? What am I? You *were* one of the Beatles! That was the frightening bit, you once *were.* I thought, God, I'm not at retirement age yet. I can't just swan off to a desert island. I've got to do something."

With more than two decades of post-Beatles work behind him, McCartney has emerged as the wide-eyed Everyman of rock 'n' roll, clinging to a deftly manufactured image of whimsy and inherited family normalcy. It is tempting to imagine him at home with Earth Mother Linda, sitting by the fire at night, toking a joint, tittering about the crafty way he's been having us on all these years, a hippie Dorian Gray living out his wildest fantasies at the public's expense. Or, is it possible he actually *is* every bit the self-effacing, good-natured Liverpool lad he's always insisted?

The rock supernova, the laid-back family man, the shepherd, the ethereal Fool of the Tarot card, effortlessly overstepping his earthly boundaries and waltzing away on thin air — the real McCartney is cleverly obscured, but partially revealed, by a facade of images. Even those who have been closest to him say that despite all the airy, Beatlesque humor, and good-natured, thumbs-up clowning, the McCartney guard is always up. With McCartney, it seems, there are no clear-cut answers, only an increasing complexity of clues.

She was a beautiful person — it came from something deep inside her. Jim adored her. I remember how he'd sometimes tell us a story he'd picked up from the businessmen at the Cotton Exchange. If it was a bit off color, Mary used to look at him and say, "Husband!"

—*Olive Johnson*—
(A longtime family friend of the McCartneys, remembering Paul's mother, Mary)

2
Every Mother's Son
Childhood

Nobody in Paul McCartney's family can remember a time when they didn't reside in Liverpool. For well over a hundred years now the clannish, closeknit, McCartneys have called England's largest seaport home.

McCartney's father, James, one of nine children, was born July 7, 1902, to tobacco cutter Joseph, and mother Florence Clegg, at 8 Fishguard Street, Everton, one of Liverpool's roughest neighborhoods. Educated peripherally at nearby Steer Street School, Jim was partial to music and taught himself piano, after a fashion, on an old upright.

"My dad was actually a pretty fair pianist, you know," McCartney commented recently. "He played by ear, his left one! Actually, he was deaf in one ear. He fell off a railing or something when he was a kid and busted an eardrum. But yes, he was definitely my strongest musical influence." As a lad of about ten Jim landed his first position, working at Liverpool's

Theatre Royal after school. McCartney remembers: "My dad used to work on a spotlight in the music halls and so he got a lot of influence from all that . . . He worked on the limelights when it was actually just a piece of lime that they burned. He had to trim pieces of lime and he used to come home after the first house . . . bring home old programs . . . Auntie Millie would iron them and he'd take them back for the second house and flog them again."

At the age of fourteen the elder McCartney entered Liverpool's then-thriving cotton industry as a sample boy for A. Hannay & Company of Chapel Street at wages of just six shillings a week. He worked diligently and, fourteen years later, in 1930, was promoted to the rank of salesman, hawking the company's wares to wholesale merchants from around the world. In his spare time he moonlighted as a gardener for the company's top brass and pursued his passion for music, forming first a swinging musical ensemble billed as the Masked Melody Makers, then later, the popular Liverpool dancehall attraction, Jim Mac's Jazz Band.

A gregarious, young man-about-town, Jim met his future wife, pretty Mary Patricia Mohin after the start of the Second World War at the McCartney family home at 11 Scargreen Avenue, West Derby. Mary, a nurse at nearby Walton Hospital on Rice Lane, was staying temporarily with Jim's newlywed sister Jin and her husband, Harry Harris, and had stopped by to visit the McCartneys that evening after work. Coincidentally, that same night the Third Reich showered Liverpool's busy harbor with bombs, forcing Jim and Mary to spend the night huddled together downstairs. "It was love under duress," Mike McCartney told me in a 1984 interview in Liverpool. "They were together ever after, even until Mum's sad passing."

Born on September 29, 1909, at 2 Third Avenue, Fazakerly, Liverpool, Mary was one of four children. Her mother, Mary Theresa (Danher) Mohin, and a baby sister died during childbirth in January 1919. Shortly afterwards, her father, Owen Mohin, married a surly spinster from Ireland called Rose. He tried hard to integrate his second wife into the family, but Mary, for one, couldn't accept the new woman in her father's life and opted instead to stay with a maternal aunt until she finished school.

At fourteen she went into nursing, accepting a junior position at Alder Hey Hospital, later moving on to a slightly better assignment at Liverpool's Walton Hospital. After ten years of devoted duty she was promoted to the position of full nursing sister. Seven years later she married Jim McCartney.

They officially tied the knot on April 15, 1941, in a full church wedding at St. Swithin's Roman Catholic Church, Gill Moss, in Liverpool. Thereafter they took furnished rooms on Sunburys Road, Anfield. Not long afterwards, work at the Cotton Exchange was suspended. Unfit for military service due to his advancing age (thirty-nine) and ruptured eardrum, McCartney found work at Napier's aircraft factory as a center lathe turner, helping to manufacture fighter planes. On the side he worked as a firefighter.

Their first child, James Paul, was born on June 18, 1942, in a private ward in Walton Hospital. As Mary had been an employee of long standing, the head nurse waived the normal visiting hours and allowed the senior McCartney to visit mother and son whenever he wished. "He looked awful, I couldn't get over it," Mr. McCartney recalled. "When I got home I cried, the first time for years and years . . . But the next day he looked more human. And every day after that he got better and better. He turned out a lovely baby in the end."

Following his stint at Napier's McCartney went to work for the Corporation of Liverpool's Cleansing Department as an inspector, making certain that the city's garbage men toed the line in their quest to keep Liverpool clean. Mrs. McCartney too soon went back to work, this time as a visiting health aid. Her second child, Peter Michael, was born January 7, 1944. By now the McCartneys had moved to a new prefab bungalow on Roach Avenue, Knowsley Estate, in Liverpool after outgrowing their old digs in Wallasey. Soon after Mike's birth Mary was stricken with mastitis, an inflammation of the breasts.

After her recovery she was appointed a domiciliary midwife and was thereby entitled to subsidized housing, moving the family first to Sir Thomas White Gardens in Liverpool's bustling city center, and later to 72 Western Avenue on the working-class Speke Estate. Paul's first memory, from around this time, is of someone coming to the door, presenting his mum with a lovely, hand-colored, plaster dog. He is not sure why, but figures it was probably in appreciation of some special kindness or concern she had shown towards one of her many new mothers. People stopped by quite often just to say thanks or maybe even leave her a little present. According to her family, that was the kind of affection she inspired. "I have another memory of hiding from someone, then hitting them over the head with an iron bar," McCartney recalls, "but I think the plaster dog was the earliest."

Intent on seeing her little family steadily move up in the world, by 1949 Mary had wangled yet another new home from the council, this one a large, reasonably well-equipped row house at 12 Ardwick Road on the outer reaches of Speke. Shortly after moving in, the little McCartney lads almost lost their lives by falling into a nearby rain-filled lime pit their father had repeatedly warned them against, made even more deadly by the fact that neither of the brothers had yet learned how to swim. After much hysterical thrashing about, Mike was finally able to grab onto an old tree limb, thus holding them both aloft until a neighbor heard their pitiful pleas for help and came to the rescue.

Their first school was Stockton Wood Road Infants' School. Although both brothers were baptized Catholic, after much deliberation their parents decided not to send them to a church-run school, opting instead for the more down-to-earth values encouraged by the state. While at Stockton Wood young Paul had occasion to view his very first flick. It was a big-screen adaptation of British radio hero Dick Barton, Special Agent. So emotionally overwhelming it was to the little boy that only a few death-defying minutes into the film he jumped up, pushed his way past his thoroughly enthralled schoolmates, and ran like the dickens outdoors.

By 1950 the mushrooming post-war birth rate had made Stockton Wood School hopelessly overcrowded. As a result, a number of children were shifted to Joseph Williams Primary School in Gateacre, a bouncy, thirty-minute bus ride into what was then still the heart of Liverpool's balmy countryside. At Joseph Williams young master McCartney grew rather portly. It was "the only time anything outwardly affected him," his brother observed, "and I remember the feeling of sheer one-upmanship whenever we had an argument, to counter with a lightning 'Fatty!' before running like hell to escape the ensuing wrath."

Despite the many petty tribulations of youth, Paul was actually quite a disciplined and committed student. Easily passing the feared eleven-plus examination, an educational must in Britain for those wishing to advance to university, McCartney was admitted to the Liverpool Institute on Mount Street in 1953. It was here that his first "artistic" expression blossomed. Going through her son's pockets one wash day, his mother happened upon an explicit drawing of a naked lady, with great care and attention having been paid by the artist to the pubic area. For two agonizing days McCartney steadfastly and convincingly held his ground. "It must have been done by my mate, Kenny Alpin," he protested over and over. In the end, however, the strain became too great and he eventually confessed. "The shame was terrible," he admitted years later. From that moment on McCartney made sure he remembered to check his shirt pockets.

Without question one of young Paul's greatest natural attributes was his smooth sense of diplomacy and persuasive charm. Apprehended red-handed perpetrating any number of naughty boyish pranks (on one occasion he and his brother almost accidentally burned down their Aunt Jin's garage while conducting an experiment to see if fire would defy the law of gravity and burn upwards), he generally managed to weasel his way out, often leaving brother Mike to take the heat. While never brutal, Jim McCartney believed in the concept of corporal punishment. On one occasion when the two brothers had crossed the line of acceptable behavior and were caught out, only the more stubbornly honest Mike was spanked. "Tell him you didn't do it and he'll stop," the cagey Paul shouted. On those rare occasions, however, when there was no possible way to avoid the inevitable, Paul would stand silent and emotionless as his father disciplined him. Afterwards, Paul would quietly engage in some tiny act of residential sabotage like sneaking into his parents' bedroom and tearing his mum's prized lace curtains almost imperceptibly an inch or two along the bottom edge. "It was just Paul's way," his dad rationalized years later.

Although not really the student his brother was, Mike too soon racked up the appropriate percentages and was admitted to the Institute. For Mary it was a triumph. Both her boys were now well on their way to respectable careers and prosperous futures. With a good, solid education behind them the sky was the limit. If they were fortunate they might even one day become teachers themselves. It was an exciting possibility. Daydreams aside, however, at the "Inny" (as the boys affectionately called it) McCartney continued to do well scholastically, eventually leaving the school with accumulated "O" levels in Spanish, German, and French.

Consistently popular with both his masters and schoolmates, Paul was voted "head boy" several times during his career at the Institute. This rare honor gave young McCartney the proud privilege of assisting teachers such as English professor Alan "Dusty" Durband with a multitude of classroom chores including roll call, delivering notes back and forth to the office, and furnishing his fellow students with the necessary school supplies. "He was always respected by the other boys," remembers Durband.

> I don't remember him playing the fool; he was a well-behaved sort of fellow. But I think he was privately what he became publicly — the person always ready with a witty comment: he would make all his mates and peers collapse with laughter at the *sotto voce* remark, rather than the public one. It was very much the Liverpool wit: he would be very much like a joker would be, making a nuisance of himself on the front row. He

was hardly a withdrawn figure. . . . He was responsible for organizing the class, but never in any bootlicking way — he was just a good executive.

Characteristically eager to please those he perceived to be in positions of authority, inwardly McCartney harbored very mixed feelings about his life at school. "Homework was a right drag," he later confessed in Hunter Davies' *The Beatles: The Authorized Biography.*

> I just couldn't stand staying in on a summer night when all the other kids were out playing. There was a field opposite our house in Ardwick and I could look out the window and see them all having a good time. There weren't many other kids from the Institute living round our way. I was called a college pudding, 'fucking college puddin' was what they said.
>
> All I wanted was women, money, and clothes. I used to do a bit of stealing, things like ciggies. We'd go into empty shops, when the man was in the house part at the back, and take some before he came in. For years, what I wanted out of life was £100. I thought with that I could have a house, a guitar, and a car. So, if money had been the scene, I'd have gone wild.

Later the footloose McCartney family moved house again. This time home was a neat and airy row house at 20 Forthlin Row, in Allerton. Notably, this was their first residence that had the benefit of indoor plumbing, quite a comfort on cold and rainy Liverpool mornings. Ensconced as they now were in such heady, lower-middle-class comfort, the conscientious McCartneys had great reason to feel confident about the future. Tragically, on October 31, 1956, Mary McCartney died suddenly after an operation for breast cancer at Liverpool's Northern Hospital.

Mike had accidentally stumbled upon his mother softly crying in her bedroom one afternoon after school. She was clutching a crucifix and a photograph of a distant relative, now a priest. Mike figured he and Paul must have done something terrible to upset her. Desperate to protect her sons, Mary never even told them she was sick. For quite awhile, apparently, she even hid it from herself, treating the intense pain with Bisodol, an over-the-counter medicine, and explaining it away to her husband as simply "the change." Deep down of course, Mary, a top-drawer nurse for twenty-three years, must have realized something was very, very wrong. Admitted to the hospital just two days prior to her death, she confided to a relative that she would have loved to see her boys growing up. Just before the end, a pair of rosary beads were tied to her wrists and the hospital priest gave the agonized woman the last rites of the Catholic church. Paul was only fourteen, Mike just twelve.

That evening the two boys cried themselves to sleep. Paul later admitted it was his mother's untimely death that initially turned him off religion; he had prayed silently for days for his loving mother to return home. "Daft prayers, you know; if you bring her back, I'll be very, very good for always. I thought, it just shows how stupid religion is. See, the prayers didn't work, when I really needed them to as well."

The week of the funeral Paul and Mike went to stay with their Auntie Jin, their father having no wish for them to see him so badly broken up. Mary was finally laid to rest on November 3, 1956, at Yew Tree Cemetery, on Finch Lane, Huyton.

Mike McCartney, perhaps more adept than his brother at expressing his emotions on a one-to-one basis, reflected on mother Mary's passing in an interview with British journalist George Tremlett:

> I think about her because she was great and I was very close to her . . . She was a good woman, and that's why I feel so sentimental about our childhood . . . really . . . At that age, you have no idea how tough you are going to have to be when you go out into the world. My mum's death was my first big knock. But my dad taught me a lot of things; we both owe him a lot . . . Of course, it would have been easy for him to have gone off getting drunk every night. But he didn't. He stayed at home and looked after us . . . he could have gone right to the top in business if he had played the rules like they are now, if he had wanted to kill . . . It would have meant neglecting us, and he wasn't prepared to do that, either . . .

It has rubbed onto both of us; neither of us has really got the killer streak. We didn't realize it so much at the time but now Paul and I are very grateful to him, and we realize what a fine man he is. We look back now, and we think of Mum, and we see how beautiful it all was, and we understand now what he must have gone through when she died. If he had gone off with other women, and gone out getting drunk, we would have been so screwed up inside.

But how did Mary's death really affect Paul? It seems he is simply more comfortable — and more effective — expressing what matters most to him through his music. His extemporaneous remarks often conceal, more than they reveal, his true feelings. "It's almost like once something really touches a nerve with him the only convenient reaction in his repertoire is to instantly recoil," says a friend. "But you can rest assured Paul's actually as emotionally vulnerable as anyone else, perhaps even more so. It's just a defense mechanism, that's all. Anyone who chooses to read it differently is simply uninformed."

Not surprisingly, after Mary died life on Forthlin Row was far different for the McCartneys. Jim, of course, was now forced to be both breadwinner and full-time housekeeper. Although his sisters, Mill and Jin, helped out when and where they could it was still a terrible strain on the fifty-three-year-old salesman. "The winters were bad," the elder McCartney was quoted as saying in 1967. "The boys had to light the fires themselves when they came home from school. I did all the cooking. The biggest headache was what sort of parent was I going to be. When my wife had been alive, I'd been the one who chastised them. I delivered the hard stuff when it was needed. My wife had done the soft stuff . . . Now I had to decide whether to be a father or a mother or both." And of course the pain of losing his wife never really went away. "I missed my wife," he reflected. "It knocked me for six when she died."

Foremost in Jim McCartney's homespun philosophy of child rearing was his concept of what Paul and Mike termed

"the two 'ations,'" short for "toleration" and "moderation."
Jim lectured that if only his sons would take these two
watchwords to heart then they would avoid hurting not only
others, but ultimately themselves as well. Remarkably, both
McCartney brothers seem to have heeded his sage advice.
Both seem to rally for the underdog, and try to avoid, as far as
possible, deliberately hurting anyone. Perhaps Mike was
right; what old Jim lacked in "killer instinct" he more than
made up for with his lifelong commitment to kindness, compassion, and a thoroughly British sense of fair play, all attributes that young Paul, in particular, would find useful in the
extraordinary years to come.

"Lose a mother and find a guitar," goes Mike McCartney's
memorable line regarding his elder brother's eventual fascination with music. In many ways, this simple sentiment says
a lot about what was going on inside his soon-to-be-famous
brother back then.

As children neither of the boys really showed any special
interest in music. Their father did sign them up for piano lessons as youngsters but made the mistake of starting them in
the summer when all their little mates were buzzing around
outside, wanting them to come out to play. After about two or
three lessons, getting them to practice became a high-stress
situation and so, reluctantly, Jim allowed them to quit. Later
he insisted Paul try out for a spot in the Liverpool Cathedral
Choir but he resisted and apparently deliberately cracked his
voice at the audition. Eventually though, Paul did sing in the
St. Chad's Choir off Penny Lane for a time but soon tired of the
choirmaster's overly regimented approach and dropped out.

Sometime later, Paul inherited from his father an old trumpet on which he learned to pick out a few tunes such as
"When the Saints Go Marching In" by ear. He was fond of listening to the radio and especially enjoyed singing old film
tunes such as "White Christmas," "Over the Rainbow," and
various Fred Astaire numbers. "I like a nice tune, you know,"
he observed in the early seventies.

The first concert he ever attended was a performance by Eric Delany's Band at the Liverpool Empire. He also occasionally went to nudie shows with his mates at an establishment called the Pavilion. "They would strip off actually starkers," he later remembered. "Some of them were all right as well. It was funny letting us in at that age."

Following his short-lived flirtation with the trumpet Paul suddenly picked up on the guitar. His first instrument, a low-budget acoustic, soon became the overriding force in his life. "It's funny, but everyone remembers their first string box," he recalls. "Mine was a Zenith. I'd no idea where it was going to lead at the time . . . I started bashing away and pretty soon had the basic chords well and truly learnt. Then I got a bit more ambitious and bought a solid Rosati (a 'Lucky Seven'). It only had two strings and when I played it it didn't produce a very melodic sound. But I kept the volume right down and it seemed okay to me." According to his brother, McCartney became obsessed: "He was lost. He didn't have time to eat or think about anything else. He played it on the lavatory, in the bath, everywhere."

One summer's holiday at Butlin's in Filey, Yorkshire, the two siblings entered something called The People's National Talent Contest, performing together, reasonably enough, as "The McCartney Brothers," squawking out what Mike has termed a "passable" rendering of the Everly Brothers' "Bye Bye Love."

Paul then launched into a raucous version of Little Richard's signature, "Long Tall Sally." Literally shivering with stage fright before, during, and after the jittery performance, Mike effectively put a premature end to the fab new singing duo right then and there by rushing offstage to throw up into the very nearest container. Paul remembers:

[At Butlin's] they used to have these talent shows, and my cousin-in-law was one of the red coats who had something to do with the entertainment. He called us up on the stage. I had my guitar with me. Looking back on it, it must have been a put-up job; I don't know what I was doing there with my guitar. I probably asked him to get me up. I went up with my brother, Mike, who had just recovered from breaking his arm and looked all pale. He had his arm in a big sling . . . We did "Bye Bye Love," and then I finished with "Long Tall Sally."

Ever since I heard Little Richard's version, I started imitiating him. It was just straight imitation, really, which had gradually become my version of it as much as Richard's. I started doing it in one of the classrooms at school; it was just one of the imitations I could do well. I could do Fats Domino, I could do Elvis, I could do a few people. I still can!

Along with McCartney's interest in the guitar came a growing awareness of rock 'n' roll. Before long it wasn't just the music that had captured his imagination but the whole freewheeling, rock lifestyle as well. A fellow classmate at the Institute, Ian James, also took up the guitar, and soon the two were cycling around Liverpool with their instruments strapped to their backs, looking for places to play. Much to Jim McCartney's dismay Paul had even taken to wearing the sort of clothes a guitar-picking teddy boy might choose. With his long, slicked-back hair, piled high above his forehead, narrow drainpipe trousers, and white, sparkly sportscoat, his perpetually innocent, choirboy face seemed incongruous. At fourteen he was far from being a tough Liverpool teddy boy, but he was also ivy leagues away from being the proper English schoolboy his father would have preferred.

Hopping on board the bus, mornings, for the dreamy, half-hour ride to school, McCartney soon made friends with the driver's son, George Harrison, who, like McCartney, was smitten with the guitar. The two soon started hanging out together after school and inevitably began the thankless job of teaching themselves the new chords necessary to carry forward their boyish fantasies of one day playing in a big group.

Those fantasies would soon move a major step closer to reality.

I had a group. I was the singer, and the leader. I met Paul and made a decision whether or not to have him in the group. Was it better to have a guy who was better than the people I already had in, or not? To make the band stronger or let me be stronger? The decision was eventually made to let Paul in and make the group stronger.

— *John Lennon* —

3

Doughnuts Over the Empire

The Teen Years

Paul McCartney's fortuitous first meeting with John Lennon officially took place on July 6, 1957, at a garden fête at St. Peter's Parish Church in Woolton. It was at the local fish and chip shop weeks earlier, however, that they actually first nodded hello. After that, McCartney recalls seeing the rebelliously attired Lennon climbing aboard the local 86 bus, bound for town. Unknown to those present at the Woolton fête, a musical miracle of sorts was secretly taking place amid the barking of Liverpool's trained police dogs, the clattery dirge of the Cheshire Yeomanry Band, and the unruly clamor of kids decked out for the day as Wolf Cubs, Girl Guides, Brownies, and Scouts.

Actually, as a rather ad-libbed, neighborhood affair it wasn't bad. Every year there was the mandatory Rose Queen parade and coronation, cheery stalls selling finger sandwiches, cold drinks, and Britain's famous multi-colored ices, as well as a fun fair featuring several daring kiddy rides, and of course a smashing musical entertainment.

That year, as a concession to the basically church-shy teenage youth of Woolton, following a blessing by the Reverend Maurice Pryce-Jones, a local group of lads known as the Quarry Men were slated to appear. Performing mostly covers of well-known rock and skiffle tunes, the five young men jived their way through a rapid-fire repertoire of numbers ranging from "Maggie May," to "Railroad Bill" and "Cumberland Gap." In those days the Quarry Men were Colin Hanton on drums, Rod Davis, banjo, Len Gary, bass, Eric Griffiths, guitar, Pete Shotton, washboard, and of course John Lennon, guitar and lead vocal. Mixed into the happily swaying crowd was Paul McCartney who'd come along for the day at the suggestion of Ivan Vaughan, a mutual friend of John and Paul. "At school one day Ivy . . . invited me to this fête the following Saturday," recalled McCartney, responding to this author's questions late in 1986.

> I remember coming up on the fête from across the field . . . John was singing a lovely tune by the Del-Vikings called, "Come Go With Me." He'd heard it on the radio but didn't quite know all the words, so he made up his own. "Come go with me, down to the penitentiary," stuff like that.
>
> His hair was greased back into a drake. With that, and his nice big sideboards, he did look a bit of a ted.

After the Quarry Men's swinging first set, Ivan led Paul across the road to the band's impromptu dressing room in St. Peter's Church Hall. Later that evening the boys were to perform again, this time alternating with a local combo called the George Edwards Band. But for the moment it was time to relax, unwind, and cool down with the aid of a few discreetly tucked away bottles of beer. "This is John," Vaughan ventured upon entering the large, sweltering room. "Hi," replied Lennon. "This is Paul." A rather ordinary beginning perhaps, but within minutes things heated up when it was discovered that McCartney not only played a pretty mean left-handed guitar, but wonder of wonders, could actually correctly tune one as well. "Neither John nor Eric Griffiths had learned how to do that yet," recalls longtime Beatle crony Pete Shotton, "Whenever their guitars went out of tune, they'd been taking them round and paying a fellow in King's Drive to do it."

McCartney further wowed the often standoffish Lennon by jotting down the somewhat convoluted lyrics to singer Eddie Cochran's classic, "Twenty Flight Rock," as well as Gene Vincent's crazy "Be-Bop-A-Lula." He recounts what happened next: "I met them in the church hall. We talked and then I picked up a guitar lying there and started to play 'Twenty Flight Rock.' I suppose I was showing off a bit. I knew all the words and they didn't. That was big currency. Then I went through all the stuff I knew. John seemed quite impressed. There was nearly two years between us, so he was a big man in my eyes."

After McCartney's departure, Lennon asked Shotton what he thought about Ivy Vaughan's obviously talented young friend and wondered out loud if perhaps he shouldn't invite him to join the group. Shotton, however, doesn't remember being exactly bowled over. "I didn't really take in Paul that first meeting," says Shotton. "He seemed very quiet, but you do when you meet a group of new blokes for the first time. I wasn't really jealous of him, not at first. He was so much younger than us. I didn't think he was going to be a rival. Me and John were still the closest pals."

Two weeks later, while cycling along Menlove Avenue in Woolton, McCartney ran into Shotton who offhandedly announced that John had been talking about him and wondered if he would like to join the band. Delicately balancing against the curb on his bike, McCartney reflected for a moment or two and then replied simply, "Okay then. See you," before shoving off back across the golf course to the willowy wilds of Allerton. McCartney was naturally pretty excited, inwardly anyway. Externally though he was typically nonchalant, hardly mentioning a word to anyone at home that night about his big break. Teacher "Dusty" Durband remembers that the day after his mother died Paul was back at his desk at school, seemingly quite normal and only a little more quiet and introspective than usual. Obviously, next to that, becoming a bona fide Quarry Man pales in comparison. Still, to the ambitious and sensitive young McCartney it was at least a milestone. At best, just what the doctor ordered to help ease his festering, raw emotion over his beloved mother's passing. From that moment on, John and Paul became virtually inseparable. Hanging out, chatting up the local wild life, and above all, making music.

While the magical team the world would soon know as Lennon/McCartney had come together, the rest of Lennon's Quarry Men were still a little undecided about their newest colleague. "I always thought he was a bit big-headed," band manager Nigel Whalley recalls. "As soon as we let him into the group, he started complaining about the money I was getting them, saying I should take less as I didn't do any playing. He was always smiling at you, but he could be catty as well. He used to pick on our drummer, Colin, not to his face — making snide remarks about him behind his back. Paul wanted something from the drums poor Colin just didn't have it in him to play."

And how did McCartney rate the Quarry Men? "Well, I thought John was good. He was really the only outstanding member. All the rest kind of slipped away, you know? The drummer was pretty good actually for what we knew then. One of the reasons I know they all liked Colin was because he had the record, 'Searchin',' and again, that was big currency. Sometimes you made a whole career with someone just because he owned a particular record!"

McCartney's first gig with the Quarry Men took place on October 18, 1957, at the New Clubmoor Club in Liverpool's Broadway. Resplendent as they were in their long, dark, string ties, black trousers, white shirts, and coffee-colored sportscoats, their performance was apparently not up to the mark. "Good & Bad" was the cryptic assessment written on the band's visiting card by dance promoter Charlie McBain following McCartney's sorry attempt at lead guitar. "He really cocked up on this one song," Lennon later recalled. "It was Arthur Smith's 'Guitar Boogie,' a tune we all especially liked. When it came time for the big solo Paul lost his bottle and was all thumbs. The rest of the evening actually went down pretty smooth. We all had a good laugh about it afterwards, everyone, that is, except Paul."

In those days virtually all of the numerous neighborhood groups played only cover versions of popular songs currently topping the hit parade. After awhile though, Lennon and McCartney found this practice not only boring and tedious, but creatively unsatisfying. It was McCartney who composed the first real tune, "I Lost My Little Girl." Lennon, massively impressed, immediately set about penning a few numbers of his own, not wanting to be outdone. Says McCartney: "Gradually, we started to write stuff together. Which didn't mean we wrote everything together . . . When I first began writing songs I started using a guitar. 'I Lost My Little Girl' . . . is a funny little song, a nice little song, a corny little song based on three chords — G, G7, and C. Later on we had a piano and I used to bang around on that. I wrote 'When I'm Sixty-Four' when I was about sixteen. I was vaguely thinking then it might come in handy in a musical comedy or something. I didn't know what kind of career I was going to take."

During the first three years of their relationship John and Paul wrote literally dozens of songs together. Unfortunately, many of them were inadvertently lost when Paul's girlfriend, Jane Asher, tossed out an original notebook containing some of the first-ever Lennon/McCartney compositions while clearing out a cupboard in McCartney's St. John's Wood home. Some of the early tunes that have been preserved are "Catswalk," "Hello Little Girl," "Hot as Sun," "Just Fun," "Keep Looking That Way," "Like Dreamers Do," "Looking Glass," "Love Me Do," "That's My Woman," "The One After 909," "Thinking of Linking," "Too Bad About Sorrows," "Winston's Walk," and "Years Roll Along," to name just a few.

Generally, these impromptu composing sessions took place

after school at Paul's while everyone was still out. After the obligatory fried egg, toast, and tea, the boys would settle back to work in the McCartneys' cluttered front room, all the while puffing away on Jim McCartney's old Meerschaum pipe filled, not with tobacco, but Typhoo Tea!

Often, when they weren't busy busking at Paul's they'd hike over to John's mother's home in Springwood for a hectic afternoon of business and pleasure at the hands of the delightfully offbeat Julia Lennon. "I always thought of her as being an exceptionally beautiful woman," says McCartney. "She was very, very nice to us all and of course, John just adored her. Looking back, I can remember two tunes in particular Julia taught us. Oddly enough, one of them was 'Wedding Bells Are Breaking Up That Old Gang of Mine,' while another was definitely 'Romana.' Much later, during the Beatle years, John and I often attempted to write a few songs with that kind of similar feeling, with 'Here, There, and Everywhere' coming immediately to mind."

During this time Paul was still quite friendly with George Harrison, who despite his tender years impressed McCartney with his strong musical presence and stirring guitar licks, a commodity very much missing from the often musically ad hoc Quarry Men.

As to Paul's initial suggestion that perhaps Harrison might be invited to join the group, McCartney isn't altogether clear of the exact circumstances. He does, however, vividly recall band leader Lennon's first reaction to the idea.

"No fuckin' way, man!" John reportedly shouted. "He's just a little kid, for Christ's sake."

"But he knows dozens more chords than the two of us put together," Paul countered. "You should hear him play, John, really. He's great. Just think about it, okay? The band could really use him."

Oscillating between the potential harm admitting Harrison to the group might have on Lennon's carefully crafted, tough guy, teddy boy image, and the obvious benefits of bringing on board a lad of such superior musicianship, Lennon finally relented when on February 6, 1958, he agreed to hear what George could do. "I listened to him play," Lennon recalled, "and I said, 'Play "Raunchy," ' or whatever the old story is, and I let him in . . . That was three of us then. The rest of the group was thrown out gradually . . . We went for the strongest format, and for equals."

Apart from George's great talent, one of the definite perks arising from his inclusion in the band was the friendly welcome the boys all received from George's mother, Louise. A hearty, good-natured woman, Mrs. Harrison was both pleased and proud to see her youngest son so involved in something as creative and individual as music. "Come along in, then, boys," she would sing out, waving Lennon's Quarry Men into the Harrisons' cosy kitchen. "How about something to eat before the big rehearsal?"

While Jim McCartney was certainly very supportive of Paul's love of music, he wasn't really all that keen on his considering anything so inherently risky as a possible career. Although McCartney denies it, there is some question of whether his mother would have approved or even allowed her precious elder son to venture into such treacherous waters. In 1986 while promoting my first book, *The Beatles: A Celebration* in Toronto, I met a woman who had known and worked with Mrs. McCartney for many years. She claimed that Mary would never have even considered that either of her sons would go into show business and had talked many times about Paul one day becoming a teacher. "If Mary had lived," she said, "I'm positive there never would have been any Beatles."

When not practising at the Harrisons', hanging out at Julia Lennon's was always a viable alternative. John's younger half-sister Julia Baird remembers: "Without a doubt, some of the most memorable episodes in the Beatles' early Liverpool period were their hilarious bathroom jam sessions with my mother at home in Blomfield Road. Our toilet was one of the tiniest in all of Great Britain, and to see John, Paul, George, Colin, Duff Lowe, and Mummy all scrambling around inside trying to find a place to sit, was truly a wondrous sight." The door shut securely behind them, they enthusiastically tucked into a bevy of now-classic tunes such as "Besamé Mucho," "Alleycat," or the sneaky theme from *The Third Man*. The raucous, musical, free-for-alls sometimes meandered on late into the evening.

Like Aunt Mimi's front porch (another old Lennon/McCartney haunt), the room gave off a kind of natural echo which somehow seemed to enhance the group's offbeat sound. "Occasionally," says Julia, "my younger sister Jacqui and I were actually unlucky enough to be taking a bath when John's buddies suddenly felt like letting loose with a little homemade rhythm and blues. In that case, we were both unceremoniously hauled out of the tub to make way for these bathroom Beethovens. Of course we didn't mind, as it meant we were allowed to go outside and play for an extra hour or so." The lineup for these unusual sessions was generally John, Paul, and George on acoustic guitars, with the others bashing along in unison, and Mrs. Lennon on her favorite kitchen pots and pans.

Being a Quarry Man, however, was not all adolescent merriment. Perpetually short of money and places to play, several times the group almost folded. For a brief while in the summer of 1958 George actually played with another local band, The Les Stewart Quartet, tired and edgy to get something happening. "Mostly we just played blokes' parties and things," recalled John, "or maybe occasionally a wedding if we were lucky. That was always a good gig as it usually meant all the free beer we could guzzle, and generally a damn fine meal to boot."

Casting off the extraneous Quarry Men along the way, the group was now down to the three hard-core members — John, Paul, and George. Any sort of reasonable drummer, as usual, was almost impossible to find, or to keep. Altogether Lennon's schoolboy group played only about twenty-five official gigs over a three-year period, more for the experience than anything else. Still, the nucleus of what would later become the Beatles was now firmly fixed.

Show business aside, Paul McCartney was growing up in other ways as well. Ever since he was old enough to understand that there were indeed two sexes, he was keenly interested in girls. His brother Mike reports that on two occasions this legendary Lothario-in-training even stooped so low as to secretly covet a couple of his sibling's first female admirers, one, a pretty "McCartney Brothers" fan from Gypsyville, Hull, named Angela, whom the brothers had met at Butlin's, the other, an exotic-looking early German Beatles fan, Ursula Milczewsky.

Paul's first legitimate crush centered on a young woman remembered simply as "Val" whom McCartney happened to notice one morning on the bus to school. Impressed with her long, pretty hair and deep-set, baby-doll eyes, he was content to admire her from afar until word went around the classroom that the young lady too was smitten. "It came along the grapevine that Val liked him," remembered Mike in a 1964 interview. "You should have seen the way he went on! He was completely knocked out! He took Val out once or twice, to the cinema, visiting friends, that sort of thing. Then the whole affair suddenly fizzled."

McCartney's initiation into manhood came at the still-tender age of fifteen in the arms of a neighborhood girl whose name history fails to record. "She was older and bigger than me," says Paul. "It was at her house. She was supposed to be babysitting while her mum was out. I told everybody at school the next day, of course. I was a real squealer."

McCartney's first real girlfriend, was Dorothy Rhone, a pretty, blonde pixie. Cynthia Lennon remembers her as "a gentle soul," who spoke in whispers, blushed frequently, and idolized Paul. Dot was from Childwall, a homey suburb very near Woolton. She worked as a clerk in a dispensing chemist's, living at home with her parents. Unfortunately, the young woman's father was exceedingly strict and so was naturally suspicious of the cheery, sometimes overly polite McCartney. Sandra Hedges, one of Dot's closest girlfriends, now a housewife in Yarm, Cleveland, recalls:

Her name was shortened to "Dot" by Paul and he wrote "P.S. I Love You" for her.

She was very much in love with Paul and he, in turn, would jealously guard her (to her chagrin) by placing her amid the group while playing. In an attempt to shake him, she returned home to her parents. Later Paul became the love of the world: the famous tickertape welcome in America, his face in every newspaper, every newscast. A year later we bade farewell to Dot when she emigrated to Canada. Ironically, I recall once saying to her: "I'm fed up with those lads from the art college practising in our front room every Sunday. You'll never get anywhere with them."

Dot, her husband, and elder daughter, Astrid, were Rolls-Royced some years later to meet up with the group when they played Maple Leaf Gardens in Toronto. When she saw Paul again, the ghost was finally laid to rest.

Despite the love affair's perhaps predictable ending, while still together Paul and Dot were a very hot item. McCartney, deeply impressed at the time with French sex kitten Brigitte Bardot (as was Lennon and, for that matter, much of the western world), requested Dot bleach her hair, which she did, much to her parents' horror. "We wanted to try and turn our girlfriends into Liverpool's answer to Bardot," says McCartney. "So my girl was Dot, and John was going out with Cynthia. I think we got them both to go blonde and wear miniskirts. Terrible isn't it, really? But that's the way it was."

On her eighteenth birthday Paul sent Dot a humorous hand-drawn, cartoon-filled card featuring himself on the cover as "THE WILDMAN OF ALLERTON." The birthday message inside read: "FROM THE LATE JAMES CROW, TO DOT, HAPPY BIRTHDAY, HIGHNESS, O GREAT SILVER BUBBLE OF THE SILVER SEAS, HANDSPUN." The sometimes fairly inscrutable McCartney magic, it seems, had netted a very willing catch.

In 1961, Dot and Cynthia embarked from Liverpool's Lime Street Station for a visit with their men while the Beatles were playing Hamburg. Traveling by boat train across the hook of Holland they arrived at Hamburg Station tired and cramped, but ecstatic at the sight of their two leather-clad lovers pacing up and down the platform, anxiously awaiting them.

Cynthia went home with early Beatles supporter, photographer Astrid Kirchherr, while Paul and Dot took up residence on an old river barge owned by Rosa, the motherly lavatory attendant at the Top Ten Club.

Several months later, Dot and Cynthia became roommates as tenants of a tacky Liverpool boarding house where Cyn first learned she was pregnant with Julian, and Dot's affair with her beloved Paul came to an end. Arriving by surprise one evening, McCartney told his long-suffering girlfriend that the romance was over, and then quick as you please, bounded down the long, shabby stairway out into the street a free man. Dot, of course, was devastated. "Poor little defenseless Dot," Cynthia recalls. "She wouldn't harm a fly but had been hurt so much that she couldn't even tell me what had happened without renewed convulsions and outbursts of uncontrollable crying."

Within a couple of days, once the reality of the situation had sunk in, Dot sadly collected her things together and went back home. "I hardly saw Dot again," says Cynthia. "It was impossible, too close to home for her to bear."

By the sultry summer of 1958 John and Paul were not only bound musically but had become exceptionally close buddies into the bargain. When Lennon lost his mother, Julia, after she was run over and killed by a drunken, off-duty policeman that July, Paul was himself deeply affected. "When I look back on Julia's death, all I really see is just the word T-R-A-G-E-D-Y written in big, black letters," McCartney reflected in 1986. "The only way I could really help was to empathize, as I'd had the same thing happen to me. I mean, there wasn't actually anything I could say that would just sort of magically patch him up. That kind of hurt goes far too deep for that."

Julia Baird remembers her mother ironically saying how sorry she felt for Paul having lost his mum at such a tender age. "Can you imagine how that must hurt?" she would comment to John occasionally over tea and toast. "And he's such a lovely, talented boy. What a pity."

Filing away his hurt and anger under an apparently impenetrable armor of emotional indifference, Lennon stoically forged ahead, intent upon turning his boyhood dreams of stardom into a life-saving reality. His bond with McCartney became even stronger. After his mother died, Lennon remained surprisingly close to Julia's party-loving, common-law husband, John Albert Dykins, or "Bobby," as he was known. McCartney remembers:

> Once in a while, John and I would pop in and visit Bobby at his new place in Woolton. We used to borrow his record player to listen to the latest Carl Perkins discs we'd dug up in town. In fact, I seem to recall catching hell from him once for accidentally damaging one of his records. He was basically a good bloke, though, and always seemed to enjoy seeing John. Frankly, I do know John had this sort of "stepfather" thing about him. I mean, he liked him alright, but he couldn't quite associate with him as his dad. Actually, it was a problem I had later, when my father remarried.

By the fall of 1959 John had finally dropped the name "Quarry Men" for the more celestial-sounding "Moondogs," and then, "Johnny and the Moondogs." It was during an on-stage audition for British television personality Carroll Levis (probably on October 18) that the boys first used the name. And although they made it into the finals (appearing for two successive auditions at the Liverpool Empire and Hippodrome theatres in Manchester), they were not ultimately chosen to appear on Levis's show.

Ever intent upon cultivating their blossoming image, the group tried on several new names over the following year, including the Beatals, the Silver Beats, the Silver Beetles, the Silver Beatles, and by August of 1960, the Beatles. Earlier that year, in January, Lennon invited his art school chum, Stuart Fergusson Victor Sutcliffe or simply "Stu" to join the band. Although a brilliant painter and designer, Sutcliffe made no pretence about being any sort of musician and was therefore obliged to up pick up the bass as he went along, a learning experience that certainly didn't ingratiate him to the perfectionistic McCartney.

By April of 1960 things were finally beginning to perk up for the band. At this point still the Silver Beatles, the boys snagged a solid two weeks work backing balladeer Johnny Gentle on a ballroom tour of Scotland. Encouraged by what for them was at least a taste of real work, they came home feeling like genuine musicians, even if their pockets were still basically just as empty as ever. "Someone actually asked me for my autograph," Paul wrote home to his dad from Inverness. "I signed for them too, three times!"

"From that day onwards," Jim McCartney later remarked, "things were never really quite the same."

Contrary to popular belief, the Beatles' initial trek to Germany came about more as a result of a lack of alternatives than of any great success in England. Thinking they had been booked at Hamburg's popular Kaiserkeller through small-time Liverpool promoter Allan Williams, they later discovered they were actually slated to appear as the new house band at the Indra, a seedy, low-life, former strip club at 34 Grosse Freiheit. Just prior to setting off, Paul McCartney rang up local drummer Pete Best on the spur of the moment and invited him to join the group as a quick fix to the Beatles' ongoing percussion problems. Best, eager to escape the hopeless tedium of attending teacher's training college the following autumn, immediately said yes. The shy, handsome young man from Hayman's Green was now a Beatle.

There was, however, still one major stumbling block to be overcome before the five eager young men could pile into Williams' battered green mini-van and make for Germany: Jim McCartney. Aware that his no-nonsense dad would never allow such an apparently foolhardy venture without a great deal of convincing, Paul, ever the politician, cleverly recruited the assistance of his brother. After Paul's stirring, fifteen-minute-speech on how his phenomenal fifteen-pounds-a-week salary would enable him to buy his beloved younger brother just about anything his heart desired, Mike was only too happy to go a couple of rounds with the old man on Paul's behalf. After all, this was a chance for high adventure. And culture! Mike just couldn't say no. "Our kid was always very good at handling Dad and getting his own way," he recalls.

> I remember coming home from school with Paul the day he told me they'd been invited to Hamburg, just casually. I said, "Wow!" But he didn't know if he should, pretending he was all undecided. I said it was fantastic! He was going to be a big star. Wow! He said, "Do you think Dad will let me?" That was very smart. I was then on his side in persuading Dad. He let me get all excited, so that I was desperately wanting him to go.

When the time came to actually make his pitch, however, Mike's impassioned pleas fell on deaf ears. Puffing thoughtfully on his ever-present pipe, Jim listened patiently before quietly lowering the boom. "I'm sorry, son, but the answer is no. The whole thing is just too uncertain."

"But he's got weeks of school holiday left," Mike went on, "and he'll be making fantastic money. I wish I had the chance to travel like that. You're always going on about how broadening it is for a man to travel."

"That may be," Jim continued, "but we haven't even had the results of Paul's A levels yet. If he were smart he'd be more concerned about that than galavanting off with some beat group."

Despite Mike's best efforts, his father remained stubbornly unmoved and so Allan Williams was brought in to try to talk sense to the naturally reserved and cautious salesman.

But there was another problem. "Allan could never get our names right," McCartney later remembered. "He would call me John." Playing on Mr. McCartney's obvious respectability, the canny Williams went on to paint a picture of the lovely Germanic scenery, good steady wages, and a chance for his son to experience new, meaningful horizons. In other words, he laid it on thick.

"Williams was really very convincing," Jim McCartney commented with a wry smile years later.

He's almost as good a salesman as myself. Maybe better! Anyway, in the long run they eventually all wore me down and I told him he could go. I remember one of my main concerns, funnily enough, was that he might not get enough to eat. From the time they first arrived I started getting these silly little postcards and letters from him reciting their menu on any given evening. I suppose that satisfied me in a way. At least he wasn't starving I thought to myself.

The reality, however, was rather grim. When the boys first arrived they were put up not in the comfortable, homey, guest houses they had been promised back home, but rather three dank, seamy rooms with bunk beds behind the movie screen of the Bambi Cinema at 33 Paul-Roosen Strasse. Stuck away in their revolting, dilapidated digs, the boys looked around in utter disbelief.

"What a fucking shit hole," Lennon finally blurted out, suddenly pacing the almost pitch-black room like a wounded animal.

"Is this supposed to be a joke?" asked Paul to no one and everyone. "Where's the bloody toilet?"

"We're living in it," George shot back sardonically.

"Not for fucking long I hope," countered Pete. "Allan should have seen to this lot."

"I'm knackered lads," said Lennon, finally throwing himself into one of the top bunks. "Welcome to the wonderful world of show business. Let's get some sleep."

Unfortunately, he spoke a moment too soon. Bone-tired from the grueling trip, disoriented and hungry, the boys were all just about to settle down for a much-needed rest when a big, burly bouncer from the club ambled in and announced that the band was expected on stage at the Indra within the hour. Groaning and cursing together almost in unison, they had no alternative but to silently gather up their ragged gear and do as they were told. All things considered, their first taste of the continent left a lot to be desired.

The next morning, after going for a quick wash in the Bambi's putrid public lavatory, the boys exploded out into the street, keen to soak up as much of the Reeperbahn's lurid atmosphere as they could. "Hamburg was fantastic," John Lennon told me in 1971 when I visited him at his Syracuse, New York, hotel suite during Yoko's *This Is Not Here* exhibit at the Everson Museum of Art.

> Between the whores and the groupies our dicks all just about dropped off. Coming from Liverpool, we basically felt like big, tough teds — until we met the Germans, that is. Virtually every night at the Indra some poor bastard was either bottled, knifed, or worse. Fortunately, as the band, we were generally left alone. I walked about legless most of the time anyway. We all did. Hamburg was where we first got into pills. Speed it was, called Prellys. Believe it or not this old bird Rosa, the lavatory attendant, used to get them for us. In Hamburg you could get anything you wanted without even trying. Usually more than you wanted.

Of all the many ribald tales of the young Beatles in Hamburg, none is more sleazy than Allan Williams' infamous charge in his book, *The Man Who Gave the Beatles Away*, that while there, at least two of the boys were involved in homosexual unions with an unnamed, glamorous, six-foot-four transvestite they met in a St. Pauli night club. Although Williams never revealed which two he was talking about, in 1975 when the book was published, John Lennon was quoted as saying that of the many Beatle books written, Williams' tome was by far the most truthful and accurate. Since that time, several so-called experts on the group have hinted at the possibility of there being at least one practising bisexual Beatle, with the allegation usually leveled at the late John Lennon. As young and basically naive as they were in those days it's entirely possible that one of them might have gone at least half way with one of these beautiful she-males before even realizing the actual gender of his date. What happened after that is anybody's guess. In the end, it's all just so much more finely ground grist for the perpetual gossip mills of London and New York.

There is, however, another Hamburg-period scandal associated with the Beatles, and Paul McCartney in particular, that's not quite so easy to dismiss, involving the daughter of a local night club owner. Erika Heubers first met Paul while working as a waitress in a Reeperbahn night spot. Almost immediately the two began dating. According to Erika, then a slim, pretty teen, with lovely, straight, shoulder-length hair, she soon became pregnant by Paul, sending the career-minded, nineteen-year-old McCartney into a chaotic tailspin. He allegedly begged the heartbroken Erika to have an abortion, a suggestion the simple, family-oriented young woman refused even to consider. Several months later, on December 18, 1962, she gave birth to a baby girl she called Bettina. Born two months premature, Bettina grew up a happy, healthy girl, blissfully unaware of her "surprise" heritage. On her confirmation day in 1975, however, her mother, then married to German Army noncom Hans-Werner Heubers, broke the incredible news to her thirteen-year-old daughter. "At the time," Bettina later told reporters, "I was collecting lots of Beatle records and was a real fan of theirs. My mother kept hinting about Paul, and then she showed me the birth certificate with his name on it. It was a shock."

Peter Brown, the Beatles' longtime personal assistant, insists that the allegations were true. He says that following the Beatles' departure from Hamburg during one of their several engagements there, legal papers were sent on to Liverpool where Brian Epstein quickly turned the matter over to David Jacobs, the Beatles' London attorney. Jacobs advised McCartney to deny all charges and allow him to send the papers back to Germany unanswered, obviously preferring the singer's chances in a plodding German tribunal to the prompt attention both the English courts and the media were likely to give such a blatantly unsavory matter.

McCartney, without exception, has steadfastly denied that he is the young lady's father. But that didn't keep him, in 1966, from paying out £2,700 towards Erika's support until Bettina turned eighteen. McCartney explains:

We were due to do a European tour. I was told that if the main-tenance question wasn't settled we couldn't go to Germany. I wasn't going to sign a crazy document like this, so I didn't. Then we were actually on the plane leaving for the tour when they put the paper under my face and said if I didn't sign, the whole tour was off. They said the agreement would deny I was the father and it was a small amount anyway. I've actually seen a letter from Brian Epstein saying it would be cheaper to sign than not go to Germany where we could make a lot of money.

It was a decision that would come back to haunt McCartney. In 1981, interviews with his alleged "love child" began turning up in tabloids around the world. Touting the teenage Bettina as the mystery "Beatle Girl" they wrote as if it were already a foregone conclusion that McCartney was indeed her father. For Paul and Linda it became an embarrassing nightmare.

What I object to most is the effect on my children. It's not fair to them. Why should they suffer?

She [Bettina] was in *Time* magazine in 1983 and there was picture of her holding one of my record covers with the com-ment, "Dad says . . . " Not even *alleged* father. My kids had to read that. You have to put it down to life being tough at the top.

Unfortunately, for McCartney things were about to get a lot tougher. On February 22, 1983, in the district court, Sch-oeneberg, Berlin, a new action by the Heubers was heard, re-questing maintenance of £375 monthly and an official decla-ration that Paul McCartney was indeed the girl's father. Under German law, if paternity could be proved, then Bettina stood to one day inherit an estimated ten percent of the former Beatle's vast estate, a potentially astronomical sum. Although the judgment would only be enforceable in Germany, if left unpaid, sizeable German royalties could be frozen by the court, a decidedly unhappy prospect for McCartney's other heirs.

In an effort to establish his innocence, McCartney agreed to submit to both blood and tissue tests later that same month.

McCartney reasoned that a negative result might serve to halt the proceedings then and there. Once again, he was wrong. That March, McCartney was ordered to pay Heubers an interim maintenance of £180 monthly despite the fact that both tests, which have a ninety percent accuracy rating, indicated he was not the father. "It seems the girl's blood contains something that is not in mine or the mother's, so it must come from the third person and he is the real father," McCartney explained at the time.

Moving to West Berlin in 1980, Erika worked at a street concession selling sausage and chips to the passing throngs, while Bettina spent her days sticking fuses into fireworks at a local factory. As soon as the story hit the papers, however, the young woman was dismissed on the grounds that her new-found notoriety was disturbing to the normal work routine of the other employees. Later, Bettina was quoted as saying that like her illustrious alleged dad, she too was intent on making it as a pop singer. "I want to have a career as a singer under the name Bettina McCartney. I have enjoyed singing for many years, and I don't see that I am copying my father or trying to cash in on his name. . . . I will do it if only to prove to my father that I have spirit."

In April 1983 full maintenance was awarded the Heubers by the court. McCartney, it seemed, was fated to shoulder the consequences of this twenty-year-old night of passion whether he was actually the girl's father or not. "One thing I think is very unfair," McCartney said at the time, "is that the judge is a woman and is pregnant herself. But I'm not going to ask for a different judge, I just want to get the whole thing settled." Not surprisingly, McCartney refused to honor the German court's ruling and did not pay the Heubers any further monies. Two months later, in June, Bettina, then twenty, attracted further international headlines by posing nude for the trashy *High Society* magazine for just a scant £600. "The pictures are very tasteful," commented Erika Heubers in an effort to defend her daughter's plummeting reputation. "She did the session because she is broke and Paul hasn't paid her any maintenance money yet." Pictured nude but for a pair of long leather gloves, and holding a clear plastic guitar, Bettina pranced and pouted her way through the sizzling eight-page spread looking very much the victim of her own tacky lust for her rightful fifteen minutes of fame.

Bettina later thought better of her unlikely quest for stardom and settled down to a job at a Berlin hair salon. She also lost two additional appeals brought on by McCartney's high-powered German attorney, Dr. Klaus Wachs. As Heubers had now officially lost her case, the poor girl was liable to pay McCartney's $60,000 legal bills, an eventuality obviously far beyond her meager capabilities. In the end, Dr. Wachs advised his client that it might be wise to go ahead and pick up the legal fees himself in an effort to quash the mortifying mess once and for all. "I advised Paul, and he agreed for psychological reasons he should by no means enforce his right for costs. It was my opinion that if he did, this would give Miss Heubers another cause to make bad publicity for him."

In a final, misguided twist to this unhappy, no-win scenario, Bettina dismissed McCartney's apparent generosity as "suspicious," saying, "I think it's very odd Paul paid these costs for us and this will be prominently brought forward in our new case." To date, nothing further has been heard from either Bettina or her mother.

Enduring a grueling four-and-a-half-hour nightly playing schedule (six hours on Saturday and Sunday), the Beatles' term at the Indra mercifully came to an end on October 4, 1960, after club owner Bruno Koschmider finally caved in to an avalanche of complaints from both neighbors and patrons not accustomed to such loud, raucous music. Having no desire to let go of his contractual stranglehold over the band though, Koschmider moved them just down the street to his sister venue, the Kaiserkeller.

Although it was definitely a better gig in terms of the actual surroundings and clientele, for the band life was still tough. For one thing, Paul and Stu, never really close, had become increasingly hostile towards each other, eventually coming to blows one night after a particularly tiring set. "I admit I had problems with Stu," McCartney once told me.

> I regret it, of course, as he is now dead, but sometimes you can't help these things if you run up against controversy. It was mainly because he couldn't really play very well which made it very embarrassing when we were on stage or having photos taken. We had to ask him to turn away from the audience or the camera, so it couldn't be seen that his fingers weren't in the same key as the rest of us, or how few chords he could play. I was probably over-fussy but I felt it wasn't a good thing for an aspiring group to have such an obviously weak link.
>
> Stuart was really a lovely guy and a great painter, but he was the one I used to have all the ding-dongs with. One time we even had a fight on stage. I assumed I'd win because he wasn't all that well built. Some extraordinary power must have taken over though because he was not an easy match, let me tell you. We were locked for what seemed ages. "I'll kill you, you bastard!" I screamed at him. "I'll bloody get you, McCartney!" he screamed back. I think they had to pour water on us in the end.

Looking back, the real bone of contention between the two might have had more to do with young McCartney's abnormally keen sense of ambition than his alleged jealousy over Sutcliffe's close friendship with John. So completely obsessed with success was McCartney that soon even his thinly veiled, nice-guy image couldn't hide his obvious lust for the limelight. No longer were the Beatles just an off-the-cuff boyhood band with stars in their eyes; by the time they realized just how rough and unrewarding life could be at the bottom, all any of them wanted was to find a way up and out, just as quickly as possible.

"Where are we going, fellas?" John would frequently cry out in an effort to boost his rag-tag group's often rock-bottom morale.

"To the top, Johnny!" they would shout back like a band of wild Apache war lords psyching themselves to do battle.

"Where's that, then?"

"Why, to the toppermost of the poppermost, Johnny!"

Sometimes, that little moment of enthusiasm was all they had. As time went by, one of the big attractions for the boys (besides sex, that is) became getting loaded. With the possible exception of Pete Best, the band were all legendary dopers, rocketing themselves up and down as the spirit moved them, fuelled by a never-ending supply of amphetamines, barbiturates, and booze. Some of the company they kept was often pretty suspect as well. Apart from the many harlots and hustlers, the Reeperbahn also attracted a decidedly more hard-core element as well. Before long the boys were rubbing elbows with a sordid collection of robbers, rapists, and even hitmen in the course of a night's entertainment. Jim McCartney, one imagines, would surely have been frantic had he known.

The scene of their most harrowing experience in Hamburg was an after-hours club they frequented when unable to sleep after their backbreaking performances at the Kaiserkeller. Sitting together around a great circular table they were quietly listening to the house band one evening with Allan Williams when, without warning, a man walked up and wordlessly pointed a revolver in the face of one of the group's German acquaintances. Before anyone even had time to react, he carefully squeezed the trigger, instantly sending a rain of blood, bone, and tissue around the room. As horrific a scene as this was, on the notorious Reeperbahn it was merely another black night in Germany's most dangerous city.

Despite the often grim reality of the Beatles' Hamburg life and times, Paul McCartney's usual party line comment regarding their days there tends to downplay the well-documented naughtiness of the place in favor of a kinder, gentler Reeperbahn. "You're in Hamburg," says Paul.

You're eighteen. You've never been abroad in your life and you've got a bit of money in your pocket. You go drinking on a

Saturday night and you end up out until Sunday morning. You do a couple of loony things like most eighteen-year-olds, or service men abroad; there's always some lunacy. But it just grows. Someone remembers and they say, "Do you recall that?" It's the old story; it grows into this amazing legend. "I remember them! They were tough days." It wasn't that much different from now. It was just a little bit more lunacy, that's all. Quite a bit more lunacy. But it was just good clean fun. Good dirty fun actually.

By far the most surprising feature of Hamburg for the boys was the inexplicable way in which so many desirable women were drawn to them. Back home they had always been reasonably popular with the ladies but nothing prepared them for the sexual smorgasbord available to them on the Reeperbahn.

Returning nights to their hovel at the Bambi Kino the boys were often waylaid by several anonymous females from the club who used to lie in wait in the almost pitch-black hallway hoping to snare a Beatle, any Beatle, on the way to their rooms. Pete Best remembers:

> There were nights when we felt so bushed all we wanted to do was head back to the dungeons and hit the sack. But we couldn't win. I would reach my cupboard-like room ready to flop — and find there was a bird already waiting outside my door. Some of them had discovered that they could enter our quarters through the cinema: all they had to do was buy a ticket, then head for the toilets, push open a crashbar on a door and there they were.
>
> When Paul and I would arrive at our doors we would hear sniggering in the darkness and suddenly become aware of the aroma of perfume — and it was a case of doing justice, no matter how we felt. Sometimes we never even saw the face of the girl who had waited in the gloom to share our beds.

According to Best, the record number of groupies the band availed themselves of on any given evening while in Hamburg was eight. After a quick huff and puff the boys would switch dates, with Lennon shouting out, "All change!" It was that wild.

We shared everything in those days, and for the nightly romp there were usually five or six girls between the four of us. During the proceedings there would come an echoing cry from John or George along the corridor inquiring of Paul and me: "How's yours going? I'm just finishing. How about swapping over? How you two doing? I fancy one of yours now!" The girls would each do the rounds with us. . . . Birds — ready, willing and able, were vying for our attention everywhere. They would even trail us to our eating haunts. We often went for a bite at a cafe called Harold's, and admiring girls would be there, happy to buy us meals — and give other delights for free later. We found ourselves having two or three girls a night each, depending on how fit we were.

The Beatles' first stint in Hamburg ended on November 21, 1960, when George Harrison was deported by immigration officials for working under the age of eighteen in a night club. Not to mention the fact that Allan Williams had somehow neglected to secure the appropriate working visas for the group. Drifting back home to Liverpool, the boys felt dejected and beaten, oblivious to the vast improvement playing in such miserable isolation had made to their music. By this time, they had raced furlongs ahead of virtually all the local competition. Leaving England, happy just to have a gig, any gig, they returned fully professional musicians able to tease the emotions of an audience with their vast reserves of talent and charisma. But they were still stone broke, an unhappy fact not lost on the overtly practical Jim McCartney. Within days Paul had reluctantly landed a "proper" job as a delivery boy for something called Speedy Prompt Delivery Service, in Liverpool. "And you'd better think about getting back to school as well," Mr. McCartney chided his thoroughly frustrated young son, "just in case things don't work out with the music."

Very similar sentiments, one suspects, were being heard in virtually all of the Beatles' households at the time. For a moment there, John's Aunt Mimi even suggested that her soon-to-be-famous nephew accept a position as a bus conductor.

Fate, it seemed, was intent upon letting the Beatles dangle just a little while longer before finally revealing to the world their extraordinary future. Waiting for a tomorrow that might never arrive is a spiky little hell all its own, a hell so diabolical as to make only a few scant months seem, to its unwilling denizens, an eternity.

The Beatle thing was fantastic. I loved every minute of it.
—Paul McCartney—

I was just so sick of it. I think we all were.
—George Harrison—

4

Glass Mountain

Liverpool, London, and the World

To no one's surprise, Paul didn't last long as a delivery boy. Within only a couple of weeks he was sacked by the powers that be as "unsatisfactory," his labors at Speedy Prompt apparently neither particularly speedy nor prompt. His major transgression, it seems, was falling asleep in the back of the van during several of the company's longer out-of-town runs. "If that were the army you'd be put up to a wall and shot!" Jim McCartney roared, only half joking when he heard the news. "I hope you still don't actually think you're going to make a living out of that beat group, son." Deep inside, Paul too was beginning to have serious doubts.

A short while later, McCartney found himself another job, this time as a lowly coil winder at Massey and Coggins, a prominent Liverpool electrical engineering company. With a whopping starting pay of seven pounds a week, it seemed this time things might really work out. Spending his days winding miles of stiff copper wire, he even considered staying on, in his mind eventually to become a high-powered young salesman. Unfortunately, McCartney lagged behind his colleagues in his winding work so significantly that he was once again let go after only a few weeks on the job. Asked about his indenture at the wire works many years later, the multi-millionaire ex-Beatle had apparently erased the entire episode from his memory with the exception of one foggy remembrance of his supervisor referring to him sarcastically as "Mantovani" because of his outrageously "long," collar-length hair.

One of the quiet turning points for the Beatles was their accidental meeting, in 1960, with future Cavern Club compere, Bob Wooler. A clever punster, the *word*wise former railway clerk first ran into two of the boys at a Liverpool bus stop. "It was on Penny Lane," he told me in 1985. "Just George and Paul. McCartney spoke first, telling me they were in a group. To be honest, I had only vaguely heard of them, but I did know their old drummer, Tommy Moore. I used to work with him on the railroad years ago. He died in 1980, you know. Most people don't realize it, but we lost two former Beatles that year, Lennon and Moore." Wooler next met up with the group at Allan Williams' Jacaranda coffee bar on Christmas day. After a couple of celebratory rounds of Cokes, Paul told Bob about their being booted out of Hamburg and wondered if perhaps he might be able to set them up with something locally. Wooler recalls:

At the time, I was doing a bit of work with a promoter by the name of Brian Kelly, so I was able to offer them a half-hour spot at the Litherland Town Hall as an extra. When I asked him [Kelly] for eight pounds he went all quiet. This is a terrible town for that, you know; everyone wants something for nothing. After regaining his composure he begrudgingly offered four, but I reminded him that with five Beatles and their driver, Neil Aspinall, that didn't even amount to one pound per man. Anyway, after a lot of hoggy boggy, Kelly eventually agreed to six and I gave them a very good spot on the bill. From the moment they first stepped out on stage the audience was transfixed. It was the beginning of what would soon become known as Beatlemania.

At this point, Stu was still in Hamburg, having fallen in love with artsy young photographer Astrid Kirchherr, which quite inconveniently left open his position on bass. To fill the gap a young chemistry student, Chas Newby, was quickly ushered in, first playing with the group on December 17 at the Casbah Club, a smoky teenage dance cellar run by Pete Best's fun-loving mother, Mona.

Almost immediately the Beatles became the hottest thing going. Soon, however, Newby left the group to continue his studies, shifting his duties on bass to Paul. Playing his battered old bass (both backwards and upside down to accommodate his stubborn left-handedness), McCartney quickly came to terms with what was actually quite a difficult instrument to just pick up and play. The Beatles' sudden home-grown success was certainly a boon to Paul's oftentimes fairly rocky life at home with his father and brother. At least now he had something positive to point to when defending his musical aspirations to his dad. "I brought home nearly twice this week what I would have been making anywhere else," McCartney would gloat in his cheery, offhand, convincing way. "We'll see, son," the older and wiser Jim muttered between puffs on his pipe. "I only hope for your sake things work out. If your mum were here she'd say the same. All I ever want is what's best for you boys."

Hand in hand with the Beatles' rapidly rising popularity began the manic adulation which was later to become the true hallmark of Beatlemania. Their sexual curiosity was at its peak, and although the money was still pretty shabby, the birds definitely were not. Paul in particular was, as they say in Merrie England, "a bit of a lad," loving and then leaving broken-hearted some of Liverpool's tastiest young maidens. One of McCartney's "fave raves" during this period was Iris

Caldwell, the pretty blonde sister of fabled Liverpool rocker Rory Storm. The romance lasted about a year and six months, during which time they both all but stopped seeing other people. Pretty heady stuff for a young man as full of hormones as Paul McCartney. Iris had trained as a dancer from the age of fifteen, appearing at local variety shows and holiday camps throughout the North. In fact, her lovely, long legs were one of her most alluring features.

Longtime Beatle buddy and respected journalist Bill Harry recalls the inception of their whirlwind affair. "I remember her appearing on one of the bills at the Tower Ballroom which featured the Beatles and several other Mersey acts. She was wearing a brief costume which highlighted her slim legs in fishnet stockings, and Paul couldn't keep his eyes off her." After Beatle manager Brian Epstein came onto the scene in November 1961, he did his best to cool off the liaison, apparently in the interests of protecting the group's guise of eligibility to their teenybopper fans. Liverpool insiders, however, hint that the covertly homosexual Epstein may have simply been jealous of Ms Caldwell's affection for the handsome and charming McCartney. Iris remembers:

> Epstein was not very pleased that I was going out with Paul, and I wasn't allowed to go anywhere with the group in case any of their fans saw me. But every night after they'd appeared at the Cavern, Paul would come round to our house, and when they went away to Hamburg he used to write me the most fantastic letters which I wish now I'd kept because they were very funny. Talking about all the things that happened to them, sometimes he'd illustrate them with a little cartoon. In those days they had funny names for people and Paul always used to call me "Harris" and he signed his letters "Paul McCoombie." I can remember one letter he'd sent in which he wrote: "We've been down to London jumping around" and he illustrated it with a little picture of himself leaping around on his bum.

Despite all the sophomoric shenanigans, says Iris, Paul was capable of displaying very real and tender emotions. A strong and passionate lover, when the spirit moved him he could also be a very good friend as well.

"Paul was very hard to dislike," she recalls. "Even in his teens there was something about him, a sort of charisma that used to strike people when they met him for the first time. And he always knew exactly where he was going, even though people often used to tell them they would never make it."

Eventually, in 1964, Iris married singer Shane Fenton (later to become seventies glitter king, Alvin Stardust), and accompanied him out on the road as part of his stage show. During her days with Paul however, there was never anyone else, at least for her. McCartney, she suspects, may have still occasionally sowed a few wild oats.

> I'm quite sure there were many other girls around but I didn't actually know he was going out with anyone else, if you see what I mean. I used to say to him, "Why don't you go out with somebody else?" though I never thought he did, and then when he came back from London once and said he had met Jane Asher, I didn't want to go out with him anymore, though we remained friends and kept a good relationship.

The Beatles' second trip to Hamburg commenced on Friday, March 24, 1961, with the boys loading their tatty gear into the baggage car of a Liverpool train and then scrambling for a seat together in second class. Arriving exhausted, three days later, they stumbled into a taxi for the ten-minute-plus ride to their new, somewhat improved digs, supplied courtesy of promoter Peter Eckhorn, four shaky flights above their latest venue, the Top Ten Club.

Their salary was a duly modest thirty-five deutsche marks per bobbing Beatle. Not a fortune by any means, but mixed in with the many attractive perks the boys enjoyed on the Reeperbahn, it was enough to scrape by. The contract, negotiated over Mona Best's telephone by the band, demanded basically the same grueling schedule of their earlier trek. They would perform nightly from 7:00 p.m. until 2:00 a.m.,

Monday through Friday. Weekends, they played an hour later, switching off their ragged amps at 3:00 a.m. Every hour on the hour they were entitled to a fifteen-minute break, plus all the free beer and booze they could manage to guzzle.

By this time, Stu had quite rightly decided to leave the band permanently in order to concentrate on his art work, not to mention his smoldering affair with Astrid. Occasionally, however, he would still sit in with the lads, and sometimes even with other visiting Liverpool groups as well. Music was definitely still very important to Sutcliffe but it was his love and respect for John Lennon that compelled him to stay close. That notion, apparently, was one of the few things he and Paul McCartney had in common.

It was at the Top Ten that the Beatles first met and later began playing with transplanted British rocker Tony Sheridan during their raucous, late-night sessions. "My first impression of the Beatles," remembers Tony, "was that they were brighter than most Liverpool people I'd known, who frankly, aren't really famous for their intelligence. Because of this I could identify with them easier than these really hard, tough guys. They weren't like that at all, despite the image Lennon had. He was not a fighter, not aggressive in that sense. On the contrary, he was a bit of a coward, actually."

Sheridan recalls the band swaggering around St. Pauli, politely telling the Germans to fuck off, betting they couldn't understand the exact nature of this peculiarly British "greeting." Fortunately for the boys, they were right. "The clubs were all pretty rough," says the singer, "the atmosphere ultra-explosive, and the waiters very aggressive. The bouncers were all ex-boxers, and virtually every night there was at least one big free-for-all. So a lot of people got injured, some very badly; it was vicious. I don't know if it was an aftermath of wartime with all the kids that grew up during the war like I did. I think that has a lot to do with the emergence of rock 'n' roll altogether — the pent-up aggressiveness we tried to express in some other way."

The unquestioned highlight of this particular visit to Hamburg had to be the Beatles' first professionally produced recording session, held, disappointingly, onstage at an infants' school somewhere in Hamburg's lookalike suburbs. Tony Sheridan recounts the momentous occasion:

> Polydor's A&R [Artist & Repertoire] man, Bert Kaempfert, came along to the Top Ten one night with this entourage of people. He brought us all over to the table for a drink and said, "How would you like to come and record an audition for Polydor?" We said all right, and as we were an entity at the time all went together.
>
> I remember John Lennon's voice conked out during the session. He was overworked, so he didn't get anything much done. I was doing most of the singing. I don't know why Paul didn't do any. Perhaps he wasn't too interested in the limelight at the time. Anyway, he was just learning bass as Sutcliffe had only recently left.

For their work on the session the Beatles received a token 300 deutsche marks each, as a one-time fee, thereby surrendering any further rights or royalties to the project. Ironically, a single pulled from the session, "My Bonnie," backed by a hardrocking Lennon rendition of "The Saints," eventually went on to sell an estimated 100,000 copies after reaching number five on the West German hit parade early that fall. The boys weren't even properly credited on the label of the disc, billed only as "The Beat Brothers," "Beatles" apparently sounding a bit too close to the German schoolboy expression for the male organ, "peedle." It wouldn't be the last time they were referred to in that regard either.

The Beatles' second trip to Hamburg ended on July 2, 1961, after their twice-extended contract with Peter Eckhorn finally came to an end. Nine days later, Paul McCartney was comfortably back home with his father and brother enthusiastically plotting for the future. They had made a record after all, something clearly beyond the reach of nearly every one of

Merseyside's hundreds of teenage bands. It was now obvious that the Beatles were something quite special, an undeniable fact nobody's uptight auntie or shortsighted teacher could ever reasonably hope to dislodge. It seemed only a matter of time now before the rest of the world would catch on.

What followed then was a whirlwind of frenzied, on-the-road activity for the still mostly skint group. Throughout the rest of the summer and early fall, they pounded out their brave new music nightly at venues everywhere from Huyton to Knotty Ash. One look at their dizzying itinerary from those days tells anyone they were in great demand. As John Lennon once told me:

> They were all good gigs because everybody loved us. But no matter where we went it was the Cavern that was home. I could tell you a thousand different stories about the place but it wouldn't matter. You had to have been there. People talk about how wonderful it was to see us performing down there, but remember, it wasn't just us four guys making it all happen. It was a lot of little indescribables all tossed together that created the magic. The smells, the crazy birds, the smoke. That was definitely a big part of it as well.

The Beatles' love affair with the Cavern first started years before, in August 1957, when Lennon's Quarry Men mounted the wooden stage to perform the rock classic "Come Go With Me," and Elvis staples "Hound Dog," and "Blue Suede Shoes." In those days, however, the club was strictly a Trad Jazz establishment, prompting the owner, Alan Sytner (obviously a purist), to send a terse note on-stage demanding that the boys "Cut out the bloody rock!" Paul McCartney, by the way, didn't join his mates onstage for that historic session, opting instead for a camping holiday with the Boy Scouts. "It was terrific!" Lennon raved to McCartney following the epic evening at the Mathew Street hot spot. "There were so many kids packed in, the walls actually started to sweat. They used some weird disinfectant stuff apparently to keep it down. Afterwards, everything — the gear, our clothes — all reeked of it. Mimi just about went spare trying to get it all out."

Paddy Delaney, the club's eternal doorman, was, as always, on duty the first time the boys ever played there as the Beatles. The date was February 21, 1961, a day forever etched into the big man's memory. "The first one I ever saw was George Harrison," recalls Delaney.

In those days hairstyles were very strict and tidy, but George's hair was down to his collar. He was very scruffy and hungry-looking. Fifteen minutes later, Paul McCartney tumbled down the street with John Lennon in close pursuit. Paul was carrying his bass guitar, and John had his hands dug deep into his pockets. I had an idea they were with George because they all had the same sort of hairstyle. A little while after they strolled in, a taxi pulled up and out came Pete Best. He was carrying the Beatles' first sound system, two cheap chipboard speakers, and a beat-up looking amplifier. He also had a set of old drums, which he unloaded by himself and took down the stairs.

From the first night they descended the eighteen stone steps of the former wine and spirits warehouse cellar, Liverpool's music-loving teens had found their band, and the Beatles' safe refuge from a grownup world of Doubting Thomases who just couldn't understand. Julia Baird remembers:

Everybody went to the Cavern, even Mimi, who was in a furious fit about it all at first. She went down to see what was going on. I think she just gave up after that, realizing John was going to do just exactly what he wanted to anyway. Personally, I didn't go as much as I might have done, but we lived quite a long way out of town and the last bus back was ridiculously early, so we couldn't stay out very late. All I can tell you was that it was the Beatles all in black leather, and lots of noise. We loved it.

The Beatles' steadily advancing career apparently well in hand, the band played on to the thunderous delight of Liverpool's legion of dance-happy teens. That fall, however, Lennon and McCartney took a well-deserved two-week sabbatical to Paris, hitchhiking south and then taking the Channel ferry to the northernmost tip of France. Even in those days hitchhiking was considered seedy and dangerous, a point not lost on either Jim McCartney or John's Aunt Mimi.

The two set off from McCartney's Forthlin Row home on October 1, 1961, on their spur-of-the-moment holiday. Funded in part by a twenty-first birthday gift of a hundred pounds presented to John by his Auntie Mater in Edinburgh, the trip proved a significant bonding experience for the two. McCartney fondly remembered the occasion during my 1986 interview:

That was one of the things I undoubtedly found very interesting about John's family. As my mother was a nurse and my dad a cotton salesman, we always lived in the nurse's house on the estate. So to actually see this sort of middle-class thing was fascinating for me. Christ, I can even recall John getting one hundred quid for his birthday off his relatives in Edinburgh I mean, I still say I'd like it now! Someone just hands you a hundred quid, still feels good to me. So I thought, "This is amazing, I've never seen people like this!" I remember John talking about people the family knew from the BBC, friends who were dentists, and uncles and aunts up in Scotland, so it was very exotic to me, all that. We went to Paris on that money. It was supposed to be Spain, but we never got past Paris, we enjoyed it so much. We suddenly thought, "We can't really get to Spain on a hundred quid." I don't really know if he was fond of me or just into spending. And I would be there for the banana milkshake! I think I actually paid my own way. We soon realized though we needed a bit of a gimmick to get people to stop so we both wore bowler hats in addition to our leather jackets. We thought they might take the edge off the kind of hoody look, or ruffian image we had then. I guess people would just think, "Whoa, look, there's a couple of daft kids in bowler hats there. You know, they don't really look like a threat." We got a bit drunk on the French beer. We had been drinking the British stuff and so we thought we could handle it, but this foreign stuff really went to our heads. It was all just so adventurous. I had never done anything like that. I'd hardly ever been out of Liverpool before. We'd been to Pwllheli, Skegness, and Lemington Spa before, but that had been the whole of my travels.

> It was very exciting to get off on your own with a mate. John
> was a great guy because he was never boring.

While in Paris, Lennon and McCartney mostly just hung out in sidewalk cafes accosting the City of Light's young female population; they also found time to attend a concert by singer Johnny Hallyday at the Paris Olympia, and took in several evenings of Parisian rock at a local beat club in Montmartre. The trek to France produced one rather significant happening in the Beatles' long and winding road to success, the unexpected birth of what the world would soon come to know as "the Beatle haircut."

The humble origins of this most celebrated object of Fab Four lore came about as a result of the band's friendship in Hamburg with Jurgen Vollmer, a beat group enthusiast and talented freelance photographer. Meeting up with Jurgen in Paris, the boys were impressed by his daring, over-the-ears hairstyle and within a few days summoned up the nerve to brush forward their formally greased-back pomp into a Caesar-like fringe. Once back home, George quickly adopted the new look with only diehard rocker Pete Best refusing to follow Lennon and McCartney's lead. It would be the first of several such differences of policy between Best and the band and the beginning of the end of his time as a Beatle.

From this point onwards events in the group's meteoric rise to the zenith of popular music rapidly gained momentum. On October 29, 1961, a Huyton boy named Raymond Jones walked into Liverpool businessman Brian Epstein's family-owned NEMS (North East Music Stores) in Whitechapel and wondered if the immaculately attired manager might have an import copy of "My Bonnie" by a local group called the Beatles. He didn't. But priding himself on NEMS ability to satisfy even the most obscure requests, Epstein immediately set about trying to find the Polydor single. Alistair Taylor, Epstein's personal assistant and longtime Apple office manager, remembers his employer's frenzied search for the hard-to-find disc.

After a hell of a lot of calling around we finally got hold of a box of twenty-five, then another twenty-five, and they just kept selling as fast as we could import them. Then a few weeks later we went down to meet this group at the Cavern. They were sensational. Not necessarily musically, as a matter of fact; they were bloody awful as musicians — then, anyway. Liverpool was full of guys like that at the time, but the Beatles had something else — charisma. I call it "Ingredient X."

Following the Beatles' performance that afternoon, Brian and Taylor met the boys backstage to say hello, but only George has any recollection of the event. The others, it seems, were unimpressed to the point of non-recall. Epstein, after all, with his posh manners and gentrified presence, was hardly the kind of person the Beatles were naturally drawn to. It was, in fact clearly the other way around. From the moment they all tramped on stage, Epstein was smitten. And not just with the prospect of perhaps one day making a buck off the band either. This was something far deeper, far more sensual. To put it bluntly, clad in their Hamburg-period, skintight black leather, these bouncy, outlandish boys quite simply turned him on.

Dining that same fateful day at the Peacock on Hackins Hey, Epstein and Taylor enthusiastically reviewed the possibilities of what they had just seen. "There's been a lot said about how Brian went around saying they were going to be bigger than Elvis," says Alistair. "But I don't remember it being as blatant as that. I mean, we were excited, of course, and talked about what we should do. It was just something new and fun." Ironically, Epstein offered Taylor two-percent-plus of the group's future earnings if he would consider lending a hand in their management, but the recently married assistant turned him down cold. "What I need is a bigger weekly salary, Brian," he offhandedly replied. "What'll I do if they never make any money?"

Paul McCartney's final assessment to me of the Beatles' manager was that, although Epstein had a definite theatrical "flair," on a business level he turned out to be rather naive and "green." The same was not at all true, however, of Epstein's dark and seamy personal life. Here was a man obsessed, a solitary figure completely torn in two over his secret yen for the "rough-trade" homosexual binges in which he frequently indulged. "He was a very complex man," confides Alistair Taylor. "And I think there's far more to it than just being gay. He wasn't happy at that. He tried very hard not to be. Twice, I had a phone call from him saying goodbye, he was committing suicide. I've often said, in many ways I would have been happier if he had."

Longtime Beatle insider Peter Brown remembers that in 1959 when Epstein was just twenty-five, he was viciously humiliated, beaten, and robbed in a public lavatory in Liverpool's West Derby, where he apparently accosted an ardently heterosexual longshoreman. Picking himself up off the floor, the terrified young man tore down the road, jumped into his smart new Hillman California sportster, and frantically drove home to his parents' house in Childwall.

Confessing to his understanding mother, Queenie, a slightly cleaned up and edited version of the tawdry episode, Brian sank down on the chesterfield, nursing a cherry brandy and a battered psyche. Within minutes of his return, however, his assailant, having discovered from Epstein's wallet how well-heeled a victim he had just bashed, rang up and demanded a significant amount of money in exchange for his silence concerning young Brian's unconventional sexual preference. Queenie, in the best tradition of British iron ladies, was not about to bend. She immediately rang the family solicitor, Rex Makin, who discussed the matter with Brian and then advised him to report the entire incident to police. A few days later, using Epstein as bait, a trap was set for the blackmailer (who turned out to be the holder of a long criminal record for similar offenses); he was charged with extortion only yards away from the Epsteins' immaculate family business in Whitechapel. It was the kind of pathetic tale told over and over again in Epstein's short and troubled life, a cross that all who were close to him were forced to bear. The morally conservative McCartney, in particular, seemed to feel that Epstein's not-so-private personal life could have a negative effect on the Beatles' image. Epstein was undoubtedly immensely encouraging and helpful to the band during those first struggling years, and frankly, there probably wouldn't have been any such thing as the Beatles without him. Later, however, he became a source of acute embarrassment and heartache for the upwardly mobile McCartney, who even today, although he acknowledges that Brian was "basically a lovely guy," maintains that Epstein's many personal trials and limited business acumen caused the Beatles much needless grief.

The Beatles themselves and their closest friends were not exempt from Epstein's homosexual advances. Pete Best remembers that one afternoon, while he and Eppy were driving around Liverpool discussing business, Brian propositioned him, asking if he might consider spending the night with him in a nearby hotel. Thoroughly embarrassed, Best quietly declined and never mentioned it to him again.

Pete Shotton, too, tells an almost identical tale in which Epstein invited him to come for a ride in order to speak to him confidentially about John. "Actually, Pete, I'm afraid I brought you here on somewhat false pretenses," Epstein began. "What I really want to talk about is you. John has told me so many wonderful things about you, I was thinking we might go back to my apartment together and get to know each other a bit better."

"I don't get it," replied young Shotton innocently. "What for?"

"I think you know what for," said Epstein, sliding over closer to the bewildered teenager.

"No way, Brian. I'm afraid that's not really my scene, mate." This incident, however, was cast aside by the former Quarry Man, and he and Epstein went on to become good friends. In his memoir, *John Lennon in My Life*, Shotton wrote that even now he considers Epstein one of the nicest people he has ever met.

Incredibly, in spite of so much indisputable evidence to the contrary, Epstein used to like to pretend that no one actually knew he was gay. "Why did you tell John that I am queer?" he demanded one evening of Neil Aspinall, who was busy unloading the group's gear at an out-of-town gig.

"Because you are, Brian. You are. You're queer and we both know it."

"I am not!" he shouted.

"Oh fuck off, Eppy. Who are you trying to kid? Me or yourself, huh?"

"I tell you, I'm not, and you had no right to ever say such a thing."

"Suit yourself then, mate. Some people just have to play their little games, don't they?"

Up until the very end of his life, Epstein persisted with this peculiar charade, despite the fact that he allegedly had a sexual encounter with one Beatle, came on heavily to another, and later freely flaunted his many lovers and boyfriends in front of just about everyone. It was unquestionably a compulsive and embarrassing aspect of his life. Such was the dichotomy of Brian Epstein, as thoroughly confused and unhappy as he was competent and hopeful.

Tony Mansfield, former drummer for the Merseybeat-era band, the Dakotas, and a latter-day NEMS talent, remembers the quiet, introspective manager with his so-called Stable of Stars.

Brian had that same flair of authority as George Martin. I remember Eppy, as we called him, used to get very annoyed at Billy Kramer occasionally. We were doing "Thank Your Lucky Stars" once, and he came running in after the show and glared at Billy, saying, "The Dakotas were lovely . . . but you, Billy, ha!" and steamed out of the room like a little boy. We were all dying to crack up laughing but we just couldn't. Sure, Brian was gay, but we never really thought of him that way, it just never came up. I don't think even Brian knew what he really was. He tried to go out with girls, didn't he? Eppy had a few girlfriends. He often dated the late Alma Cogan. We met him out one night with her at a posh London restaurant.

Tony (the brother of popular sixties singer Elkie Brooks), eventually left the Dakotas to open a Manchester boutique after several uneasy years playing sideman to the only marginally talented Billy J. Kramer. At one point, prior to Ringo Starr's ascension to the throne as the Beatles' easygoing drummer, Mansfield says that he was actually considered for the job but turned it down. Tony, whose real last name is Bookbinder, looks back fondly on his days hanging out in the Beatles' inner circle, but like so many reared under Brian Epstein's motherly wing, still isn't all that sure that what Brian did, he actually did for them.

> I was always a bit frightened of Brian. I could never speak my mind to him. We looked up to him like you would a schoolmaster. We were very much manipulated by him, I think. He was trying to help us and he got very well paid for it, but I don't think he really put the interest into us that he should have. Now you can't give somebody something if they don't already have it, but Brian could have groomed Billy a bit better.
>
> I mean he was a nice enough person to the degree that he always remembered your birthday and made sure he bought a present. . . . Actually, he bought all the acts presents on their birthdays or at Christmas time. He was very meticulous in the way he looked and always bought extremely expensive clothes. With the normal calibre of personal manager running around at the time being the fast-talking, cigar-smoking type of guy, Brian was a real gentleman. The business wasn't used to a Brian Epstein and didn't always know how to treat him.

Epstein officially became the Beatles' manager in January 1962, through a contract, incidentally, which the former record store executive never actually signed. Now all he had to do was to find them some sort of a deal. Any deal. A tall order for a guy who only a few miserable months before had confided to his younger brother Clive that he actually felt quite depressed about his future.

By January 1, 1962, things had moved along considerably. Guitars in hand, the Beatles traveled down to London for a recording test with Decca Records at the request of A & R man Mike Smith, who had first heard them rip it up at the Cavern. During the session, Paul in particular laid down several exciting lead vocals, but the label ultimately turned them down with recording manager Dick Rowe's memorable line, "I'm sorry, Mr. Epstein, but groups with guitars are definitely on the way out."

Although by now Stuart Sutcliffe had well and truly put his Beatle days behind him, he and John still maintained a close relationship through an exchange of long, chatty letters. Once or twice Sutcliffe related that, for some unknown reason, he was having very severe headaches. Not every day, but still often enough to cause some concern. Even as far back as Christmas of 1961, during a visit home to Liverpool, Lennon had silently noted just how pale and sickly his old friend looked. When he fainted once at the art college in Hamburg, Astrid and her mother realized there must be something seriously wrong. The family doctor was called and Sutcliffe sent for an exhaustive series of X-rays, but nothing untoward showed up.

In addition to the now-devastating headaches, Sutcliffe was experiencing terrible temper tantrums. Increasingly abusive and violent for no apparent reason, he became difficult for the Kirchherrs to cope with. After coming home one afternoon from an appointment with yet another specialist, he sat staring blankly out the window, into the empty street below, and observed calmly to Astrid: "I don't want a black coffin like everyone else. I saw a lovely, bright white one today in a window. I want one like that." Needless to say, such morbid talk was extremely upsetting to the dedicated and loving woman. Allan Williams, a faithful and caring friend, remembers the last bleak days of Sutcliffe's brief, eventful life:

Stuart was complaining to me about his recurring headaches and fits of depression. He spent many sleepless nights literally beating his head against the wall to stop the pain . . . Stu agreed with me that the headaches stemmed from injuries he had received when he was beaten up by a gang of hostile youths outside Lanthom Hall after a Beatles gig. Paradoxically, Stuart's work improved immensely in this period, though it took on a somber, ghost-like quality.

Now securely under the tutelage of Brian Epstein, the Beatles cut a significantly more professional image due in large part to their new manager's well-honed sense of style and passion for the theatrical. Henceforth, they were strictly forbidden to swear, chew gum, or, God forbid, drink or eat on stage, prohibitions particularly irksome to the naturally rebellious Lennon. McCartney on the other hand, ever the promoter, clearly saw the wisdom of it all and actively encouraged the group to toe the line. "At least until we get what we want," he would mutter under his breath to John.

It was these new improved Beatles who jetted off to Hamburg on April 10, 1962, to begin their third stint on the Reeperbahn. This time, thanks to Epstein's fastidious advance planning and skillful PR, they would play the Star Club, then one of Hamburg's most upmarket, high-paying venues. Just as they were about to leave for Speke Airport, however, an urgent telegram was received from Astrid. Cut down by another blinding attack at the Kirchherr's home in Altona, Stu was rushed by ambulance to the hospital, unconscious and only barely alive. He never made it, dying enroute, cradled in Astrid's arms.

At first, the cause of the young painter's death was a mystery. Listed on his German death certificate as cerebral paralysis, it wasn't until almost two years later that the truth was finally uncovered. Following his death and the return of his body home to Liverpool, his mother, Millie, donated the cadaver to scientific research, hoping that their work might provide some answers. As it turns out, Sutcliffe suffered from a tiny benign tumor housed surreptitiously in a small depression in the skull. Carefully examining the exposed brain tissue, doctors confirmed the Beatles' theory that the growth was probably the direct result of a swift, traumatic blow to the head, just like the one he had suffered outside Lanthom Hall in Seaforth on May 14, 1960.

Pete Best remembers: "Stu had just walked outside and a couple of so-called hard knocks were giving him a good going over. Anyway, John and I immediately stepped in and broke it up. A lot of people have turned around and said, no, it was a direct result of Stu overworking himself in Hamburg. I don't really know. I'm sure that didn't help things any, but for my money what happened that night definitely seems the most likely." In that terrifying instant, Stuart Sutcliffe became the very first victim of out-of-control violent Beatlemania. Sadly, he was not to be the last.

The devastating news hit the Beatles like a bomb. John burst into hysterical laughter, unable to stop. George became predictably quiet, while Paul, despite his long record of run-ins with the former Beatle, appeared genuinely shocked and upset. So did Pete. That same day, Paul, Pete, and John flew on to Germany, meeting Astrid at the airport for a somber, tearful reunion. George, Brian, and Millie Sutcliffe, meanwhile, arrived the next afternoon, joining Astrid and the other three for an unusually demonstrative, emotionally charged encounter in the arrivals lounge. Grasping for something comforting to say to Mrs. Sutcliffe, Paul reportedly told the grieving fifty-four-year-old woman that within six months of his mother's passing, most of the deepest hurt had disappeared. Millie smiled weakly. "That's because you are young," she replied softly through her tears. "It's different when you're my age, Paul."

Years later, Astrid summed up her still-tender feelings for her lost love to author Ray Coleman in his masterful 1984 work, *Lennon*. "I know Stu would have preferred to have died rather than go on in the pain he was suffering. But the loss to me was great, and to anyone who knew him, because he was a genius, with a great mind and an original talent as an artist. He would have been outstanding if he'd lived. How John got over that period I'll never know."

Within days of the Beatles' solemn arrival in Germany, Lennon and McCartney, still enthusiastically pursuing their songwriting partnership, had penned a tune then called "Love, Love Me Do." Both knew it was a good song, "a keeper," as Lennon put it, and he went right to work creating a catchy harmonica riff for the intro. The duo was beginning to take its composing duties a little more seriously than before, soon amassing a considerable portfolio of well-structured, upbeat material.

To everyone's complete surprise and delight, an urgent telegram was received from Brian Epstein in London on May 9, 1962, after he had finally secured a provisional recording contract for the group with Parlophone, a small subsidiary of the vast EMI empire: "CONGRATULATIONS BOYS. EMI REQUEST RECORDING SESSION. PLEASE REHEARSE NEW MATERIAL."

The four young men were on top of the world. This was it, the big break they had all been waiting for. And Eppy had made it happen.

"I told ya he was alright," said Lennon, gleefully jostling Paul as they read and then re-read the stiff white paper. "Oh right, you bastard. Who's been pushing you lot to go along with all his bullshit? You can thank me for this, lads."

"Now all we gotta do is come up with a hit," said George, his usual pessimistic self.

"Don't worry about that," McCartney replied. "We'll do alright. I know we will. But first things first. Anyone for a drink?"

Upon their return from Hamburg seven weeks later, the boys immediately began to ready themselves for their London trip, whittling down to a fine point their already razor-sharp musical instincts during a private, closed-door practice session at the Cavern the first week of June. Several days later,

Brian and the boys arrived at EMI House, Manchester Square, London, to sign their contract. Though strictly provisional, if the sessions turned out well and the music and material measured up, the Beatles had themselves a deal. Forty-eight hours later they were bounding up the stone steps of 3 Abbey Road, St. John's Wood, to meet producer George Martin and begin work on what would eventually become their very first single, "Love Me Do," backed by the romantic ballad, "P.S. I Love You."

The whole Parlophone experience was a significant high point in the Beatles' ever-advancing assault on the music-loving youth of the world, but behind the scenes there was big trouble brewing. Pete Best, long regarded as the group's most handsome and sexy member, was soon to experience an excruciatingly cruel twist of fate. After four years of virtually full-time, mind-bending commitment and hard work, the quiet, gentlemanly drummer was about to be cheated out of his one and only shot at the big time. All things considered, the sacking of Best from the Beatles was a very nasty business, heartless naughtiness engineered, some suggest, by no less a personality than Paul, due to Pete's amazing popularity with the Beatles' female fans. Mike McCartney, however, hastening to the aid of his big brother, disagrees:

> Actually, it could have been any one of them fate chose to go. George could have been the one, you know. None of them was that fucking strong. But when they all got together, that's when the magic happened . . . The other three were very quick on the street level, but Pete was very moody, magnificent, and good-looking. The girls screamed for him and that was a big asset. They wouldn't have sacked the sod for that! Think about it. That would have been much bigger. A good-looking drummer out of the way behind with Paul, John and George fronting it. It was basically down to his drumming ability in the end. There were quite a few very good drummers around Liverpool then and I used to go home and tell Paul about Ringo. I used to see him play with Rory Storm. We didn't think about how ugly

he might have been, or about the white streak in his hair. Those things weren't important. It was just that this guy with Rory was a very inventive drummer. He goes around the drums like crazy, right? He doesn't just hit the drums, he invents sounds. He moves around the kit, and he's unusual. His feel is a little different and he can deliver the goods . . .

No matter what the motivation, changing drummers midstream was definitely a very tricky maneuver for the band at such a critical stage. And a controversial one.

Vaunted New York record producer Bob Gallo, Best's mentor following his split with the Beatles, remembers:

I always felt Peter had a very big challenge in life just to try to overcome what had happened to him. He did say that there was a hell of a lot of jealousy between him and Paul in the early days. Of all the Beatles, Paul and Peter were certainly the best looking. When they played the Cavern, apparently the girls would scream for him while Paul was singing. Now the story I got from Peter was that McCartney became very tired of all this and wanted to get rid of him for stealing his thunder. He also said that the Beatles went to Brian Epstein and told him Peter was taking pills, and that became one of the reasons he was dismissed as well. The fact is Peter might not have had the charisma Ringo had. The story goes that when they were considering tossing him out of the band, Paul went around Liverpool trying to find the ugliest drummer he could that had his own drum kit. Now, to be honest, technically Best is probably a better drummer than Ringo. His timing and feel are exceptional and as a producer doing a whole album with Pete, I can tell you he is a *very* talented player. The point is, according to Pete, it was jealousy that started the whole thing, not musicianship.

Too much of a gentleman to make a fuss, Pete quietly caved in to his former friend's betrayal and resigned his role as a Beatle. Although a few years later he was pushed by Gallo and his partner to sue and then settle for a relatively small sum with the band, he walked away terribly torn and confused about both his past and future. When I first met him in 1986, he still seemed hurt by the ordeal, and his faithful mother, Mona, was still reeling with anger over her son's unceremonious sacking from the greatest rock 'n' roll band of all time.

"Tell him about that Ringo, Pete!" she shouted from the stone stoop of her surprisingly grand West Derby home. "Why don't you tell him about the times we paid for him to go to the pictures when he didn't have a penny to his name! People forget he was your friend as well. The little bastard!"

"Please, Mum," the obviously embarrassed Best replied, smiling helplessly to his incensed mother. "Just forget it. It still upsets her," he apologized, "even after all this time." Sitting in the spacious back garden once filled to overflowing with sweaty teens seeking a bit of fresh air after dancing themselves to distraction in Mrs. Best's Casbah, Best waxed philosophical about his crazy days as a Beatle.

GEOFFREY: Was there a competition between you and Paul throughout your entire term with the Beatles?

PETE: Not unless Paul had taken it onto himself that there was a rivalry. Of course a lot of people have said there was a significant jealousy factor. My answer to that is, if he was jealous then it was bloody stupid. Personally, I was never vying to be number one.

GEOFFREY: Did you ever sing lead?

PETE: Yeah, I sang a couple of numbers — "Matchbox," "Roses Are Red," "Peppermint Twist," — that's about it.

GEOFFREY: To this day, do you know for sure exactly why you were kicked out of the group?

PETE: I wish I did. A lot of it is the fact that they didn't want me being a focal point in the band. Remember, I was the drummer. And it must have hurt knowing I was taking attention away from them.

GEOFFREY: It seems to me you were a very strong complement to their wild aggressiveness, being so laid-back and cool.

PETE: We were a unit. As far as I was concerned, if the birds screamed and paid more attention to me it didn't make any difference. They were just contributing to what the Beatles were. It all just added to the atmosphere.

GEOFFREY: I think it must be said that as a drummer it seems as though you were certainly as good, if not better, than Ringo Starr.

PETE: I've always advocated that. Even other drummers from that period have said to me over the years that as a Liverpool drummer I was top dog.

GEOFFREY: Obviously, all this must have been hell for you. I mean, you're world famous now as the guy who wasn't good enough. It's got to really hurt.

PETE: But there's two sides to it. That's the way I look at it. Sure, by a Kiffey trick, I was ousted. I wasn't there to share in the fabulous wealth and acclaim we all worked so hard for. But the other side of the coin is that now I have a great family and good friends. I can basically do what I want now without fear or trepidation.

GEOFFREY: They certainly can't. I mean, look at what happened to poor John.

PETE: As far as I'm concerned, that counts for a lot. I'm still a happy guy.

GEOFFREY: I suppose it must have taken quite a long time to really come to terms with the disappointment though?

PETE: Many years of heartache and resentment.

GEOFFREY: Did you ever personally speak to the other Beatles about it?

PETE: Never saw them. It was a funny thing. Of course my new band played on the same bill as them on two occasions, but nothing was ever mentioned. There was a stone-cold silence. And from that day to this that's the way it's remained.

GEOFFREY: It's well known you were very good friends with Neil Aspinall since day one. Did that friendship go out the window then as well?

PETE: The funny thing was Neil was with me the day I was let go. He'd driven me down in the van that afternoon I met Brian. When I came out of NEMS he looked at me and said, "Peter, what's happened? You went in happy as Larry, and you've come out like you've been kicked in the crotch." "Basically," I said, "that's what happened; they've kicked me out." So Neil turned around and said, "Well, that's it. If you're out, I'm out!" I remember we went out for a couple of pints and I said to him, "Look, Neil, they're going places, you can feel it. What's the use of cutting off your nose to spite your face? Stay with them. You've worked too damned hard to quit now." And of course he did, and he's with them to this day as executive director of Apple.

GEOFFREY: What do you think you'd say if you happened to meet Paul McCartney again after so many years?

PETE: Well, as far as I'm concerned the animosity was gone long ago; only the good memories are left.

GEOFFREY: You wouldn't want to sock him would you?

PETE: (Laughing) No. That would ruin everything! Meeting him again would probably be very embarrassing for both of us. But I should imagine, knowing Paul, it would probably just be a case of, "Hi, how ya doin', man?" Where the conversation would go from there, I don't know.

GEOFFREY: How did you react when John died?

PETE: You know a lot of people have said to me, "What difference should it make to you? You hadn't seen the guy in twenty years." What they fail to remember is that I still harbor very affectionate memories of the guy. I knew him for three or four years. I spent a lot of time alone with him. We fought fights for one another. We swapped birds with one another in Germany. I had a lot of respect for him. I always will.

Despite a fairly bumpy transition between drummers, the Beatles' hometown popularity continued to skyrocket. On October 5, 1962, the "Love Me Do" single was released in

Great Britain, eventually climbing to number seventeen on the charts. Several weeks later, the group traveled down to London once again to begin sessions for what would later become their second single, "Please Please Me."

Julia Baird recalls the impact of hearing her big brother's band's first recordings:

> I remember tramping up the stairs of the Cottage to [our cousin] David's room, clutching John's demonstration disc of "Love Me Do." What a thrill it was to finally hear on record the fruit of the band's many years of struggle. Another big occasion for us all was hearing the Beatles on Radio Luxembourg for the first time.
>
> Unfortunately, the reception was absolutely dreadful so we were all crouching down around the wireless trying to pick out the music from all the terrible static coming through the tiny speakers. Still, that was my big brother on the radio there and I couldn't help thinking how Mummy would have loved being part of our happiness. Another time, I remember hearing Jimmy Saville introducing "Please Please Me" by saying, "Well, here it is, the big new record from Liverpool's Beatles, and I hope it pleases somebody out there, 'cause it sure isn't me!" I wonder how many times he's lived to regret that rather hasty assessment of Britain's greatest gift to the world of show business!

Despite deejay Saville's skepticism, "Please Please Me" soon became the number one tune in England, conquering the summit of the coveted *New Music Express* charts on January 11, 1963. Twenty-four hours later it would do the same on the Disc chart. The Beatles had finally, and forever, arrived.

Meanwhile, back home at Forthlin Row, Mike McCartney was beginning to think seriously about his career as well. A super-talented all-rounder, Mike was himself a fine singer, writer, illustrator, and wit, eventually forming the highly original musical comedy troupe, the Scaffold, with Liverpool poet Roger McGough and funny man John Gorman.

The genesis of this legendary fool's paradise was typically as offhand as the trio's sly, infectious humor. Mike, who for want of anything better to do had offered himself as an apprentice performer in the 1962 Merseyside Arts Festival, was asked by Gorman to play the part of an old man in a comedy sketch with him and McGough. At first he declined, politely insisting that he "didn't do that sort of thing," but after a little gentle coaxing his comedic talent soon blossomed. Listed in the official program as "Mike Blank," the principled younger McCartney had no wish to try to cash in on his Beatle brother's newfound success, and so adopted this reasonably dotty pseudonym for the event.

From there the three irreverent loons became the Scaffold, performing initially in minor-league reviews all over Merseyside, including Allan Williams' Blue Angel club, various local political gatherings, and even, rather incongruously, the Cavern. "We didn't actually go down too well," says Mike, "because they were used to pop groups and we'd come out spoutin' poetry and bloody comedy."

Riding the crest of a wave wrought by the popular British television institution, "Beyond the Fringe," and the lesser-known "American Happenings," the zany Scaffold soon began to catch on. During the heady heights of Beatlemania, Britain's ABC television even offered the group their own seven-week series. "The first TV Scaffold ever did was our most successful in terms of the public," remembers Mike. "I only ever go on the public. That's the criteria because if they remember you years after the event, then you've done something that is unique . . . We came up at about the same time as the Beatles."

Despite his relative success, Mike was still standing in the giant shadow cast by Paul, and so, in 1963, unofficially changed his name to Mike McGear. "To protect the innocent and retain a little dignity amongst the absolute chaos, I decided to change my more-than-ample, historically proud family name (I can assure you it was that crazy)," McCartney/McGear wrote in his 1981 family biography, *Thank U Very Much*. "And it wasn't only the desire not to cash in on my brother's new found Beatle fame that made me do it. You see, my parents had taught me certain ethics, standards, pride, whatever you call it, which were impossible to go against, even if I wanted to."

As it became clear to everyone that indeed both McCartney boys were exceptionally gifted, Brian Epstein suggested to Mike that perhaps he too might consider climbing aboard the NEMS bandwagon for a go at the big time as a pop singer. McGear, however, quite astutely declined. "This was when [NEMS] was just getting Gerry [Marsden] and Cilla [Black] organized," he remembers. "I said, 'Brian, you must be jokin'. We've got one up there already who is doin' rather well, thank you.' To try and emulate that, to try and put myself up there and draw on Paul as a comparison would be a pretty dumb thing to do. I'm as good as him. He's a natural singer, a natural player of instruments and things. I'm a natural singer, too, though I've never been relaxed enough to let anybody hear it."

McGear and his fellow Scaffolders did eventually sign a record deal with EMI, releasing a commercially disappointing first effort with the nonsense ballad, "Two Days Monday," in 1966. One year later, EMI's gamble on the batty trio paid off with an easy number one — their off-the-cuff, bouncy comedy classic, "Thank U Very Much."

On June 7, 1968, McGear married Angela Fishwick in a high-spirited family ceremony in the tiny village of Carog, North Wales. Paul was best man, accompanied for the afternoon by his intended bride, popular British actress Jane Asher. That same month the Scaffold was booked into London's Royal Albert Hall joining show business greats Cleo Laine, Sammy Davis Jr., and Jonathan Miller, for one of the first-ever anti-apartheid concerts, entitled "Come Back, Africa." Later in the year, the irreverent comedy consortium played the famous London Palladium, meeting and later schmoozing with the likes of Princess Margaret and her then-husband, Anthony Armstrong-Jones.

That Christmas the Scaffold received a very special present: their latest musical offering, an uptempo satirical masterpiece, "Lily the Pink," became their second British number one, prompting even the usually tight-lipped Paul to break a long-standing personal resolution not to comment publicly on anything to do with Mike's up-and-coming career. When he first heard the happy news he told reporters:

> That's terrific! I've always given Mike brotherly advice because I reckon I know something about recording. But my advice to him has always been wrong! When the Scaffold recorded "Thank U Very Much," I told him not to sing about the Aintree Iron because it was too obscure — yet that became a big talking point about the song. And I also told him I wasn't too sure "Lily the Pink" was the right thing to record either!

On December 17, 1968, the BBC presented a show, dedicated to the collective lunacy of the Scaffold, entitled "The Talk of the Town Scaffold Special." It was the beginning of a reasonably long and prosperous career for the three on British TV. Children, it seemed, were especially fond of their somewhat . . . well . . . childish humor, which led to their very own kids' series. "How about that? Talking about drugs, we called our show 'SCORE with the Scaffold!'" Mike recalls. "But the BBC thought it was very innocent you see. They thought it was SCORE POINTS. We had these big badges on, saying, 'Score Now Kids.' It was the BBC, and they couldn't understand an innocent little thing like that could have two meanings."

Unfortunately, the lighthearted appeal of the group eventually began to dissipate: their incredible popularity with the British public was short-lived. "One of the biggest problems with the Scaffold," McGear reflects, "was that we were always the *next* 'That Was the Week That Was,' the *next* 'Beyond the Fringe,' the *next* 'Monty Python.' We were never '*it*'! We were always the *next* one. McGough's writing is just too clever. He used to write this verbal poetic imagery stuff, that was far too advanced for its time. One day you'll all catch up though."

Quite apart from his duties in the Scaffold, Mike was also making significant inroads as an author. His first work, described by him as a "children's/adult" book called *Roger Bear* sold well, paving the way for his next two — *Thank U Very Much*, and most recently, *Mike Mac's White and Blacks*, an oversized trade paperback of his justly famous, mostly Beatle-era photographs.

Towards the end of its time, the Scaffold amalgamated with former Bonzo Dog Doo Dah Band refugees, Neil Innes and Vivian Stanshall to form "Grimms" in the early seventies. Together this unholy tribe of unpredictable musical fools performed live throughout England, recording two superb albums for Island Records, *Grimms* and *Rockin' Duck,* before they imploded and dissolved into the outer reaches of pop history.

All things considered, McGear did pretty well for himself with the Scaffold, creatively, if not financially. It is important to note that any success he has won hasn't been because of his big brother's incredible achievement, but rather in spite of it. "The only way to survive was to choose a theatrical comedy concept," he explains. "If I'd chosen pop music I'd be dead now. It's like young Chris Jagger. I did a TV show with him in Munich recently. I mean, he's practically on the dole. He's into acting now; he got out of pop music, luckily. Now he's trying to survive as an actor."

Although Mike later went on to record a few solo albums as a singer, he is best remembered as the Scaffold's cheery, effervescent straight man. The group attempted one final reunion in 1984 as part of an outdoor show filmed in New Brighton, but things didn't quite work out as planned: "The sound was so bad nobody could hear," Mike recounts. "Everything was done at the last minute — bad news. Anyway, at least the three of us have a tape of us working together again. . . . The producers liked us. It just didn't go well. They ended up taking our segment out of the film — and I'm glad, to tell you the truth."

On June 18, 1963, Paul McCartney legally, and officially, became a man, finally turning twenty-one. No small event in anyone's life, let alone the number-one teen heartbreak in Britain's number-one band. To celebrate, a full-tilt blowout was held a few days later beneath a colorful marquee in the back garden of his Auntie Jin's home on Dinas Lane, Huyton. Tony Mansfield was one of the guests: "The Shadows were all there. I think even the Beatles would tell you they looked up to Cliff Richards and the Shadows. The party went on all night as I recall. It wasn't really an outrageous piss-up, but we were certainly all enjoying ourselves. I don't think anybody was too drunk or disorderly, except maybe John Lennon."

Lennon's "disorderly" conduct was the talk of Liverpool for weeks afterwards. Having had far too much to drink, he exploded like an artillery shell after Bob Wooler insinuated that he and Brian had engaged in a homosexual union while vacationing together recently in Spain. Wooler reportedly referred to Lennon's well-deserved respite from the rigors of Beatlehood as his "Spanish honeymoon." Lennon answered the accusation by pummeling the stocky compere, mercilessly hitting and kicking the poor sod almost into unconsciousness. Epstein immediately drove him to the hospital where he was admitted with a black eye, torn knuckles, and several bruised and battered ribs.

Of course, this kind of violently aggressive behavior was totally abhorrent to the gentlemanly McCartneys. Paul was definitely very annoyed with his out-of-control songwriting partner, as was Mike. It was Jim McCartney, though, who was the most upset, and despite the fact that Lennon fancied himself one of Jim's great mates, the elder McCartney cooled towards John from that night on.

Despite John's violent protest at the time, Pete Shotton recalls that years later Lennon actually confessed that he and Brian did indeed consummate their relationship while on holiday together.

> Eppy just kept on and on at me, until one night, I finally just
> pulled me trousers down and said to him: "Oh, for Christ's
> sake, Brian, here, just stick it up me fucking arse, then."
>
>   And he said to me, "Actually, John, I don't do that kind of
> thing. That's not what I like to do."
>
>   "Well," I said, "what is it you like to do?"
>
>   And he said, "I'd really just like to touch you, John."
>
>   And so I let him toss me off . . . Yeah, so fucking what! The
> poor bastard. He's having a fucking hard time anyway. So what
> harm did it do, then, Pete, for fuck's sake? No harm at all. The
> poor fucking bastard, he can't help the way he is.

After he came to his senses, John reportedly felt remorseful
about the incident with Wooler and instructed Epstein to fire
off a telegram, apologizing for the whole stupid mess. It read
as follows: "REALLY SORRY BOB. TERRIBLY WORRIED TO
REALIZE WHAT I HAD DONE. WHAT MORE CAN I SAY. JOHN
LENNON."

Fortunately, this and a token settlement of £200 seemed to
put the unseemly matter to rest, but not the continuing allegations of Lennon's rumored homosexuality. Paul McCartney,
however, has steadfastly denied the rumors, insisting that after having spent so many years in Lennon's company he
would have surely picked up on it if his famous colleague
were in any way so inclined.

Following "Please Please Me," "From Me to You," scored big
for the Beatles, giving them yet another number-one tune on
April 26, 1963. Their next musical coup, the hard-driving, boy/
girl mantra "She Loves You," rocketed to the top of the *Melody
Maker* singles chart on September 7, 1963. Written by Lennon
and McCartney in the music room of Jane Asher's parents'
house in London, the wild success of "She Loves You" proved
once and for all that the Beatles had real staying power as
artists. After all, three successive top-flight number-one singles could hardly be called a fluke. Perhaps McCartney's biggest personal thrill of that incredible, eventful year was the
Beatles' October 13 appearance on what was then Britain's
top television show, "Sunday Night at the London Palladium."

True to the end, the boys' many London fans virtually surrounded the venerable Argyll Street theatre, prompting police to call in hundreds of extra forces to help cope with the crunch. Predictably, the uproar attracted the attention of Fleet Street and virtually filled the pages of Britain's newspapers with exacting accounts of the phenomenal show both inside and outside the legendary hall. From that moment on, virtually everything the Beatles did became front-page news, at least in Great Britain. America, of course, was another story altogether.

It was not until the Beatles' heralded appearance at the Royal Variety Performance on November 4 that much news about the charismatic new teen group taking England by storm finally filtered across the sea to America. It was a great honor, to be sure. Jim McCartney was reportedly almost in tears that his son was about to personally perform before the Royal Family. "Wouldn't Mary be proud," he wondered to his sister Jin, the morning of the grand event. "She is, Jim, she is," came the reply. It was perhaps the single happiest moment Mr. McCartney had known since those first carefree days with his young family back in their humble two-bedroom home on Roach Avenue in Liverpool.

By the time the curtain rolled up at The Prince of Wales Theatre that evening, it seemed almost certain that a successful American invasion by the group could only be a matter of time. The sense of optimism and control was almost palpable. Lennon's visionary "toppermost of the poppermost" was finally, and impossibly, true.

"We'd like to thank Sophie Tucker," said Paul, nodding his head in the direction of the hefty songstress who had only seconds before left the stage to thunderous applause. "She's probably our favorite American group!" To which the entire theater exploded in laughter. The Queen Mother, speaking to them after the show, wondered where they were playing next. "Slough," answered Paul. "Oh," she replied, quite unintentionally delivering one of the evening's most memorable quips, "that's very near us."

McCartney remembers the event:

> Obviously the main thing about a Royal Command show was telling your family, imagining all your parents, uncles and aunties seeing you meet the Queen. On the way to the thing, John said, "Oh God, we've got to have some announcements; what are we going to say?" Then he said, "Oh, I'll do something about clap your hands," because he used to do a thing on stage about, "Those at the back, clap your feet and stamp your hands!" So he did a variation of that, coming out with the famous line, "Everyone stamp your feet, clap your hands," and then added, "and those of you at the front just rattle your jewelry." We met the Queen afterwards and she was great. We were quite elated because we'd gone down well and we'd all been so scared.

At the end of November their fifth single, "I Want to Hold Your Hand," was released in England and shot directly to number one. A few days later, the group's second LP, *With the Beatles* also came out, amassing immediate advance orders of 2.5 million. Not even Elvis had ever been able to do that.

By the winter of 1964, America was more than ready for the Beatles. Midway over the Atlantic on board Pan Am flight 101 to New York, Paul McCartney was untypically somewhat apprehensive about the reception they might receive. "America has always had everything," he confided to record producer Phil Spector. "Why should we be over there making money? They've got their own groups. What are we going to give them that they don't already have?"

Any lingering doubts were magically swept away when at 1:35 on the afternoon of February 7, 1964, they touched down on Kennedy Airport's long, icy runway. As the plane inched its way to the terminal, the shrill sound of over ten thousand teenage voices, all chanting and screaming for the Beatles, penetrated the hull of the aircraft like gunfire. Peering out of the frosted windows of the DC-10, the Beatles saw for the first time the wild reception America had in store for them. McCartney, for one, was almost in a state of shock. Ultimately, the boys were led to the airport press lounge where they held the largest and most disorganized conference in the history of New York City. John Lennon yelled at everyone to shut up and the entire room applauded! Beatlemania now held the entire world in its grasp as an untold number of hustlers, con men, and copycats all clamored to jump on board the bandwagon.

After the press conference, the Beatles were ceremoniously driven into the city and installed in a palatial suite of rooms at the Plaza Hotel. George had come down with a bad case of strep throat and was definitely not impressed by either the room service or the food. The management wasn't particularly bothered as they didn't really care for the Beatles and their fifteen thousand crazed fans tearing up their hotel. This it rather ungraciously made known to the entire world by offering the group to any other five-star hotel that would have them. George's older sister, Louise, remembers the madness:

> George asked me to meet him at the Plaza, so I checked in and headed up to the Presidential suite. The security man said, "Where do you think you're going?"
>
> I said, "I'm going to meet my brother."
>
> "Have you any idea how many times that's been tried today?" the whole crowd just laughed. Reporters, fans. I was shocked.
>
> "Is your name on the list?" he said.
>
> "List?" of course, George never thought about putting my name on any list. I was standing there, looking like a dummy. Then one of the reporters went up and got George. He ran down the corridor and hugged me and spun me around. And then everyone applauded.

The Beatles' famous appearance on "The Ed Sullivan Show" two days later confirmed the smiling, winking, precocious Paul McCartney as the "sexy one" of the group. It was a label that fit as well, discreetly squiring, as he was, a long line of stewardesses, fans, and even complete strangers he happened upon, from London to Miami Beach. One of those ten-minute liaisons came back to haunt him when, in the spring of

1964, a young Liverpool woman, Anita Cochrane, gave birth to a baby boy, Phillip, she claimed was fathered by the amorous McCartney. That March, the girl and her mother visited one of the Beatles' associate attorneys, D. H. Green, Esq., of Liverpool, and let it be known that they wished the famous Beatle no ill will and only wanted enough money to buy a decent pram for her young son. Anita's mother, Vi, commented on the allegations in a rare 1983 interview in the British press. "They would go out together regularly, although it was not really serious," she said. "Then one day she confessed she was pregnant by Paul. It was a bombshell to the family."

Accordingly, McCartney's London counsel, David Jacobs, was in the midst of putting together a small, one-time settlement for the girl when her maternal uncle involved himself, demanding what he termed "proper compensation" be paid to his broken-hearted niece — £5000 was the sum he had in mind for the family's continued discretion. Brian Epstein, meanwhile, felt that even if the money were offered there could be no real guarantee that down the line they wouldn't elect to come crawling back for more, or worse, sell their story to London's infamous gutter press. In the end, a £3000 payment was made with no admission that McCartney was the boy's father. Additionally, Anita was prohibited from ever making any further claims against the millionaire Beatle, and if she did the entire amount would be forfeit.

Although mother and son appeared to be satisfied, the disgruntled uncle, who had personally received only £5 wasn't. During the Beatles' triumphant Liverpool homecoming that summer for the grand premiere of *A Hard Day's Night*, Anita's uncle reportedly distributed handbills among the crowds, alleging McCartney's paternity. Despite David Jacobs' threats to press extortion charges against the man, he persisted for the next three years by sending long, cynical poems to the local newspapers concerning his niece's alleged relationship with McCartney. Cynthia Lennon later summed up the whole unsavory episode: "It appeared from the evidence on the solicitor's desk that Paul had been a bit of a town bull in Liverpool.

Claims for paternity suits rolled in . . . Whether the claims were true is anybody's guess."

Young Phillip, meanwhile, wasn't told about any of this until he reached his late teens and then steadfastly refused any comment to the media. His family did say, however, that he was not interested in any of McCartney's money and preferred instead to try to make his own way. "My daughter just wants to forget the whole business and so does Phillip," Mrs. Cochrane later commented. At the time, Anita was happily married with two young children and had no interest in reopening old wounds. "We just want to forget the past," her husband, Christopher, told reporters.

In a curious postscript to this affair, a diehard teenage McCartney fan outside his Soho Square office in London told me that he had been out one afternoon in the early eighties waiting for Paul to arrive, when a middle-aged woman and a boy approached the singer, screaming, "This is your son! This is your son! Don't you care, you bloody bastard?" So infuriated was the unidentified woman that she actually attacked the thoroughly astonished McCartney, ripping his shirt to tatters before his roadies, Trevor Jones and John Hammel ran over and pulled her off. No charges of any kind were ever filed.

Such intensely personal and disturbing episodes aside, 1965 saw the Beatles just as popular as ever, playing to jam-packed houses everywhere they went. Julia Baird remembers a typically frantic concert at the Astoria Theatre in Finsbury Park on December 1: "I remember riding into London with John that evening and commenting on how nervous he seemed.

" 'Just because I've been doing this rubbish since I was fifteen is no reason not to be edgy,' John explained to his kid sister. 'You've no idea what these shows are really like, Ju. Twenty minutes of out-of-tune madness played to an audience of blithering idiots. None of us really like it, you know.' "

Of all the Beatles, it was Paul McCartney who seemed to most enjoy the pleasures and privilege of playing in the planet's number-one band. By far the friendliest and most accessible of the four, Paul worked just as hard at being helpful and congenial, as Lennon did at being oblique and inscrutable. Alistair Taylor says that if one of the boys were needed to perform some sort of immediate promotional activity it would most likely be Paul who volunteered. Immaculately attired and ever ready with a sly smile or a slap on the back, the diplomatic McCartney definitely knew how to push people's buttons. To him, being a Beatle wasn't so much an inconvenience (as it often was to the others) as a hard-fought-for honor. To call him the "yuppie Beatle" might be a little unkind, but it's frankly not too far off the mark either. At the very least he was (and is) a dedicated overachiever, "It does seem to have fallen my role to be a bit more kind than the others," McCartney has said.

> I was always known in the Beatle thing as being the one who would sit the press down and say, "Hello, how are you? Do you want a drink?" and make them comfortable. My family loop was like that . . . But you're aware you're talking to the press. You want a good article, don't you? So you don't go slagging the guys off. . . I'm not really tough. I'm not really lovable either, but I don't mind falling in the middle. My dad's advice: moderation, son . . . You don't love everyone you meet, but you try and get on with people, you know? You don't try to put 'em uptight; most people don't anyway. . . I mean there's nothing wrong with that. Why should I go around slagging people? I really didn't like that John did.

When the Beatles learned that they would be inducted as Members of the British Empire and awarded the coveted MBE at Buckingham Palace by the Queen herself, Lennon, not untypically, thought it was a load of bollocks and shoved the invitation into a pile of papers at the bottom of a drawer. Paul McCartney, conversely, was ecstatic. "In the beginning it was a constant fight between Brian and Paul on one side, and me and George on the other," Lennon recalled.

Brian put us in neat suits and shirts and Paul was right behind him. We had to do a lot of selling-out then. Taking the MBE was a sellout for me. You know, before you get your MBE the Palace writes to ask if you're going to accept it, because you're not supposed to reject it publicly and they sound you out first. I chucked the letter in with all the fan mail, until Brian asked me if I had it. He and a few other people persuaded me that it was in our interests to take it, but it was hypocritical of me to accept it.

The investiture took place on October 26, 1965, in the Great Throne Room of Buckingham Palace. Standing on a dais, dressed in a golden gown, the Queen broke into a wide infectious smile upon seeing the boys. At a pre-arranged signal from an usher they bowed low and took exactly four paces forward. A moment later, they bowed again as Lord Chamberlain Cobbold officially announced their arrival.

THE QUEEN (to Paul): How long have you been together now?
PAUL: Oh for many years.
RINGO: Forty years.
THE QUEEN (to Ringo): Are you the one who started it?
RINGO: No, I was the last to join. I'm the little fellow.
THE QUEEN (to John): Have you been working hard lately?
JOHN: No, we've been on holiday.

After the big event the Beatles were ushered into the royal courtyard where they cheerfully faced off against the press.

PAUL: We've played many palaces including Frisco's Cow Palace. But never this one before. It's a keen pad and I like the staff. Thought they'd be dukes and things but they were just fellas.
REPORTER: What about the Queen?
PAUL: She's lovely, great. She was very friendly. She was just like a mum to us.
REPORTER: Were you nervous?

JOHN: Not as much as some of the other people in there.

REPORTER: How did the other medal recipients act toward your award?

JOHN: One formally dressed, middle-aged winner walked up to us after the ceremony and said: "I want your autographs for my daughter, but I don't know what she sees in you." So we gave him our autographs.

REPORTER: How did you know what to do during the ceremony?

JOHN: This big fellow drilled us. Every time he got to Ringo he kept cracking up.

REPORTER: What will you do with your medals?

PAUL: What you normally do with medals. Put them in a box.

After a time, the rigors of the road began to catch up with the band. John and George were especially adamant: if running around like monkeys on a stick from one concrete baseball stadium to another was all they had to look forward to in playing before live audiences, then forget it. Following the Beatles' final bows at San Francisco's Candlestick Park on August 29, 1966, they said goodbye to touring forever and with it the uncontrolled, scrambled lunacy of their kamikaze fans.

Only Paul McCartney harbored doubts. Too long out of the spotlight, he reasoned, and people might begin to forget — an eventuality that, quite frankly, scared the wits out of him. He had, after all, worked damned hard at being a Beatle.

The Paul which the public sees is not the real Paul. He has a built-in PR man: the facade is there all the time. Behind it is a very serious man. He gives off that pleasant little-boy-lost image. But behind it is a highly intelligent and extremely hardworking bloke. He always knew what he was doing, and was very, very money conscious. Not tight, but careful, extremely careful. He was very astute and business-like, and very organized. But the facade was this little-boy-lost, wondering what it was all about and thinking, "Isn't this fun?"

—*Brian Sommerville*—
(The Beatles' first press officer)

5

A Conspiracy of One
McCartney Behind Closed Doors

F ollowing the Beatles' appearance on the BBC special, "Swinging Sounds '63," on April 18, 1963, the more-than-eligible McCartney enthusiastically homed in on lovely Jane Asher, the popular seventeen-year-old British acting star, who earlier in the evening had posed with the Beatles for a *Radio Times* photographer.

For the decidedly upwardly mobile young bachelor, Jane Asher was as close to a perfect match as possible. Born in London on April 5, 1946, she was the daughter of prominent London physician Richard Asher and his wife, Margaret, a professor at the prestigious Guildhall School of Music. The bloodlines secure, there was Jane herself, a professional actress from the age of five. Her early screen credits include *Alfie, The Greengage Summer, Mandy, The Masque of the Red Death, The Prince and the Pauper*, and *The Quatermass Experiment*. She has also appeared in countless theatrical productions and on many of Britain's top television programs, including "The Saint," as well as in TV adaptations of Dostoevsky's *The Brothers Karamazov* and George Eliot's *The Mill on the Floss*.

The stunningly beautiful redhead was everything McCartney had ever envisioned in a woman, and certainly worlds apart from the numerous other young ladies he had known. Lovely, talented, gracious, and refined, Jane Asher was the perfect royal consort to one of England's princes of rock 'n' roll. From the beginning theirs was a match made in heaven, love so strong, only fate, time, and buxom, pushy American heiress Linda Eastman could even begin to nudge. From almost the moment they first met they began regularly and exclusively dating. Jim McCartney was thrilled with what he considered to be his son's first official girlfriend. Nothing would have made him happier he said, than to see them wed. Even brother Mike was smitten. Remembering their first meeting, Paul later recalled: "We [the Beatles] all said, 'Will you marry me?' which was what we said to every girl at the time. [She was a] rare London bird, the sort we'd always heard about. We thought we were set."

After the gig, Paul met up with the young starlet at his hotel, the Royal Court on Sloane Square, for a coffee. Later Paul, John, George, an old mate, singer Shane Fenton, and journalist Chris Hutchins took Jane to Hutchins' flat on the Kings Road where they sat on the floor, polishing off a bottle of good Irish whiskey and actively flirting with the somewhat overwhelmed young actress. After a respectable, collective schmooze, Paul and Jane retreated to the bedroom where much to the amazement and wonder of the other four, they spent the evening talking about their favorite foods and what consistency they preferred their gravy. "They couldn't believe I was still a virgin," Asher later recalled. Even macho man Paul was unusually candid when it came to that first time together. "I knew this was the girl for me," he told Hunter Davies in 1967. "I hadn't tried to grab her or make her. I told her, 'It appears you're a nice girl.'" As the night wore on, Fenton suggested that he and the three Beatles go on to a West End night club he knew, dropping Jane off at her home on the way. As she was stepping out of the singer's big American car, Paul gently grabbed her by the arm, asking if he might ring her the next day. She said yes, that would be fine, and quickly scrawled her number on a scrap of paper pulled from the bottom of her purse.

Over the next few weeks they became inseparable, roaming the streets of Mayfair, arm in arm. Ironically, in those days, it was the radiant young actress people tended to recognize, not Beatle Paul, which caused more than a few ripples in the ill-fated relationship. For the moment, though, the couple were both head over heels in love, so much so that, unknown to his many female fans, McCartney soon accepted an invitation from Jane's mother to move into the Ashers' smart family home at 57 Wimpole Street in London.

Jane's brother Peter, half of the hit sixties singing duo Peter and Gordon, remembers Paul as a considerate house guest whose few possessions could be divided into three basic categories: expensive camera and recording equipment, a pop star's wardrobe of trendy clothes, and cash. McCartney, apparently drawing on his conservative family roots, had a habit of stashing wads of tightly wrapped ten- and twenty-pound notes all over the top-floor rooms he shared with Peter. Asher, who went on to become a much-sought-after record producer, remembers uncovering McCartney's wages under the Beatle's seldom slept-in bed, and even tucked away in the lauded bassist's sock drawer. Asked to comment on his rather idiosyncratic banking system, McCartney jokingly replied that he was just grateful Asher never helped himself to any of his hard-won bread. McCartney and his well-known yen for money, it would seem, go back a long way. Although Paul lived in the same house as Jane, they kept separate rooms and were always extremely discreet regarding their personal affairs. McCartney, in particular, was very mindful of Jane's parents' wish that their talented daughter's reputation remain spotless under the watchful eye of London's Fleet Street gossip mongers.

Not surprisingly, Brian Epstein was less than thrilled that the group's number-one heartthrob was making himself at least psychologically off-limits to a generation of admiring girlhood. Brian Sommerville, the Beatles' early publicity manger, recalls the conflict:

> There was a considerable difference of opinion over the Jane Asher situation. Brian made a terrible fuss about it, saying it would offend the fans, but, in effect, Paul just told him to mind his own business. Brian was probably just being over-cautious, and Paul more far-sighted, knowing that sort of thing didn't really matter. But at the time it was a textbook rule of publicity that the artist must appear single and available.

Tony Barrow, longtime promo man for NEMS, confirms Sommerville's assessment of Epstein's displeasure over the McCartney/Asher affair:

> Epstein himself admitted to me on more than one occasion that McCartney was the Beatle who gave him the greatest headaches, pushed him to the limit, and usually got his own way. Epstein certainly went out of his way to avoid upsetting Paul. Behind McCartney's back though, Eppy disliked the amount of public interest that surrounded the romance. He asked me how my press office might cool the situation. I had to admit that it was not the type of story one could cover up — especially with so many public appearances of the pair at celebrity functions where the press had been invited in ad lib numbers. Overruling everyone's wishes to the contrary, of course, was McCartney himself. As far as he was concerned, sooner or later he and Jane would marry, despite his constant, "just good friends" posturing to the news media.

Suggestions that McCartney was attempting to enhance his social status through association with the picture-perfect Asher hardly seem valid in view of his lifetime of championing working-class people and values. As Brian Sommerville, now a successful attorney, points out: "He just found himself in a set of circumstances, loved the girl, and fell naturally into those circumstances as if he'd been brought up in the Bloomsbury set all his life."

While discretion was definitely the watchword for the much-written-about romance, occasionally one or the other of the young lovebirds would venture into print on the subject. Interviewed for the splashy British teen rag *Fabulous* in February of 1964, Asher faithfully endorsed the Epstein party line regarding her by-then passionate affair with McCartney. "We aren't engaged!" she began, in a fruitless effort to try to stop the rumors, "and we certainly aren't secretly married. We're just dating. I like Paul. He is very nice. But it is impossible to date him without everyone spotting him as he wears his hair the same way all the time. And whenever the Beatles pop round to my father's home, the street soon fills up with people. We don't get much chance to be on our own."

Throughout their time together, Asher continued to accept acting jobs, determined not to allow the Beatles' brilliant aura to obscure her blossoming career. McCartney tried his best to be big about it, but eventually began to resent her devoting so much of herself to working. Never a big fan of the stage, he nonetheless faithfully attended most of Asher's opening nights and backstage cocktail parties, but never really connected with the arty, serious types who seem to gravitate to the boards. "The only thing the theatre ever gave me was a sore arse," he once complained to the late playwright Joe Orton during his Asher days in London. It would become another significant, though not overwhelming factor in the relationship's eventual disintegration.

For the time being at any rate, Paul and Jane were basically happy. Curious and anxious to experience the finer things in life, McCartney, somewhat atypically, allowed himself to be schooled by his upper-crust girlfriend in the airs and graces of London's gentry. Whether it was practicing his stilted schoolboy French in fancy restaurants, or frequenting London's finer tailor shops, the provincial Beatle was eager to advance himself culturally. "I don't want to sound like Jonathan Miller going on," he commented to the London *Evening Standard* at the time, "but I'm trying to cram everything in, all the things that I've missed. People are saying things, painting things, and composing things that are great, and I must know what people are doing." Despite his newfound high cultch, he wasn't about to renounce his modest origins. When the same interviewer happened to mention he was reading William Burroughs' *Naked Lunch,* Paul replied that he was himself currently ploughing through *The Packed Lunch* by Greedy Blighter.

As for Jane Asher, she was simply a young lady very much in love with someone she desperately wanted to see happy and content. It is important to remember, however, that it was Paul, and not *Beatle* Paul who had captured her heart. In direct contrast to the manhunting Linda Eastman, the introspective redhead could never be accused of being a groupie.

Not surprisingly, one of the first things McCartney did when he began to make some big money from the band was to buy for his father and brother a fine new family home, "Rembrandt," on the Wirral, Baskervyle Road, Heswall, in Cheshire. Purchased in July of 1964 for a respectable £8750, the five-bedroom bungalow among other things boasted its own rambling wine cellar. Intent on seeing the place made as comfortable as possible, McCartney immediately sunk in an additional £8000 for decorating and furnishing the place, even installing a first-class central-heating system, something of a rarity in Britain even today. One of the great advantages of being a homeowner for McCartney was that he now had someplace relatively private to be alone with Jane. Summer afternoons were spent picnicking in the large back garden, downing a pint or two at their favorite local, or casually motoring along Cheshire's winding back roads on matching motor scooters.

But all was not roses. For Asher an especially irksome facet of McCartney's Beatle business was his perhaps overly attentive catering to the fans. She was more embarrassed than jealous of the hordes of screaming girls who gathered whenever Paul was around. Being from the theater, Asher didn't particularly have to worry about her professional life overflowing into her private world. When the curtain fell it was time to switch off and be herself. The same could not be said though for a Beatle. As such, McCartney was hounded from dawn to dusk, pursued and put upon by willing females from six to sixty, and he quite frankly loved it. Tony Barrow remembers: "Jane refused to accept that the Beatles' fans were of any long-term importance. She objected to Paul depending so much on the adoration of 'Beatle People.' On one occasion she lost her temper in my hearing and asked why Paul did not see for himself that the affection of the fans was trivial and short-lived while her true love for him was deep and permanent."

An example of how this kind of devotion to the fans can carry with it potential for trouble at home is a little encounter remembered in Beatle historian Bill King's superlative *Beatlefan* magazine, by aficionada Marianne Goldsmith:

> My sister and I lived with our parents in St. John's Wood, which was close to Paul McCartney's house and the Abbey Road studios. One evening a party was going on next door and an Aston Martin was parked in our driveway. I had to go and ask if the car could be moved. Guess who it belonged to? Yes, Paul. So he came out with Jane Asher and said he was just going. I managed to say, "Please can I have your autograph?" And he turned to Jane and said, "Have you got a thingy?" And she gave him a pen. I produced an envelope for him to sign. His hand glided across it. He put, "To Marianne, Love Paul McCartney xxx." As he handed it to me my hand touched his and I stuttered, "Thank you very much. I don't know how I can thank you." He said, "What about a kiss?" I think he had been drinking. So I leaned into the car, forgetting about Jane, and kissed him. My head swooned, and before I knew it, he had driven off into the night.

Eventually, things began to get a little crowded for the couple at the Ashers', prompting the upper-echelon young professionals to go house-hunting. After a long string of false leads, pricey real estate catalogs, and running about, McCartney ultimately settled upon a fine three-story Victorian townhouse at 7 Cavendish Avenue, in London's prestigious St. John's

Wood. When he purchased it for £40,000 late in 1966, McCartney didn't really do too much with it at first. On the contrary,
he seemed to delight in allowing the large, rectangular back
yard to revert to an overgrown state, a condition the tidy and
orderly Jim McCartney found most annoying.

After a time, McCartney was persuaded that he needed a bit
of help with the place, so he hired an elderly couple, Mr. and
Mrs. Kelly to oversee its day-to-day operation. He drew the
line however at hiring a secretary, insisting that he could
handle all of his personal business quite well on his own. The
couple's life in St. John's Wood soon settled into a hypnotic
domesticity centered around their need for privacy and
space. Jane generally did most of the cooking, and was said to
be quite a culinary whiz although Paul tended to prefer a good
hearty Liverpool fry-up to anything too fancy. After Linda
Eastman moved in following McCartney's stormy split with
Asher in 1968, Wings insider Jo Jo Laine reports that the once-
elegant townhome was soon reduced to a smelly, dog-hair-
covered "shit hole," completely taken over by the sexy
American photographer's uninhibited love of all things free
and natural. But for the moment, anyway, Asher's eminent
good sense and taste reigned supreme. "Jane spent a huge
amount of time decorating Paul's new home to her personal
taste," says Tony Barrow, "selecting fresh wallpaper throughout and choosing beautiful carpets to match. Everything
pointed towards a wedding. Paul and Jane soon started to entertain visitors and throw small but lavish dinner parties just
like an old married couple."

Unfortunately, despite their finely tuned domesticity, living
virtually in the heart of London tended to attract the fans.
Completely surrounded by a high brick wall, the London
hideaway also sported a menacing-looking front gate covered
in thick iron sheeting. The gate opened mechanically from the
inside after prospective visitors had been cleared via an in-
tercom. More evenings than not the intrusive buzzer would
sound every few minutes, poked at by fans and all manner of
wandering loonies and brazen opportunists. True to his public,

however, McCartney would generally drop what he was doing and trot out to sign autographs or pose for a quick snap from a blinding sea of clattering cameras.

To those closest to the couple it now seemed a certainty that they would soon marry, a sentiment publicly encouraged by Asher herself in several interviews granted to the media at the time. "I am not Paul's wife — but yes, we are going to get married," she told the *Sunday Mirror.* "We won't be married for a while yet, but when it happens we've got a family planned. First we want a boy and then — come what may. There's no particular reason why we are not getting married right away, except that we're both pretty young . . . . I shan't give up my career unless it interferes with our being together." In a 1967 interview in the *Daily Express,* she had this to say about her future plans with McCartney: "I love Paul. I love him very deeply, and he feels the same. I don't think either of us has looked at anyone else since we first met. . . . I want to get married probably this year and have lots and lots of babies. I certainly would be surprised indeed if I married anyone but Paul."

At Asher's insistence, McCartney had also bought a 183-acre rural retreat in June of 1966 called High Park Farm near the tiny hamlet of Machrihanish, very close to the equally tiny village of Campbeltown. The farm's original owner, Janet Brown, recalls meeting the big-city buyers: "Our farm had been up for sale for quite awhile, but what a surprise my husband and I had when we saw the famous pair. Paul told me that it had always been his ambition to own a farm in Scotland."

McCartney and Asher's time away from the non-stop grind in London and the Beatles did them both a world of good. The living conditions on the bare-bones farm were rough, which prompted McCartney to learn a bit about carpentry.

They even went so far as to make their own primitive furniture out of several old wooden packing crates they had found piled in the barn. (Playing poor up on his Scottish farm has remained one of McCartney's favorite pastimes even to this day.) Bathing at first in an abandoned stainless steel dairy trough set on a concrete slab, the pioneering pop star eventually ordered an old tub installed in the house. It would remain one of the very few conveniences he would add to his private hippie/gypsy paradise.

"Jane cooked our meals on a horrible old electric cooker we'd picked up cheap," recalls Alistair Taylor, one of Paul and Jane's few semi-regular house guests. "She's a super cook and you'd never know what a primitive kitchen she was working in. . . . We did a little bit of decorating as well. All that chocolate brown paint makes the farmhouse look like the inside of an Aero bar. Paul, at last, decided he'd had enough of it, so we went down to Campbeltown and bought lots of packets of colored pens. The three of us spent the next few hours just drawing little doodles in all these colors, spreading them all over the wall trying to relieve the gloom." So much for lifestyles of the rich and famous!

Surely the most exotic trek McCartney and Asher took together started in February of 1968 when they left Heathrow Airport for the extravagant Himalayan home of the giggly, mixed-up mystic, the Maharishi Mahesh Yogi. The eagerly anticipated Himalayan high, however, soon fell short of expectations when the garrulous guru supposedly came on hot and heavy to celebrity meditator Mia Farrow. Questioned upon his return to England five weeks later about their magic carpet ride to inner peace in Rishikesh, McCartney would say only that at first the Beatles figured the Maharishi was somehow superhuman, but soon found out he was as fallible as anyone else. Asher, a side of whom was inclined towards things spiritual, appeared genuinely disappointed that their quest for nirvana had ended on such a sorry, negative note.

Still, 1967 was definitely an eventful year for the pair. In January Asher left London for an extended tour of America as part of the Bristol Old Vic. Upon her arrival in the U.S., however, it was clear that the media was far more interested in her relationship with McCartney than in her sterling acting ability. "I don't need the publicity," she chastised one particularly aggressive reporter from the *Sunday Express*.

> I don't want it — and I don't like it. It puts me at such an awful disadvantage, you know . . . it upsets me and I hate being upset. Because when I'm upset I'm no good at my work or anything. I know that most people think I basically love it all, and am secretly overjoyed and revelling in the gossip. But they're wrong. The press just doesn't understand about actresses and the theatre. I've become a publicity freak, and this I resent. How do I begin to tell you what it means to an actress who is trying to make it on talent alone?

While in America Jane turned twenty-one. Flying from London, McCartney caught his girlfriend's performance in *Romeo and Juliet* and then joined her for a big birthday bash.

Still, McCartney had some difficulty accepting the "working woman" in Asher. Interviewed by author Hunter Davies, the couple discussed the conflict:

"I've always wanted to beat Jane down," McCartney confided.

"I've refused," said Asher. "I've been brought up to be always doing something. And I enjoy acting. I didn't want to give that up."

"I know now I was being silly," McCartney replied, aware of his selfishness. "It was a game, trying to beat you down."

Asher also indicated to Davies changes she observed in the relationship following her return home after the Old Vic tour. "When I came back after five months, Paul had changed so much. He was on LSD, which I hadn't shared. I was jealous of all the spiritual experiences he'd had with John. There were fifteen people dropping in all day long. The house had changed and was full of stuff I didn't know about."

Unshared experiences notwithstanding, the relationship continued. McCartney had never really abandoned his playboy lifestyle and was out in the clubs trying his luck virtually every time Asher went off somewhere. Eventually, waking up, as he put it, to "old drinks and strange ladies," began to wear him down, and on Christmas Day 1967, he presented Jane with an exquisite diamond-and-emerald engagement ring and finally asked her to become his wife. She accepted. New Year's Day they motored up to Rembrandt and broke the news to his dad. "I'm thrilled," Jim exclaimed, beaming. "And Jane, my love," he said, giving her a fatherly peck on the cheek, "welcome to the family." For all Jane knew within months she would become Mrs. James Paul McCartney and lay to rest, once and for all, the many unhappy times she had been forced to endure as simply Paul's girlfriend. If she were his wife after all, things would surely become more stable, more certain. It wasn't to be.

In 1968 Francie Schwartz was a pretty twenty-four-year-old advertising copywriter living in New York. Like so many other young show business hopefuls, she yearned for a shot at the big time, and when it was announced that the Beatles' Apple Corp. was on the lookout for new talent and more than willing to back it all up with its mighty power and prestige, she was on the next plane out to London.

Making a beeline to Apple's headquarters on Wigmore Street, Schwartz happened to catch sight of Beatle Paul as he made his way through the company's austere lobby on his way to a late-morning meeting with his lawyers. Francie had found her moment. "Excuse me, Paul!" she sang out over the general din of the Beatles' eccentric seat of power. "Hi! I'm Francie from New York. Could I possibly speak to you for a moment?" Always a sucker for a pretty girl, McCartney ambled over and the two began to chat. "I'm a writer," Francie began. "That is, I'm trying to become a screen writer. I've been working on this film script for quite some time now, and I was wondering if you'd have a look?"

"Sure," said Paul, turning on the charm. "And what's this?" he wondered, reaching for a long manila envelope sticking out from under her arm.

"Oh, just a picture of me and my bio."

"Well, we've gotta have a look at that as well. May I?"

"Yes, of course. You know, it's really great to finally meet you," the young lady gushed, suddenly so nervous she almost dropped everything onto the carpet.

"So, anyway, how can we reach you?" Paul asked.

The next afternoon the still jet-lagged Schwartz was suddenly wakened by a loud knock at the door. It was a motorcycle courier with a letter from Apple. Carefully peeling back the beautiful cream-colored envelope bearing the striking, mysterious, levitating Apple logo, she took a long deep breath and began to read the hastily scrawled note: "Come, call, do something constructive." It was signed, "With love, Paul." Rooting in her purse through the unfamiliar English coins, she literally ran down the stairs of her cheap cold-water flat to the phone box in the foyer. After the mandatory Apple third degree and a ten-minute wait, Francie finally got through to her man. A few hasty "hellos" and "how are you's" later, McCartney told her to hop in a cab and come right over, he had something important to discuss.

Ushered into Apple's sacred inner sanctum, it soon began to dawn on the somewhat naive young woman that the famous Beatle might actually be more interested in her as a potential conquest than as a brilliant new discovery in the world of film.

Without a lot of fuss, he suddenly announced that if she wanted to be with him she'd have to be willing to remain "on call" twenty-four hours a day. Not exactly the most romantic of propositions. Still, she was interested enough to give him her number and patient enough to go home and wait. One month later to the day, the phone rang, and McCartney invited her to attend a late-night Beatle recording session at EMI studios.

Sitting next to Paul for hours, fascinated by the opportunity to witness the Beatles at work, Francie gently rubbed his shoulders while he and John worked on an early version of "Revolution." Not too surprisingly, Francie also remembers a lot of strong black hash being smoked by just about everyone there.

After the session Schwartz was limoed home without so much as a tender hug or a kiss from her potential new lover. The next morning, out of complete frustration, she dashed off a note to Paul at Apple saying, "Dear Mr. Plump: I think I'm going to have to go home soon. When am I going to see you?" A couple of days later, she received a reply in the form of a telegram stuck in among the morning milk bottles on her front stoop: "Make it Monday, Mr. P." "Tomorrow," she said to herself as she kneeled in her doorway, twirling the paper over and over. "Tomorrow."

Early the next morning the doorbell rang as she was taking her shower. Struggling to make herself presentable, she rushed down the stairs and flung open the front door. "It's fuck day!" shouted a jubilant, unshaven Paul McCartney as he and his ever-faithful sheepdog, Martha, bounded up the stairs. "It's fuck day!" As the two of them fell together in a heap on a bedside chair, the lusty Beatle bachelor began tearing away at her still-damp clothing, all the while kissing her passionately. Coming up for air a few frantic minutes later, Francie asked, "Do you love me?" "I don't know," the rough and ready McCartney intoned without missing a beat. It was the one and only time love was ever mentioned.

Later that evening, Francie once again accompanied him to the studio and afterwards home to St. John's Wood. Over a couple of very stiff drinks, McCartney began to brood about his relationship with Jane. "I don't know what the hell to do with her, you know," he began. "Why can't she understand how important it is for me to have a full-time lady? I just don't see the big fascination with her fucking career all the time. I can easily give her anything she really needs. What do you think?"

Schwartz listened patiently and none too subtly hinted that if she were ever in Jane's shoes she would stand by her man. "Would you really?" said McCartney, suddenly focusing on the real live woman in front of him.

"I'd be willing to try."

Without saying another word McCartney tenderly led her

up the stairs into his dark, spacious bedroom where the couple spent the next few hours making love. As far as Francie was concerned anyway, this was, without a doubt, the real thing.

From that day on, Schwartz's "on call" services really came into play. She was expected to look after the house, though not to seriously tidy up. Paul apparently didn't like people going through his belongings. "Just leave things the way you find them, okay?" he would growl if she ever accidentally went too far in her house-cleaning chores. "You're a nosey parker aren't you, then?"

In addition, she was also expected to ring up Paul's local connections and arrange for them to deliver his weekly supply of hash and grass. Then there were her other various kitchen and bedroom duties. All things considered, it was a rather one-sided relationship. Still, for the moment at least, the young New Yorker felt a kind of strange satisfaction in knowing that she was helping someone she cared for, someone important not only to her, but to the entire world as well. If only, she thought to herself, Paul would begin to reciprocate.

That is not to say, however, that Paul and Francie never had any good times together. In her memoirs, published by *Rolling Stone's* Straight Arrow Books, she reflected that they "often visited friends in the country and even ran barefoot in the rain." But such truly romantic interludes, it seems, were fairly few and far between. She observed that as a lover he was "either terribly good or terribly bad," and claimed that on several occasions, coming home very late and very high, he used to go on about how women secretly liked being knocked around, and that even the super-refined Jane Asher seemed to get turned on by a little of the old rough stuff.

Perhaps the most humiliating experience she endured during her stint as Paul's paramour occurred late one evening after the couple had partied with friends at the trendy London nightspot, Revolution. Driving home, McCartney suddenly pulled over to the curb and told the confused young woman to wait in the car for a few minutes. As it turned out they were outside the home of one of Paul's old girlfriends with whom he had maintained a long and steamy affair. Fifteen minutes later, he returned to the car without saying a word and turned off in the direction of St. John's Wood.

"You fucking bastard!" Schwartz suddenly blurted out, no longer able to contain her emotion. "Couldn't you have at least taken me home first?"

No answer.

"Why Paul? *Why?*" she said, choking on her tears.

"I don't know," McCartney said under his breath.

Meanwhile to the gentle, faithful Jane, the Francie Schwartz intrigue was about to become the final straw. Returning to St. John's Wood unexpectedly that July, following an Old Vic tour of the provinces, Jane motored onto Cavendish Avenue and glided to a stop just outside Paul's front gate. Margot Stevens, a die-hard McCartney devotee and longtime Apple Scruff, who happened to be hanging around outside, frantically pushed the buzzer in an effort to warn Paul that his fiancee was approaching. As it happened, Paul himself answered the call.

"Yeah?"

"It's Margot. Listen, Jane just pulled up. What about Francie?"

"Do you think I was born yesterday?" he said sarcastically. "Why don't you lot leave off for a bit. Don't you think I'd know if Jane were coming over?"

Stepping onto the curb, Jane said a quick hello to the fans and then, using her key, let herself into the cobblestone courtyard. Entering the house, she set down her purse and slowly walked up the stairs to the bedroom she shared with Paul. For some reason she stopped short of opening the door and quietly knocked. Inside, McCartney bolted straight up as if he had been stuck with an electric cattle prod.

"Who's there?" he asked, suddenly filled with frantic anticipation.

"It's Jane, silly," Asher replied, obviously happy to hear her lover's voice again.

Springing to the doorway, Paul carefully slipped out into the hall, his heart pounding. Peering into the darkened room, Jane suddenly zeroed in on Francie, standing next to the bed, clad only in the fine oriental silk dressing gown Jane had given Paul for Christmas.

"Uh, look . . ." Paul started, anxiously rubbing his brow.

Broken-hearted, Asher looked him in the eyes for a moment, the tears welling up even as she turned away and ran back down the stairs and out of Paul's life forever. The whole thing played like a scene from some B-grade British movie, but unfortunately there was to be no happy ending. Francie now moved up the ladder in Paul's mixed-up love life. Convinced momentarily that she was definitely the one, he even took her home to meet his father. Despite his reputation for diplomacy and tact, Jim was not impressed and all but ignored his son's new love throughout an uncomfortable and embarrassing weekend.

In time the affair came to an abrupt end. Francie simply left one morning while the great Beatle was out. "Paul," she said later, "was an outrageous adolescent, a little Medici prince, powdered and laid on a satin pillow at an early age. But he was so pretty."

Francie Schwartz wasn't McCartney's only sexual transgression in his five-year relationship with Jane Asher. He was also known to have been intimate with folk singer Julie Felix and, of course, Linda Eastman.

From day one, McCartney and Asher's romance was tempestuous. Tony Barrow says that behind closed doors they often fought like cats and dogs. Although a diehard showbusiness professional, Jane was, unlike McCartney, basically very quiet and shy. On July 20, 1968, she appeared on the BBC television show "Dee Time," and offhandedly announced that the engagement was off. She later told reporters, "I know it sounds corny, but we still see each other, and love each other, but it hasn't worked out. Perhaps we'll be childhood sweethearts and meet again, and get married when we're about seventy."

After nearly a twenty-year silence on the subject, in a 1986 interview given to promote his critically disastrous *Press to Play* album, McCartney had this to say about his long-suffering lost love:

> We nearly did get married. But it always used to fall short of the mark and something happened. And one of us would think it wasn't right, for which I'm obviously glad now. Jane and I had a long, good relationship — I still like her. I don't know whether she likes me, but I don't see any reason why not. We don't see each other at all.

McCartney achieved a measure of notoriety when, in late June of 1967, American televangelist Billy Graham knelt down in his plush Washington hotel suite and began to pray for the redemption of the wayward Beatle's soul. Billy's inspiration had been McCartney's sensational statement in *Life* magazine that he had taken the dreaded hallucinogen LSD several times and, worse still, enjoyed it. "I am praying for Paul," Graham confirmed to reporters, "that he finds what he is looking for. He has reached the top of his profession and now he is searching for the true purpose of his life. But he will not find it through taking LSD."

McCartney's first trek into the uncharted territories of his mind via LSD had taken place after a Beatles recording session. Lennon had taken what he assumed was a handful of uppers, realizing too late he had accidently ingested several thousand micrograms of powerful White Micro Dot. Teetering precariously close to the edge, he panicked during a vocal overdub and was whisked outside in an effort to calm him. "I can't remember what album it was," he recalled later.

> But I took it and I suddenly got so scared on the mike. I thought I was going to crack. I had to get some air, so they took me upstairs on the roof and George Martin was looking at me funny, and then it dawned on me I must have taken acid. I said, "Well, I can't go on, you'll have to do it and I'll just stay and watch." You know, I got very nervous just watching them all. I was saying, "Is it all right?" and they were saying, "Yeah." They had all been very kind and carried on making the record.

As the session progressed, John, lost in inner space, became increasingly edgy, prompting the others to pack it in for the evening. They soon realized no real work could be accomplished with their leader in such a hyperkinetic, electric state.

"I think I'd better take John home with me," Paul confided to George, as Harrison carefully wiped down, and then packed away, his Gretsch Country Gentleman electric.

"Good idea," said George, "He might need a little looking after." Plodding through EMI's long, narrow hallway, Lennon felt his legs turning to spaghetti. Looking down to examine the trouble, his feet suddenly seemed miles away, two tiny pinheads unwinding like a spool of kite string on a blustery spring day.

On their way to Cavendish Avenue in Paul's purple Mini Cooper, Paul decided it was now or never. "You haven't got another hit there, have you?" he asked, observing John in the back seat through the rear-view mirror.

"Yeah, sure," croaked Lennon, rustling through his coat pocket for another bright white tab. "I could use the company."

Sitting together cross-legged on McCartney's huge oriental rug in the diningroom at the rear of the house, the two men stared intensely into each other's glazed eyes for what seemed an eternity. "I know, man . . ." McCartney trailed off after at least an hour of this time-honored psychedelic ritual. "I know."

Now that Paul had finally followed suit and entered the doors of perception, he emerged a changed person. "God is in everything," he observed to a journalist friend a couple of weeks later. "God is in the space between us. God is in the table in front of you. It just happens I realize all this through acid. It could have been through anything else." In Liverpool, Jim McCartney was unimpressed.

By the time the Beatles' hallucinogenic adventures hit the papers, McCartney was convinced that if not an outright psychic panacea, LSD was, at least, a powerful catalyst in the spiritual evolution of the species. Straining with the evangelical zeal of the neophyte, he eagerly discussed his acid-induced insights with both reporters and friends, praising to the skies the wonders of this accidental derivative of the humble ergot fungus. Not surprisingly, it led him into tangles with the media:

REPORTER: So, now you seem to be encouraging your fans to take drugs!

PAUL: No, I don't think my fans are going to take drugs just because I did. That's not the point anyway. I was asked whether I had [taken LSD] or not, and from then on the whole bit about how far it's going to go, and how many people it's going to encourage, is up to the newspapers, and up to you.

REPORTER: But as a public figure surely you've got a responsibility to . . .

PAUL: I'm not trying to spread the word about this. The man from the newspaper is the man from the mass media. I'll keep it a personal thing if he does, too, you know. . . It's his responsibility for spreading it, not mine. You are spreading it now at this moment. This is going into all the homes in Britain, and I'd rather it didn't. You're asking me the question, you want me to be honest, I'll be honest. But it's you lot who've got the responsibility not to spread this.

As usual, the canny McCartney demanded and got the final word.

Days later, in a scathing editorial entitled "Beatle Paul, MBE, LSD and BF (Bloody Fool)," the *Daily Mirror* charged that he had behaved "like an irresponsible idiot," and suggested that he should see a psychiatrist.

Racing to the aid of his charge, Brian Epstein granted several interviews to journalists the following month, defending the Beatle's statements about the drug. "Paul rang me to say he had told the press he had taken LSD," he explained to one reporter.

I was very worried. I came up to London knowing I was going to be asked to comment on Paul's decision. I finally decided that I would admit I had taken LSD as well. There were several reasons for this. One was certainly to make things easier for Paul. People don't particularly enjoy being lone wolves. And I didn't feel like being dishonest and covering up, especially as I believe that a lot of good has come from hallucinatory drugs.

In a 1984 interview, Alistair Taylor, a lifelong opponent of drug use, reflected on what he felt were the deeper reasons behind the Beatles' turning on.

Look, if you weren't there you can't begin to understand the pressure and their way of life. I can't convey to you what it was like. It was unbearable and they just had to do something. Imagine, you can't walk down the street, you can't go out in a car, you can't do anything without being torn to shreds, day in, day out, you know? The real development, I think, came about as an escape. It was fun, they could afford it, and they mixed with people who said, "Hey, try this." I mean, Lennon spent weeks trying to persuade me to go on a trip, but I never did. I had nothing to do with drugs. I tried a joint about twice, and I decided it was an idiot's game, quite frankly. Who needs it? But John and Derek [Taylor] would spend hours trying to persuade me. "We'll be with you, it's great." It was all done in fun, really.

Towards the end of McCartney's relatively short-lived fascination with acid he began to think twice about having been so keen to sing its praises publicly and backed off from stirring up any further controversy. "I don't recommend it," he told the papers. "It can open a few doors, but it's not any answer. You get answers yourself."

John Lennon, ever the cynic, later charged that it was simply McCartney's inbred squareness that led him to recant his earlier position on the unholy sacrament.

In L.A., the second time we took it, Paul felt very out of it, because we were all a bit slightly cruel, sort of, "We're taking it and you're not!" But we kept seeing him, you know? I think

George was pretty heavy on it; we are probably the most cracked. Paul is a bit more stable than George and I. I think LSD profoundly shocked him — and Ringo. I think maybe they'll regret it.

McCartney, however, offered another, less critical assessment of his crazy acid days to Hunter Davies in *The Beatles*. "Me — I'm conservative. I feel the need to check things out. I was the last to try pot and LSD and floral clothes. I'm just slower than John, the least likely to succeed in class."

In 1986, Lennon's prophecy that McCartney might one day regret his flirtation with the drug was realized when he told Britain's *Q* magazine: "I was given a lot of stick for being the last one to take acid. I wish I'd held out in a way, although it was the times. . . . I remember John going on the old 'Grey Whistle Test,' saying, 'Paul only took it four times! We all took it twenty times!' It was as if you scored points."

Although he ultimately rejected LSD, McCartney did go on to sample all manner of other under-the-counter pharmaceutical delights from fine Afgani opiated hash to Colombian cocaine. In a 1986 interview with *Rolling Stone* he claimed to have been experimenting with cocaine at the time of *Sgt. Pepper*, before any of the other Beatles and the record industry generally, but abandoned it because of its severe downside: "I could never stand that feeling at the back of the throat — it was like you were choking, you know? So I knocked that on the head. I just thought, 'This is not fun.' "

Despite his claims to the contrary, Paul's penchant for the infamous "Devil's Dandruff" didn't end with the collective lunacy of the sixties. Jo Jo Laine remembers an incident from McCartney's 1976 Wings Over Europe tour: "One time in Liverpool for one of the New Year's parties we had some, and we all had a snort. It was Denny and I, Jimmy [McCulloch], Henry [McCullough], and Paul. It was mine. I'm the one who brought it. Paul didn't do a lot, but I remember thinking, 'He's not as straight as everybody thinks he is.' "

Recreational activities aside, the latter half of the sixties also saw McCartney increasingly concerned with the pursuit of serious art. Although John Lennon has the reputation of being the "artistic" member of the group, it should be noted that the inspiration and planning for the albums *Sgt. Pepper's Lonely Hearts Club Band*, *Magical Mystery Tour*, much of *The White Album*, and the operatic side two of *Abbey Road* belong almost solely to McCartney.

Long after John, George, and Ringo had retreated to the staid placidity of London's pastoral suburbs, McCartney was burning the midnight oil with the likes of junkie author William Burroughs, beat poet Allen Ginsberg, heralded LSD manufacturer Michael Hollingshead, *International Times* founder Barry Miles, and Marianne Faithfull's husband, John Dunbar, who owned and operated the celebrated Indica Gallery and bookstore on Southampton Row. Through Dunbar, McCartney began to look at art in a new way. Giving himself up to Dunbar's gentle guidance, he soon became a devotee of avant-garde filmmaker Michelangelo Antonioni and a patron of Greek sculptor Takis and his bizarre collection of magnetic machine art. "He wasn't especially interested in the art scene at first," remembers the handsome, bespectacled Dunbar. "He was just generally being turned on to things. Acid had come along by that time and it made a big difference."

Together, McCartney and Dunbar began making their own underground films, stalking around London with twin 16 mm cameras, shooting just about anything they considered freaky or far out. Back at St. John's Wood, the two spaced-out cinematic pioneers would carefully dub in a soundtrack of McCartney's own electronic music, often working late into the night like a couple of mad scientists in Frankenstein's lab. Although nothing of any great importance surfaced from all this frantic activity, McCartney did have fun. He recalls the phase:

> I had a very rich avant-garde period which was a buzz, making movies and stuff. Because I was living on my own in London, and all the other guys were married in the suburbs, they were very square in my mind, and they'd come over to my pad

where there'd be people hanging out and weird sculptures and I'd be piecing together little films and stuff.

As the years pass, it seems increasingly important to McCartney to be remembered as the "arty" Beatle or at very least the first of the four to dabble in experimental film and music. Even ten years after John Lennon's death, his larger-than-life presence weighs heavily on Paul who despite his post-Beatles accomplishments still seems to resent John's image as the band's cultural trailblazer. "I was making 8mm movies and showing them to Antonioni," he told *Q* magazine in 1986.

> I had all sorts of theories of music. We'd put on a Ravi Shankar record to our home movies and it'd synchronize and John used to come from Weybridge, kind of looking slightly goofy and saying, "Wow! This is great! We should do more of this!" I used to sit in a basement in Montague Square with William Burroughs and a couple of gay guys he knew from Morocco, and that Marianne Faithfull – John Dunbar crowd, doing little tapes, crazy stuff with guitar and cello. But it didn't occur to me the next NME interview I did to rave about William Burroughs. Maybe it would have been good for me to do that.

Not surprisingly, McCartney's "artier than thou" ideas didn't go down well with the rest of the group.

The closest the public ever got to viewing any of Paul McCartney's deliberately obscure *cinéma vérité* was in 1968 when a writer from Britain's *Punch* magazine wrote about the dubious honor afforded him at Cavendish Avenue. There he viewed two of McCartney's LSD-inspired epics: *The Defeat of the Dog* and *The Next Spring Then*. "They were not like ordinary people's home movies," he wrote.

> There were over exposures, double exposures, blinding orange lights, quick cuts from professional wrestling to a crowded car park to a close-up of a television weather map. There were long stillshots of a grey cloudy sky and a wet grey pavement, jumping Chinese ivory carvings and affectionate slow-motion studies of his sheepdog Martha and his cat. The accompanying music, on a record player and faultlessly synchronized, was by the Modern Jazz Quartet and Bach.

▲ Paul's official school portrait as a teen.

▲ McCartney's boyhood home in Liverpool.

▼ Paul on stage at the Norwich Carnival, July 1963.

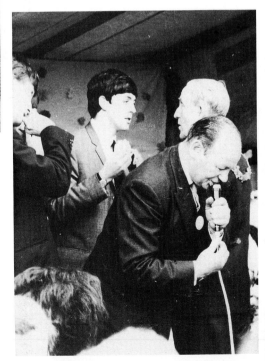

The Fab Four, circa 1967.

▲ Paul and Martha passing the time between takes at an outdoor recording session for Apple's Black Dyke Mills Band, 1968.

▲ McCartney front and center with his mates at the historic global satellite, "Our World," featuring the Beatles performing "All You Need Is Love," 1967.

▶ Beatle manager Brian Epstein and Paul together at EMI, 1966. Although he respected Epstein's theatrical flair, McCartney was unimpressed by his limited business acumen.

▼ Paul, Jane Asher, and Cynthia Lennon together in Rishikesh, India, 1967.

▲ McCartney hitting the skins on location during the filming of the *Magical Mystery Tour*. Owing to the particular costume he is wearing, the widespread rumor that Paul was indeed the Walrus can now be confirmed. Removing the heavy latex head for a bit of fresh air must have provided welcome relief.

▼ John and Paul during a break in shooting for the *Mystery Tour*.

▲ Lennon and McCartney, to many the greatest songwriting partnership of the century

▲ The lovely Ms. Asher in her bedroom at her parents' stately Wimpole Street home, 1967.

▶ Paul and Jane during McCartney's dashing psychedelic period.

▶ Arriving home from a Greek holiday with tiny Julian Lennon in tow, 1967.

▼ New York "Apple girl" Francie Schwartz shadows her man during a late-night Beatles recording session at EMI's Abbey Road studio, 1968.

Forget anything you've read to the contrary. The canny Yoko Ono is definitely the person who contributed more than any other to the unhappy breakup of the Beatles. She is seen here with two of her celebrated victims.

Paul and Jane, the romantic "perfect couple" whose much-publicized relationship hid a lot of deeply private pain.

▲ In Scotland with Jane . . .   . . . and with Linda Eastman. ▼

▲ McCartney conducts the Blackdike Mills Band in Bradford, June 1968.

▼ Off to New York to launch Apple.

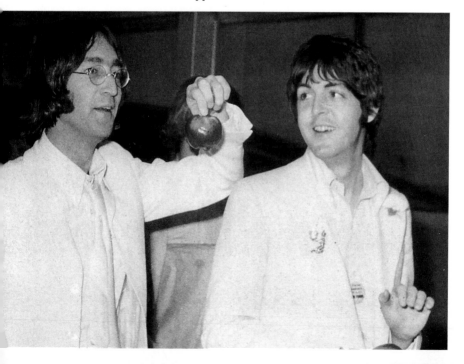

LINDA L. EASTMAN
Advertising Club 4;
Chorus 1, 2, 3, 4;
Pep Club 3, 4.
"Strawberry Blonde"
....Yen for men
....Shetlandish.

▲ The future Mrs. McCartney as she appeared in her high school yearbook.

▼ A rare pic of Paul and Linda (together for only the second time) taken during the press launch for *Sgt. Pepper's Lonely Hearts Club Band* held at Brian Epstein's posh London townhouse in Belgravia, 1967.

▲ The happy couple during the first hot and heavy days of their relationship.

▲ Paul and Linda stop by for a quick blessing from the local vicar in St. John's Wood following their wedding, March 12, 1969.

▼ Running a gauntlet of fans and well-wishers.

The McCartneys arrive home at 7 Cavendish Avenue at the end of the big day.

Having made the difficult decision to commence litigation against his three former colleagues in an effort to formally dissolve the group, McCartney was faced with an extended and complicated legal battle. He is seen here with Linda, leaving a London court in 1970.

▲ Arriving at the Beatles' international corporate headquarters, Apple, housed at 3 Saville Row, just off Piccadilly.

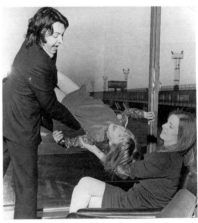

► Playing daddy to Linda Eastman's little girl, Heather See, while en route to visit Paul's dad, 1969.

▼ Say what you like about Paul and Linda; for the last two-decades-plus they've shared a touching and committed love.

◀ Mary Hopkin, McCartney's sensational Welsh singing discovery, relaxes with John and Yoko during the annual Apple Christmas party, 1968.

▼ Wings plays an impromptu gig at London's Hard Rock Cafe, March 18, 1973.

▲ John and Yoko at a trendy London art show opening, 1968.

▶ Linda and Mary hit the road in the early seventies.

▲ For Paul McCartney, home and hearth have always remained at the very heart of almost everything he does. The ladies in his life (left to right, top to bottom), Linda, Stella, Heather, and Mary.

◄ Peter Michael McCartney, known formally as Mike McGear, Paul's super-talented younger brother.

Despite Paul's penchant for all things new and exciting, there were definite limits:

> [John and I] had dinner one night — just a friendly dinner, just bein' mates — and I remember him saying he was thinking of having this trepanning thing done: drilling a hole in the skull. The Romans or the Greeks or somebody used to do it, so that gave it a validity in John's mind, I think. And he said, "Would you be up for that? Do you fancy doin' that? We could go and get it done." I said, "Why?" He said, "It relieves the pressure on your brain." So I said, "Look, you go try it, and if it's great, you tell me, and maybe I'll do it."

For a while, the privacy and freedom afforded the Beatles by their rejection of the road was a balm, a breath of fresh air for the stressed-out quartet. After five frantic years of being together night and day, often for months on end, each of them now had the option of wandering off on his own for awhile.

Following the unbridled success of their films *A Hard Day's Night* and *Help!*, the Beatles' music became noticeably more introspective, interesting, and intricate.

As early as *Rubber Soul* Paul McCartney had asserted his colossal talent for melding strong lyrics with widely appealing melodies, as in "You Won't See Me," "I'm Looking Through You," and "Wait." All three tunes seem a kind of oblique invitation to his oft-absent lover, Jane Asher, to emotionally ante up and settle down with him once and for all.

The Beatles' next album, *Revolver*, further showcased McCartney as a musical painter with a wonderfully full and varied palette. Here, for the first time, emerges a truly compassionate Paul, wounded by an uncaring world that capriciously casts aside the broken and lonely, as he portrays in "Eleanor Rigby" and the hauntingly beautiful "For No One." "At first I thought ["Eleanor Rigby"] was a bit like 'Annabel Lee,' but not so sexy," reflects McCartney.

> Then I realized I'd said she was picking up the rice in church, so she had to be a cleaner; she had missed the wedding, and she was suddenly lonely. In fact she had missed it all — she was the spinster type.

Jane was in a play in Bristol then, and I was walking round the streets waiting for her to finish. The thought just came: "Eleanor Rigby picks up the rice and lives in a dream." So there she was. The next thing was Father MacKenzie. It was going to be Father McCartney, but then I thought that was a bit of a hang-up for my dad, being in this lonely song. So we looked through the phone book. That's the beauty of working at random — it does come up perfectly, much better than if you try to think it with your intellect. In the next verse we thought of an old feller going through dustbins; but it got too involved — embarrassing. That was the point anyway. She didn't make it, she never made it with anyone, she didn't even look as if she was going to.

At the opposite end of the spectrum, *Revolver* re-affirmed McCartney's more familiar, optimistic self, in cuts such as "Good Day Sunshine" and the Tamala Motown-inspired "Got to Get You into My Life," with a good-natured subtlety that both stimulated and assured the listener.

Then came the album that was to define the music of the entire decade, the iconoclastic *Sgt. Pepper's Lonely Hearts Club Band*. The album, recorded at EMI Studios between December 1966 and April 1967, was McCartney's answer to, or perhaps grand elevation of, the Beach Boys' eclectic *Pet Sounds* LP, but also gleaned more than a little inspiration from the Mothers of Invention's startling *Freak Out*, which McCartney later called "the first pop album that was not simply a set of singles all strung together."

Always uppermost in McCartney's mind was to keep the Beatles at the very pinnacle of all that was exciting and different. With *Sgt. Pepper* he set out not just to bruise the barriers of popular music but to obliterate them. "Normally a Beatles album would just be a collection of songs with a nice picture on the cover, nothing more," says Paul. "So the idea was to do a complete thing that you could make what you like of, just a little magical presentation."

Aiding and abetting McCartney in his grandiose schemes to tie together the entire package of music and album graphics into a unified concept was Mal Evans, who is said to have originated the album's unforgettable title. He also helped out on the lyrics to the album's title track and assisted Paul with the tune "Fixing a Hole." Although he remained uncredited, the former telecommunications engineer from suburban Liverpool did receive an unspecified royalty for his efforts.

The first *Pepper* composition the Beatles committed to tape was Paul's "When I'm Sixty-Four," work commencing at 6:45 p.m. on Tuesday December 6, 1966. Although, the Beatles used to perform a version of this vaudevillian ditty at the Cavern occasionally, when their amps broke down, Paul may have included this number as a tribute to his father who on his next birthday would turn sixty-four.

The next track to see daylight was the hauntingly ethereal, "A Day in the Life," tentatively entitled "In the Life of . . ." on the first day's tape log. John and Paul recalled the genesis of the work. "I was writing the song with the *Daily Mail* propped up in front of me on the piano," said John.

> I had it open at the "News in Brief" section or whatever they call it. Anyway, there was a paragraph about four thousand holes in Blackburn, Lancashire, being discovered, but there was still one word missing in that particular verse when we began to record. I knew the line should go, "Now they know how many holes it takes to . . . the Albert Hall." It was a nonsense verse really, but for some reason I just couldn't think of the bloody verb! It was actually Terry Doran who finally said, "*Fill* the Albert Hall, John."

Paul McCartney remembers:

> There'd been a story about a lucky man who'd made the grade, and there was a photograph of him sitting in his big car, and when John saw it he just had to laugh! That's all just a little black comedy, you know. The next bit was another song altogether, but it happened to fit well with the first section. It was really only me remembering what it was like to run up the road to catch the school bus, having a smoke, and then going into class. We decided, "Bugger this, we're going to write a real turn-on song!" This was the only one on the album written as a

deliberate provocation to people. But what we really wanted was to turn you on to the truth rather than just bloody pot!

The album's title track was started on February 1 and by 1:45 a.m. the next morning a rough demo remix was already in the can, enabling acetates to be made for further review and work by McCartney at home.

One week later, the Beatles moved across London to Regent Sound Studios on Tottenham Court Road for work on Paul's surreal "Fixing a Hole." After a prolonged rehearsal, the band forged ahead, recording three complete takes of the finished song, eventually settling on the second as their final choice. McCartney comments:

> If you're a junkie sitting in a room fixing a hole then that's what it will mean to you, but when I wrote it I meant if there's a crack, or the room is uncolorful, then I'll paint it. It's about fans too: I invited one in once, and the next day she was in the *Daily Mirror* with her mother saying we were going to get married. So now we just tell the fans, "Forget it."

McCartney's "Lovely Rita" was recorded chiefly on February 23 and 24 at EMI with overdubs added in March. The whimsical tale of a London civil servant who "allows her heart to be towed away" at the end of every romantic evening, "Lovely Rita" is based on a real-life encounter between McCartney and a St. John's Wood traffic warden, who ticketed the Beatle's illegally parked Mini on Garden Street in 1967. "Lovely Rita" is in reality Lovely "Meta," today a retired nineteen-year veteran of the force. "He saw that my name was Meta," remembers Constable Davis, "and he laughed and said, 'That would make a nice jingle, I could use that.' We chatted for a few minutes and then he drove off. I didn't think anymore of it, but later, the song came out and although I knew the record was about me I never bought a copy."

"Getting Better," a frank rock 'n' roll confessional from Paul, was laid down on March 9 with serious work beginning at one o'clock in the morning, (although the band was officially booked to start at seven). Paul has often commented that the song is a textbook example of how the Lennon/McCartney compositions were strengthened by the collaborators' differing, and complementary, perspectives. When McCartney sang "I've got to admit it's getting better," Lennon caustically added, "It can't get no worse."

The next McCartney track to be laid down was the schmaltzy "She's Leaving Home" with six takes of the complicated string arrangements recorded on March 17. "It's about a much younger girl than Eleanor Rigby, but the same sort of loneliness," recalls McCartney. "That was a *Daily Mirror* story again. This girl left home and her father said, 'We gave her everything, I don't know why she left.' But he didn't give her that much, not what she really wanted when she went away."

The final, mostly McCartney track on the album, "Sgt. Pepper's Lonely Hearts Club Band (Reprise)," was recorded in one intense eleven-hour session on April 1. As Paul was due to fly out to the U.S. two days later, it would also be his final *Pepper* session, although taping continued for a full three weeks under the steady hand of George Martin and sporadic appearances by the other three. "I think the reprise version of the song is more exciting than the first cut of *Sgt. Pepper*," says Beatles recording engineer Geoff Emerick. "There's a nice quality about it. We recorded the Beatles in the huge Abbey Road number one studio which was quite hard because of the acoustics of the place. It's difficult to capture the tightness of the rhythm section in there."

The next challenge was to create an album jacket that would appropriately reflect and package the work's progressive musical content. The Beatles had commissioned The Fool, an aberrant tribe of hippie designers from Holland, to do the job, but McCartney's friend and advisor, art expert Robert Fraser, convinced them that The Fool's splashy, swirling designs would date far too quickly, possibly impeding the record's longevity. In addition to their work on the front cover, The Fool also submitted graphics for both the inside gatefold spread and a psychedelic liner sleeve to hold the actual disc. The inside artwork, however, didn't align properly with the newly commissioned photo put together by artist Peter Blake, and so was dropped at the last minute in favor of the famous portrait of the Beatles by twenty-five-year-old Chelsea photographer Michael Cooper. By way of consolation for The Fool's efforts, however, their electric red-and-pink liner was used.

Neil Aspinall recalls some of the pitfalls of working with The Fool:

> They hadn't somehow checked on the album size and their design was just slightly out of scale. So they said, "Oh, O.K., we'll put a border on it." So we now had this design which was too small and a border being added just to fill up space. I said to the fellows, "What are we selling here, a Beatles album or a centrefold with a design by The Fool which isn't even ready? Hadn't we better get a picture taken of the four of you, and stick that in so we can see who you are?"

In order to expedite matters, at the Beatles' behest, EMI hired Robert Fraser for £1500 to oversee the production of *Sgt. Pepper's* by-now wildly ambitious sleeve. He, in turn, brought in Peter Blake who set about designing and assembling the collage of famous faces to be used as a backdrop against which the Beatles would be photographed. "I went along to [Peter's] house with Robert," Paul recalls in the lavish give-away-program to his 1989/90 world tour:

> Because originally the idea was gonna be that this group was being given a presentation by a Lord Mayor on a kind of grassy knoll with a floral clock, which is very typical of Cleethorpes in Lancashire and all the parks — the floral clock. It was going to be that, and that might have said, "Congratulations, Beatles" or something. And we were going to be standing receiving a silver cup or something from this guy. I drew it all out — little sketches (being sold at Sotheby's regularly, these sketches, they got found). I took this to Peter Blake and he started developing them. He said instead of the floral clock, couldn't we have all these heroes that we'd written these lists of.

From there each of the Beatles was asked to submit the names of twelve personalities they would like to see mixed in amongst the pantheon of famous faces being assembled at Chelsea Manor Studios on Flood Street.

Finally, after two weeks of almost continuous work by Blake and his wife, sculptor Jann Haworth, the outrageous set was completed and the photo session held on March 30, 1967, commencing at 11 p.m. It took Michael Cooper just a little over three hours to get the shots he needed for both the front and back covers as well as the interior gatefold photo.

The next afternoon, Blake returned to the studio to help pack away all the various bits and pieces, only to find that almost everything was already gone, picked over by various assistants and friends of the group. Two decades later, one of the sixty-plus cardboard heads still occasionally turns up at Christy's or Sotheby's and is immediately snapped up by wealthy Beatle freaks from Tokyo to L.A.

It is little known that in addition to the album, a *Sgt. Pepper* film was also planned, with a distinct scenario envisaged for each of the thirteen spectacular tunes. The project, to have been produced in association with the London-based Peacock Productions Limited, went as far as being officially planned and budgeted with a confidential production report signed on Tuesday, September 26, 1967, by producers Hathaway and Peacock. Included in the document were particulars relating to the location, studio, and editing facilities needed for the fifty-two-minute film which was promised for completion late that November. The locations were listed as follows:

A. Longleat/Country: Sgt. P & Reprise
B. Kew Gardens: Lucy
C. Circus: A Little Help
D. Fun Fair: Mr. Kite
E. Air Field: Sixty-Four
F. Modern Middle C House: Leaving Home
G. London Streets Etc. Rita
H. School: Getting Better
I. Factory/Offices/Lifts: Within
J. Studio: 40% of Within and Good Morning
K. Studio/Meditation Room: Fixing A Hole

L. Observatory/Planetarium: Lucy
M. Recording Session: Day in the Life Parts I, II, III

Why the film, which was to be shot in Eastman color for "color television presentation," was never made remains a mystery never publicly commented on by either the Beatles or anyone close to them. In the late seventies, however, an obscure film clip began surfacing occasionally on television around the world. It was later identified as a segment from the ill-fated project. As the cinematic counterpart to the epic "A Day in the Life," the fragmented footage was indicative of the acid-soaked era that spawned it. Apple insider Peter Brown explains:

> It was a mess. The guy who arranged it, Vic Sing, was involved with the movie *Wonderwall* and it was he and Paul who set the whole thing up. They filmed the last session at Abbey Road which was the one with the London Symphony Orchestra. As everyone arrived, most of us were given 16mm cameras and hand mikes and told to film whatever we liked. But no provision had been made by either of them for any straight film taking, so everything that was done was just off-the-wall. There was nothing long enough — just people playing around the cameras.

The idea for *Magical Mystery Tour* first occurred to McCartney while in Denver Colorado with Mal Evans to help celebrate Jane Asher's twenty-first birthday. The concept was simple: the Beatles would invite a select group of close friends, fan club secretaries, bizarre character actors, midgets, and circus freaks to travel around the English countryside with them in a rented coach and just see what happened. "Getting quite excited about planning the television film," Evans wrote in his diary during the trip. "Idea going at the moment is make it about some sort of Mystery Tour (Roll Up! Roll Up!). Paul is getting lots of ideas and we're jotting them down as we go."

Flying home on Tuesday, April 11, 1967, McCartney began working on the lyrics for the project's title track, mapping out further ideas with Evans for the proposed one-hour special. Borrowing some paper from one of the stewardesses, McCartney carefully drew a large circle and then divided it up into several equal sections. He then pencilled in various ideas as to the film's content and structure, leaving several blanks for his colleagues back in London to work out. Nine days later, the Beatles began recording the song "Magical Mystery Tour," but were soon sidetracked by their promised participation that June in the global satellite telecast, "Our World," on which they performed "All You Need Is Love."

On Thursday, August 24, just a couple of days prior to Brian Epstein's tragic death from an accidental overdose of sleeping pills, he and the Beatles met to discuss the group's plans for the rest of the year. He is said to have been very keen about Paul's idea for the *Mystery Tour* film and advised his charges to carry on with their plans. Within three days, Brian Epstein was dead. Thrown into a tailspin by this totally unexpected turn of events, the Beatles decided to postpone further work on the film until returning from a three-month meditation course they had promised to attend at the Maharishi's Rishikesh ashram. A few days later, however, they changed their minds, reasoning that it would make more sense to postpone their holidays until after the filming had been completed.

On Friday, September 1, a meeting was held at Paul's to discuss the particulars of the ambitious project. Neil Aspinall remembers:

> While everyone added ideas, Paul sat at his typewriter and with one over-worked finger put down a list headed "Main Points." Underneath he put: "Coach Tour (Three Days) with people on board. Week beginning Sept. 4 — Cameraman, Sound, Cast, Driver. Hotels to be arranged for 2 nights. 'Magical Mystery Tour' Emblem to be designed. Yellow coach to be hired (Sept. 4 to Sept. 9). Microphone system in coach. Must be good all-round vision. Tour 'staff' — Driver, Courier, Hostess. Three staff uniforms required. Coach destination — Cornwall??? After coach — Shepperton Studios (One Week)." On another sheet he typed out a sequence of arrangements to be made: "Write outline script. Decide cast. Engage cast. Decide when shooting starts. Sets for studios. Fix completion date."

Ringo, listed in the credits as "Richard Starkey, MBE," was ostensibly director of photography, and although all of the Beatles contributed to the final editing of the film, it was mostly Ringo and Paul who supervised production. Setting off enroute to Cornwall together on Monday, September 11, the Beatles and thirty-nine others began the arduous task of filming without benefit of any real script, competent technical advice, or even much of a clue as to where they were heading. Needless to say, right from day one, the Magical Mystery Tour was an unqualified disaster.

One of the most unfortunate setbacks had to do with shooting the dreamy "Fool on the Hill" sequence in Nice on October 30, 1967. Jetting off solo, Paul soon realized he'd not only forgotten his passport but his wallet as well, leaving him in difficulty with French customs officials. A series of frantic phone calls resulted in the document's being rush-delivered by air freight several agonizing hours later. To make matters worse, someone at NEMS had forgotten to include any money with the passport, and McCartney's hotel refused to accept his signature for the room or advance him any credit. Once again the international phone lines were buzzing.

As for McCartney's contribution to the score, it is perhaps his soulful "Fool on the Hill" that is best remembered although his post-*Pepper* music-hall offering, "Your Mother Should Know," also stands up well. Unfortunately, it was the film itself that people had problems with. Lennon observed:

> Paul made an attempt to carry on as if Brian hadn't died by saying, "Now, now, boys, we're going to make a record." Being the kind of person I am, I thought, "Well, we're going to make a record all right. . . ."
>
> Paul had a tendency to come along and say well, he's written these ten songs, let's record now. And I said, "Well, give us a couple of days, and I'll knock a few off," or something like that. . . . Paul said, "Well, here's the segment, you write a little piece for that," and I thought, "Bloody hell," so I ran off and wrote the dream sequence for the fat woman and the whole thing with the spaghetti. George and I were sort of grumbling

about the fuckin' movie but we thought we'd better do it as we had the feeling we owed it to the public to do these daft things.

Magical Mystery Tour was first aired on Boxing Day, 1967, on BBC. The *Daily Mail* called it "blatant rubbish," while the Los Angeles *Times* reported, "Critics and Viewers Boo: Beatles Produce First Flop with Yule Film." Paul McCartney commented that if the film had been shown in color as originally intended, rather than black and white, it might have made more sense. Nevertheless, American network officials ultimately canceled their option to broadcast the film in the United States. Twenty-odd years later, the *Mystery Tour's* critical and commercial failure still seems to nag McCartney.

We didn't worry about the fact that we didn't know anything about making films and had never made one before. We realized years ago you don't really need any knowledge to do anything. All you need is sense. It started out to be one of those kind of things like *The Wild One*, with Marlon Brando. At the time it couldn't be released. The interest in it came later. *Magical Mystery Tour* was a bit like that. So all of those things work out well. You've got to be patient. I think it was a good show. It will have its day, you know.

The White Album signaled the beginning of the end for the Beatles as a group. Although they were still working together, they were beginning to grow apart. No longer was Beatle music the cohesive, joint effort it had been in earlier years; rather, it was usually Paul or John with a backing group. Recorded under the working title *A Doll's House*, the album featured a stark, all-white cover designed by artist John Kosh, with the title "The Beatles" embossed across the front. Inserted inside the two-record set were 8" × 10" head shots of the four Beatles and a phantasmagoric, collage-style poster (which doubled as a lyric sheet) by Richard Hamilton. Years later, John Lennon reflected that of all the Beatles' albums this one stood out as his personal favorite. Paul too, was partial to the impressive thirty-song opus.

But even as they were at their most creative as a group, the inevitable death knell had already been sounded; the band played on, unwilling troubadors at their own musical wake. "They attempted to be nice to each other when they were laying down the basic tracks," remembers Ken Scott, one of their engineers from the early days of *A Hard Day's Night* and *Help!*

> But there was one time, when we were putting bass on one of Paul's songs. . . . Everything was going real well, and then John and Ringo walked in and for the half hour they were there, you could have cut the atmosphere with a knife. It was awful. At one point Ringo quit the band for a couple of weeks — he had reached that point, and he walked. When he came back, they filled the entire studio with flowers and big WELCOME HOME banners. They wanted him back.

The Beatles' ever-faithful father figure, George Martin, was beginning to show signs of strain and took a well-deserved three-week holiday in the middle of recording, bringing in latter-day Who producer, Chris Thomas, to oversee the continuing work. In his absence the pace accelerated and a full ten tunes were recorded by the time he returned. "The fastest track we did was 'Birthday,'" engineer Scott recalls. "We started it in the afternoon, then we all went round to Paul's house to watch one of the old rock 'n' roll movies, *The Girl Can't Help It*, that was being shown on TV. That gave everyone a new lease on life, and we went back in the studio and finished the song that night."

McCartney's thirteen-plus tracks on *The White Album* are the work of a punchier, more mature composer intent on stretching his songwriting and performing talents to the limit. In "Back in the U.S.S.R." he mimics not only the perpetually sunny Beach Boys but also himself through a rapid-fire succession of vocal gymnastics only the most limber of rock performers could ever hope to match.

"Ob-La-Di, Ob-La-Da" is Paul's surreal, reggae-inspired ode to a Jamaican friend. "I might have given him a couple of lyrics," John recalled in December of 1980, "but it's his song, his lyric."

Also included on *The White Album* are three of Paul's outstanding miniatures. Perhaps insubstantial in themselves, they work admirably in the context of the expansive two-record set. The first, "Wild Honey Pie," was originally just a typical McCartney off-the-cuff ad lib which was later edited down and fitted between "Ob-La-Di, Ob-La-Da" and Lennon's silly "Bungalow Bill." Of "Wild Honey Pie" Paul has said, "This was just a fragment of an instrumental which we weren't sure about, but Pattie [Harrison] liked it very much so we decided to leave it on the album." Steve Holly, virtuoso drummer for Wings in its last, fragile incarnation, remembers Paul often working up and recording several similarly offbeat compositions including a ditty about going for a pee, aptly entitled "Call of Nature." The next unfinished McCartney gem on the album is the reasonably obscene, "Why Don't We Do It in the Road." None of the other Beatles performs on this peculiarly barren track; Paul screams out the mantra-like lyrics with a gritty rasp reminiscent of his delivery on the *Abbey Road* opus, "Oh! Darling." Finally, the twenty-seven-second "Can You Take Me Back" may be one of the spiritually richest lyrics McCartney has ever created.

Harkening back to McCartney's early music-hall influences are his tribute to his beloved sheepdog, Martha, in "Martha My Dear," and the big-band-inspired "Honey Pie." "Only someone like Paul could ever get away with doing that sort of lame-ass shit," John Lennon complained to me in 1971. "That's all due to his father, Jim, of course, who I must admit I've always rather liked. His brother Mike too. It's just Paul who sometimes gets my goat. Especially when he's intent on doing his fucking Cole Porter routine all the time like on 'Honey Pie'."

More subdued are "Blackbird," "Mother Nature's Son," and the beautifully simple "I Will." Even the often critical Lennon had to admit that McCartney's acoustic guitar work was excellent, his light touch cascading around his deeply felt lyrics like wind over water. Denny Laine, for one, has always acknowledged "Blackbird" as one of his former partner's greatest compositions. "It's such a simple melody to play," he

would often say, while doodling around on his guitar. "Whenever I show people they just can't believe anything that
sounds that good can end up being so damn simple. But it is.
And that's a big part of Paul's incredible genius." Of "Mother
Nature's Son" John recalled: "That was from a lecture by Maharishi where he was talking about nature, and I had a piece
called, 'I'm Just a Child of Nature' which turned into 'Jealous
Guy' years later."

Perhaps Paul's least-inspired track on *The White Album* is
the inane B-western spoof, "Rocky Racoon." Like his early
Wings single "Mary Had a Little Lamb," the popular mid-
seventies tune "C Moon," and his as-yet-unreleased "Rupert
Bear" ballad, "Rocky" is more a zany children's song rather
than anything one would expect to find on a straight-ahead
Beatles album. "I saw Bob Hope doing it once on the telly
years ago," John once recalled. "I just thanked God it wasn't
one of mine."

Finally, Paul's two token pre-heavy-metal rockers, "Birthday" and "Helter Skelter," are stirring examples of the Beatles
at their hard-driving best. In spite of the fact that American
mass murderer Charles Manson adopted "Helter Skelter" as
his anthem of terror during his 1969 killing spree in Los Angeles, the manic tune has not been compromised and remains
one of McCartney's finest vocals.

Although not released until after *Abbey Road*, *Let It Be* was
the next full-fledged Beatles project. A fine semi-live album, it
also spun off into an intriguing motion picture documentary,
and even an excellent picture book. "In a nutshell it was time
for another Beatle movie or something," recalled John:

> Paul wanted to go on the road. He sort of set it up, and there
> were discussions about where to go and all that. I was stoned
> all the time anyway so I didn't really give a shit. Nobody did.
> We put down a few tracks and nobody was in it at all. The tape
> ended up like the bootleg version. We didn't want to know
> about it anymore, so we just left it to Glyn Johns and said,
> "Here, mix it." We got an acetate in the mail and we called each

other and said, "What do you think?" We were going to let it out in really shitty condition. I thought it was good to let it out and show people what had happened to us, we can't get it together, we don't play together any more; you know, leave us alone.

Despite the turmoil surrounding the production, *Let It Be* contains several classic McCartney cuts, foremost among them his two heartfelt ballads, "The Long and Winding Road" and the majestic "Let It Be." Paul illuminates the genesis of the latter:

> I had a lot of bad times in the sixties and we used to sort of — probably all the drugs — lie in bed and wonder what was going on and feel quite paranoid. I had a dream one night about my mother. She died when I was fourteen so I hadn't really heard from her in quite awhile, and it was very good. It gave me some strength. "In my darkest hour, Mother Mary comes to me." I get dreams with John in, and my Dad. It's wondrous, it's like magic. Of course you're not seeing them, you're meeting yourself, or whatever. . . .

Another significant McCartney creation recorded for what the album jacket touted as this "New phase Beatles album" was "Get Back." In the high-powered track McCartney sings about a character he calls simply "Jo Jo." According to Jo Jo Laine, McCartney was referring to her. During the first, dizzying heights of Beatlemania the starstruck young lady ran across Paul's home address in a fan magazine and began writing her hero dozens of affectionate, flowery letters. After a couple of years she stopped, never having received a reply and all but forgot about her mad crush on the baby-faced Beatle. Although McCartney never acknowledged his devoted follower later, Jo Jo likes to think that when he was writing the lyrics for the tune he may have obliquely referred to the long-distance groupie. She further claims that Linda told Denny about it all some years later when the ravishing Boston model was first dating Laine. "I don't really think she liked it much at all," says Jo Jo. "As a matter of fact, every time they played that particular tune Linda used to stare daggers at me whenever Paul got to the bits about me."

Finally, McCartney's good-natured "Two of Us" echoes back to a time of innocence when it was John and Paul, not John and Yoko, a long-distant time when two teenage boys from suburban Liverpool struggled to find the sound that would one day change the face of popular music. "From 'Love Me Do' to 'Let It Be,' wasn't really such a big step," recalled Lennon in 1971. "Just a gradual awakening of the lives we were all living at the time. I can never let it go completely because it was my youth, you know? A very special youth that only Paul and I were there to share."

Originally entitled simply *Everest*, the *Abbey Road* LP was the Beatles' final studio album and, in retrospect, their last hurrah together as a band. McCartney recalls the titling of the work:

> We were working a lot in there at the time, always wondering what we were going to call it and Geoff Emerick, the engineer, always used to smoke Everest cigarettes, so we were thinking of things of like *Ever Rest*. It was kind of working out to be a biggish album — and it was going quite well and then everybody started saying that it wasn't a very good title really. We were in Studio 3, the little one at the front which used to have record covers on the ceiling in those days and looked like a record shop, and said, "Why don't we call it *Abbey Road* and have a picture of us on that crossing outside?" It was the simplest thing to do. For everyone that didn't know the name of the studio, that would imply something kind of mystical — Monastery Avenue sort of thing.

The sessions for *Abbey Road* began in earnest in July of 1969 with all four Beatles eager to bury the hatchet and get back to making music the way they once did, as a team. At first George Martin was skeptical and only agreed to be coaxed back from his work at his own successful AIR Studios on the condition that the Beatles allow him to direct the sessions as a producer rather than in the relatively subservient fifth-fiddle role he had played on the previous few albums. "*Let It Be* was a miserable experience and I never thought that we would get back together again," Martin recalls. "So I was very surprised when Paul rang me up and said, 'We want to make another record. Will you produce it for us, really produce it?' I said, 'Yes, if I am really allowed to produce it. If I have to go back and accept a lot of instructions which I don't like I won't do it.' It was really good, even though the boys tended to do their own items, sometimes in different studios at the same time, and I had to be dashing from one place to another."

After assurances from Paul that all would be well, the sessions commenced at 2:30 p.m. on July 1, with McCartney overdubbing a lead vocal for "You Never Give Me Your Money." Arriving well before the others the next day, he laid down the twenty-three-second acoustic track, "Her Majesty," moving on to "Golden Slumbers" with George and Ringo later in the day.

The next McCartney composition to be recorded was the whimsical "Maxwell's Silver Hammer" on July 9. This turned out to be John's first appearance at this round of sessions; he and Yoko had been waylaid in Scotland after crashing their car into a ditch while visiting with Lennon's Aunt Mater near Durness. Pregnant and under doctor's orders to stay in bed and rest, Yoko was happily accommodated by John who ordered a large double bed be brought into the studio to help facilitate her recovery. Setting up the microphones for the session that morning, the engineers were astounded at this latest Lennon eccentricity. Sometime later, Yoko arrived by ambulance and was carefully lowered onto the mattress by two uniformed attendants. The other three Beatles were not amused. To make matters worse, Lennon insisted a microphone be hung directly over his ailing lover's face in case her highness felt moved to participate! Of course if for some reason John had to pop into one of the other studios for a moment or two for a quick overdub, the bed was simply rolled alongside wherever Lennon happened to perch. All in all vintage Yoko Ono.

On July 17, a lead vocal for another McCartney tune, the brilliant fifties-inspired "Oh! Darling," was recorded. This version was ultimately discarded in favor of a stronger, gutsier rendition sometime later. Alan Parsons, now a respected musician in his own right, happened to be second engineer on that particular afternoon. "Perhaps my main memory of the *Abbey Road* sessions," he told Beatles historian and author Mark Lewisohn, "is of Paul coming into Studio 3 . . . to do the vocal on 'Oh! Darling.'"

> That was a feature of the *Abbey Road* sessions: you very rarely saw all four Beatles together . . . But Paul came in several days running to do the lead on "Oh! Darling." He'd come in, sing it and say "No, that's not it, I'll try it again tomorrow." He only tried it once per day, I suppose he wanted to capture a certain rawness which could only be done once before the voice changed. I remember his saying, "Five years ago I could have done this in a flash," referring, I suppose, to the days of "Long Tall Sally" and "Kansas City."

"The End" is just that, Paul's final bit of homespun cosmic truth tacked onto the tail of this moving, four-part medley by the four, perfectly tying together and encapsulating eight years of inspired music from the band the world refuses to forget.

Most people thought I was due to marry Jane Asher — I rather thought I was too. But I just kept remembering Linda, this nice blonde American girl. I twisted her arm and finally she agreed to marry me. Linda was afraid it wouldn't work out. And I kept telling her, "Aw come on, it will be fine." I'm still telling her that.

—Paul McCartney, 1985—

I consider myself a peasant. I guess I rebelled against the privilege I was born into. To tell you the truth, I never had a friend in my life until I moved to Arizona, except one person. I always got along very nicely with animals. My kids are my best friends.

—Linda McCartney, 1985—

6
Hands Across the Water
Paul and Linda

I f Linda Eastman started out as just another silver-spoon groupie from Westchester County, she ended up an integral and important part of Paul McCartney's lifelong search for security and love. Without her, one suspects, he would never have done so well for so long, or been quite as able to bear up under the incredible pressure of being the popular icon he has become.

As Linda McCartney, this eldest child of a successful show business attorney and a wealthy Cleveland heiress, she is today a mature, creative, socially concerned woman with no illusions about either her complicated place in pop history or her role as a responsible, caring citizen of Spaceship Earth.

Unlike the snaky, condescending Yoko Ono, these days Linda is generally exceptionally kind and polite and routinely affords even the most spaced-out McCartney freaks a friendly smile, a quick word, and a moment or two of reflected glory for those poor, fragile creatures so inextricably tied up in someone else's fabulous life.

On the family farm near Peasmarsh, Sussex, the McCartneys' down-to-earth rural residence is very much her domain. Aggressive fans intent on an afternoon of up-close McCartney-watching inevitably have to get through her first, a maneuver worthy of only the most skilled and clever rock 'n' roll commandoes. Once, in 1985, when Julia Baird was trying to get in touch with Paul after nearly a thirty-year gap and asked one of the McCartneys' neighbors to please amble over and give him a message, Linda came to the door literally screaming at the poor woman. "I don't care who wants him!" she cried. "How dare you come here uninvited for any reason. Get out, now!" Later, the totally mortified young mum insisted to Julia that the whole time she "felt" Paul was cowering just inside the only partially opened front door.

On another occasion, however, a couple of diehard English fans experienced just the reverse, when, after they turned up at the former Beatle's front gate, Linda came barreling out, motioning them to hurry up and get into her car.

"It's a good thing for you Paul's gone out for a bit," she told the two boys. "He gets really upset about people hanging around down here. It's not so bad in London; he's used to it. But this is our home. Can you understand that?"

Driving the unwelcome admirers directly to the train station in nearby Rye, the pretty, gently aging McCartney softened up as the two disappointed and embarrassed teens collected together the pile of albums and 45's they had lugged down from London in the hopes of getting signed. "Listen, guys," she said. "I know Paul appreciates the fact that so many people love him. He's very grateful to his fans; you know that. It's just that we really value our privacy, what little we have. So anyway . . . I guess we'll see you up in London sometime, okay?"

Born Linda Louise Eastman on September 24, 1941, Paul's photographer wife was raised against the affluent backdrop of Scarsdale, New York and the family's other opulent homes in

East Hampton and Manhattan. Her father Lee, was a Harvard graduate who officially changed his name from Epstein to Eastman following the completion of his decidedly upper-crust education. "My family was very close," Linda confided to Britain's *Women's Own* magazine in the early seventies. "My father's parents — they're dead now — were Russian immigrants, very warm, down-to-earth, working-class people. My dad just happened to be born intelligent and worked his way through Harvard Law School." One of four children (three girls and a boy), Linda was always especially close to her mother, formerly Louise Linder, daughter of the founder and CEO of the famous Linder department store chain.

With her father working closely with so many of the big-name artists of the day, young Linda often came down to dinner to find the likes of such celebrities as Hopalong Cassidy, Hoagy Carmichael, Howard Arlen, Tommy Dorsey, and even abstract artist Robert Rauschenberg tucking into one of her mother's sumptuous gourmet meals. In 1947, while still only six years old, she had the honor of being the inspiration behind the Jack Lawrence tune, "Linda," the copyright of which he had traded to Mr. Eastman in exchange for some legal work. First recorded by Buddy Clark, the catchy, upbeat melody was turned into a certified American classic in 1963 by surf music stars Jan and Dean.

Linda admits to having been perpetually restless as a child, and curious about life outside the perimeters of her parents' isolated world of prestige and wealth, remembering that she often felt like "the black sheep" of her large, loving family. "I was forced to learn piano," she complained in an interview several years ago. "And like a lot of children forced to do something against their will, I rebelled against that, learnt nothing — and finally got my way."

Although Linda wasn't really keen to take the time to try to learn a musical instrument that is not to say she wasn't interested in music. Like most red-blooded American teens in the late fifties, Linda felt a close covenant with both the music and the artists of that pop-cultural renaissance. "I was into

R&B in high school," she is quoted in her husband's slick 1990 world tour program.

> At home in Scarsdale, New York — which was out in the coun-
> tryside then, although it's a suburb now — I listened to the
> Alan Freed rock 'n' roll show on the radio every night of the
> week, 7 to 10. He never played a bad record. The Dells, The
> Doves, The Moonglows, I was into them all. I wasn't in a band
> but me and some of the girls used to sing doo wop together for
> fun up in our school's Music Tower.

Graduating from Scarsdale High School and then moving on to both the exclusive Sarah Lawrence and then Princeton, studying history and art, the young woman's life was suddenly shattered when her beloved mother was killed in a plane crash.

Shortly after the tragedy, Linda met and married fellow student Melvin See, an aspiring geophysicist, and together they moved to Colorado to continue their studies. Early in 1963 Linda became pregnant and gave birth to their only child together, Heather, on December 31. The couple were incompatible, however, and when, after his graduation, Melvin wanted them to move to Africa so that he could undertake some field work, Linda informed him that there was little point in continuing the relationship and that she wanted a divorce. Altogether, the marriage lasted less than a year.

Moving on to Arizona with little Heather, Linda, at odds about what to do next, enrolled in a photography course given by wheelchair-bound instructor Hazel Archer at the Tucson Art Center. It was to be the beginning of a whole new way of viewing the world for the young mother, and her first halting steps towards an eventful career. "When my marriage broke up, I decided to get away from everything I had ever known before," Linda has recalled. "I moved down to Tucson, staying with friends, studying photography at a local college, and spending much of my time riding on the edge of the desert . . . For the first time I started going round with artists, actors and writers, and all that helped me to discover who I am. It changed my life, meeting so many interesting, intelligent people."

Eventually moving back home to New York, Linda landed a job as a receptionist at the upmarket *Town & Country* magazine, where in 1966 she intercepted an invitation to a party for the Rolling Stones aboard a yacht on the Hudson. Grabbing her trusty Pentax, she hopped into a cab and the rest, as they say, is rock 'n' roll history. . . . "I stood there on the quay with my long blonde hair and, I guess, a mini-skirt," Linda remembers.

> I must have caught the band's eye because a woman came down the gangway and said I was the only photographer they would allow on board. I got well into it, using black and white. Then back on the quay all the journalists came up and gave me their cards because they needed the pictures. I got them back from the lab and, lo!, they were wonderful. After that I started to get a lot of work with bands like the Jimi Hendrix Experience, Lovin' Spoonful, The Doors, Jefferson Airplane, The Grateful Dead and The Beatles. One reason is, I was the cheapest photographer in town! Give me a credit and pay for the film and I'd do it!

Linda's next big score was being named informal house photographer at the famous Fillmore East. There she met and mixed with virtually every big-name group of the day, establishing herself as one of rock's hippest and prettiest photographers. She was linked romantically with such luminaries as Steve Winwood, Tim Buckley, Warren Beatty, Eric Burdon, Stephen Stills, Mike Bloomfield, and Al Kooper. According to Linda, the first time she met her future husband was backstage at Shea Stadium in 1966: "It was John who interested me at the start," she recalls. "He was my Beatle hero. But when I met him the fascination faded fast and I found it was Paul I liked."

At the invitation of author J. Marks she flew to London in the hope of photographing some big-name groups for his intended book, *Rock and Other Four-Letter Words*. In a meeting with Island Record publicists a few days later, Linda was granted a private session with the supergroup Traffic, one of the few times the camera-shy musicians acquiesced to such a request. Following the session, Linda decided to hang out for a few days visiting some clubs and generally soaking up the high-energy atmosphere of swinging London, circa 1967.

One evening, she accepted an invitation from ex-Animals bassist Chas Chandler to accompany him down to the Bag O' Nails, a celebrated superstar watering hole on Kingley Street. Georgie Fame and the Blue Flames were playing that night, a particularly popular crowd pleaser which brought out more than the usual number of London's glitterati. Paul McCartney too, had dropped by for the show, little suspecting that within hours he would meet his future bride: "Paul was at a table almost next to us. You know it's the old story. A little flash from him, a little flash from me. Yeah, love at first sight. It was *something* at first sight, I don't know if it was love."

For the flirtatious McCartney, eyeing yet another pretty young lady at yet another crowded club was an almost-nightly occurrence, and certainly nothing to get too excited about. Still, jaded as he might have been to his almost uncontrollable attraction to the opposite sex, this time it was somehow different. "We were both with other friends," says Paul. "I saw this blonde across the room and I fancied her. So when she passed my table, I said something stupid like, 'Hello, how are you? Let me take you away from all this.' Linda happened to know one of the friends I was with. So after chatting for a bit, we left and went to some other club."

The "other" club was the Speakeasy, perhaps the quintessential hippie gentry hideaway, high over Leicester Square in the heart of Central London. Once there, Linda found herself rubbing elbows with such royal rockers as Pete Townshend, Brian Jones, Keith Moon, Eric Clapton, and Roger Daltrey. And to think that the single greatest catch of all, Beatle Paul was her date! Although she went home alone that night, for supergroupie Linda, it was a memorable night's work.

The next afternoon, Linda rang NEMS and asked Peter Brown if she might come by and show him her portfolio in the hope of winning a spot as a photographer at the upcoming *Sgt. Pepper* press party to be held at Brian Epstein's ultra-fashionable Chapel Street townhouse in Belgravia. Ever the gentleman, Brown agreed and, frankly, very much liked what he saw. Eastman's pictures had, by this time, developed a basic integrity and simplicity that belied her sometimes overly aggressive, all-too-American veneer. Upon leaving, Linda presented Peter with a large blow-up of Brian Jones as a gift. Brown had a little surprise for her as well. "So I'll see you at Brian's then in a couple of days," he mentioned casually as she was zipping up her portfolio. "And don't forget your camera."

Here at last, was Linda's big chance. Not quite the private, exclusive session she had hoped for, but a prestigious gig all the same. Besides, she knew that this was the kind of plum assignment that would inevitably lead to a lot of other work. Important work. Work that could further her reputation as an up-and-coming artist.

In a 1990 interview, Barrie Wentzell, photographer-in-residence from 1965 to 1975 for *Melody Maker,* Britain's most prestigious and authoritative rock magazine of that era, remembers that despite all the hoopla, he and his colleagues were granted only a scant half hour in which to get their precious shots. Derek Taylor, he says, was directing the carefully orchestrated proceedings, making sure that each of the twenty or so Fleet Street shooters got a fair shake at zeroing in on the Beatles, who were reportedly in quite a jolly mood throughout the party.

Peter Brown remembers the grand occasion in his 1983 work, *The Love You Make*:

> The girl that turned up at Chapel Street that May nineteenth wasn't the same sloppily dressed girl I had seen in my office a few days before. . . . She wore impeccably applied makeup, including long, fluttering false eyelashes. . . . It wasn't long before she zeroed in on Paul. . . . He watched as Linda sank to her knees in front of his chair and began snapping photos of him. Although she tried to manage otherwise, she left with all the other photographers.

Later, Linda tried unsuccessfully to phone Paul at a private number given to her by one of Fleet Street's finest. Unfortunately, the number actually rang through to the home of Harry Pinster, financial adviser to Apple Corp., who, for what Brown calls "security reasons," had all of the Beatles' home phones billed to his account. Several times the diplomatic Pinster patiently explained to Linda that there was no Mr. McCartney at that exchange, but the determined Ms Eastman would typically not take no for an answer. In the end, the disgruntled executive had to unplug his telephone. A few days later, Linda Eastman packed up her gear and reluctantly caught an early morning flight back to Manhattan.

Friends say that from the moment she arrived home the lovesick Linda did little more than hang around her apartment, pining for McCartney. Lilian Roxon, a New York writer and friend of Eastman's, somehow ran across a photo of Linda and Paul taken at the *Pepper* press launch and posted it to her as a keepsake. Linda responded by blowing it up to half the size of a roadside billboard and then plastering it proudly across her livingroom wall. Linda Eastman was out to get her man. Back in London bachelor Paul's carefree days were clearly numbered.

The next great installment of this transatlantic cat-and-mouse saga came almost exactly one year later when John and Paul flew to America to formally announce the formation of the Beatle's Apple Corp., and thus, the rock band's gallant Utopian struggle for what Lennon termed "Western communism." Suffice to say, there was still apparently quite a lot of high-potency hemp in the air.

Talking her way into the strictly invitation-only press conference on May 15, 1968, Linda surreptitiously slipped Paul her phone number, which McCartney dutifully rang later that afternoon with plans for them to meet that evening after the two Beatles had finished taping an appearance on the popular *Tonight Show,* with guest host Joe Garagiola. Paranoid to have the preppy-looking blonde meet him at his suite at the opulent St. Regis Hotel for fear one of the ubiquitous paparazzi might photograph them together, thereby alerting Jane of his philandering, McCartney "borrowed" Beatle associate Nat Weiss' flat where the two secret lovers happily hid out together for the next few days. So intertwined were they that Linda even accompanied John and Paul to the airport upon their departure from New York so that she and McCartney could savor every last possible second they could have together.

Returning home to St. John's Wood, McCartney sat pensively on the cold, stone steps leading into his weedy and tangled back garden and found his thoughts returning to America. That he genuinely loved and cared for Jane was never in question, but there was something truly wonderful about Linda, a sort of indefinable wildness that he found compelling, forbidden, and very, very sexy. Within days a courier arrived at the tall iron gate with a package from New York. Inside was a poster-size blowup of Paul with his arms tangled around Linda's little four-year-old daughter. That was another plus about Linda versus Jane. Not only would the solitary Beatle get a girlfriend, he would inherit a ready-made family as well.

Several weeks later, towards the end of June, Paul was once again back in the U.S., this time as key speaker at Capitol Records' annual convention in L.A., a decidedly unBeatlesque endeavor that only PR man Paul would even consider. Tony Bramwell remembers the highly unlikely event in the NEMS-approved *Beatles Monthly Book*:

> Other than the heads of Capitol, not a soul knew a Beatle was coming to Los Angeles. . . . Eventually, as the convention drew to a close, came the special announcement from the stage and Paul was brought on. . . . Everyone went berserk and gave him a fine welcome. And the Apple promotional film was screened showing the Beatles at work in the Apple offices, in the recording studio and so forth. . . . On Saturday night we went to the home of Capitol's president for cocktails and then to the record company's barbecue in the open air beside Century Plaza fountains.

This obviously G-rated version of the trip differs significantly from rumors that, holed up with him in his cozy bungalow at the Beverly Hills Hotel was a black Hollywood superhooker, as well as an unnamed white young actress he was also squiring.

On Sunday, June 22, the relentless Linda had at last tracked down her elusive lover and rang up, announcing that she was at that moment not five hundred yards away, in the lobby of the posh hotel. "Come on over, then," said Paul. The fact that he currently had two only partially clad young women in the room apparently never for a moment phased him. "It'll be great to see you."

After Linda arrived, McCartney quietly got up and knocked at the bedroom door, offhandedly instructing his two lady friends to get dressed and hit the road. Ten minutes later, they both stormed out in tears as Paul and Linda sat chatting on the overstuffed leather sofa in the lounge of the luxury hotel cottage.

After a hot romantic night and a fine day of sailing on Warner Brothers executive John Calley's yacht the next day, Paul, Linda, Ivan Vaughan, and Apple label director Ron Kass caught a late-afternoon flight to New York and on the way almost landed themselves in deep trouble with the Federal Bureau of Investigation. Peter Brown recalls the near catastrophe:

> Marijuana, it turned out, was one of Linda's favorite vices. Ron Kass became aware of this while the four of them were waiting in the VIP Ambassador Lounge at Los Angeles International Airport. It was announced over the public address system that because of a bomb threat all carry-on luggage would have to be searched.
>
> Kass immediately turned to Paul and said, "Do you have anything in your bag that would embarrass us?" Paul shook his head. Then Kass turned to Linda Eastman. She seemed surprisingly complacent as she informed him that she had "a couple of kilos" in a Gucci bag sitting at her feet.

Infuriated at Eastman's blasé attitude about something so potentially damaging to someone she claimed to care about,

Kass quickly kicked the damning evidence under a row of chairs and then led the tiny entourage through the FBI search. Adding insult to injury, after the awkward inquisition, Linda somehow managed to slip back through the dragnet and scarf up her precious reefer, sauntering casually on board the plane as if she were carrying baked goods for the church bazaar.

Upon McCartney's return to London, Linda attempted to maintain her grip on the often impressionable Beatle through a veritable barrage of late-night phone calls and steamy love letters. In the end, however, the sex-mad McCartney resumed his old ways, pairing off with both Francie Schwartz and London dolly bird Molly Migivern for yet more off-the-record close encounters.

As the St. John's Wood summer faded into fall, thoughts of the lovely Linda again consumed the fickle McCartney. Now that his five-year liaison with Jane had effectively fizzled out forever, it was clear to him that the only-too-willing Linda must now truly be the one. "I persuaded Linda to come to London for a visit," Paul recalls, a visit Linda remembers her father, Lee, wasn't all that keen on her making. "It's a pity you can't go," he told her. "You've got to take the child to school."

"I thought, 'What do you mean I won't be able to go?' Anyway, I came over and we lived together for awhile. Neither of us talked about marriage. We just loved each other and lived together."

One of the unkindest scraps of gossip concerning Linda is the outrageous allegation that shortly after coming to England on Paul's invitation she sent a postcard to one of her girlfriends in New York saying only, "I bagged a Beatle!!!" Interestingly, the story comes via someone currently involved in working on one of Linda's more commercially successful projects. The source goes on to say that above and beyond all the many other artists she has dealt with in the course of her career, Linda McCartney is far and away the most unpleasant, pushy, and overbearing.

After a time, both Linda and Paul began to miss having Heather around, culminating early one morning in McCartney phoning his little daughter-to-be. "I rang Heather in New York and said, 'Heather, will you marry me?' She was five. 'No, don't be silly,' she said. 'I'm too young.' 'Well I can't wait,' I said. So we went to New York and brought her back to London to live with us."

For five months Paul and Linda stayed together at Cavendish Avenue. Being an almost-married man felt good to McCartney who approached his role of husband and daddy with the same sense of enthusiasm and commitment he applied to everything he undertook.

Unfortunately, according to at least one reliable source, Linda might not have been always the tender, loving mum she went out of her way to appear. In an interview with George's mother, Louise Harrison, journalist Alana Nash recalls her intimating that, to her mind anyway, Linda was a stuck-up bitch who could on occasion brutalize her daughter. Mrs Harrison reflected:

> We were up to see Jim for dinner one night and Paul and Linda were there, and they'd brought Heather, Linda's little girl. Linda barely spoke to us. We arrived quite a long time before dinner, and Heather was begging for something to eat, but Linda just ignored her.
>
> Finally, she gave her something, and Heather spilled it or dropped it or something, and Linda grabbed her up, screaming and cursing at her. She upset the child terribly. When the meal was finally on the table, Linda told Heather she couldn't have anything to eat because she'd been naughty. Paul had to take over and give her some food. Shocking!
>
> I always liked Cynthia [Lennon] very much. Yes, she was lovely. And so was Jane. I don't know what Paul wants with Linda.

Towards the end of his Jane Asher days, McCartney visited a clairvoyant in Brighton who told him that he would soon marry a blonde and have four children. By February of 1969 doctors confirmed that Linda was indeed pregnant. This convinced McCartney that he should cease playing house and make Linda his wife. To his utter amazement, the headstrong Ms Eastman at first declined. "I had been pressured by men all my life," recalls Linda. "I rather liked being on my own, making my own decisions. I had actually sworn to myself that I would never get married again."

McCartney kept on pitching, and on March 11, 1969, the Apple press office announced the forthcoming nuptials. Fifteen years later, Paul remembered the general anti-marriage mood that seemed to prevail at the time:

> People started to say that family life was finished, that the family as a unit was gone. We saw all that talk come and go: "People don't want to get married anymore; women are asserting themselves." We just didn't go for it. We knew that was supposed to be the fashion.
>
> Many of our friends were not getting married but were having common-law marriages and calling their kids funny names like Zowie or Wow or Moondust. Can you imagine a kid at ten with a name like Zowie? All the other kids in school would make fun of him.
>
> It was a media trip. Maybe some journalists or some artist friends of mine in London weren't getting married, but everyone I know in Liverpool was. And I'm sure Philadelphia steel workers were still getting married. They didn't listen to all that rubbish.

As soon as word hit the street about the Beatle's impending, next-afternoon wedding, it seemed as though every young would-be Mrs. McCartney within a fifty-mile radius of St. John's Wood was on Cavendish Avenue. By early evening just slightly over three dozen sobbing females had turned up to mark the solemn occasion, standing like statues in the rain in front of the dark brick wall which protected their idol during this, his final night as a free and available entity. Every few minutes or so, the wailing women would fall silent until one of the spurned, teenage spinsters recalled a particularly tender memory of her beloved Paul and her agonized sobbing would set off the others. "God, it was awful," remembers Margot

Stevens. "Just awful. We went to his house and Rosie [his housekeeper] told us he got upset because he could hear the girls outside his gate, crying. He went out and told the girls 'You knew I had to get married sometime!' He was on the verge of tears himself." Many years later, Paul revealed that the night before the wedding he and Linda had a whopping great row and almost canceled the whole thing right then and there, but has never said why. Sources close to the couple speculate it may have had something to do with Linda's reaction to all the girls outside. "She has always been extremely jealous of anyone outside the family getting too close to Paul," says a lifelong friend of the pair. "I hate to be unkind, but in the beginning she and Yoko both had the reputation of treating the fans like dirt." Linda offers her perspective:

> The girls went to war when I married Paul. Looking back I think I took on a battle when I should just have said that I understood, and tried to talk to them. But it was difficult. I had been a free woman in New York. When I married Paul I suddenly felt fenced in. We would go home at night and find about twenty girls outside who had been standing there for five years! They each felt as though they were Paul's wife. They would say "I hate you. You're horrible. Why didn't he marry Jane Asher, at least we knew her!" They painted nasty things all over our walls and played their radios real loud at night outside our house.

On March 11, 1969, Mike McCartney was in Birmingham performing with the Scaffold at not less than two area nightclubs. Back in his hotel room after the exhausting shows he poured himself a small scotch and proceeded to tuck himself in for the night when the phone rang. It was Paul. "Hey, Gaf!" he said, obviously in high spirits. "Lin and I are getting married tomorrow. How about coming down to be best man? And for fuck's sake, don't dare tell anyone, okay?"

The next morning at precisely 9:45, McCartney and his rather frumpily attired bride-to-be arrived at Marylebone Registry office along with Mal Evans. There to greet them were hundreds of teenybopper fans and reporters, all clamoring to squeeze that much closer to the happy couple. Once safely inside it was hurry up and wait as Michael was a full one hour late due to his train breaking down at Birmingham's Newstreet Station.

"Where the bloody hell have you been, then?" asked Paul under his breath to his panting little brother.

"Never mind that now. Am I too late?"

"We waited for you, didn't we?"

"Hope you got the ring?"

"I do."

"Not *yet,* lad."

Within ten minutes the "private" civil ceremony was over and after a round of hearty hugs and handshakes the wedding party braced itself for the rugged return trip to the car. That night McCartney was neither out celebrating nor at home honeymooning with his new missus; rather, he was just down the road at EMI producing a session for Apple crooner Jackie Lomax and Billy Kinsley. McCartney has commented on some of the stresses put upon him and his new bride:

> To the world, of course, she was a divorcee, which didn't seem right. People preferred Jane Asher. Jane Asher fitted. She was a better Fergie. Linda wasn't a very good Fergie for me and people generally tended to disapprove of me marrying a divorcee and an American. That wasn't too clever. None of that made a blind bit of difference; I actually just liked her, I still do, and that's all it's to do with.
>
> I mean, we got married in the craziest clothes when I look back on it. We didn't even bother to buy her a decent outfit.

All things considered this was a particularly stressful time for everyone in the Beatles' camp. Only hours after Paul and Linda tied the knot, Sgt. Norman Pilcher and a squadron of his Scotland Yard goons mounted a particularly aggressive assault on George and Pattie's Esher home, Kinfauns, intent upon uncovering the Beatles' secret drug stash. After thoroughly turning the place inside out they found a quantity of hashish.

Both of the Harrisons were arrested and arraigned later that evening, nipping home just in time to change clothes and barrel into London to party with Princess Margaret and Lord Snowden. "Pretty shitty to do it on Paul's wedding day, anyway," George told me in 1983. "Ripe bastards!"

Eight days after the McCartney/Eastman wedding, John and Yoko followed suit and were married on the British-held island of Gibraltar. It was the first time in Paul's recent memory that he had actually managed to pull something off before his old mate got the drop on him, and it felt great.

Mary McCartney, Paul and Linda's first child together, was born at 1:30 a.m. on Thursday, August 29, 1969, at the Avenue Clinic in St. John's Wood. Weighing six pounds, eight ounces, the beautiful baby quickly became daddy's little girl with her proud papa showing her off to the world on the cover of his now-classic *McCartney* album. Grandad Jim, needless to say, was delighted, as was Linda's father, who first saw his granddaughter some three months later in New York during a family visit home.

Deeply in need of a little relief from all the media hype and nonstop lunacy of Apple and the Beatles, late in 1969, Paul took off with the family up north to Scotland for a little isolated R&R. After being so very visible for so long he needed a break, a chance to collect himself and plan for the future. It was at this time that the reprehensible "Paul Is Dead" notion was born, providing virtually unlimited fodder for a legion of pot-smoking idlers around the globe to further squander their limited lifetimes from that day to this.

The contention was made that a young McCartney lookalike by the name of William Campbell had secretly taken over for the fallen Beatle (allegedly decapitated in a fiery car crash in the autumn of 1966) at the behest of the other three. Soon, frantic fans everywhere were studying the group's covers in an effort to force the imposter and his three Beatle accomplices to fess up. On *Magical Mystery Tour*, for instance, the configuration of stars that spell out the word BEATLES on the front cover was imagined to be a London telephone exchange, 537-1438, somehow printed upside down. Later, American dee jay Russ Gibbs rang the mysterious number on the air with the intention of confronting the imposter. The phone was answered by an extremely perplexed British journalist who, following a fervent denial of having an alter ego, wisely had the number disconnected the next day.

Another variation on this theme had the Beatles slyly hinting at their departed comrade's untimely demise by forcing the pseudo "new" McCartney to turn his back to the camera on the back cover of *Sgt. Pepper* while the other three stared squarely into the camera. The reason? McCartney double Campbell's extensive facial plastic surgery was not yet completed. In addition, it was thought that a patch on the right arm of "McCartney's" *Pepper* jacket included the letters OPD, which was said to stand for "Officially Pronounced Dead." In actual fact the letters were "OPP," representing the decidedly less dramatic Ontario Provincial Police, a souvenir given to McCartney by a Canadian cop.

The whole stupid mess soon became a phenomenon that even McCartney could no longer comfortably ignore. Tracked down in Scotland by *Life* magazine London correspondent Dorothy Bacon and a staff photographer early in November, Paul at first warned them off, screaming at them to turn around and go back, but within a couple of minutes thought better of it and reluctantly invited them in for a chat. On the condition that Linda provide any and all pictures for the story, McCartney cozied up to a cup of strong Earl Grey and once and for all sought to lay the story to rest:

> Perhaps the rumor started because I haven't been much in the press lately. I have done enough press for a lifetime and I don't have anything to say these days. I am happy to be with my family and I will work when I work. I was switched on for ten years and I never switched off. Now I am switching off whenever I can. I would rather be a little less famous these days. . . .
>
> What I have to say is all in the music. If I want to say anything I write a song. Can you spread it around that I am just an ordinary person and want to live in peace? We have to go now, we have two children to look after.

Despite the Beatles' "all you need is love" politics, privately, the fierce rivalry between John and Paul was rapidly reaching catastrophic proportions. Apple insider Ritchie Yorke remembers that in those days if you valued your position there was no way to be friendly with both men. "It was bitter. Very bitter," he says. "John wouldn't go near Paul. He always sent Ringo to do any dirty work with McCartney."

There were exceptions, unfortunately, perhaps the least known and most potentially horrific of which was the time Lennon actually physically attacked Linda McCartney during a particularly volatile Apple meeting towards the end of 1969. Witnessed by several Apple Scruffs, the violent "assault" took place around 5:30 in the afternoon in Lennon's all-white ground-floor office facing the street. "We couldn't hear what she actually said that upset him so," says one of the Scruffs. "But whatever it was must have been brutal. John leapt to his feet like a madman, waving his clenched fists over his head like an angry gorilla. Paul threw himself in the middle of the fracas just at the nick of time. Seconds later and Linda definitely would have been out cold."

This wasn't the only time Lennon had lashed out so violently either. During the recording of *Abbey Road* Paul on one occasion chose not to attend an early-evening session as it was apparently the first anniversary of his initial meeting with Linda. John, reasonably enough, felt this a rather lame excuse to inconvenience so many people, and after hanging about a couple of hours for the delinquent Beatle, finally raced around the corner for a confrontation.

Screeching to a halt out front, Lennon didn't even bother ringing the bell, opting instead to climb up over the eight-foot-high gate in a fit of fury. Once inside the cobblestone courtyard, he sprinted up to the large red door and began banging without cessation for several tense minutes. Eventually Paul opened up. "Just what the bloody hell are you playing at, McCartney!" John shouted, pushing his way inside the front hall. "You must have fuckin' known before now that you couldn't make it. What about us lot then? Ringo, George and I all drove in from the country for this thing and you don't have the motherfuckin' decency to turn up?"

"But it's our anniversary tonight," McCartney replied weakly.

"Bollocks!" Lennon screamed. "You don't see me canceling anything for my anniversaries with Yoko. Why don't you grow up? Those fuckin' bastards at the studio have all got to be paid as well, you know. None of it comes cheap either."

With that the irate Lennon bolted into McCartney's living room and snatched from the wall a favorite painting he had done for his partner and ceremoniously put his foot through it. "Happy anniversary, mate!" he said as he turned to leave. For Paul it was a deeply hurtful and embarrassing episode.

By the summer of 1970 it seemed inevitable that the Beatles as a group were almost certainly finished. In June, Lee Eastman (who, along with his son John, now handled McCartney's business affairs) wrote to Allen Klein (John, George, and Ringo's manager) politely requesting that the Beatles' partnership be immediately dissolved.

Hoping that the group could somehow settle their difference amicably and carry on making music, and millions, Klein tried to sidestep any confrontation with Eastman by simply ignoring his letter. McCartney, however, was by this time adamant, and dashed off a terse note to John suggesting that the Beatles break up once and for all. Several days later, McCartney received a postcard from Lennon reading simply, "Get well soon." It was the last straw. Paul remembers finally coming to terms with the painful prospect of taking his three former partners to court:

> My lawyer, John Eastman, he's a nice guy and he saw the position we were in, and he sympathized. We'd have these meetings on top of hills in Scotland, we'd go for long walks. I remember when we actually decided we had to go and file suit. We were standing on this big hill which overlooked a loch — it was quite a nice day, a bit chilly, and we were searching our souls. Was there any other way? And we eventually said, "Oh, we've got to do it." The only alternative was seven years with

the partnership — going through those same channels for seven years . . . People said, "It's a pity that such a nice thing had to come to such a sticky end." I think that too. It is a pity. I like fairy tales. I'd love to have had the Beatles go up in a little cloud of smoke and the four of us just find ourselves in magic robes, each holding an envelope with our stuff in it. But you realize that you're in real life, and you don't split up a beautiful thing with a beautiful thing.

Paul McCartney formally filed suit on Thursday, December 31, 1970, his stepdaughter, Heather's seventh birthday, petitioning the London High Court to order the Beatles' partnership dissolved and demand an accounting of all partnership assets and liabilities. Neither John, George, nor Ringo were in any way amused and sought to legally block the move by retaining their own counsel for the long, unpleasant road ahead.

The next big blowup came, predictably, following Paul's first-round victory with the appointment of an official receiver to monitor the group's ever-flowing millions. Henceforth, all of the Beatles were forced to cut back their expenditures at least temporarily, in an effort to maintain not only their rapidly rotting Apple empire, but also their own lavish lifestyles. There was, however, another potentially ruinous problem, the taxman. The delicate matter was examined in the January 20, 1971 edition of the London *Times:*

> The financial affairs of the Beatles partnership, whose estimated annual earnings are between £4m and £5m, are in a grave state, counsel said in the High Court yesterday.
>
> "The latest accounts suggest that there is probably not enough in the kitty to meet even the individual Beatles' income and surtax liability," Mr. David Hirst, Q.C., declared. He added that "on a conservative estimate" the four's surtax liability must be £500,000. . . . Each Beatle has a five percent interest in the partnership. Apple Corp. holds the remaining 80 percent.
>
> Mr. Hirst told Mr. Justice Stamp that the group's manager, Mr. Allen Klein, had instructed accountants not to give Mr. McCartney information about the group's financial affairs. He said of Mr. Klein: "He is a man of bad commercial reputation.

Mr. McCartney has never either accepted him as a manager or trusted him. And on the evidence his attitude has been fully justified."

Counsel gave three main reasons for the claim for dissolution:

(1) The Beatles had long since ceased to perform together as a group, so the whole purpose of the partnership had gone.

(2) In 1969 Mr. McCartney's partners, in the teeth of his opposition and in breach of the partnership deed, had appointed Mr. Klein's company, Abkco Industries, Ltd., as the partnership's exclusive business managers.

(3) Mr. McCartney had never been given audited accounts in the four years since the partnership was formed. Counsel said the partnership agreement was entered into in April 1967, before the death in August that year of The Beatles' manager, Mr. Brian Epstein.

In May 1969, the other three insisted on appointing Mr. Klein, or rather Abkco Industries, Inc., as exclusive director. Mr. McCartney opposed and protested strongly. But Abkco were appointed managers "at a fee of no less than 20 percent of the gross income."

On the afternoon of the court's appointing a receiver, John, George, and Ringo were together in Lennon's sparkling white Rolls when the bespectacled Beatle got an idea. "Excuse me, Anthony," he said to his chauffeur. "Take us round to Paul's would you. I've got a little going-away present for the cunt." Arriving at the smart address some thirty minutes later, Lennon bounded out of the car and in a single agile leap pulled himself over the famous wall. Seconds later, the latch clinked from the inside. Grinning from ear to ear, Lennon peeped his head out to the others. Walking silently around the classic Phantom Five, he opened the trunk and produced two perfectly new bricks which he then carried the few steps back inside Paul's entrance way. By this time, George and Ringo had stepped out of the car and were standing in the street, their eyes now carefully following John's every move.

Without a moment's hesitation, Lennon drew back his arm and flung one of the bricks through a downstairs window. Almost before the din had subsided he fired off another, smashing an adjacent pane. Flinging open the front door, McCartney stopped dead in his tracks as soon as he saw the culprits. All at once George burst out laughing hysterically, followed by Ringo and John. Seconds later, the three superstar vandals were motoring joyfully down the street, leaving poor McCartney alone on his front stoop, frozen with anger.

The disintegration of the Beatles as a band was hardest on Paul. So very much of everything he does is directed at being accepted and loved and it hurt a lot when his three closest mates began to outgrow the circumscribed world of Beatlehood. From almost day one the Beatles had meant everything to him. Although John started the group, as time went by he gradually relinquished the reins of power to Paul, who has hung on mightily ever since. For McCartney the preservation of the Beatles' music, mystique, and lore is a life's work.

He has commented that, apart from the death of his mother when he was fourteen, the breakup of the Beatles was the worst thing that ever happened to him. After it was all finally over, he was left feeling useless and impotent, a lone, out-of-work musician, so long part of a band. "If it wasn't for his family," says a friend, "I'm not sure that he would have ever made it." If it wasn't for his family, maybe he wouldn't have wanted to.

After over ten years of playing with Paul and Linda it would have been nice to feel that I'd worked with the McCartneys rather than simply for them.

—Denny Laine, 1989—

It was a hassle going on the road with Paul. It was like taking the whole Shrine Circus on tour.

—Joe English—

7

Pastimes

Paul McCartney and Wings

A lthough Linda McCartney occasionally ventured into the studio with the Beatles (she and Mary Hopkin sang harmonies on "Let It Be"), it wasn't until Paul's strictly solo *McCartney* that her presence became at all musically significant. Released on April 17, 1970, the popular, largely homespun album, showed that even on his own McCartney was still a force to be reckoned with. Despite his role in the extended dissolution of the Beatles, his solo effort (complete with album graphics and backing vocals by Linda) nevertheless reached a wide audience curious to see what kind of magic an individual Beatle could conjure. Obviously, the commercial acceptance of the work was extremely important to McCartney who, now that his old group seemed almost certain to split forever, was naturally anxious about the future. Just to make sure everyone knew exactly where McCartney stood, Peter Brown at Apple sent over a list of forty questions for him to answer regarding his decision to break away from the band. This, along with a blow-by-blow account of the making of *McCartney*, was then released to the world media in the hope of softening the blow of the Beatles' final goodbye to their fervent fandom. The net effect, however, was to point the finger at McCartney as the originator of the Beatles' demise as a group.

After the initial shock of the break-up and his searing estrangement from John, McCartney picked up the pieces of his life and began to think about getting back to work. With no band, and no great desire to rush out and start one, working with his new wife seemed the simplest and best alternative.

The McCartneys' first real joint effort was the heartfelt single, "Another Day," issued on February 19, 1971. The story of a young girl lost in a maze of one-night stands and broken dreams, the song was a compassionate statement about the displaced and alienated in society. An auspicious start to McCartney's solo career, the record reached all the way to the number one slot on the British charts.

Flying to New York in January for a visit with Linda's family, the couple decided to lay down some tracks for a new album. Auditions were secretly held in a dingy Manhattan rehearsal hall to try to find some local musical talent to play with them in supporting roles. One of those who came along to the invitation-only proceedings was New York session drummer, Dennis ("Denny") Phillip Seiwell. Seiwell remembers some third-rate equipment haphazardly set up in one corner, complemented by the absolutely shoddiest kit he had ever seen.

"A lot of the boys were really put out at being asked to audition," he remembers. "Paul just told me to play, as he didn't have a guitar. McCartney wanted more than a drummer; he was looking for a certain attitude, too. Anyway, I just played . . . . I always say that if you can't get it on by yourself, you can't get it on with anyone."

Much to the drummer's surprise, he was informed the next day that he had blitzed the other eight percussionists invited

to perform and was in. McCartney recalls his reason for settling on the towering 6-foot, 2½-inch native Pennsylvanian:
"Well actually it was his tom-toms. That may not sound like
much to anyone who is not a musician . . . but if you see a
drummer playing tom-toms, you learn a lot about him." With
Seiwell in place, the McCartneys needed to locate a couple of
top-flight guitarists who soon presented themselves in the
persons of David Spinoza and Hugh McCracken.

Only twenty-one at the time of the audition, Spinoza was already a recording-studio legend of sorts, turning pro at the
age of just seventeen. In those days, the standard fee was a
mere ninety dollars for a three-hour session, but the super-
talented Spinoza was generally taking home more than $1500
for the same work. Among the many artists he played with
over the years are John Lennon, Yoko Ono, Freda Payne,
Carly Simon, and B. B. King.

Spinoza later recounted the humble beginnings of his totally unexpected stint as the former Fab's first guitarist:

> All I remember is getting a phone call from Linda McCartney
> identifying herself as "Mrs. McCartney" and I said, "Who?" She
> said, "My husband would like to meet you." So I said, "Did I
> ever work with your husband before?" Finally she said, "This is
> Linda McCartney, and my husband is Paul McCartney," like I
> was supposed to know Paul McCartney was calling my house.
> She didn't make it clear what she wanted me for — I thought it
> was a meeting or a recording session — but it turned out to be
> an audition.

Cabbing it down to a crummy 45th Street loft a few days later,
Spinoza was surprised to learn that the grueling tryouts had
already been going on for a full three days before he arrived:

> You had to be called; you couldn't just walk in off the street
> with your guitar. . . . Paul played a blues, a solo, some folk, and
> said he wanted me to do that. So I played everything and then
> he just says, "Sorry I couldn't spend more time with you but I
> have a lot of people to see." As soon as I got home the phone
> rang and Linda wanted me to do the sessions the following
> week.

Booking time at Phil Ramone's A&R Studios, the totally unre-
hearsed quintet charged ahead, recording no less than
twenty-one of Paul and Linda's new tunes. According to reports, the sessions started out smoothly enough, but soon ran
into difficulty when the McCartneys began spacing out on the
day-to-day business of organizing and overseeing the dates.
Spinoza recalls:

> I'd told them I couldn't keep every week open because when
> McCartney goes back to England there are other people that
> call me, and they are going to keep me eating, not him, al-
> though I'd love to do his sessions.
>
> I said I could make two of the days but not all five, and Linda
> got very indignant. I got vibrations like, "It's Paul McCartney's
> session, you're supposed to keep your life open indefinite-
> ly. . . ." She really speaks for him, and handles all the business.
> She wouldn't let me talk directly to him to sort out what he
> wanted.

Musically, Spinoza felt right at home playing with the creative
and orderly McCartney, but complained that his well-known
penchant for perpetually trying to push the river did tend to
make the others feel rather like second-class citizens. It is a
charge that has been leveled against the sometimes annoy-
ingly perfectionistic musician since his early days in Liverpool. "I think the whole album was done in the same format as
the *McCartney* album," says Spinoza, "only we played the
parts for him, there was no freedom. We were told exactly
what to play. . . . Paul sang us the parts he wanted and the
tune developed as we went along. We made suggestions, but
he rarely took them, and if he did, always modified it into a
'Paul McCartney'-sounding thing. . . ."

For David Spinoza, perhaps the least attractive feature of
playing with McCartney was the nearly constant presence of
Linda who, apart from being Paul's wife, didn't seem to have
a very productive reason for being around at all:

> Linda didn't have much to do in the studio, she just took care
> of the kids. . . . They brought the whole family every day to the

studio. . . . If he was there until four in the morning, everybody stayed. I thought to a certain degree it was distracting. I don't know what Linda did in the studio apart from sit there and make comments on what she thought was good and bad. . . . I mean she can sing fine — like any girl that worked in a high school glee club.

In the end, Spinoza was politely let go by Linda, who rang him up one evening and told him not to bother coming in the next day as they were doing some last-minute vocal overdubs and he wouldn't be needed. He half-expected them to phone in a few days and invite him back, but the call never came, his thinly veiled disapproval of Mrs. McCartney perhaps a little more obvious than he'd imagined. Still, Spinoza was happy to have been part of the sessions and remembers the experience today with mixed emotions:

Working with Paul was fun, inasmuch as it was good to see how he works and where he's coming from. But as a musician there was no challenge. . . . McCartney is definitely a songwriter, not a musician, but he composes beautiful tunes. In the studio he's incredibly prompt and businesslike. No smoking pot, no drinks or carrying on, nothing. Just straight ahead. He came in at nine every morning. We'd listen to what we'd done the day before then it was eight hours of just playing. He's not a very loose cat. He just wants to make good music.

The arduous, extended sessions eventually reached the public as *Ram*, one of Paul McCartney's most innovative, original, and poetically offbeat works. Two other musicians, Ron Carter and Richard Davis, also participated, playing bass on several of the album's twelve eccentric tracks. The McCartneys also enlisted the aid of the New York Philharmonic whose lush string section enriched the songs "Uncle Albert/Admiral Halsey," "Back Seat of My Car," and the haunting "Long-Haired Lady." In addition to the sessions at A&R, the tapes were further refined at Columbia Studios with final mixing and sweetening carried out at Sound Recording in Los Angeles.

Altogether six tracks were credited to "Paul & Linda Mc-Cartney," and six solely to Paul. Unfortunately, bigwigs over at the Beatles' old publishing house, Northern Songs, and Sir Lew Grade of ATV, found it difficult to accept that the musically untrained and unaccomplished Linda should be listed as co-composer alongside the great Paul McCartney, and on that basis slapped the couple with a whopping million-dollar lawsuit in defense of their interests in the former Beatles' publishing. As it stood, on those six tracks Linda was entitled to collect half the writers' royalties which normally would have gone entirely to Paul to be shared with his publisher. Mrs. McCartney, however, was not one of Northern's clients and therefore that little bit of flesh would have been denied them, an intolerable prospect for the already well-fed corporate conglomerate. McCartney explains:

> I said, "Well, look! If my wife is actually saying 'change that' or 'I like that better than that' then I'm using her as a collaborator." I mean, John never had any input on "The Long and Winding Road," and Yoko still collects royalties on it. You've gotta flow with these things. The joke at the time was that Linda was the only one getting paid in our household, because we were all held up with Apple being subject to litigation! I wasn't seeing any money. . . .
>
> Every businessman I had ever known was suing me. I felt, "I'm damned if she's not gonna get paid for it; I'll put in a bill for her services!" They weren't major checks, but it was the only money we were seeing because she was the only one free of all contracts in our house.

With no wish to further legally entangle himself, McCartney agreed to film a television special for ATV in exchange for their dropping the suit. Additionally, Linda would get to keep her royalties. Released in Great Britain on May 21, 1971, *Ram* was not the hit Paul felt he needed in the face of the flak he had been subjected to for initiating the disbanding of the Beatles. He was disappointed but determined to have another go at it. This time, however, he figured it might work out better if he took the plunge and formed his own group, something that had been in the offing for some time.

Originally, he had wanted to call his new band "Turpentine," but was subsequently talked out of the idea by an indignant fan. Then it was the "The Dazzlers," but that too was dropped at the last minute in favor of the more commercially viable "Wings." According to popular legend, the inspiration behind the name came to Paul as he silently prayed for the safe arrival of his second daughter, Stella, asking that the child be delivered "on the wings of an angel." McCartney adds:

> Linda and I were having our second baby. . . . It was a difficult pregnancy and I had to be with her a lot. So I got myself a camp bed and kipped in the hospital. Eventually one of the matrons told me I couldn't sleep there, so I said, "We're gonna use another hospital!" So we looked around until we found one that would have us. . . . Our baby was in intensive care. . . . It was dodgy at the time, so rather than just sitting around twiddling my thumbs, I was thinking of hopeful names for a new group, and somehow this uplifting idea of "Wings" came to me.

As for the group's lineup, McCartney immediately settled upon Denny Seiwell as his drummer, ringing the good-natured American with the news from his farm in Scotland. Seiwell, honored to have been remembered thus by the great Beatle, hopped on a plane with his wife, Monique, and within hours was sitting down to dinner with the McCartneys at High Park.

Next came the matter of choosing a suitably inventive rhythm guitarist. The insubordinate David Spinoza was definitely out, despite his virtuoso performances, and McCartney was casting about, attempting to put a face to his vision of the flash, good-looking player he was hoping for. He finally hit upon his old friend Denny Laine. "It's one of those things when you're starting a band," says McCartney, "Several ideas go through your head, different names are suggested to you, and then I remembered 'Go Now.' That was the single Denny made with the Moody Blues, and it has always been one of my favorite records."

Born on October 29, 1944, the youngest of five children of Eva and ex-boxer Herbert (Herbo) Hines, in Birmingham, Brian Frederick Hines, known professionally as Denny Laine, grew up a quiet, creative child attracted to folk music, jazz, skiffle, and later, down-home American rhythm and blues. When he was twelve his mother enrolled him in tap dancing lessons at a local conservatory, but he eventually dropped out after suffering a continuous barrage of insults from his mega-macho dad. Shortly thereafter, Herbo went out and quietly purchased his artistically inclined offspring a cheap acoustic guitar for the princely sum of three pounds and encouraged the boy to learn to play. After only a few months of intense work, Brian was strumming along like an old pro. "My mum used to play a little bit of piano after the war," recalls Laine.

> In those days everyone made their own music. It seemed as though there were old pianos in virtually every front room in England back then. My sister was into singers like Frankie Laine, Johnny Ray, people like that. She was a record collector, that was her thing. Through her I was exposed to a lot of really great music. Later, I was put into a tap dance company as a kid. We used to do pantomimes and other little shows. At the time I was also listening to Buddy Holly a lot. He was my first real inspiration I guess. In fact, the guitar lick on "That'll Be the Day" made me want to learn to play. Anyway, my dad bought me a guitar and I eventually worked out a few little skiffle tunes. In between acts with the tap company I sometimes did a solo spot on my guitar, singing.

Laine's first group was called Johnny and the Dominators, already a reasonably well-respected Birmingham area band by the time he signed on with them as lead singer.

> You see in those days groups used to just make up names that sounded good, like Ricky and the Rebels. "Johnny," of course, was whoever the singer happened to be. So, of course, I eventually became "Johnny." Looking back, I suppose my school

work suffered because I was always so much into the music. I wasn't thick by any means. I was fairly good, but music was definitely my preference.

Later in 1960, Laine formed his own band, Denny and the Diplomats. Performing semi-regularly at various neighborhood functions, the Diplomats gradually became one of Birmingham's most popular homegrown groups, eventually winning a coveted recording test with Petula Clark's producer, Tony Hatch, on behalf of Pye Records. Although they were never signed, back then even being heard by a real record company was big news, so much the bigger if it happened to be a label as respected and popular as Pye. "I could tell he liked what we were doing," recalls Laine, "but we weren't really original enough. That was the main problem. Too much emphasis on other people's material I think."

Despite the setbacks, being in the Diplomats went a long way towards shaping the young musician. He changed his name to Denny Laine, thinking it sounded more confident and professional.

I thought of the name because I had my own den in the back garden, like kids have tree houses. My mates use to come to this den so it became kind of a nickname that I was called "Denny." Not by everyone, just a few close friends in our little club. The name "Laine" came from Cleo Laine, who I always thought was brilliant. Actually, I was influenced quite a bit by the jazz thing. In fact, some of my first major influences were people like Django Reinhardt and Stéphane Grappelli. I was into jazz, gypsy music I guess. So "Denny Laine" eventually became the one.

Within three years of their getting together, Denny and the Diplomats were appearing on the same bill as many of the biggest-name groups of the day, including the Beatles. Laine, of course, later went on to become the initiating powerhouse behind the formation of the Moody Blues, scoring a British number-one hit with the now-classic "Go Now."

Although during the mid-to-late-sixties McCartney and Laine had been good mates, by the end of Paul's frantic Jane Asher days the two had all but lost touch. Linda too, apparently, was keen on the inclusion of the laid-back Laine, later admitting to several journalists that he had been a big favorite of hers when he sang lead for the Birmingham-based Moodies.

Typically, Laine was unruffled. Sleeping on an old mattress in a back room of his then-manager Tony Secunda's Mayfair office, he wasn't even sure whom he was speaking to when the telephone call first came through. "Paul *who*?" he barked into the receiver, not especially thrilled at rising prior to his customary one o'clock wakeup from Secunda.

"McCartney, you daft sod. How are you, mate?"

"I'm okay. Jesus. Listen, sorry about the mixup, I had a bit of a late night. It's great you called though. So what's up?"

"I'm forming a new band to go out on the road," Paul explained. "Are you interested?"

"Too right I am," said Laine. "When do we start?"

Laine caught a late flight to Glasgow and was met at the airport by Denny Seiwell who joined him on the brief twenty-minute run up to Campbeltown, the nearest airfield to the McCartneys' sprawling Kintyre farm.

Seiwell took Laine to his own place first for a couple of quick drinks before cruising over to Paul and Linda's just a few miles up the rocky dirt road. "I was amazed he was living in the back of beyond in a very small farmhouse he'd only just started to work on," remembers Laine. "I liked the fact that we could go and live that sort of lifestyle and still get things done."

Asked to recall his first impressions of Linda, Laine patiently explained that he had always liked the earthy blonde, and therefore wasn't surprised to see her as an unaffected young mother preparing a late dinner in the tiny kitchen for her hungry tribe. "Linda was doing some cooking, I remember, and said she admired my work in the Moodies. She'd heard a Coca-Cola ad we'd done she thought was pretty original. I got on with Linda all the way through Wings."

Although at first the plan for the new band was a typical male macho lineup, McCartney later suggested that the musically inexperienced Linda come in on keyboards. Like Stuart Sutcliffe joining the Beatles to play bass without benefit of any prior musical expertise, Linda similarly became a member of Wings with nothing to fall back on except her immense desire to please her husband and the keen, competitive spirit of the upwardly mobile Eastmans.

"The main reason she was there," says Laine, "was she was Paul's wife and they wanted to be together. . . . I always resented it because I thought we could have been a better band a lot quicker if we had a proper keyboard player. Not that I minded Linda being around, but as a musician I wasn't too keen on the idea." Laine recalls that Linda actually agreed with him concerning her new role in the group. "She never wanted to be in Wings. . . . I think she would have liked to be part of it, yes, but as a photographer. . . . She certainly wasn't an idiot by any shake of the stick, though. She reminded me a bit of John Lennon; she had that same kind of attitude. If she believed something, nobody was going to change her."

After a couple of hard-rocking days together on the farm, McCartney's rag-tag Wings flew to London and cloistered themselves at Abbey Road to begin recording their premier album together, *Wild Life*, originally intended as a concept album with the faster tracks collected together for dancing on side one, and the slower, supposedly sexier numbers (for "necking" said their first tour program) snuggled up on the other side.

Altogether Paul and Linda co-wrote seven of the eight tracks on the LP, tacking on the Everly Brothers/Buddy Holly hit, "Love Is Strange" as a tip of the hat to their teen years. Produced by Paul, and engineered by the soon-to-be-famous Alan Parsons, the album also contained what McCartney later termed his least favorite tune of all time, the innocuous "Bip Bop." "It just goes nowhere," he later commented. "I still cringe every time I hear it."

Working at lightning speed, the fledgling group laid down the basic tracks within days, interrupted only by the caesarian birth of little Stella Nina McCartney on September 13, 1971, at London's King's College Hospital. In all *Wild Life* was made in just over two weeks from start to finish, and was previewed to the eagerly waiting media on November 8 at a gala party held at the Mecca Ballroom in Leicester Square.

Among the pop luminaries in attendance at the "buy your own drink" extravaganza were Keith Moon, Sandy Denny, Mary Hopkin, Terence Stamp, The Faces, Jimmy Page, Deep Purple, John Entwistle, Elton John, Mungo Jerry, Gilbert O'Sullivan, and Sandie Shaw. Dancing to the big band sounds of Ray McVay's Orchestra, the one-thousand-plus invited guests thrilled to a spirited display of formation dancing and boogied the night away until 3:00 a.m.

Sadly, like the flamboyant *Ram*, the barebones album was generally very poorly received, inching its way up to number eleven in Britain and only a notch higher in the U.S. For the first time in his career, McCartney was forced to allow that not everything he touched automatically turned to gold. "*Wild Life* is another album we could have done better," said Linda in 1976. "Some of the songs are very good but we only did it in about a week. It's funny, the band was so new but we didn't take care. . . . It wasn't really a group when we did *Wild Life*."

The album's back-to-nature front cover, although striking, was completely devoid of any word of just who this faraway band of hippie musicians really was, further contributing to the record's dismal sales. Eventually a small green-and-gold sticker was affixed to the front jacket. It simply said "Wings Wild Life" and did little either to promote the band or salvage the record. In the end, even McCartney himself had to admit failure. "I must say you have to like me to like the record. . . . It wasn't that brilliant as a recording. . . . We'd been hearing about how Dylan did everything in one take. I think in fact often we never gave the engineer a chance to set up a balance."

Following the release of *Wild Life*, Paul and Linda jetted off to Jamaica for a short holiday, eventually linking up with the two Dennys in New York for a bit of promotion, plus a fair amount of rehearsal in the same West Forties rathole where the first faint echoes of the band were born. In addition, they laid down an as-of-yet unreleased instrumental blues track in anticipation of one day using it as a B-side to a possible maxi-single.

After the inevitable mad McCartney Christmas rush, the group finally got down to some serious rock 'n' roll first thing in the new year with daily rehearsals in London aimed at pulling together material for both a new Wings LP and a concert tour planned for sometime in 1972.

Initially, Paul had envisioned Wings as strictly a four-piece unit, but changed his mind and added Denny Laine's old mate, Irish guitarist Henry Campbell Liken McCullough on lead guitar. By the time he joined Wings in January of 1972, McCullough was an almost legendary figure back home in County Derry, having worked in a number of Irish showbands before joining the popular Dublin group Jean and the Gents, fronted by a black South African lead singer. He then played with the innovative Eire Apparent, later discovered and groomed by Jimi Hendrix mentor, Chas Chandler. Thereafter, McCullough drifted through a succession of hard-rocking bands including Sweeny's Men and the Grease Band. He remembers being called up for service in McCartney's Wings:

> In fact it was Paul's roadie who rang, saying, "Do you fancy sitting in?" After the Grease Band I didn't know what the hell was going on so I went down and had a play. That was Tuesday and afterwards things were left at that — nothing was said. Then I had another call on Thursday to go down again and afterwards Paul said, "Do you want to join our group?" Although I knew Laine, I'd never met McCartney before. Once I got used to seeing him there in person, he turned out to be a great bloke.

The first track utilizing McCullough's top-flight talents (and, incidentally the first Wings single) was the controversial though musically uninteresting McCartney tune, "Give Ireland Back to the Irish," released in Britain on February 25, 1972.

Banned by the conservative BBC as being a bit too far left, the thumping anti-English ballad nevertheless gave McCartney something he had secretly coveted all his life: instant disrespectability. Having written a direct response to the terrible Bloody Sunday massacre in Northern Ireland that January, the song allowed Paul to feel every bit as heavy and potentially radical as his old nemesis John, at least for a while. "Our soldiers, my country's army had gone in and killed some people," says Paul.

> And I'd grown up with this thing that the Irish are great, they're our mates, our brothers. We used to joke that Liverpool was the capital of Ireland. Suddenly we were killing our buddies and I thought, wait a minute, this is not clever and I wish to protest on behalf of the people. . . . I did that song and was rung up by a lot of people who said, "Please don't release this. We don't need this right now." And I said, "Yes we do. Gotta have it."

Despite McCartney's late-blooming crusading, however, the backwater skiffle tune failed to impress just about everyone other than the uptight Auntie BBC, and fell to earth with a resounding thud like so many other of Paul's immediate post-Beatles releases. Denny Laine remembers:

> Paul was quite innocently trying to solve a problem which obviously can't be solved with a song. A lot of Irish people took umbrage at it which was a bit frightening. . . . As a result we did get a lot of picketing at gigs. At one point, I had to put my toe down and drive through some people, forcing them to jump out of the way, to get us out. And I think Henry's brother was beaten up in Southern Ireland because of it. It's very difficult when you're writing songs not to be controversial sometimes. You're obviously going to upset someone, but that's one instance I'm not particulary happy about, or wasn't at the time, certainly.

The next great chapter in the life of Wings commander McCartney was his impromptu university tour of Great Britain, commencing February 8, 1972. Gathered together for this dangerously ill-planned series of unannounced musical encounters were Henry McCullough, Denny Laine, Denny Seiwell and his wife, roadies Ian and Trevor Jones, three dogs, and of course, Paul, Linda, Heather, Mary, and Stella McCartney. Their gear packed into a rented lorry, the wandering minstrels headed north along the M1, initially following signs for a place called Ashby de la Zouche, solely because they liked the sound of the name. While enroute, they discovered the tiny hamlet of Heather nearby, where they tried without success to buy a small pony tied to a post on the village green.

As impossible as it seems today, McCartney was intent upon touring without benefit of advance publicity, proper venues, or even pre-arranged gigs. Wherever they stopped at the end of the day was where they played, the more unexpected and informal the better, a plan which, incredibly, Paul had envisioned for the Beatles in 1969. Their first show, held in the student union of Nottingham University on February 9, went well, due in large part to the solid back-up provided by the school. From there, McCartney's roadshow rumbled on to York where they played the dining hall of a local college, having dropped by without sufficient notice to secure the use of the university's splendid theater.

Wings' next surprise performance was in Hull where McCartney remembers everyone somehow seemed to be expecting them, having already set up a first-class sound system in the school's formal concert hall. After the gig, the exhausted travelers booked into a third-rate bed-and-breakfast, where, far from treating them like stars, the uptight owner didn't even know who they were. Laine recalls:

> I remember we were all having fish and chips. The landlord was a bit of an asshole as well. We were just another group to him. Anyway, we accidentally left some rubbish on the bar and he came down the next morning and was shouting about it to one of the roadies. Paul was very pissed off but bit his tongue and didn't say anything, realizing the old boy didn't recognize him. So Paul nudged him in the nose with his elbow, accidentally on purpose, as he was so fed up with this guy's attitude.

He just sort of nicked him really. Of course he threatened to call the police, but we just sort of breezed out like nothing happened.

From there the band pushed on to Scarborough where they all sat in their rooms for the day listening to roadie Ian's makeshift recordings of the previous gigs. Huddling around the twin reel-to-reel tape recorders borrowed from Abbey Road, it became obvious that as a band Wings had a long way to go before becoming the slick professional group McCartney so wanted. Their date in Leeds, for instance, was almost marred by a musical *faux pas*. Paul recalls: "We were doing the tune 'Wild Life' and Linda was to start with the chords on electric piano. I looked around and said: 'One, two, three . . . ' Nothing. She had a glassy stare in her eyes and she's looking at me, mouthing, 'I forgot the chords.' The audience thought that it was part of a comedy routine we were working into the act. So I walked up to the keyboards, showed Linda the chords and got a great laugh."

In Salford, near Manchester, the band played a local theater, where a play was currently running, and caused the management some concern lest their pounding rhythms topple the scenery — they didn't. Motoring on to Liverpool, McCartney decided to stop in at his father's home where the road-weary crew spent the night before moving on to Birmingham the next day. "We went to Denny's [parents'] place first," says Paul, "then played a university slightly out of town. It wasn't the best gig."

For two weeks the band criss-crossed the country, splitting up their meager earnings in cash at the end of every evening, just like the Beatles had a thousand lifetimes before. "We only had two or three hours a day to ourselves," Denny Seiwell recalled. "It wasn't easy getting six rooms in a place that took dogs, with no notice. And you'd get fish and chip shops up to here . . . "

Wings played their final gig of the tour on February 17 at Swansea in Wales. Originally, they had planned another full week, but even this novel approach to performing was beginning to wear a bit thin. "It was tiring being on the road twenty-four hours a day," recalls Henry McCullough. "The excitement and fun drained the old brains out."

The thoroughly knackered group turned back into Cavendish Avenue a couple of days later. "It all seems a wee dream," McCullough quipped. Still, McCartney had realized a twelve-year ambition to get back out on the road minus all the hassles that travel hand in hand with being a big star.

It is tempting to speculate how things would have worked out if it had been the Beatles crammed into the back of that van and not Wings. McCartney too must have at least considered it. Of course, he wasn't talking. "That was then," he would often say to people around him. He must have wondered if things would ever be the same.

Wings' second single, an only slightly rearranged version of "Mary Had a Little Lamb," brought down yet another hail of ruthless criticism on McCartney, who quite reasonably, after ten-years-plus of catering exclusively to the young adult market, only wanted to put out a tune children might enjoy. As far back as 1968, he had wanted the Beatles to do something specifically for children, originally considering a full-length feature based on Alfred Bestall's well-loved character, Rupert the Bear. That particular project, unfortunately, never quite came off, although Paul and Linda did manage one trailer-length cartoon, "Rupert Bear and the Frog Song," later released in conjunction with *Give My Regards to Broad Street* in 1984. All things considered, the critical reaction to "Mary Had a Little Lamb" was not only grossly unfair, but typical of much of the self-righteous, quasi-intellectual claptrap masquerading as critical journalism both then and now. Happily, the quaint, infectious little tune sold well, eventually working its way up the charts to a very respectable number six.

Now reasonably well-knit as a band, Wings hit the road again in July of 1972, this time heading out in a gaily appointed, open-top, London double-decker bus, bound for the outdoor festivals and opera halls of the continent.

Their first gig, at the Centre Culturel at Chateau Vallon in France on Sunday, July 9, went down brilliantly. Everyone was in exceptionally fine form, breezing through a rapid-fire succession of several rare, heretofore unreleased Wings' tracks including "I Would Only Smile," "Henry's Blue," "1882," "Momma's Little Girl," "Suicide," and "Best Friend," as well as the Denny Laine classic "Say You Don't Mind."

By the following Wednesday, the band had moved on to Juan les Pins, playing to a capacity crowd appreciative of their funky, wide-eyed pop. Attending that night's performance, with friends, was Joanne Patrie, a highly paid American fashion model then gracing the runways of the better couturiers of Europe. As flirtatious as she was beautiful, Jo Jo (as she preferred to be called) remembers watching the band parade off stage and wondering which of the three stunning guys with McCartney might be single.

Fortunately, her traveling companions were friends of one of the roadies whom she remembers only as "Mick," who invited her to join him in the crew car for the upcoming German and Swiss legs of the tour. Always a super Beatles fan, Patrie was knocked out at the prospect of spending the next ten days in such close proximity to Paul and Linda, not to mention the rest of the band. She recalls rumbling down the Autobahn, smoking up with the road crew, and periodically pulling alongside Wings' bus where she caught sight of Denny Laine staring at her from the transport's windy open deck.

A couple of nights later, Jo Jo, who had been bedding down with roadie Mick, was taking a bath when Laine walked in.

"It's extremely naughty for a gentleman to interrupt a lady's bath uninvited," the precocious Jo Jo teased.

"Well, we wouldn't want to be naughty now would we, luv?" Laine replied sarcastically, as he turned and left.

Seconds later, Jo Jo leapt to the door and pointedly locked it with a loud "click." She sank back into the tub, intrigued by the guitarist's cheek.

Meanwhile, in the roadie's adjoining suite, the usual after-show party was in progress amidst a fog of sweet-smelling black hash and no shortage of high-priced booze. Arriving a short while later, Jo Jo spied Laine, sucking on a particularly gigantic joint. She sat down beside him, and after a few minutes of polite chit-chat, he motioned with his eyes towards the door, rising almost in unison with the widely smiling Jo Jo.

"Like to go back to my room for a smoke," Denny asked demurely as they cuddled together in the hall.

"There's plenty of great shit in there," said Jo Jo, playing just a little hard to get.

"Not like I've got," said Laine, kissing her deeply for the first time.

Five minutes later, they were back in Laine's room, passionately making love. They would not let go until very early the next morning, Jo Jo's face made raw by the unshaven Laine's impassioned kisses.

From that night forward Denny and Jo Jo were inseparable. Backstage, on the bus, in the hotel, everywhere, the attractive couple were about as close as two people can become, a proximity that caused Linda to feel suspicious of Jo Jo and uncomfortable about the liaison between her and Laine. "The McCartneys were very nice to me at first," says Jo Jo. "I really thought they liked me. A few days later, though, Denny came into our room after a gig and told me to sit down as he had something he wanted to talk to me about."

"Look," said Laine softly, hanging his head slightly, like a little boy caught out at something naughty. "I've just been in Paul and Linda's room, and to be honest, they're very uptight about you being around."

"But why?" asked Jo Jo, crushed that her childhood idol had so callously rejected her. "What did I do?"

"It's Linda. She reckons you're a groupie and that you're after Paul. She says you're only using me to be near them."

"Denny . . . " she said, now sobbing. "Of course I think Paul and the Beatles are wonderful. But I'm here because of *you*. If you want me to leave though, I will, and I don't care what this woman is saying."

"She says you're trying to flirt with Paul," Denny continued, obviously torn in two over the unpleasant dilemma.

"That's a lie," Jo Jo insisted. "I hate them for what they're trying to do."

"Well I fuckin' don't know what to think . . . " Laine trailed off. After a few dreadful minutes of silence Jo Jo told her boyfriend that under the circumstances it would probably be better if she flew out to London in the morning. As upset and confused as he was, Denny reluctantly agreed.

"I was so hurt because I always looked up to Paul," recalls Jo Jo. "They were both so nice to me that night before, driving back to the hotel in the limo. It would have been better if they hadn't been so friendly, building up my hopes and making me feel wanted. Deep inside, I'm sure Denny knew I couldn't possibly be faking my feelings for him, but you've got to remember what a manipulator Linda is."

The next evening, after the Zurich gig on Friday, July 21, Jo Jo was backstage with Denny and the McCartneys when Rolling Stone love interest Anita Pallenberg unexpectedly showed up in the dressing room, ready to party. "She was on the pull for Denny," says Jo Jo. "I thought I might as well start packing. I mean this girl was so beautiful, so extremely sexy, I even remember wondering how Paul was able to keep his eyes off her."

Feeling well and truly defeated, Jo Jo went back to the hotel with Mick to get her things out of Laine's suite. Minutes later, Denny was standing in the doorway.

"Where do you think you're going?" he said, sitting down on the edge of the bed.

"Well I just thought you'd want to be with Anita tonight, that's all," the distraught model said through her tears.

"Nonsense," said Laine, tenderly taking her in his arms. "Anita's just a friend from my old Brian Jones days. I mean, if you weren't here I might have considered it, but not now. You're not going anywhere."

Two kids and six years later, Denny and Jo Jo were married

on a party boat docked just outside of Marblehead near Boston. The McCartneys chose not to attend the formal ceremony, sending along neither their well wishes nor even a gift. Some time later, says Jo Jo, one of the roadies dropped by their home and delivered the McCartneys' wedding gift to the young couple, an unwrapped pair of silk sheets and pillow cases with no card, still in the original shopping bag.

The first major unpleasantness of the twenty-six city, ten-country tour happened on August 10 in Göteborg, Sweden, when police intercepted a parcel of seven ounces of dope addressed to Denny Seiwell at the hotel and swooped down upon the McCartneys, Seiwell, and Wings' traveling secretary, Rebecca Hinds, immediately following the last note of their gig at the Scandinavian Hall. Boldly switching off the band's sound system, the Swedish cops sternly requested the presence of the alleged ringleaders down at the local jail where they were relentlessly badgered and harangued until they finally confessed to the deed. "We told them we had found the cannabis in a letter," commented a police official.

> At first they said they knew nothing about it. But after we questioned them for about three hours they told the truth. McCartney, his wife and Seiwell told us they smoked hash every day. They said they were almost addicted to it. They said they had made arrangements to have the drugs posted to them each day they played in different countries so they wouldn't have to take anything through customs themselves.

Fortunately, local prosecutor, Lennart Angelin, not wishing to bring down the wrath of the world's youth upon his peaceful little country, chose not to press for further charges, in exchange for the McCartneys' paying a reasonably hefty £1000 fine. Despite Paul and Linda's indignation at being brought to task over their passion for smoking cannabis, the fun-loving couple would go on to face similar charges five times over the next eighteen years, all in the name of having a quiet toke with friends to help shake off the pressures of life at the top.

"You can tell everyone that we're not changing our lives for anyone," McCartney mouthed off to reporters in Lund, Sweden, the night after the bust.

> We smoke grass and we like it, and that's why someone sent it to us in an envelope. . . . At the end of the day most people go home and have a whiskey. . . . Well, we play a gig and we're exhausted, and Linda and I prefer to put our kids to bed, sit down together and smoke a joint. . . . That doesn't mean we're heavily into drugs or anything. Neither Linda nor I have gone further than grass. You simply couldn't if you want to get out there and entertain people. But you can't expect us to pretend we don't smoke for the sake of our fans. . . . But now that I've been caught I'll say, "Yeah, it's true. . . . " People will be looking at us and wondering what we've got with us. And we're not the kind of people who can't go on without it. We wouldn't go on tour if we were. We're just easy people who like to smoke if we can, but now that's out of the question and I'm sorry.

After the humiliation of this first arrest the Wings gang were committed to never getting popped for anything again. It's not that anyone quit smoking dope; from that point on everyone was just more careful, that's all. Jo Jo explains: "Paul would say, 'Look, lads, we're coming to the border, so we've got to get rid of the shit.' So we all sat there on top of the bus, cleaning and smoking it up as fast as we could. As we got closer we would grab big handfuls of the stuff and start flinging it over the side, watching it scatter to the wind. It was so sad, rather like a funeral, spreading someone's ashes away. I remember being tempted to keep a few joints myself but Denny said, 'Don't you dare!'"

Other measures, apparently, included the McCartneys tucking away a good-sized bag of reefer inside the hood of little Stella's coat (something witnessed by both Denny and Jo Jo), and, a few years later, secreting it away in son James' diaper, a rather distasteful practice to say the very least.

There were other difficult times too on this, Wings' first full-blown outing as a functioning touring band. One particularly disturbing incident happened in Sweden when a young man walked up to Paul and Linda in a basement nightclub and calmly threatened to blow the superstar away with a revolver he claimed to have tucked away in his coat. McCartney sat frozen with fear as the youth slowly walked to the other side of the club and leaned up against the bar, all the while grinning menacingly. Five minutes later, in walked Laine and McCullough who sidled up to the couple in high spirits, ready for a good night out.

"So what's happening, kids?" asked Denny as he signaled one of the waiters for a drink.

"Some guy's just said he's got a gun and he's gonna shoot me," Paul whispered.

Without a moment's hesitation, McCullough silently pulled a long thin knife from inside his boot, hiding it carefully in his lap. "Where?" asked the veteran Dublin brawler.

"The guy at the bar in the green suit coat," McCartney answered. "But don't look . . . "

"Leave it to us, mate," said Henry, soundlessly slipping out of his seat while Denny went around the other way, joining up on either side of the leering, would-be assassin.

"Got a problem, lad?" McCullough asked, sitting down next to him on an adjacent stool.

"No, why?" said the kid, suddenly quite meek and mild.

Seconds later, the two guitarists had him securely on the floor, searching his pockets for any sign of a weapon.

"Okay, leave off," the obviously off-balance "fan" bellowed. "You're hurting me. I didn't mean anything by it, I swear. It was a joke, that's all."

"Some fuckin' joke, you wanker!" Laine growled angrily, violently grabbing him by the hair for one last scathing tirade. "Clear off now, before my friend here loses his patience and puts the boot in. Understand?"

Not even stopping to brush away the slime on his clothes from the bottom of the bar, the pimply faced punk ran for the door. Ten minutes or so later, the four musicians quietly left the nightspot and returned to the security of their hotel, McCartney badly shaken by the experience.

But there were also moments of comic relief on the tour. Denny Laine recounts the time that Wings' bus driver helped himself to a luxury meal of caviar, lobster, steak, several bottles of obscenely expensive champagne, and a dozen or so hand-rolled Cuban cigars, all at his famous employer's expense. Walking into the diningroom of their five-star hotel, Paul and Linda were horrified to see the hulking Londoner living it up on their tab. A word or two to tour operator John Morris, however, and the gluttonous chauffeur was summarily dismissed. Well fed, but out of work.

Even more memorable for Laine was the time the McCartneys' famous sheepdog, Martha, soiled a priceless antique oriental carpet in the foyer of a hotel in Italy where Wings was quartered. Without missing a beat, a waiter making his way through the lobby scooped up the foul-smelling lump and stashed it away under the sterling cover of a dinner platter he then lifted aloft as if it contained an exotic culinary delicacy prepared by one of the hotel's *cordon bleu* chefs. Walking a neat ten paces behind the extended McCartney clan with their three kids, two dogs, and half-dozen bellboys, he followed the procession up to their suites where he dutifully deposited the prize in the commode and then held out his hand for a tip. "That was Paul and Linda," Denny recalled, laughing, as he sat with me on my boat in 1989, reciting the silly little tale, "just a couple of salt-of-the-earth millionaires from the dark side of the moon. However much they pissed me off they always made me laugh as well."

When the caretaker at High Park Farm, Duncan Cairns, got wind of the McCartneys' recent brush with the law in Sweden, he immediately drafted a letter of resignation. Working for the famous rock 'n' roller was one thing; associating with suspected "drug addicts" something else entirely. Another local piqued by the news was Campbeltown police constable Norman McPhee, who, having recently graduated from a drug identification course in Glasgow, decided to drive out and nose around the McCartney farm on the off-chance he might ferret out yet more of the menacing killer weed.

McPhee would not go away disappointed. Making a routine sweep of Paul's run-down greenhouse, there, mixed in amongst the tomatoes and marigolds, he spotted several pointy-leaved plants which seemed to match his instructor's description of marijuana. Quickly grabbing a few specimens, he hotfooted it back down to headquarters to positively identify the suspect substance. Several hours later, the keen-eyed constable returned to the unoccupied farmhouse with seven of his nosiest crimefighters, thoroughly turning the place over in an effort to uncover further incriminating evidence. Fortunately, no more was found. Charged on September 20, 1972, with three counts, which included both growing and possessing marijuana, McCartney was given a court date for the following March. Pleading a definite not-guilty on the two possession charges, he explained through his high-priced solicitors that a thoughtful fan had sent him an unmarked packet of seeds through the post which he merely planted out of curiosity to see what would spring up. This argument, however, wasn't quite good enough, and the wayward ex-Beatle ended up submitting a guilty plea on the cultivation issue for which he received a fine of £100. The other two charges were subsequently dropped. "I was planning on writing a few songs in jail," said McCartney at the time. "You have to be careful. I look on it like Prohibition but you have to recognize the law. I think the law should be changed, make it like homosexuality with consenting adults in private. I don't think cannabis is as dangerous as drink. I'm dead against hard drugs."

Finished with touring for awhile, Wings retreated into the studio where they churned out the paralyzing rocker,"Hi, Hi, Hi," released during the latter half of 1972. Once again, the uptight BBC took offense and promptly banned the record, this time citing what they termed the "inappropriate lyrical content" of the rousing celebration of youthful sex, drugs, and rock 'n' roll. McCartney explains:

> There was controversy over a supposed phrase in the song —
> "body gun." But in actual fact I used a really mad word from a
> surrealist play by a man called Alfred Jarry . . . He was a real

nutter who used to cycle around Paris on his bike and had this thing called the Pataphysical Society. It was nothing but a drinking club but a Professor of Pataphysics sounds great. I used the term in "Maxwell's Silver Hammer." . . . Jarry wrote this theatre sketch which has the character Ubu, who's always going around worried about his "polyhedron." . . . So I put a line in where I said, "Lie on the bed and get ready for my ——
—." I wondered what I should put here, so I said "polygon." . . .
The people taking down the lyrics for us thought I said "body gun," which I thought was better. And that's the basis the song got banned on.

Fortunately, the prurient British Broadcasting Company did little to affect either the popularity or the sales of the high-energy forty-five which clocked in at number ten on the American *Billboard* chart.

Holed up at Abbey Road, Morgan, and Olympic Studios with his band, McCartney laid down some of his most enduring post-Beatles work during this period, including the explosive theme to the James Bond sleeper, *Live and Let Die*, as well as the romantic "My Love." Much of the material culled from these sessions eventually appeared on *Red Rose Speedway*, perhaps McCartney's most accessible LP to that date. Although he originally intended it to be a double album, Paul eventually abandoned the idea in favor of coming out as strong as possible after the relative commercial failure of both *Ram* and *Wild Life*. Although the album was rumored to have been named after the McCartneys' housekeeper, Rose Martin, McCartney refuted the idea in an 1988 interview.

Denny Laine remembers there being considerable tension in the air during the sessions because McCartney and secondary producer Glyn Johns often failed to see eye to eye on the project's often complicated musical issues. "He and Paul didn't hit it off at all," says Laine.

Paul always likes to be his own producer anyway, but at least if he's going to bring one in they've got to be able to see Paul's point of view. I could understand him, but when he's trying to come up with new sounds you might get a producer set in his ways who will not accept that this crazy new idea is ever going to work. That's what happened with Glyn. As a result though, we did experiment a lot more. We would try for different sounds, going into funny little rooms to get weird guitar noises and stuff. . . . In some ways the fact that they were in competition actually helped the album.

Issued in Great Britain on May 3, 1973, the brilliantly packaged LP climbed only as high as number four in the U.K., yet did manage a short stint at the top of the charts in the U.S.

Having decided that a British tour was in order to bolster the release of *Red Rose Speedway*, McCartney and Wings set out on a bus to Bristol on May 11. Opening up for the band was Brinsley Schwartz, a cult group with a small but loyal following, often seen on the London pub circuit. Nick Lowe, then playing bass with the group, remembers his first impressions of the magnificent McCartney. "There was always this veil in front of him: you got the impression that he was thinking about something else to what he was telling you. And whatever happens, he's having a nice day all the time: if any nastiness crops up it's like he never sees it. I don't think this veil was anything to do with smoking pot, although he did seem to smoke it pretty much all the time."

Lowe, who was great friends with Henry McCullough, remembers that McCullough was often very rude to Linda in front of everyone, which certainly didn't bode well for his longevity in the group. In addition, the high-living Irishman actually vomited on stage once during the taping of a promotional clip for "My Love" on "Top of the Pops." Strike two.

Altogether Wings blitzed twelve cities during the brief two-week tour, playing an additional four dates early in July.

Quite apart from McCartney's various musical endeavors, 1973 saw him involved in work on several film projects. The first, a partially animated documentary tentatively entitled "The Bruce McMouse Show," was to chronicle Wings' first European tour from the point of view of a tiny mouse who lived underneath the stage with his wife, Yvonne, and their kids, Soily, Swooney, and Swat. Beyond the Wings tune "Soily" (first performed on the 1976 Wings Over America tour), nothing further has ever surfaced from the project other than some very early animation roughs of the main characters which were offered for sale by a prominent New York memorabilia dealer several years later.

The film that many people did see of course, was his exuberant, "James Paul McCartney" special, first airing on American television on April 16, 1973. Despite generally poor reviews, the hour-long program neatly showcased McCartney's varied musical talents. It was capped by a rollicking Wings mini-concert finale. Called "overblown and silly" by Britain's *Melody Maker,* the eclectic special was defended by McCartney in a series of interviews in which he discussed his decision to act out his often clearly middle-of-the-road fantasies. "You could say it's fulfilling an old ambition," he told reporters. "Right at the start I fancied myself involved in musical comedy. But that was before the Beatles. Don't get me wrong. I'm no Astaire or Gene Kelly and this doesn't mean the start of something big. I don't want to be an all-rounder. I'm sticking to what I am." Shown periodically on television over the years, "James Paul McCartney" seems to have mellowed considerably with age, and stands today as an interesting, though by no means balanced, overview of its subject. Incidentally, this was the production done in settlement of Sir Lew Grade's 1971 publishing royalties suit brought against the McCartneys by ATV and Northern Songs.

Wings was definitely Paul McCartney's band. Whatever Paul wanted, he got. The feelings and opinions of those around him were largely incidental, especially when it came to allowing his band mates to express themselves creatively. Always image-conscious, McCartney at least tried to appear interested in his colleagues' thoughts and feelings. But it was all a sham; he would simply wait for the others to stop talking and then do exactly as he pleased.

Sometimes, however, people with a bit of spunk would beat him to the punch and tell him to get lost. It didn't happen often, but when it did, it inevitably left the egocentric composer dumbfounded. A case in point was Henry McCullough's departure from the band while rehearsing at the McCartneys' farm in July of 1973. Always skeptical about Linda's inclusion in the group, Henry apparently drew the line when the heavy-handed McCartney tried to tell him how to play the guitar. Jo Jo Laine recalls that Paul insisted McCullough play a certain riff in a way the veteran musician felt, was, in her words, "bubble gum." After tossing the ball back and forth for a few minutes, Henry calmly laid down his guitar, switched off his amp, and called to his wife. "Sheila! That's it. Get the car and start packing. We're getting outta here!"

Storming out of the barn, never to return, McCullough had asserted his artistic integrity before the McCartneys in a way few others had dared — a fairly heroic stance for a basically unknown, financially strapped musician who might have gone far had he simply shut up and toed the line. Of the many musicians McCartney has courted over the years, it is interesting to note that the vast majority have ended up taking a walk after bottoming out on his oppressive attitude, not to mention the ever-critical eye of wife Linda.

"I'm sure Paul wanted to say to poor Henry, 'Okay, man, do it your way,'" says Jo Jo. "But it was too late. They were both locked into their trips and neither one was about to give in."

Her husband, however, views Henry's departure a little more philosophically. As far as Laine is concerned, McCullough was most likely looking for an excuse to bail out after having gone as far as he felt he could with McCartney's mainstream music. "Henry quit because he'd made enough money to buy a house and a nice car, and he wanted to relax awhile," said Denny. "He didn't really like the big time. He couldn't handle it. . . . Henry was a bit of a problem. He wouldn't want to do certain things, as he was basically into one style and we liked to kind of play the field, so to speak. . . . He was a bit of a rebel, that's all. It was hard work to get him to do things sometimes." Ringing up a few days later, Henry confirmed that he was indeed leaving for good, which reportedly quite upset McCartney.

Eager to go off and record their next album in some exotic locale, Paul eventually settled on Lagos, Nigeria, where EMI had their own studio. Now that McCullough was gone, however, he and Denny would have to try to take up the slack on guitar, a prospect McCartney secretly found exciting. As the days slipped by he grew increasingly keen about the African trip. "Think about all the wild rhythms and things they've got going over there," he would say to his mate, Denny. "We're gonna have the time of our lives — you wait."

For Laine, life as Paul's sidekick was fraught with exhilarating highs and devastating lows. He stuck it out with the often difficult McCartneys for ten long years, far longer than anyone else. Apart from John Lennon, no one has ever been as close, worked so intimately, or been included almost as family. But after it was all over, Laine too walked away, just like so many others, everything he ever put into the band washed away, almost as if it had never happened. According to Jo Jo, McCartney returned Denny's unquestioning trust with false promises and subterfuge, his faith with lies, his friendship with pretense. She remembers:

> Denny and Paul were up on the hill near his farm having a joint one evening at sunset and Paul started talking about the album [*Band on the Run*]. It was the first time Paul had ever offered Denny any royalties. He said something like "Just think, man, you'll get like a quarter of a million . . . " I don't remember the exact percentage, but later, when the money came in, it wasn't what Denny thought. Paul had definitely told him it was to be a certain amount because I remember Denny came home and was hugging me as he was so excited. He said, "Just think of the money we'll have from that alone, if it goes gold or platinum or anything like that." We were both very happy. But then when the album came out, although Denny got a lot of money, he said to me, "Jesus, that isn't what Paul said to me on the farm that night."

Jo Jo insists that right up until *Band on the Run,* Paul, never exactly lauded for his generosity when it came to paying the hired hands, kept Denny on a salary so measly the young couple were forced to kip in their van when and where they could. "When I first met Denny in '72 he made £35 a week," she recalls.

> I think later he did get one raise to £75 per week. Everybody got paid the same. I remember there was an article once when Linda was busted for something, and she said she couldn't pay the fine straight away because she only got £75 a week. Knowing Paul, that's probably all he was paying his wife as well.

Money wasn't the only complaint the unpopular Mrs. Laine leveled against the McCartneys either. Asked whether she ever got the feeling that either of the couple had a wandering eye, she replied, "Yes, Linda!" Questioned further if she felt (as rumor sometimes had it) that Linda had a crush on Denny, the answer again was a definite "Yes." "Denny was the only other male allowed to spend so much time around Linda," she recalls.

> Even Denny wouldn't tell me the personal things they discussed. Sometimes she'd get very upset about how she didn't really want to be in the band and would cry on his shoulder. . . . I remember one time I rang up the hotel when they were on tour in Europe and she was in his room. Anyway, she tried to make it look like he was preoccupied, not necessarily with her, but she was in Denny's room and answered the phone. So she said, "Well, he's really kind of busy right now, Jo." So I said, "Oh well, he's a good fuck, isn't he, Linda?" Then she immediately said, "Hang on a second, I'll just get him." She was playing games with me so that I would get paranoid. . . . Now I don't think for one minute they ever had an affair, but there was definitely a flirtation there.

On August 9, 1973, as Wings was about to leave for Lagos, Denny Seiwell called to say he didn't really feel like going to Africa, and was quitting the band. (Privately, Seiwell too had grave doubts about Linda's role in the group.) All things considered, Paul paid a heavy price for his almost neurotic need to have his consort constantly by his side. Like his old Liverpool girlfriend Dot, ensconced amidst the Beatles as they thumped about in the Cavern, Linda wasn't to venture out of McCartney's sight, at least while he was performing. No matter what the critics, the public, the band, or even Linda herself had to say, on this point McCartney's word was law.

Now that Wings was unexpectedly reduced to a trio, the challenge of making a successful album was significantly greater. Still, if Paul and Denny were forced to get by without a proper lead guitarist then they would also somehow muddle through *sans* a drummer. Always a passable percussionist, McCartney decided to pick up the sticks himself, and to the surprise of many did just fine. "It looked like it was going to all be a disaster," he recalled in 1977. "One hour before we were due to fly out from Gatwick our drummer telephoned and said, 'Sorry, man, I won't be able to make it.' But, thank God, Denny Laine turned up. They were even building the studio when we got to Lagos. I was faced with doing the drumming and we would have to share the guitars and harmonies. It was a weird feeling of being in the wrong place at the wrong time and believing that nothing can go right."

From the moment the aeronautical trio touched down in Africa things went wrong. For one thing it was still the tail end of the monsoon and the place was awash in a rolling river of mud. It was also crawling with bugs, which petrified their insectophobic engineer, old Beatles ally, Geoff Emerick.

Apart from the many mundane inconveniences, however, there were some very real threats. One day, while the band was busy laying down some bed tracks in the studio, McCartney suddenly crashed up against the mixing console, unable to breathe. Grabbing at his throat, he fought to suck down even the tiniest bit of air. Rushing to his side, Linda and Denny were convinced the thirty-two-year-old singer was having a serious heart attack. When he passed out moments later, Linda ran screaming for a doctor. After regaining consciousness Paul was sure death was imminent. Linda, Laine, and a local physician tried their best to calm him. He was later diagnosed as having had an acute bronchial spasm, probably brought on by his heavy smoking. He spent the next few days recovering at Ikeja, near the airport, in one of the houses rented for the band.

Scarier still was the night Paul and Linda were accosted by a gang of knife-wielding hoods on a dark Lagos street. The McCartneys had been walking on the sidewalk when a decrepit car containing five youths pulled up alongside and started to follow them. At first they were not particularly alarmed; starstruck locals often spotted them.

Pulling up to the curb, the five thugs jumped out of the car and swarmed around them. "Don't kill us, please!" Linda screamed through a torrent of tears. "We're musicians, you know? He's Beatle Paul!" McCartney glanced over at Linda who was tight against the wall with a very nasty blade pressed hard against her throat.

"Give it up, bastards!" one of the more menacing shouted.

"Okay, fine. *Fine*. Take the lot," shouted McCartney. "Just don't hurt us, that's all. We don't care about the money."

Grabbing everything of value the rich white couple were carrying, the thieves made off with not only their jewelry and cash, but also two of Linda's favorite cameras and, most upsetting of all, the cassette demos of the songs for the new album.

Attempting to compose themselves, Paul and Linda cautiously made their way to the nearby studio where the staff summoned the police. "It's a lucky thing you are both white," one of the constables confided as the couple nursed drinks aptly provided by Denny. "Otherwise they would have surely cut your throats. You see, they know that to you all blacks look alike, and so they did not fear being identified. Here, the penalty for such a crime is execution, so they had nothing to lose by killing you. You are very lucky people." Laine elaborates on the incident: "He was warned about going out after dark. . . . You see, it's a military set-up over there, so when they finally catch the guys they just take them down to the beach, tie them to a pole and shoot them publicly. . . . Anyway, Paul just thought, 'Well, we don't listen to things like that,' and they set out on foot over to my place. . . . It could have been extremely nasty."

In the studio too, there were problems. "Half the stuff was just hanging out of the walls," says Laine.

> Nobody knew where to plug it in. We'd give a guy twenty dollars to go out and get a pack of cigarettes and he'd come back with no change. . . . Ginger Baker was always trying to get us to use his studio, but then Paul felt we might be somehow unduly influenced by the whole African thing happening there. . . .
>
> Paul would sit around with an idea for a song and I'd learn it. Then I would play guitar and he'd look after the drums. Of course, Linda was taught her little bits as well. . . . The beauty of that album, everybody says, is the feel. It proved Paul and I had a very sharp needle edge, a keen eye for what we wanted. . . . The fact that it was just the two of us showed we didn't really need anybody else, although I felt we should think about getting a band together to go back out on the road.

Troubling too, was the interjection of popular native musician, Fela Ransome-Kuti into McCartney's African mix. A close friend of Ginger Baker's, Kuti met the former Fab following his high-energy set at a Lagos nightclub. The musically militant Nigerian immediately laid into the astonished McCartney over his very presence in the country. Fearing the megastar might somehow spirit away the cultural essence of his people's music, he warned him not to attempt any undue exploitation of the exotic rhythms he found there. "Maybe you should just go back to England where you came from, man," Kuti remonstrated to the pop icon. "The people don't need you here."

"Listen, mate," McCartney retorted. "We've done okay without Africa so far. We're not here to rip anybody off." Thereafter, Paul and the self-appointed custodian of African musical culture formed a tenuous, if uneasy friendship. In fact, McCartney has always secretly admired those who have dared stand up to him.

"He was apparently a kind of prince," says Denny.

Son of a chief of some tribe who had his own little set called Africa Seventy. He accused us of stealing his music, which is absolute bullshit. Talk about somebody who owns the rights to the world! If you like a piece of music and you go and sing it, that doesn't mean you're stealing it. Obviously we were influenced; we were influenced everywhere we went in the world, but he tried to cause trouble.

About the only comic relief in the extended African nightmare was the appearance on the front lawn of an entire traveling market, complete with camels and other exotic livestock. Laine recalls: "One morning we got up, drew the blinds and they were all out on the grass like the Saturday market on Portobello Road. This one guy who hitched onto me wanted to come back to England as my man Friday. *Everything* was for sale in Lagos."

Out of the adversity of Wings' African safari was born what stands today as the group's finest album, *Band on the Run*. It encompasses the very best of McCartney's work, both as a musician and a composer, heralding a deeply genuine partnership between himself and the vastly underrated Denny Laine. The album's ten tracks represent a Paul McCartney unencumbered by the dictates of a career concentrated on generating "hits" as opposed to simply making fine music. Even today, McCartney admits that the skyrocketing "Jet" is one of his favorite Wings tunes. It was one of the few Wings songs he performed on his 1989/90 world tour. Laine, on the other hand, is a little less sentimental about the triple platinum bestseller. "All it meant to me was I made a little bit more money and everybody was giving us gold albums," he reflected ruefully in 1989, "although of course, I was happy we'd made a good record."

The outlaw edge of *Band on the Run*, even if more in title and packaging than between the grooves, gave McCartney a refurbished image, light years away from the mushy lightweight lolly-pop he had been proliferating in his recent past, and paved the way for the majesty of more substantial works such as *Tug of War* and the critically panned, but progressive, *Flowers in the Dirt*.

The fall of 1973 saw the final reunion of the Beatles when John, Paul, and George joined forces to help their old pal Ringo boost his then-dismal solo career by contributing to what would later become his popular *Ringo* album. Paul's offering, the syrupy love-gone-wrong tune "Six O'Clock," worked well within the narrow perimeters of Starr's vocal range, as did Lennon's "I'm the Greatest" and Harrison's three — "Sunshine Life for Me," "You and Me (Babe)," and the hit single, "Photograph."

Denny and Jo Jo, meanwhile, were busy putting down roots. Their first child, Laine, a boy, was born in August of 1973 in Campbeltown Hospital, Scotland. The Laines had been visiting the McCartneys' farm where Denny was rehearsing with Wings. The night before little Laine's arrival everyone sat around a makeshift campfire listening to the McCartneys' romantic and sentimental tales of the births of their children. Jo Jo felt a warmth towards Paul and Linda she had previously thought impossible. Hours later, her water broke, prompting Denny to dash outside and unpack their overflowing van in the middle of the night so that his girlfriend might have somewhere to lie down during the five-minute ride to the hospital. The labor was short and the delivery without complications. Proud almost to the point of tears, Denny decided to immediately drive down to Birmingham to bring back his parents so that they too might meet their newest grandson.

"Are you sure you'll be alright, luv?" he asked, softly stroking his lady's beautiful auburn hair.

"Of course I will," whispered Jo Jo, exhausted by the birth of her first child. "Paul and Linda are only a couple of miles up the road. I'm sure they'll be looking in soon."

"Sure they will," Denny replied, bending over for one final look at his tiny son. "Hang in there. I'll be back before you know it."

As Jo Jo lay there in the quaint country hospital, the only visitor she entertained was an old Guernsey cow who stuck her mammoth head through the lace curtains one afternoon as the all-but-abandoned new mum nursed her infant son.

> They knew Denny was gone. I had no visitors, no money . . . and still they didn't come. The only thing I got was a card from Heather with pictures of horses drawn on it, which I still have. It said something like, "Congratulations on the birth of your baby boy. Love, Heather and the Macs." I would have thought they could have sent a nice telegram at the very least. By that time though, I wasn't really all that shocked by their selfishness. It was pretty much par for the course.

Denny, however, feels that many of the problems between his missus and the McCartneys stemmed, at least initially, from Jo Jo's own insecurity and paranoia.

> I don't believe the shit that you have to go around sending flowers to everybody all the time. Our way of life wasn't like that. I mean, Paul didn't even go to his old man's funeral. I can understand it in a way, and yet a lot of people can't. I don't think the McCartneys went out of their way to be nasty to her — a lot of that was just Jo. If she hadn't been quite so paranoid of them it wouldn't have been so bad. After all, she was invited to things. We went to Paul and Linda's house for barbecues many times . . . even though they were unfair in some ways. . . . I was protective of her, but I also saw their point of view.

In June of 1974 McCartney decided to replace the departed Henry McCullough on guitar. Of several possibilities contemplated, he finally settled on young Jimmy McCulloch, a feisty, hard-drinking Scot from Glasgow, born June 4, 1953.

McCulloch had been something of a rock 'n' roll prodigy, joining his first hometown band, One in a Million, at the age of thirteen. "My folks helped us get a truck and backed us all the way," he later recalled. Three years on, after moving south to London, he shared in the spoils of Thunderclap Newman's smash, "Something in the Air," after being discovered by Pete

Townshend in 1969. He was then hired as lead guitarist for John Mayall, taking over a position formerly held by rock legends Eric Clapton, Jeff Beck, Mick Taylor, and Peter Green. Although he quit the group after only a short time, Jimmy left his mark on the famous blues band, garnering some of the grandest reviews ever lavished on one so young. In 1973, he briefly joined the generic band Blue (managed by Robert Stigwood) before taking over for the late Les Harvey in Maggie Bell's Stone the Crows, after Harvey was tragically electrocuted while performing onstage. "It wasn't all glamor being a child rocker," he recalled. "I had to rely on cabs and public transport. I went for a Jethro Tull audition on the tube once. It was the Piccadilly line from Wood Green to Leicester Square, and I had to stand with my guitar upright in a packed tube. Then it turned out I was too young for the audition."

McCulloch first crossed paths with the McCartneys in Paris in 1972 when he joined in on sessions for Linda's pleasant South Seas ditty, "Seaside Woman," playing with obscure Wings sideman, Davy Lutton on drums. Two years later, the five-foot-three-inch powerhouse was retained by MPL to appear on Mike McCartney's landmark *McGear* LP, produced and co-written by Paul. For all McCulloch's press as an egotistical, immature little brat, Mike remembers Jimmy fondly as someone who often had difficulty coping with the stress of life at the top. "With his first wages from Wings he bought himself a new Rolls-Royce," recalls Mike.

> And for some reason Paul rang me up and asked if Jimmy could crash at my place as he had been drinking heavily and was out of his head. I warned him not to think about driving himself over, but he insisted and within a little while showed up at the door. Leading him to his room I told him, "Listen. Just get your head down, son. Don't do anything else but sleep. Okay?"

Gently closing the bedroom door, McCartney saw to it that his entire family tiptoed around the house well into the next afternoon for fear of disturbing the well-oiled guitarist. "About noon I walked down to the shops for the paper," says Mike, "and noticed the Rolls was no longer out front, so I shot back into the house only to find the bed well and truly empty." He learned later that the outrageously intoxicated McCulloch had soundlessly slipped out of the house and driven all the way back to London, still thoroughly smashed out of his tree. "Jimmy always liked his ale," McCartney summed up.

McCulloch's first real assignment as a member of Wings was playing on Paul's famous Nashville sessions in June and July of 1974. While in the States McCartney also produced an album for American songstress Peggy Lee (which included the McCartney track, "Let's Love," released in October 1976). Ms Lee recalls the collaboration:

> Paul and Linda McCartney are two people I sincerely like. I remember once when I was playing London I invited them up to the Dorchester[hotel] for dinner when Paul said to me, "Instead of bringing you a gift or a bottle of champagne I'm bringing you a song." It was called "Let's Love," and I was very thrilled about it. Anyway, when I got back to the United States, he and Linda came over to help record it with me, which was lovely. Later in the studio he played on the song for me and even conducted it; that whole side was all his. Unfortunately, due to an unexpected merger between my label, Atlantic, and Electra Asylum, the tune never quite made it out as a single, but one thing's for sure, that man has loads of class and we had a wonderful time working together.

While in the U.S., however, the creative juices began to flow, with the band laying down not only the classic "Junior's Farm," but also the obscure Jim McCartney instrumental, "Walking in the Park with Eloise." Later released under the Wings alias, the Country Hams, it is now perhaps the rarest of all McCartney-related cuts. In addition, "Country Dreamer," the little-known B-side of "Helen Wheels," was also recorded, along with the twangy "Sally G" and several other unreleased country standards involving the likes of Chet Atkins and Floyd Cramer. "I've been in the business a long time," McCulloch later recalled, "but it never occurred to me I'd ever play with

McCartney. I met a guy who worked in a studio and he told me Paul was looking for a guitarist to work on some sessions. I went along to chat about it but it was like some kind of dream. Paul was there chatting happily and I just kept staring at him, thinking to myself, 'Christ! He used to be a Beatle. And here he is talking to me like I matter.'"

Also on board for the Nashville trip was Wings' newest probationary member, cockney drummer and black belt karate champ, Geoff Britton. Invited to audition for the post along with no less than forty-nine other top-flight percussionists at the Albery Theatre, St. Martin's Lane, London, on April 26, 1974, the fair-haired Britton buried the competition, including former Jimi Hendrix drummer, Mitch Mitchell. "Mitch was on a head trip that day," says Denny. "Maybe he resented the fact that we'd asked him to audition and he wasn't getting the star treatment, which in some ways I feel a bit guilty for. Anyway, the one guy that shone at the end of the day was Geoff, and that's the truth of it."

Despite Britton's stellar performance that afternoon, the general consensus later was that allowing him in the band had been a mistake. "He was a lovely guy," Jo Jo remembers. "But he should have stuck to the karate. He was way too straight for this crowd, believe me. I mean, he didn't even smoke dope. And with potheads like Paul and Linda that in itself was grounds for immediate dismissal!" Often turning up for work clad only in his karate suit, Britton soon became the butt of innumerable jokes from the sometimes painfully cynical McCartney crowd. "What are you gonna do," Denny used to chide the ultra-confident young musician, "play the drums or chop them in two?" Musically too, Britton's take-no-prisoners drumming style didn't really mesh with Wings' concentric swirling rhythms. "It was a disaster basically," Laine recalls. "He was always talking about, 'When I get my big house . . . ' And when people start talking like that, they're out the door, pal. . . . The guy was an opportunist, what can I say?"

While in Nashville, Wings set up camp at the luxury home of good ol' boy Junior Putnam, hence the origin of McCartney's

▲ Wings in their final configuration in the highlands of Scotland.

▼ Backstage in the McCartneys' dressing room.

▲   A promotional shot taken during filming for the "James Paul McCartney" television special, which aired in America to very mixed reviews on April 16, 1973.

▼   Denny, Linda, and Paul posing in front of but a few of the countless gold, silver, and platinum records they received for their musical accomplishments in Wings.

▲ Denny Laine outside one of the ramshackle stone outbuildings the frugal McCartneys expected the band to inhabit during their frequent treks to Scotland to rest and rehearse, 1972.

▲ Wings' two Dennys: drummer Seiwell and rhythm guitarist Laine, passing the peace pipe.

▶ Henry and Denny onstage somewhere in Europe during an early Wings gig, 1972.

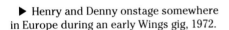

▼ In the studio with veteran engineer Phil McDonald.

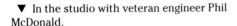

▶ Denny Laine takes the young daughter of Simon and Marijke of the Dutch design team The Fool, for a pony ride, 1976.

◄ Clowning around at Mardi Gras, New Orleans, 1975.

▼ Jo Jo and Paul kick up their heels at a reception for Wings in New Orleans.

▲ Hamming it up with the Campbeltown Pipe Band, gathered together for the promotional film for the mega-hit "Mull of Kintyre."

▼ Denny's famous double-neck guitar in action.

▲ Together in L.A., 1977.

▲ Linda, super-roadie Trevor Jones, and Jimmy McCulloch.

▼ Laine with McCartney's longtime, long suffering housekeeper, Rose Martin (right) and her twin sister.

▲ Wings commander McCartney onstage in a look reminiscent of his bygone *Sgt. Pepper* days.

▼ MPL executive Allan Crowder and Linda aboard the good ship *Fair Carol* in the American Virgin Islands during sessions for Wings' impressive *London Town*.

The beautiful Joanne Alice Patrie marries Brian Frederick Hines at
Marblehead, near Boston, Massachusetts, November 5, 1978.

▲ The Laines' home, "Yew Corner," a palatial Victorian manor in Laleham village, Suffolk.

◄ Denny and Jo Jo during their first, "poor but happy," days together, aboard their houseboat, Searchlight, in Chertsey, on the Thames.

▲ Heidi Jo Hines, the Laines' beautiful and talented second child, on the ferry en route to France, August 1991.

◄ Jo Jo Laine, as she is today, displaying a memento of her wild Wings days.

◀ Backstage following a Wings gig in the mid-seventies.

▼ Recording *Tug of War* in Monserrat.

▼ Killing time in Paul's Spirit of Ranachan Studios on the farm in Scotland.

▲ Heather McCartney posing with a friend at the family's estate/farm near Peasmarsh, Sussex.

▶ Mary Louise McCartney, Paul and Linda's first child together.

▶ Stella Nina McCartney, their second child.

▼ Inside the stables with Mary and Stella.

▲ Mike poses with his three young daughters and niece Mary McCartney (second from right).

◄ "Waterfalls," the McCartney's eccentric first home in Sussex.

◄ The toney St. John's Wood address, London.

Definitely the most photogenic incarnation of Wings, the final "Steve Holly/ Laurence Juber" configuration.

◄ McCartney playing the fool at Lympne Castle on a Break from the rigors of the recording.

▼ Smoking a joint in the studio.

▼ The couple that sings together, Wings together. Trodding the boards during the disastrous 1979 British tour.

▲ Heather and Linda at Denny Laine's birthday party, 1976.

▲ Wings à la chez McCartney. Breakfast in Scotland.

◀ After his controversial split with Wings in 1980, Denny sought refuge in Spain where he spent his days partying, learning flamenco guitar, and working the land at his rugged five-acre farm near Madrid.

▲ The one and only, the original, the incomparable Jo Jo Laine.

▲ Perhaps the finest drummer in rock 'n' roll today, Steve Holly is also a concerned family man with a big heart and a deep regard for his former boss, Paul McCartney.

▲ "Free Paul" button circulated during McCartney's Japanese incarceration, 1980.

▶ Denny Laine and the author at the superlative Mark Recording Studios in Clarence, New York, late 1989.

▲ Superfan and Beatle entrepreneur extraordinaire, Charles F. Rosenay!!! presents Linda with a copy of his top-flight fanzine, Good Day Sunshine, backstage in Liverpool, 1990.

▼ Onstage during the high-stepping Flowers in the Dirt tour, 1990.

popular single "Junior's Farm." At the sprawling ranch the group fell into a breezy routine centered around recording, partying, and otherwise enjoying the great American outdoors. "We were in a place called Lebanon," Britton recalls, "a dry county. There was no liquor allowed so there was moonshining in the hills around us. Guys came into town in old pick-up trucks and hung out all day whittling on bits of wood. It was straight out of a movie."

Almost from the very beginning it was apparent that the hard-driving Britton's days were numbered. Not surprisingly, Geoff has a slightly different version of his rise and fall through the politically supercharged pecking order that was Wings. "There was a controversy once over the day's rehearsal. Everyone was a bit stoned and so it got heavy. Jimmy insulted Linda and there were tears. Then I told Jimmy what I thought of him." Walking out, slamming the door behind him, Britton tried to hit up one of Wings' management team for enough money to allow him to see a bit of the U.S.A. before returning home to England. Although various members of the road crew tried to calm him down enough to go back in and pick up the sticks, Britton says he was adamant about his decision to leave the band.

The next afternoon, however, Paul and Linda personally expressed their desire that he continue in the group, an act which, for the moment anyway, allowed Wings to resume working in the converted garage they called home. "It's alright if a band has come up together and they are all millionaires," reflected Britton some years later. "They can talk to each other as equals. But with Wings there were these incredible imbalances which manifested themselves in so many ways. For example, we were offered a gig to play a festival with Stevie Wonder for half an hour. The money being offered was a fortune. I instinctively said, 'Let's do it!' My cut of that alone would have bought me a house! I said, 'Fucking great!' But Paul didn't want to do it. So as a result I didn't do any live gigs with the band."

Interestingly, a rare film account of Britton's Wings days

exists in the form of *One Hand Clapping*, a long-unreleased documentary of Paul and the band in rehearsal. Directed by David Litchfield and backed by MPL, the hour-long peek into the private world of Wings has only recently made its way into the hands of collectors, selling briskly on the underground bootleg market for up to a hundred dollars.

Following their month-long stint in Tennessee, the band flew home, where apart from a November 20 appearance on Britain's "Top of the Pops" to promote "Junior's Farm," nothing of much significance occurred until their January 15, 1975 departure for New Orleans to record tracks for the *Venus and Mars* album. In spite of the gaiety of Mardi Gras and the excitement of working in such a creatively stimulating atmosphere, all was not well amongst McCartney's musical cohorts. Britton remembers: "It was very fragile. Words would be said and Linda inevitably got upset. Jimmy would say something about the chords being wrong, and the worst thing you can do to a musician who is struggling is to put them under pressure. . . . Jimmy would be short with Denny too about his tuning. If he came in wrecked and hung over everything about him would be negative."

While it's true that tensions amongst Wings' inner circle were at an all-time high during this period, the public had no idea of just how deep the wounds were. Once again, Geoff Britton:

> I was so depressed. I dreaded going to New Orleans with them. It should have been the happiest time of my life. But I was miserable and hated it. There was no sincerity in the band and every day it was a fight for survival, a fight to re-establish yourself. Denny could be very cruel. He and Jimmy were supposed to be close muckers who would go out boozing together and yet, when the chips were down, he tried to get Jimmy shafted out with a knife in the back. He's a bastard. I should have chinned him. I regret it now.

Although no one had yet actually resorted to physical violence, the dramatic dislike Wings' new drummer held towards

Jimmy and Denny was certainly more than mutual. "They definitely thought I was a fly boy, a bit of a Herbert," says Geoff. He recalls:

> They were pretty ignorant guys really, just good players and that was it. They were into heavy drinking and over-the-top drugs. And of course I didn't participate in anything. . . . We would go to parties and the tables would be laid out with coke, and anything you wanted was there. So everybody got absolutely legless, on the knowledge that I would drive them all home. . . . Unfortunately, I let it slip a few times, with the Londoner's attitude, about the "thick Northerners." And I definitely thought they were thick Northerners, that's for sure.

Geoff Britton was formally "terminated" from Wings by the McCartneys, who came into his room one morning during the sessions for *Venus and Mars* and casually broke the news. There weren't any gut-wrenching scenes, however, as Britton also realized that things had indeed reached the point of no return: "When I first joined I was promised royalties and we talked in telephone numbers. Then it became just session fees and bonuses. . . . Maybe I should have given McCulloch and Laine the pasting they both deserved. Maybe then Jimmy wouldn't be dead now and we'd all still be with Wings."

Once again, smack dab in the middle of an important project without a proper drummer, McCartney was forced to look about for a replacement. It was Tony Dorsey, leader of Wings' occasional horn section, who first suggested burly-bearded American, Joe English for the job. Born in Rochester, New York, on February 7, 1949, Joe was eighteen when he joined a local band, Jam Factory. Touring the country for the next six years, English and his fellow Factory workers became well known as a first-class support group, regularly opening for such pop luminaries as Jimi Hendrix, the Grateful Dead, and Janis Joplin. When the group split up in 1973, English's life was on the rocks. With Joe securely out of work for what seemed like millennia his wife left him, taking their two young children with her.

Settling in the unlikely musical mecca of Macon, Georgia, Joe met and fell in love with a pretty young girl named Dayle. It was strictly love in a garret though, as the easy-going drummer was still not exactly in high demand. "I was on the bottom," says English. "But Dayle stuck with me, kept my spirits up, and helped me get through the year." Joe was rehearsing with singer Bonnie Bramlett for an upcoming tour when the call came through, inviting him to meet with Paul in New Orleans in anticipation of joining Wings. He readily accepted, but first made sure he found a steady replacement for his old boss, Bramlett.

After working with Wings for the first two months of 1975, Joe followed them to Los Angeles where they went to work overdubbing and mixing down the new album at Wally Heider Studios. Driving with him to a session one day, Paul turned to the drummer and asked if he'd like to join up permanently, to which English replied simply, "Yes." "In the studio," says Joe, "Paul made it so if you wanted to come in every day and be part of the recording, mixing, ideas and putting it all together, you could. He really gave everyone a lot of freedom. Of course, if he thought something should be played a certain way, he'd tell you to do it, and ninety-nine percent of the time I'd go along because it was usually the right thing. But if I came up with something better, I'd tell him and he'd go for it."

Wings' stay in Los Angeles was punctuated by an appearance of Paul and Linda at the Grammy telecast where they scooped up an award for *Band on the Run* as album of the year. Ensconced in several luxury suites at the Beverly Wilshire Hotel the band partied lavishly. For once, says Jo Jo, the sky was the limit, with absolutely no restrictions placed by the normally frugal McCartneys on either room tabs or the band's extravagant hire cars. As a matter of fact, Joe English's brand new Porsche was stolen from the hotel's parking lot. Jo Jo can't quite recall if it was ever recovered. "It was a fantastic time." She remembers: "*Venus and Mars* turned out to be such a great album, and after the phenomenal success of *Band on the Run*, Wings were virtually the most sought-after group of people in Hollywood. My sister and I were pursued by Warren Beatty; I was wined and dined by Rod Stewart and made more than comfortable with a steady stream of the best pharmaceuticals the city had to offer."

Paul and Linda also partook of California's good life. On March 3, 1975, the couple once again ran afoul of the law when their late-model silver Lincoln Continental ran a red light and was pulled over by a highway patrolman. Leaning through the window, the officer noticed the strong, pungent odor of what he correctly assumed to be marijuana, subsequently uncovering all of seventeen grams of the weed from Mrs. McCartney's purse.

Initially, both Paul and Linda were placed under arrest, prompting Linda to protest violently, swearing to all that was sacred that the contraband was hers and hers alone, McCartney's two preceding pot busts having already made it a legal nightmare for him to obtain the necessary visas to enter the U.S. Charged at the West Los Angeles police station with possession of marijuana, the indignant strawberry blonde was held for two hours before being released on $500 bail. Ironically, the multi-millionaire McCartney had only $200 on him at the time, and was forced to track down old Apple man Peter Brown at the Beverly Hills Hotel for a loan. To make matters worse, there was some concern that another charge, of contributing to the delinquency of a minor, might be leveled against her, as the three McCartney girls were also in the car at the time of the incident.

Although the charge was eventually dropped, the judge ordered Linda to attend six drug counseling sessions with a London psychiatrist. "The only real unfortunate thing," Paul later commented about being busted, "is that it starts to get you the reputation as a kind of druggie."

In the McCartneys' case, of course, the reputation was well deserved, as Laine recalls:

> He and Linda did smoke a fantastic amount of the stuff by anybody's standards. They smoked joints the way ordinary people smoke cigarettes. Really, I don't think smoking that quantity of

cannabis did Paul and Linda any good. Sometimes smoking a little pot helps to give you good ideas, but so much of it makes you very indecisive and takes away your self-confidence. That's why Paul's albums take him ages and ages to make. He just cannot be decisive about anything. It's very frustrating for people working with him because he changes his mind so often.

Dope or no dope, *Venus and Mars* was a certified smash. Soaring almost immediately to number one in Britain and America, the clever, well-crafted, impressively packaged album contained such memorable, listenable tunes as "Listen to What the Man Said," "Letting Go," and "Rock Show" as well as Denny's stirring "Spirits of Ancient Egypt" and, ironically, the Jimmy McCulloch anti-drug opus "Medicine Jar."

Altogether, three singles were culled from the album throughout the year, racking up further incredible royalties for the "just plain folks" McCartneys. Some of the Wings natives, however, were growing restless. According to an undated MPL memo titled "Fees for Artists' Services" obtained in the research stage of this work, Paul's right-hand man, Denny Laine, while reasonably well paid for his creative input, took home nothing close to the millions of pounds his celebrated employer was steadily making off the band. In 1973, it says, Laine was paid a "retainer fee" of ₤5,730. The following year this dropped to a surprisingly paltry ₤3,408. A further entry states: "Services up to August 1974 to include albums to *Band on the Run* and singles to "Junior's Farm" . . . ₤40,000."

By 1975, Laine was apparently doing a bit better, taking in a cool $100,000 for his work on *Venus and Mars* and the singles "Listen to What the Man Said," "Letting Go," and "Rock Show." Still, by rock star standards, and considering the incredible number of units these records were selling, Laine and his family were just about ready for the bread line.

In February of that year Denny purchased Yew Corner, a marvelous gothic estate in the tiny village of Laleham, Suffolk, for the bargain-basement sum of just ₤37,500. According to Jo

Jo, MPL and the Eastmans bought the property first on the musician's behalf so that the family could move in right away. Later, after the appropriate financing had been arranged, Laine was to buy it back for a sum based on a monthly mortgage. Jo Jo recalls:

> They wanted to set it up that way for tax reasons. And although we were in the fortunate position of being able to pay cash for the place, old man Eastman insisted that it would be better in the long run to have a mortgage. Maybe he was right. But, when the money began slowing down after a few years, making the payments became almost impossible. I realize now that if we had simply kept it free and clear like we wanted, we would probably still have the house today.

Although of the Wings "family" Jo Jo Laine has been the most publicly critical of the McCartneys, the usually magnanimous Denny has occasionally vented his spleen as well:

> McCartney was always making excuses for not paying us properly by saying his money was all tied up in the Beatles' company, Apple. Finally, I got so sick of it I blew up and said I was going to leave — so he gave me £30,000 . . . I was kept in the dark all the time about money, just given a check now and again. You can't pin Paul down. He treated me like a youngster, the way he treats his own younger brother, like a kid. His attitude was, "Stick by me and you'll be alright!" But I don't believe I was getting a fair crack. When I pushed him into a corner he'd say: "Talk to so-and-so." It was never his fault. I began to hate the whole thing. At the end of the day I feel he used his business machinery to confuse me.

It was around this time too that Denny and Jo Jo started having their share of personal difficulties as well. Both of them always rather sexually precocious, Jo Jo was sure Denny was having an affair with a young woman by the name of Consuela he had met in Nashville. According to Jo, after Wings' return from Nashville she found a collection of Polaroid photos of Laine and this new lady secreted away in Jimmy McCulloch's bags. "It was one of the worst moments of my life," she remembers. "I felt like my heart was being ripped out of my nose. The pictures were real cozy too. There was Denny with his arm around this gorgeous-looking Spanish girl. So I started screaming and freaking out so much the doctor had to be called who fortunately gave me a sedative. I almost gave birth to Heidi Jo [the couple's second child together] right then and there."

Six months later, Jo Jo happened to spy the Mediterranean beauty in New Orleans while Wings were in town working on *Venus and Mars*. Without missing a beat, the insanely jealous Jo Jo leaped onto her leggy rival in a restaurant, tearing out her long black hair by the handful and digging her tapered ruby-red nails into the poor girl's flesh with murderous intent. Fortunately, one of her girlfriends was also there and somehow managed to pull the outraged Jo Jo away from the terrified young woman. Needless to say, this was hardly the kind of profile the conservative McCartneys had in mind for their band. Throughout the long, checkered history of rock 'n' roll, Jo Jo Laine stands firmly as one of the art form's most colorful and determined bit players.

After *Venus and Mars* finally hit the stores and duly spun its way to the top, the high-flying McCartneys made their inevitable migration home to England, this time to their new family home in Sussex. First spotted by Paul in an upmarket real-estate catalog, the tiny, perfectly round three-bedroom cottage was the ideal country retreat for the unostentatious McCartneys. Peter Brown comments:

> The house is circular, like a large gazebo, with the rooms cut up like pieces of pie. This odd architecture leaves little privacy, as you can hear every sound from room to room. There are few trappings of a rock star or even a rich man. The gold records and expensive stereo equipment are in his offices in London. The furniture in the house is simple and well worn, the floors littered with newspapers, magazines, and children's toys. There are so many books, plants, and knick-knacks every-

where that it's easy to miss the black baby grand piano in the corner.

That summer (1975) Wings rehearsed like demons in a dere-lict movie house in the nearby town of Rye for what Paul en-visioned as a worldwide "tour to end all tours." Originally, the plan was to kick off the overseas shows in Australia, moving on to Japan, always a Beatles stronghold. Unfortunately, be-cause of McCartney's previous marijuana convictions the straight-laced Japanese government would not grant him a visa, citing his "criminal record" in England.

The band decided to test the waters by going out first at home, playing eleven dates between September 9 and Sep-tember 23. The meticulously orchestrated concerts were well received, bolstering everyone's enthusiasm for the tour ahead.

On October 28, 1975, Wings jetted via Qantas Airlines to Australia. Altogether they did nine shows, commencing at the Entertainment Centre in Perth on November 1. From there they rumbled on to play two shows in Adelaide, two in Sydney, two in Brisbane, and a final two in Melbourne. McCartney re-members this, Wings' first major international outing: "We had fab fun. . . . The audiences were great and we just dug playing. It was more like a holiday."

So wildly successful were the concerts that tickets were being scalped on the underground for upwards of $500, or, what McCartney playfully called, "Sinatra prices." It soon be-came clear that Wings' incredible popularity had gone through the roof, forcing the band to film one of the shows and air it on TV for "all the people who couldn't get to see us." McCartney also made sure a copy was sent to Japan, just to show all the folks there what they'd missed. The two-hour broadcast was followed by a long, drawn-out panel discussion on the pros and cons of smoking marijuana. Yawn.

Jo Jo subsequently described an incident in Australia as "The Cruelest Thing Linda Ever Did." Out with the band for an afternoon of sightseeing on one of Wings' few days off, Paul invited almost the entire entourage for a coach trip to take in some of the local sights, including a visit to a nearby zoo to see the koala bears. Mixed in amongst the roadies, management personnel, and band members was Rose, by far the McCartneys' most trusted and loyal employee. Conservative, middle aged, cheery, and cockney to the core, she showed up ready for the big day decked out in her sportiest summer wear complete with an ancient Kodak and a surprising new coiffure she'd had done especially for the grand occasion. According to Jo Jo, as everyone was climbing onto the bus, Linda made a point of calling out to the excited housekeeper, "Oh no, Rose. Not *you!* You're not going. I've put aside some mending for you upstairs. Some of the children's things. They've needed doing for ages now."

Hurt and embarrassed beyond words, the submissive Rose stepped down off the coach and scooted off without a word. "Everyone was stunned at Linda's complete meanness," says Jo Jo. "Even Paul felt a bit funny, I think. Rose always used to tell me what a lady Jane Asher was. I wouldn't like to repeat what she used to say about Linda."

Making their way back to England, Paul and the band booked themselves into Abbey Road in January of 1976 to begin work on their next album, later called *Wings at the Speed of Sound.* "The idea of that LP," says Denny, "was to try and showcase each member of the band."

> Of course, I'd already had some promotion, having done the Buddy Holly project with Paul. As an individual, I suppose, I was a little bit more well known than the other guys. The idea was to try and take some of the pressure off Paul as far as it being just "Paul McCartney and Wings" all the time. He wanted to promote it as a proper band as well. Perhaps if we had done another album with that sort of line up we might have ended up a tighter all round band. Who knows?

Speed of Sound remains a tribute to Paul McCartney's wish to accord his musical cohorts at least a smattering of recognition as individual artists with their own creative agendas. It came off rather well too, despite the tedious, unfocused cover art by Linda McCartney and Clive Arrowsmith. "This is much more of a group album," said Paul at the time. "I always felt that the tunes Denny was producing weren't really big enough for him, so I wanted to write something that was a bit more epic. So we recorded 'The Note You Never Wrote,' and then took it from there with the rest of the group." Linda McCartney sings "Cook of the House" while Joe English performs "Must Do Something About It." Jimmy McCulloch's contribution is "Wino Junko" which, like "Medicine Jar," he co-wrote with Colin Allen. "With Denny it was very natural for him to sing leads," McCartney continued, "because he's really a lead vocalist anyway. I don't like the idea of me doing all the vocals and Denny just harmonizing, because it seems a waste. With the others it was just a thing that happened, and if it didn't come off we'd just skip it; I could always fill in with something else. But they all seemed to work."

Issued in May 1976, the album did well, eventually spawning two popular singles, "Silly Love Songs" backed by "Cook of the House" that April, and "Let 'em In" sporting the sassy Motown-inspired, "Beware My Love" on the B side, released in July.

After his wife passed away in 1956 Jim McCartney stayed close to home, caring for his two sons. When the Beatles hit it big, however, and Mike began to have some success with the Scaffold, Jim began to think about his own future. Quitting work at Paul's behest in the wake of the first great wave of Beatlemania, Jim settled into his new life, moving with Mike to Rembrandt in 1964. For the first time in his life the senior McCartney had time on his hands. Although Paul insisted he employ two part-time gardeners to help with the reasonably extensive grounds, Jim himself maintained a first-class greenhouse on the property and tenderly cared for a mind-boggling assortment of flowering shrubs and fancy grapevines. Another of his favorite pastimes, now that he was officially a member of the landed gentry, was bird watching. Trekking into town regularly for afternoons of gentle socializing in the pubs, he would often nip into the local library and pick up a book or two on ornithology.

On November 24, 1964, Jim married a thirty-four-year-old widow named Angela Williams to whom he proposed after just three nights out together. At first, Angie, as she liked to be called, was somewhat dubious about the May-September romance, but was lonely after her husband's tragic death in a road accident several years before. "We were two lonely people," commented the elder McCartney some years later. "It was nice to be really close to someone again, after all those years on my own."

He was especially pleased that Angie brought with her to the marriage her charming little five-year-old daughter, Ruth, whom Paul reportedly nicknamed "Scabby." Jim doted on her. Once, after she broke her leg in an accident, Paul presented her with a puppy they named Hamish. Recalling that first meeting with her famous stepbrother, Ruth reflects: "One night I remember a man coming into the bedroom with mother and lifting me onto his lap. When I became fully conscious I saw it was Paul McCartney. I fainted clean away."

Although Paul and Mike would later reject both their new stepmum and kid sister, in the beginning the family was quite close. Ruth remembers being taught to ride her bicycle by Jane Asher and racing around the front yard with both sheepdog Martha and Paul in hot pursuit. To McCartney's credit, during those early Beatle years his father wanted for nothing. As was the case with all the Beatles' parents, an account was established from which the elder McCartney could draw funds at any time. "The change was a bit sudden, coming as it did when I was sixty-two," Jim remembered in 1967. "It took a while to get used to it. Now I've taken to it like a duck to water. I haven't started saying 'glaas' or 'baath,' but I'm enjoying everything. It's as if I've always been used to it."

According to Angie McCartney, however, after Linda Eastman appeared on the scene things began to deteriorate. Speaking in the London papers following Jim's death, she, like so many others once close to the former Beatle, complained bitterly about not only her stepson's penny-pinching, but also what she suggested had been an apparent change in his affections towards his own father. Claiming that after Jim died she and her daughter were forced to move out of Rembrandt due to dwindling finances, Angie also noted that during Paul and Linda's frequent visits north she had to make do on a scant twenty pounds per week housekeeping money, while Linda had her family's groceries shuttled in by train from Fortnum and Mason's in London.

She also claimed that on the few occasions Jim and Angie went to stay at the McCartneys' farm they were forced to sleep on dirty mattresses thrown haphazardly across the cold, concrete floor. In addition, said Angie, the whole place was so dirty and unkempt that flies and other insects continually fell from the ceiling into people's dinners.

Angie confided to Mike McCartney that shortly before Jim's death at his home in Heswall on March 13, 1976, from complications of his crippling arthritis, he raised himself up a little in bed and said softly, "I'll be with Mary soon." A few days later, James McCartney was cremated and his ashes interred at Landican Cemetery in Liverpool during a brief family ceremony. Mike was late; Paul didn't show. Whatever Paul might have felt, he opted for his business-as-usual demeanor in the face of grief. There's no doubt, however, that McCartney definitely loved and respected his father, perhaps more than anyone else in his life. But somewhere deep inside him was still the Liverpool boy who lost his mum at too early an age. It was a wound that had covered over but never really healed. From his mother's death forward, it was safer just to try to look the other way. In his mind no one he loved would ever die again. The emotionally vulnerable pop star just couldn't make it through any other way.

A regrettable postscript to the Angela Williams McCartney story is her sale of Paul's birth certificate to a U.S. investor for an unknown amount. In November of 1990 the document was sold for $18,000 at an auction in Houston, Texas. After his successful bid, Brian Taylor, 26, of Washington, D.C., observed that his passion for Beatles memorabilia had perhaps "gone a little too far."

Two days after McCartney's father died, Wings began a brief European tour as part of their on-going global assault on the youth of the world. Playing their first show at Copenhagen's Falkoner Theatre, the band then moved on to West Germany where they gave a particularly stunning show at the Deutschlandhalle in West Berlin. Finally, Wings touched down in Rotterdam for an appearance at the Ahoy Sportpaleis before jetting home to England.

The famous Wings Over America tour was scheduled to have begun at the end of March 1976, but had to be postponed due to Jimmy McCulloch's fracture of his index finger during a barroom brawl in Paris. About a month later the tour kicked off with a show at the Tarrant County Convention Center in Fort Worth. Denny Laine recalls some of the rigors of the demanding series of gigs: "We would base ourselves in an area and then take a private plane or 'starship' as they used to call them, to the gig. Afterwards, we'd come off stage, still in our stage gear, get in the limo, go to the plane and fly back home. We did that twice a day for weeks on end, using our plane like you would a car. Most of the fun, unfortunately, inevitably goes with the roadies."

To help relieve the tedium of the road, individual band members would often sneak off into the cockpit for a quick turn at the wheel, on one occasion sending the deluxe, specially equipped aircraft into a tailspin. McCartney, who had been playing cards with Linda and a couple of the road crew at the back of the aircraft, ended up in a very unhappy heap in the center aisle, screaming bloody blue murder at the high-flying, spaced-out pranksters. Laine, who himself had a go, was piloting the plane on the basis of a book he was then reading called *Anyone Can Fly*, later the title of one of his most interesting solo albums. He comments: "When you take anything off automatic pilot it goes all over the place for a moment or two. At one point, Steve [the brass player] took the

plane into a terrible dive, sending everybody at the back flying inside the plane. . . . Paul was very pissed off about that,
yeah. Then he found out we'd all been flying for weeks. His
bottle went, as they say."

Not all of the high flying was confined to the air. Around the
time of Wings' two sold-out concerts at San Francisco's Cow
Palace on June 13 and 14, Jo Jo ran across an old coke connection. While Denny didn't mind a neighborly toot every now
and then, he drew the line when it came to either foolishly
shelling out big bucks or running the risk of putting either
himself or his famous boss in jeopardy. Jo Jo, on the other
hand, simply liked to party. Next to that, any other considera-
tions ran a consistent and pitiful second. "I couldn't ask
Denny for the two thousand dollars I needed for the ounce,"
the often outrageous goodtime girl recalls. "At first I thought
of telling him it was for a new dress, but he never would have
believed it. I'd already brought along more clothes than Paul
and Linda combined." Sneaking into an empty dressing room,
Jo Jo happened upon a briefcase belonging to one of the road
managers, filled with dozens of primo front-row seats reserved for the McCartneys' invited guests and family. Unwilling to
overlook such a karmacally golden opportunity, Jo Jo
scooped up her booty and left.

Having made up her mind to go outside and scalp the
prized seats, she now faced a serious dilemma. What if, God
forbid, she were recognized? Imagine, Denny Laine's old lady
busted for hustling stolen tickets to her boyfriend's own concert. The headlines could be brutal. Not to mention what it
might do to her already terribly rocky relationship with the
ever-scandal-conscious McCartneys. "I just couldn't go out
there looking like my normal glamorous self," recalls Jo Jo,
self-mockingly. "So I grabbed an old raincoat and a head scarf
from one of the cleaning ladies, messed up my hair, and dis-
guised myself as a kind of rock 'n' roll bag lady." Not surprisingly, the premium tickets were all gone in one chaotic rush,
leaving Jo Jo with more wadded-up bills than a crack dealer
on a Saturday night. "Anyway, I had more than enough for the

coke which I used to put in smaller packages so that no one actually sussed how much I had. Old Jimmy [McCulloch] and I, especially, used to like having some blow around, as did Denny. . . . Fortunately, we then had enough coke to keep us all going for a bit more of the tour. I wouldn't say that the band was strung out, but everyone certainly enjoyed a good buzz." Finally, Jo Jo reveals that she didn't actually offer any of the stimulant to McCartney, fearing he might wonder how she got it. Besides, she figured, what if he suddenly put two and two together regarding the tickets? Linda, on the other hand, was apparently a different matter altogether:

> Once on the airplane we did it in the ladies' room. Linda asked, "Do you have some coke?" So I said, "Do you want to do some?" And she replied, "Sure." So we went into the ladies' room and had a good snort. That was one of the few pleasant memories I have of Linda because she was like a buddy, and genuinely so. That's why it's so confusing being with those people, because when you actually got a good feeling from them it went right through your soul. But then, the next day, there they were, looking down at you all over again. That was the only time I ever did it with Linda on the tour. In Liverpool though, I had some and we all enjoyed a snort. Even Paul.

By June 24, 1976, Wings Over America was history. The night before, at the Forum in L.A., Ringo Starr had walked on stage during the group's final encore and presented his old bandmate with a bouquet of flowers. It was a touching scene that seemed to suggest, at least as far as Ringo and Paul were concerned, that the bitter feud over the Beatles' legacy was finally over. At least on a personal level.

Altogether Wings played twenty cities during the six-week tour, reaching over three million rabid fans who often queued for hours to win the chance of seeing the one-time Beatle go through the paces with his new band. While extravagant multi-million-dollar tours are now the order of the day, Wings Over America was the first big show to utilize not only lasers and truck loads of other space-age equipment, but also computers and the expertise to pull it all off. All told there were over a hundred people out on the road with Wings at any given time, an astounding number to both coordinate and maintain. The seas of humanity washing around the venues also created problems for the often harried Wings entourage as well. Road manager Trevor Jones explains: "The first thing I had to do every day was to look into security chop-off points of access, and make sure that the hall staff understood the general plan. There were a lot of people with backstage passes and they had to be looked after diplomatically. The crew had to have room to work, but people mustn't be hassled. Only once did an accident occur, when someone kicked one of the power cables and cut out half the sound system." Culled from the concerts was a live three-record set (released in December of 1976 as *Wings Over America*) and a thoughtfully produced, entertaining television special, *Wings Over the World*, first aired on CBS in America on March 16, 1977.

Despite Paul's king-size concern for always looking good in the eyes of his fans, there are those difficult moments when being congenial is clearly not enough. If, in the course of one of these little five- or ten-minute "dreams come true" for a fortunate McCartney loyalist, Paul feels suddenly uneasy or trapped, he will casually reach down and scratch his elbow, a sign to one of his ever-present minders to immediately excuse the singer on the basis of some (imaginary) pressing engagement. Such a plan is of course perfect for the Teflon-coated star: it allows him to evade any personal responsibility for abruptly ending the interview, and to skate away on a pretense of embarrassed apologies, looking daggers at the naughty blighter who dared interfere with this all-important encounter between McCartney and his public.

During his off-hours Denny Laine had always been particularly enamored of boating and the sometimes unpredictable but generally laid-back lifestyle that accompanies it. One of the first things he bought with his newfound relative riches from the band was a forty-foot cabin cruiser he called the *Louis*

Phillipe after Jo Jo's father. For a time, he kept the vessel in Rye harbor in Sussex, learning the ropes, every once in a while taking out his mate Paul for a spin along the tiny seaport's jagged coast. On Laine's birthday one year, Paul and Linda presented him with a plaque which boldly declared: "A Boat Is a Hole in the Ocean Surrounded by Wood in Which a Man Continually Pours Money." It was a good laugh alright, but turned out to be the source of inspiration for one of Wings' most memorable and unusual professional interludes, the recording of their *London Town* LP while camping out on the chartered yachts *Fair Carol, Samala, Wanderlust,* and *El Toro* in the American Virgin Islands.

Although much of the initial work took place at Abbey Road between February 7, 1977, and the end of March, it was the sessions on the *Fair Carol* (for one month starting on May 1) that truly shaped the tone of the ambitious project. McCartney recalls: "After a few phone calls to the Record Plant in L.A. to organize the equipment which would be taken on board the *Fair Carol*, we were off to St. Thomas. From there we sailed to St. John's, a neighboring island, and just after sunset coasted into Watermelon Bay which had been selected as the least choppy spot around."

Another more practical reason McCartney may have had for recording in such an unorthodox location was the ever-present problem of tax. Although he suffered mightily under the exacting tax laws of Great Britain (paying at times as much as 98 percent of his gross income), at least it is his home and there is the off-chance that the money might eventually be used for some public good. When it comes to paying tax elsewhere in the world though, McCartney tightens his grasp significantly. Recording, as he was, anchored in international waters there was the possibility that, taxwise, he might fare a little better.

Although Linda joined her husband on the working vacation, according to Jo Jo, none of the other Wings wives or girlfriends were invited to tag along. "At the time Linda was very pregnant and I think she was intimidated by the girls perhaps wearing a bikini around Paul," she reflects. "Jimmy's girlfriend was the Playmate for February 1976 so we would have both gone down there looking pretty terrific. I remember Linda saying, 'Well, some women look lovely pregnant.' Still, if a woman is pregnant she doesn't generally wear a bikini, but Linda sure did! She never shaved or anything, either. I can recall Denny going on about her 'dog' hair hanging out everywhere. It must have been dreadfully embarrassing."

Once again the McCartneys were pestered by the police. This time three of the boats in their control were apparently visited by suspicious U.S. customs officials, prompting charter boat liaison Peter Baker to write MPL executive Alan Crowder a terse letter threatening to cancel their contract if the band were caught with any illegal drugs. McCartney's 1982 song "Wanderlust" from the *Tug of War* album alludes to the unhappy incident.

Musically, too, there were problems. The sometimes painful particulars of multi-track recording aside, trying to get decent sounds aboard a bobbing boat was almost impossible. At one point, pothead Paul wondered what it would be like to try to play with the boat actually underway. He found out. Ten minutes later, the roadies were still trying to extricate Joe English from his drum kit. Even when things went well there were still plenty of hassles. One evening, as the band was wailing away, nailing down some new material, they were visited by rangers from the St. John's National Park Commission for breaking the park's rule banning any amplified music after 10:00 p.m. What a bummer.

On the same expedition Alan Crowder broke his heel after slipping down a narrow stairway and had to be rushed to a local hospital by water ambulance. The same day, Denny was taken to Caneel Bay for treatment of a severe case of sunstroke while Geoff Emerick electrocuted his foot in a control room mishap. Jimmy McCulloch suddenly went deaf in one ear, while Record Plant advisor Jack Crymes developed a painful throat infection. To top things off one of the crew even lost his false teeth overboard. So much for a weekend in paradise.

Despite the traumas and distractions, Wings did manage to get down to work. Mark Vigars, at the time an assistant engineer with EMI, recalls the band's daily routine:

> By Monday, May 2, 1977, serious recording began and a pattern emerged of three- or four-hour sessions in the morning, the same from late afternoon to evening, interspersed with yet more swimming, water skiing and fantastic meals on *Samala*, prepared by no less than the captain, Tony Garton, a sound seaman but also a superb chef. On the morning of the 5th, Paul recorded a track playing acoustic guitar on the stern deck looking out over a sun-splashed sea. A dolphin surfaced to enjoy the super sound and splashed around the boat for some time.

London Town turned out to be quite a fine album. Even Denny was pleased, given as he was the chance to include two solo compositions. "I thought that was a really good record," Laine recalls. "At the time I was going through this thing of not being able to see my children as much as I would have liked, so artistically I was preoccupied by those kind of themes." His "Children Children" was, according to Jo Jo, originally titled "Laine and Heidi" but at the last moment the title was nixed by Paul as "too sentimental." The other, thematically related, Laine track, was "Deliver Your Children."

Like *Band on the Run*, *London Town* was more a joint effort by Paul and Denny than the collective effort of Wings. Linda's creative input was minimal, while Joe English and Jimmy McCulloch acted essentially as session men. Among the tunes worked on in earnest by McCartney and Laine were the title track itself, "Morse Moose and the Grey Goose," "Famous Groupies," and the ethereal "Don't Let It Bring You Down."

Following Wings' extended day in the sun, the band moved on to AIR Studios in London where they continued working through the first half of December. In January of 1978 they returned to Abbey Road, polishing off the last few bits of the album by January 23.

Now that *London Town* was safely in the can, the group lay back for a bit to plot their next move. Everyone, that is, except

Jimmy McCulloch who had left the band on September 8 of the preceding year after a row with his Beatle boss on the farm in Scotland.

For all his music business millions, Paul McCartney seemed somehow compelled to feign poverty by living in the most modest digs possible. Of course, having the luxury of his money to fall back on made the humble life that much easier. If he wanted to go and stay on his muddy, rat-infested farm for a while, no sweat; he could always beat a hasty retreat back to the sanitary sanctity of St. John's Wood if things became just a bit too spartan. Not so, however, for the rest of Wings. Although each had at least his own apartment down south, only Denny really had a proper home. And financially, despite McCartney's pretense at running the band democratically, the Grand Canyon gulf between his paycheck and theirs was almost embarrassing. Although as old hippies, the boys in the band could in a way appreciate their leader's need to isolate himself from the prying eyes of the world, being cloistered at the ass end of the earth wasn't always easy. "The place they expected us to stay in was more like a barn than anything resembling a house," recalls Jo Jo. "The walls, floors, everything, was all cement. I remember Jimmy used to call it 'the bunker.' There was no carpeting, only a couple of old chairs and some ragged pee-stained mattresses." Apparently, the "Cottage," where the roadies lived, was no better, with walls so bare that, one night, after a dozen or so strong hash-filled spliffs the downtrodden road crew rebelled by drawing a television set on the wall and then gathering around, pretending to watch it.

Meanwhile the band's shanty was devoid of hot water; any washing-up or serious cooking had to be done either at the roadies' or in an adjacent outhouse. Jo Jo Laine:

> I thought to myself, "I bet Paul and Linda are living in luxury over the hill." But their place was actually smaller than the one we were living in. All they had to their advantage was a television set. They didn't live much better except that they had hot water. I guess when some people have so much money it's like

a sickness — they have to try and prove they didn't do it all strictly for the cash. I mean, their children would have odd socks on, for Christ's sake. And I know for a fact that many of the dresses Stella had worn were the same little frocks I saw Mary in. I remember there was that one famous red-and-white-checkered dress. I'm sure there's been loads of pictures taken of both the girls in that. I must say, however, the kids were always reasonably happy, or at least appeared to be.

While the rest of the band were older and took a lot of the day-to-day inequities in stride, Jimmy McCulloch was never quite so charitable. The first major falling-out between McCartney and the five-foot-nothing guitar player occurred during Wings Over America, backstage at the Boston Garden on May 22, 1976. According to the Laines and other credible sources, the two got into an argument over McCulloch not wanting to go back out on stage for a second encore. Jo Jo explains: "Something pissed him off. I think maybe the sound went wrong. It certainly wasn't because the crowd wasn't responsive. Anyway, he just said, 'No. I'm not going out.' He and Paul were both swearing like crazy and then before you know it, Paul had him on the ground and just whacked him one in the face. I'm fairly sure he ended up going out there after that."

The final straw, however, came as a result of Jimmy protesting the decidedly un-showbiz way McCartney elected to treat his superstar cohorts. "We were staying in a pretty run-down cottage," says Denny, "but again, it wasn't that bloody bad. It's just that Jimmy and the roadies got drunk one night and wrecked the place even more than it was." Being a true country mama, Linda prized her homegrown chicken eggs, which she and Paul took great care to collect each morning at the crack of dawn. On the day in question, Jimmy, in a drunken huff, decided to redecorate the cottage's shabby kitchen by slamming a couple of dozen of Linda's finest against the dank, dirty walls. "Linda started to cry and was apparently really upset," Jo Jo remembers. "So Paul went to try and calm him down but then freaked out himself when he saw the terrible mess."

"You apologize to Linda!" McCartney shouted at the pissed-up little Scot, "or get off the farm."

"Fuck you, you bastard. I'm getting off your fuckin' shit-hole farm. I've had enough of both you lot." At that point, says Jo Jo, Paul had the pathetically plastered muso securely by the throat, loosening his grip only after McCulloch made a definite move towards the door.

McCartney certainly didn't enjoy these horrific little scenes, and was basically only reacting to Jimmy's tantrums. McCulloch, it seemed, often brought out the worst in people. "We were always putting Jimmy in his place," Denny recalls. "I would shout at him to grow up, literally. Once he'd sobered up though he was quiet as a mouse. I guided Jimmy through lots of things, you know. I even got him out of jail for drinking and driving. We were with Frank Zappa once and he fell over the table, face down on the floor. I mean we've all done it, don't get me wrong. We've all had our moments, but Jimmy seemed to have more moments than anyone else."

Determined not to allow the often overbearing McCartney to have the final word, after Paul and the others had cleared off to the other side of the farm, Jimmy walked calmly to his guitar case and pulled out a small nickel-plated, pearl-handled revolver he kept secretly hidden in one of the soft side-pockets. "Just let the cunt fuck with me again," proclaimed McCulloch to the same four walls that had oppressed him so during his unhappy term on the farm. "Let's see them laugh this one off."

Sitting alone in the deserted, cold stone hovel, Jimmy propped himself up against one of the picnic tables in the so-called dining area and meticulously began cleaning and then recleaning his illegally purchased .22 caliber handgun, all the while downing great gulps of scotch. He had his mind on only one thing: revenge. "I'll get my own back on the bastard," he ranted, getting up only occasionally to pace back and forth across the cement floor. A little past eleven, McCulloch took one last long swig from the bottle, smashed it against the wall, and rose, shoving the gun into his coat pocket. Switching off the light, he made his way out into the dark starry night, stumbling in the direction of the McCartneys' one-story bungalow.

About halfway there the hopelessly stoned guitarist tripped over his own feet, making just enough noise to alert the McCartneys' several dogs of the presence of an intruder. Rushing close by, the animals whimpered for a second at the sight of the diminutive McCulloch, but silently turned away as he quietly called them all by name. Taking a moment to gather himself, he rose soundlessly and continued his deadly stroll right up to the McCartneys' partially opened bedroom window. Peering into the darkened room, he saw the former teenage heart throb and his Shetlandish wife sleeping soundly, cuddled together in a comfortable tangle. His heart pounding so loudly he was afraid it might wake them, he carefully reached into his pocket, slowly drawing out the fully loaded weapon. Pausing not for a moment, McCulloch pointed the gun at McCartney's face, later telling Jo Jo he had planned to shoot the sleeping Beatle through the eye, and then do the same to Linda. His arm outstretched through the window, within a few seconds his hand began to shake, at first almost imperceptibly, and then fully, violently, until even holding onto the tiny revolver seemed impossible. Summoning up the courage to make good on his mental threat, Jimmy began slowly pulling back the trigger, measuring its progress by the tiniest fractions. Watching the shiny hammer tediously pulling itself back, gathering up the momentum to launch the explosive charge that would free him once and for all from the oppressive McCartneys, McCulloch suddenly changed his mind at the last micro-second and caught it with his thumb.

Panicking, he turned and ran furiously towards the narrow winding creek that cut through McCartney's farm on its way to a swollen pond at the bottom of a nearby gully. There, without really thinking about it, he put the gun into his mouth, intent that the terrible night should not end without bloodshed. Just then he was distracted by the harpooning lights of

Denny and Jo Jo's van, stretching across the night sky. Dropping the gun, he felt suddenly drained beyond words. There was no point in carrying on, he thought to himself. Why bother? He was already dead.

We were worried about that Jap business, though, the family. We were very concerned here in Liverpool. When one of your own is incarcerated in a Japanese prison cell, you worry, you know? We've only seen the war films . . . They may be little, but they've got bloody big swords.

— Mike McCartney, 1984—

8

Standing Alone
Nine Days in a Japanese Prison

On September 12, 1977, Paul McCartney was finally granted his secret wish for a son when James Louis McCartney was delivered by caesarian section at a London nursing home, weighing in at six pounds, one ounce. Eight days later, the proud parents released an "official" photograph of this, the first male issue from rock's royal family. "I'm over the moon!" Paul told the evening papers. "When I knew the baby was a boy I really flipped. I was waiting outside the door while he was being born. He has fair hair and looks like Linda. She's still a bit tired, but otherwise smashing. I don't know how she does it."

Bearing in mind Jimmy McCulloch's maniacal bid to wipe out the peacefully snoozing McCartneys only some four days prior to the auspicious birth, little James was lucky to be around at all. After McCulloch's split with the band he soon sank into a debilitating routine of late nights and over-the-top drinking and drugs in London's fast lane. With the money he earned from the Wings tunes "Medicine Jar" and "Wino Junko," he set himself up in a swank Maida Vale flat done up by the same design team that provided the interior for MPL's offices in Soho.

At the time of McCulloch's departure from Wings, the media, never having had a clue as to the real reason behind the split, ran a few lukewarm stories indicating that Jimmy merely wanted to branch out musically, having outgrown Wings' featherweight sound. Even McCulloch's own carefully worded rhetoric belied the lunatic intensity of what had happened back on the farm:

> With Wings I was virtually an employed musician, working mainly in the studio. With the birth of the McCartneys' son I realized it would be some time before we ever toured again. And that's the side of a musician's life I like best. I left amicably. I don't think anyone was too upset about the parting. We had some very good times together. Though Linda doesn't know much about music, she's really a nice chick. And I certainly learned a lot over the past two years.

Initially, Jimmy attempted to make a home for himself as one-fifth of the newly re-formed Small Faces. Business, however, was disappointing and he left after only a short time. Thereafter, he sought to form his own band called the Dukes. Latter-day Wings drummer Steve Holly remembers that the guitarist called him late in 1979 to ask if Holly might come up to Wales and do a bit of recording. "Sure," said Steve, and he waited for McCulloch to ring back with the particulars. The call never came. Two days later he read in the papers that Jimmy had been found dead.

A day or two after Jimmy failed to show for a rehearsal at London's Dingwall Club, his elder brother and road manager, Jack, decided to investigate. Arriving at the flat, he knocked loudly. After a few minutes, he decided his brother was out and turned to leave when he noticed a peculiar odor coming from under the securely locked door. Concerned that there might be a smoldering fire inside, he threw himself against the large mahogany door, never for a moment suspecting the horror awaiting him inside. "Jimmy's gonna be bloody pissed I broke the lock," he thought, as the door jamb splintered slightly under the weight of his shoulder. A moment later, McCulloch discovered his brother's body, leaning back in an easy chair with a burned-out joint still resting between his fingers. Jimmy McCulloch, one of rock 'n' roll's brightest shooting stars, was dead. "I don't know how my brother died," Jack was later quoted as saying. "I am deeply upset."

An inquest held in November recorded an open verdict, which left room for definite suspicions of foul play. "There are certainly some odd circumstances and because of this I think an open verdict is the proper one," Deputy Coroner Dr. Paul Knapman told reporters. While the autopsy uncovered traces of morphine, cannabis, and alcohol in the musician's blood, none of the offending substances (other than the single spliff) was anywhere to be found in the flat. In addition, a security chain across the door had been broken by someone other than Jack McCulloch. "I'm sure somebody was in that apartment when my brother died," he later commented, "and I'd like to find out who it was." To date nothing further has ever been revealed about the tragic incident, but speculation within the industry has always hinted that the pint-sized head banger was eliminated by someone with a colossal grudge. "It just doesn't tally up," Jo Jo Laine mused during interview sessions for this book. "Jimmy was an experienced drug user, not at all the sort to accidentally O.D. As far as I'm concerned, it was definitely either murder or suicide. Still, you have to ask yourself, how many people kill themselves with other people in the room?"

Despite McCulloch's fame as a former member of Wings, the British papers all but ignored his passing. The October 3, 1979, edition of the *Daily Express* did, however, carry the following:

STARS' TRIBUTE TO GUITAR MAN JIMMY

Stars from around the world sent wreaths for yesterday's cremation of Wings guitarist Jimmy McCulloch. Jimmy, 24, was found dead a week ago at his flat in London. An inquest has been adjourned. His brother Jackie said yesterday: "He had nearly 100 messages. It has made it a bit easier for us." Among those who sent tributes were Paul McCartney, Kenney Jones of The Who, and a top U.S. group, The Beach Boys.

In the Wings camp, meanwhile, McCulloch's passing was pretty much taken in stride. No one from the exclusive clan even bothered to turn up for the funeral with the exception of Rose Martin and Jo Jo, who blustered and cried all the way through the grim proceedings. "Maggie Bell was there," says Jo Jo, "as well as all the band [Stone the Crows]. About fifty Wings fans were there too, though they never talked to anyone. Nobody really screamed; everyone was very solemn. I brought along some lovely flowers. Denny wouldn't go with me. He was very cold about it, saying, 'Well, he's dead now, so that's it. We're all going to die sometime.' For some reason Denny always thought I had an affair with Jimmy."

Late in 1989 Denny himself recalled the day of McCulloch's cremation:

> I was going. I was all dressed up and ready, but I was doing something for *Wings Over America* — overdubs, I think it was . . . Anyway, to be honest, I was of two minds about it. I was pissed off with Jimmy over lots of things and I'd kind of fallen out with him . . . I know it sounds funny to say, but when somebody dies you can still be angry with them. In the end, I didn't attend because I was told to go to the studio and carry on with what I was doing. Besides, I didn't want to upset Paul.

McCartney's only official recognition of McCulloch's death was a slim notice in Wings' official fan club publication, *Club Sandwich*:

JIMMY McCULLOCH
His Music Lives On

Wings and MPL were shocked and very sad at the news that ex-Wings guitarist Jimmy McCulloch was found dead last month. I'm sure you will agree that Jimmy's unique style and flair contributed greatly to many favourite Wings tracks both in concert and on record. Any of you who saw Wings touring in 1975/6 will probably never forget the sensitive but powerful guitar riffs from Jimmy — a real talent who will be sadly missed. Our very sincere condolences to his family, especially Jack and Bella.

On the very next page, however, a huge banner headline boldly proclaimed: "IT'S PARTY TIME AGAIN," the accompanying copy going on to chronicle some half-baked MPL function reserved for London's well-connected elite. In McCartney-land any expression of grief lasting longer than your average joint was still strictly a no-no.

Eleven years later Paul had this to say about his fallen comrade:

> Jimmy McCulloch was an erratic personality to put it nicely. He was a terrific guy, great little player, lovely bloke. Been brought up in Glasgow, so he was a boozer *par excellence*. Jimmy wanted it all and he wanted it now . . . You'd want to get your kip and he'd be in the next hotel room blasting music. He'd come in off the piss at four in the morning and put his stereo on as he was so out of it. If anything, from the perspective now, it's lucky we ever held a band together.

Joe English elected to leave the band around the same time as McCulloch. Reportedly also a bit strung out on a number of forbidden fruits, he was desperate to get back to the comparatively sane and pastoral American South. According to inside sources, Joe's wife, Dayle, was also fed up with the scene in England and had returned to the U.S. some months earlier, leaving English to rack up huge transatlantic phone and airlines bills through his repeated efforts to visit with his family.

Filling the gap left by McCulloch and English were two of the most talented alumni to pass through Wings' revolving door: lead guitarist Laurence Juber and drummer Steve Holly. Coming in as they did at the tail end of things, they were free of any pent-up hostility or prejudice and so had no difficulty in getting down to the business at hand.

Juber, born November 12, 1952, in London, had always

aspired to be a musician. Picking up the guitar at eleven, he took a few primary lessons but then taught himself by listening to the recordings of his early heroes — Hank Marvin, Chuck Berry, Andres Segovia, and Eric Clapton. His first real gig was playing with an eight-piece jazz/rock band called Gramophone.

Moving on to serious study at Goldsmith's College and later the University of London, Juber eventually joined the National Youth Jazz Orchestra where he became fluent in many musical styles. Graduating with a Bachelor of Music in 1975, he went on to play with, among others, Cleo Laine, Shirley Bassey, John Williams, and Jimmy Rafferty. "My ambition," says Laurence, "was to be a studio guitar player because that was the top of the line. But I had this dream: 'Wouldn't it be wonderful to work with Paul or play with the Beatles.' It was a typical kid's dream, except I got it realized, which was quite amazing." His eventual association with Wings came about as a result of playing back-up for Denny Laine on the BBC's "David Essex Show" during a solo rendition of "Go Now." Impressed with what he heard, Laine told McCartney about the bright young player. A few days later Juber got a call from MPL, inquiring whether he'd be interested in meeting up with the band for a little jam: "I went along without really knowing what to expect, and as it turned out, we played nothing more than rock 'n' roll tunes like 'Johnny B. Goode' and things like that. I thought to myself, 'Is this an audition?' and then I was offered the gig the same day. So obviously I was what they were looking for. We started working a couple of weeks later."

Steve Holly first banged a drum at the age of five. His father, the leader of a popular swing band, actively encouraged his musical interest as did his mum, a one-time singer. Born in Isleworth, Middlesex, on August 24, 1953, Steve always knew he wanted to be a drummer, salting away his school savings certificates for a trap set from the time he was eight. The first record he ever played on was called "Look at Me Now" for Mungo Jerry star, Paul King, in 1970. One of Holly's first bands was the innovative G.T. Moore and the Reggae Guitars who toured the college canteen circuit for a brief while in the early seventies. Later on he played with Elton John and Kiki Dee. Then in March 1978 he started sitting in with Wings, invited by his longtime friend and drinking buddy Denny. He soon developed a casual, "just mates" relationship with the band, never seriously considering the prospect of joining up full time. Traveling down to London with Laine for his formal audition the same afternoon as Juber, Holly had to cool his heels for nearly three hours, waiting for Paul and Linda to breeze in from the country. "We played a good long time," he recalls, "and then Paul just said, 'Fine. That's a good group. Sounds great. Let's go.' He made his decision right there and then, which is the fastest I've ever personally been through any audition. Denny and I went out afterwards and had a few drinks to celebrate. A few days later, we all flew to America where Laurence and I met with Lee Eastman to discuss the terms of our contract and salary."

On June 29, 1978, work began on *Back to the Egg*, Wings' last all-new studio LP. Laying down the basic tracks at Paul's Spirit of Ranachan Studios on the farm in Scotland, Juber and Holly proved a valuable addition to the band, mixing well with the gilt-edge poppiness of Denny, Linda, and Paul. One evening, after work, as Steve and Linda were relaxing with a cup of coffee by a nearby stream, she gazed contentedly over the rugged Scottish countryside and said, "You know, I could stay here forever. This is all I really need. The band, the biz, all the rest of it, doesn't really mean that much to me. All I truly want is to be here with my family."

Working like devils on the new album, Wings pulled out all the stops in the hope that *Egg* might just be the vehicle to toughen up their cream-puff image with a legion of rock watchers weaned on so-called heavyweight acts such as Pink Floyd and the Who. It was not to be. Fragmented, over-ambitious, and sporadic, *Back to the Egg* shipped out to record stores like gangbusters and limped back a couple of months later, a fifty-cent record in a two-dollar sleeve, its failure heralding the end for the band.

That's not to say that the album didn't contain some interesting material. The sultry R&B-inspired "Arrow Through Me" rings with convincing emotion, an immaculate piece of soulful pop. The bumpy "Old Siam Sir," on the other hand, showcases McCartney the storyteller, summoning up yet another appealing collection of surreal characters and mindscapes. (Steve and Denny almost came to blows over this one. Holly still insists that one of the main riffs in the tune was "borrowed" by Denny from him for the arrangement prior to Paul's coming in for the session that day, although at the time the argument was settled in Laine's favor.)

Perhaps the album's two most celebrated tracks arise from the superstar collective known as "Rockestra" which laid down a heavy-handed anthem of the same name, as well as the flashy "So Glad to See You Here." Among the elite participants were John Bonham, Kenney Jones, and Steve Holly (drums); Paul McCartney, Ronnie Lane, John Paul Jones, and Bruce Thomas (bass guitar); Linda McCartney, Tony Ashton, Gary Brooker, Paul McCartney, and John Paul Jones (piano and keyboard); Howie Casey, Tony Dorsey, Thaddeus Richard, and Steve Howard (horns); Morris Pert, Speedy Acquaye, Tony Carr, and Ray Cooper (percussion); Pete Townshend, Dave Gilmour, Hank Marvin, Laurence Juber, and Denny Laine (guitars).

Gathering at Abbey Road on October 3, 1978, at 11:30 a.m. for the session, things started cooking as Paul led the band through a final rehearsal and then five full takes of the "Rockestra Theme." After a brief time-out for refreshments and a quick playback, work then began on the second tune. Technically, of course, the big-time event was a nightmare. All together sixty microphones were utilized along with two mixing consoles as well as both a twenty-four and a sixteen-track recorder synched together by a new system known as Tape Lock. In addition, the event was filmed by director Barry Chattington who brought along his own full sound crew as well as the manpower necessary to operate the five Panavision 35-mm cameras enlisted for the cause. Jo Jo Laine remembers it as one of the wildest afternoons ever in Wings' nine-year history, with several pop stars literally queuing up to get into the studio's tiny restroom for a line of coke.

In the end, even such heroic measures could not rescue *Back to the Egg*. Although it briefly made the top ten in both Britain and America the album was almost universally panned and sold poorly. "We went to great lengths to try and make that record a hit," says Steve. "After working in Scotland we recorded at Lympne Castle in Kent, later moving on to Replica Studios (in the basement of MPL). It was only during the final mixing stage at Abbey Road that it began to dawn on any of us that there might be some problems. The maddening thing is that, taken apart track by track, it seems to work. It's just when you hear it all together you begin to lose focus."

One of the saddest occasions of 1978 for almost everyone around the McCartney camp was the unexpected death of Who drummer Keith Moon, an old flame of Jo Jo's, a drinking buddy of Denny's, and an all-around good mate of Paul and Linda's. The tragedy was brought even closer to the McCartneys by the fact that only hours before Moon's passing he had been partying with them at London's Peppermint Park restaurant in celebration of the film premiere of *The Buddy Holly Story*.

British television personality David Frost remembers that Keith (who was seated throughout the evening at the same table as the McCartneys) was "really delightful company," even announcing his engagement to longtime girlfriend, Annette Walter-Lax. Gently sipping red wine, the thirty-one-year-old Moon seemed to be on a definite upward swing. Having drastically cut down on the drugs and booze that had inspired much of the out-of-control behavior of his youth, Keith seemed to be settling in nicely with his approaching middle age.

About forty-five minutes into the star-studded private screening Moon excused himself to the McCartneys, saying he was feeling a little ill and that he'd ring them in a few days. Returning home with his fiancee to his flat in Curzon Place,

Moon popped in a video of *The Abominable Dr. Phibes* and had a bite to eat. He then washed down a couple of strong sedatives and fell asleep.

Early the next morning Keith nudged Annette, saying that he was hungry and fancied a steak. Still a bit shattered herself, the stunning Swede somehow pulled herself together and prepared what was to be Moon's final meal. After eating he took several more tablets, telling his girlfriend he wanted to get a bit more sleep before attending a band meeting later in the day. Lax also went back to bed. When she awoke that afternoon, around two o'clock, she discovered Moon's body. Altogether the flamboyant drummer had taken a staggering thirty-two tablets over the previous twenty-four hours. Like all grief within McCartney's sphere Paul ignored it. "He's a moral coward of the highest order," charges Jo Jo. "I wouldn't be surprised if he's working on a plan to hire someone else to die for him."

According to Denny, a lot of Paul's troubles might have been avoided if he had been able to relax a bit more with his great success and not feel such a need for total control.

> His worst trait is getting involved with people and then not giving them enough scope to flourish creatively . . . He was too much of the boss in the office as well, but it was his money, and he certainly deserved to have a say. A lot of people who worked for us could have made life a little easier if they had been allowed more input. He wasn't the greatest person in the world moneywise either, as everyone seems to think. If it hadn't been for his father-in-law he obviously wouldn't have done so well. Paul is frightened of going out into the world and mingling with ordinary people. If he did, I think he might be a happier person. As a result of his fame and fortune he's become a bit of a recluse as well. If he wasn't, I think he'd be a more approachable, less sensitive person.

One of the happier events of 1979 for Wings was the successful release of McCartney's first decidedly disco single, "Goodnight Tonight." Issued in Britain on March 23, 1979, the catchy tune did well, reaching as high as number six at home and five in the U.S. What made the project special, however, had less to do with the music than the spectacular, spare-no-expense video filmed to promote the release on Tuesday, April 3, at the meticulously preserved Hammersmith Palais Ballroom in London. Produced by MPL and directed by Keef McMillan of Keef & Co., the concept was deceptively simple. The band dressed up in elegant, 1920s-style evening clothes as Paul did his best Rudy Vallee, crooning into an imposing antique radio mike. Judiciously intercut were segments with the group as they were in the present, getting down hard in all the right places. Seldom shown in its entirety anywhere, it is a clever clip that represents McCartney at his eclectic best and expresses the dialectic at the heart of his music — Cole Porter cloaked in the guise of a good time rock 'n' roller.

The record's acoustic B side, incidentally, "Daytime Nightime Suffering" remains Paul and Linda's all-time favorite solo track. Ironically, it is one of the artist's most obscure, virtually never-played, tunes. Steve Holly remembers that a few days prior to recording the song Wings was hard at work trying to come up with the new single at Replica Studios, when Paul generously announced that if any of them could invent a strong enough tune over the weekend, the band would put it out, thus almost assuring its composer a small fortune in writer's royalties for years to come. Holly spent the entire weekend banging away at his old piano, trying to come up with something, as did Denny, Laurence, and reportedly even Linda. By Monday morning though, Paul had recovered from his momentary lapse of reason and offhandedly told them the deal was off as he himself had whipped up "the one." "Daytime Nightime Suffering" was recorded then and there. Steve remembers bashing away on his drums from the sanctity of the kitchen while the Leslie cabinet for the organ was placed in the elevator shaft of the sub-basement in order to take advantage of the apparently naturally superlative acoustics therein.

By late autumn Wings was ready to once again hit the road. On November 16, their cutesy holiday single, "Wonderful

Christmastime," backed by the virtually unlistenable stinker, "Rudolf the Red Nosed Reggae," was released, complete with a jingle bells video on which the band members appeared as four rocking Father Christmases (along with one blonde Mrs. Father Christmas). A week later at Liverpool's Royal Court Theatre, the band began a nineteen-date tour with a free concert for the entire student body and staff of McCartney's *alma mater*, the Liverpool Institute, and a group of severely handicapped young children. They played the next three nights at the popular Liverpool venue, which McCartney, to his credit, had specifically chosen in the hope of helping to save from the wrecker's ball.

Included among the familiar Wings hits performed on the tour were such reasonably oddball numbers as Linda's "Cook of the House" and "Again & Again & Again" from Denny, as well as the rock classic "Twenty Flight Rock," and the *McCartney* album throw-away, "Hot as Sun," from McCartney himself.

Steve Holly recalls stopping by Paul and Linda's dressing room one evening during the tour to remark how great he thought the show had gone over that night. "It sucked," replied McCartney, suddenly as depressed as the drummer had ever seen him.

"Paul hated the whole tour," Steve commented to this author during a 1990 interview. "He felt all the performances were bad. About a quarter of the way along I got the distinct feeling that he was just going through the motions. Musically, there were definite problems with some of the band as well. I think Paul felt he was rather 'dragging the dresser,' to quote an old northern phrase." Holly also speculated that after the triple platinum success of Wings Over America, McCartney might have been expecting a bit too much. "Maybe we just went out too soon. I know Paul was under pressure not to lose any of his new fans." Holly also stresses that originally the tour was rehearsed and staged for smaller venues, while they ended up playing four nights at places such as Wembley Arena. "We were like tiny little ants up there on that great stage," he remarked laughingly. "A lot of it was very tough going, but it wasn't all terrible, looking back. There were actually quite a few fine magic moments as well."

According to both Holly and Juber one such evening was Wings' on-target final performance of the tour at the Apollo Theatre in Glasgow. Tramping back on stage for an encore at the end of their set, Paul banged out the first familiar chords of "Mull of Kintyre," by this time almost a second Scottish national anthem. At precisely the right moment, recalls Holly, the entire Campbeltown Pipe Band came marching out from under the stage, instantly bringing the already blissful audience to its feet. "It was just one of those incredible emotional highpoints you can never really adequately describe," Steve recalls. "I, for one, remember becoming a little teary-eyed myself, and I'm not even a Scot. I think that, more than anything, begins to explain the absolute magic of the man."

Denny Laine's recollections of the song are less magical. Originally issued as what's known as a "double A side" to Wings' "Girls' School" single, "Mull of Kintyre" was the type of laid-back, sentimental fare one would hardly have expected to become any sort of super hit. When it did, however, its phenomenal success only served to damage the relationship between Paul and Denny. Laine remembers:

> We sat outside with a bottle of whiskey one afternoon in the hills of Kintyre and wrote the song. Paul had written the chorus. But we wrote the rest of it together, and most of the lyrics were mine. He made tens of thousands from the song. It was number one for sixteen weeks and sold millions of copies. But I personally got very little out of it. I was on wage when we wrote it, not a percentage of the sales. Of course I was promised more, but it never came. When I asked Paul for a special deal on the tune his answer was virtually: "Look, I'm Paul McCartney, and anyone who writes with me is privileged." I told him that it was time he trusted me and that I wasn't going to take him to the cleaners. All I wanted was to see in writing what was selling and how much my part would be. If the records didn't sell, I didn't want the money. I was being treated as little more than a highly paid session man and felt the insult keenly.

Supporting Denny's contention that he was denied the better part of his rightful proceeds for the song is yet another MPL memo to the singer retained by this author, stating clearly that Laine was paid a mere $20,000 for both his work on the solo *Holly Days* album and his contributions to "Mull of Kintyre." Even the Campbeltown Pipe Band felt shafted, complaining bitterly until old Macca (a longtime McCartney nickname) begrudgingly dispatched each of the lads the somewhat meager sum of £200 as a belated peace gesture.

And what did Paul McCartney take home for his afternoon's work, drinking with Laine in the shadow of the Kintyre peninsula? Released in Great Britain on November 11, 1977, "Mull of Kintyre" sold over a million copies within a month. Oddly enough, comedic actor Dan Ackroyd happened to be the lucky purchaser of the millionth pressing, finding a slip inside the sleeve notifying him he was to be presented a special Christmas hamper by Denny Laine as well as a gold disc from EMI. Not until Band Aid's "Do They Know It's Christmas?" in 1984 was the song's staggering sales record overtaken.

Responding to Laine's oft-repeated charges concerning McCartney's widely rumored frugality, Paul had this to say in a 1989 issue of *Rolling Stone*: "Okay, let's take Denny. I've got receipts in the office for a million pounds paid to him. Now, you tell me a guy in any group who got that for the period we were together. Now, okay, if you think I sound mean after that, I've got to disagree with you. I mean, these people like Denny say, 'He didn't pay us enough.' Well, what I think is, 'Yeah, well, I did.' I know exactly what I paid him. It's a million. And that was worth more than a million is worth now."

Laine, however (these days living comfortably in upper-crust Windsor with his new lady, Helen Grant, pretty daughter of Led Zeppelin mentor Peter Grant), takes some consolation from the fact that while he has been successfully "sprung" from his crusty internment in Scotland, his old mate McCartney still walks the windswept moors quite alone with all his big bucks. "The Mull," says Laine, "was where this old lighthouse was, and for my money was actually the worst shithole in the world one could ever visit. You wouldn't go there with your worst mother-in-law. All it had was this lighthouse, a cemetery, and this shitty hotel where the band sometimes stayed. I wouldn't wish the place on my worst enemy." Apparently, he doesn't need to.

By the late seventies there was generally a lot of loose talk floating about concerning a potential Beatles reunion. Responding to a non-stop barrage of questions from the prying media, the ex-Beatles often made matters worse by cryptically saying "no" in such a way as to imply the opposite. Of course, the Beatles themselves had not made any final decisions concerning the idea. Paul, especially, would have loved to see his old band back together, if only for one rousing night of music tucked away in the privacy of an obscure rehearsal hall or studio somewhere. John, too, was basically game, often confiding to friends that he found the possibility intriguing. Only Dragon Lady Ono, it seems, felt compelled to keep the famous feud going. "She was threatened," says a close family member of Lennon's.

> It was obvious she had no place within the private men's smoking club that was the Beatles, and deeply resented it. To my mind, she only ever convinced two people into believing she had any sort of artistic talent: John and herself. The other three Beatles weren't so easily duped, and would never have tolerated her interference. As a result, she kept up a near-constant tirade against the idea right up until poor John's death.

The odious Ms Ono's meddling aside, a lot of people gradually became convinced that if the cause were important enough, or the money right, a reunion just might happen. One such person was Kurt Waldheim (long before his nagging Nazi troubles), at the time Secretary General of the United Nations, who drafted a conciliatory letter to each of the four, asking them to consider getting back together for a concert in aid of the starving masses in war-torn Kampuchea.

McCartney's response was equally diplomatic: he nixed the Beatle idea, offering instead a benefit concert by Wings. So it was that on the evenings of December 26, 27, 28, and 29, 1979, London's Hammersmith Odeon became the site of the Concerts for the People of Kampuchea, McCartney's most overtly humanitarian venture to date. Expanded to include other acts such as the Pretenders, Elvis Costello and the Attractions, Queen, Robert Plant, Rockpile, the Who, the Clash, the Specials, Matumbi, Ian Dury and the Blockheads, and, of course, Wings, the series of manic shows ended with the ever-evolving Rockestra performing three numbers, "Lucille," "Let It Be," and the spectacular "Rockestra Theme."

Viewed by many in the international music media as a kind of bargain-basement Bangladesh, the cause, admirable though it was, didn't ignite with the public in the way future shows such as Live Aid and the 1986 Amnesty International Conspiracy of Hope tour did. Even as it was happening, says Steve Holly, the mood backstage was more cynical than serious with the performers literally unable to move for the hordes of pointless VIP guests and inevitable hip hangers-on. "It was one hell of a long day let me tell you," remembers the drummer. "Once you were there in the morning there was no getting out all night." With the artists trapped in their dressing rooms for twelve hours, Holly says, Wings co-commander Denny was "almost comatose" from the non-stop drinking that had been going on all day. "I remember I was trying to wake myself up with hot coffee before we went on," he adds. "Our performance too, unfortunately, left quite a lot to be desired because of all the partying. Not Paul though. He may have had a scotch and Coke or something, but never to the point of being drunk. He was always the consummate professional."

There was, amid the chaos, an amusing incident involving Pete Townshend, which took place on the final evening. Holly spins the yarn: "It was during Pete's over-the-top cognac-drinking days. Just before we all went on, the poor wardrobe girl popped into Townshend's dressing room to make sure everything was okay, when, to her horror, she discovered he wasn't wearing the gold lamé top hat and tux jacket Paul had made up for everybody, and what's more, had no intention of doing so." "I'm not wearing that fucking shit," the often surly guitarist roared. Townshend was certain Paul was having him on, and never actually expected that anyone else intended to appear on stage in the admittedly tacky-looking outfit. Of course, everyone else was wearing the get-up, which left Pete paranoid about being out of step with his colleagues.

By January 12, 1980, Paul McCartney felt on top of the world. Springing back mentally after the relative failure of both *Back to the Egg* and Wings' recent British tour, he was literally ready to take on the world, flying to New York aboard the Concorde on his way to a long-awaited engagement in Japan. After a brief, four-day visit with Linda's dad, and an aborted attempt to see John Lennon, the McCartneys checked out of their luxury suite at the Stanhope Hotel and boarded a TWA jumbo jet bound for Tokyo's Narita International Airport.

On the flight over, all McCartney could think about was how the maneuvering, vindictive Yoko had snubbed his efforts to make contact with his former partner. All he wanted to do, after all, was hang out for a couple of hours and blow a few joints for old times sake. But Yoko was adamant.

"This isn't really a very good time," she cooed condescendingly into the telephone, seemingly thrilled to be the bearer of such inhospitable tidings. "We're very busy these days, you know. Maybe next time, okay?"

McCartney, no slouch himself when it came to repartee, instantly retaliated by boasting that while in Ono's homeland they planned to set up shop in the posh presidential suite of the astronomically expensive Okura Hotel, John and Yoko's permanent home away from home while in Japan. This he knew would pique the always insanely jealous Yoko no end. "Right. Ta ra, then, luv," he said, hanging up the receiver. "Cow," he muttered, just loud enough for Linda to register a sly smile.

Landing in Tokyo fourteen exhausting hours later, Paul and Linda emerged from the aircraft all smiles, thrilled to finally be playing Japan. Inside the customs hall they were greeted by a hail of flashing cameras all zeroed in on the great man lugging little James in one arm as he mugged predictably for the delighted media. As they stepped up to the long, low inspection counter, a customs officer indicated to the couple to open their carry-on luggage. "Sure," replied McCartney, revealing no perceivable emotion. Linda, on the other hand, suddenly seemed panicky, her eyes darting back and forth between the small rumpled bag and her unsuspecting husband.

Sitting inside what has been widely reported as Linda's overnight case was a small, fist-sized plastic bag obviously containing several ounces of primo pot.

"When the fellow pulled it out of the suitcase," said Paul, "he looked more embarrassed than me. I think he just wanted to put it back in and forget the whole thing, you know, but there it was." A senior officer pushed his way out from behind and immediately ordered the pop star detained. He then radioed for the Narcotics Control Bureau to come and get their man.

"It's all a mistake," Paul said feebly as the Tokyo vice boys slapped on the cuffs and began leading him away. "A serious mistake." To the morally conservative Japanese, McCartney's transgression was indeed a serious matter.

Within minutes, news of the bust rocketed through the entire city, prompting well-known music commentator Ichiro Fukuda to lash out angrily at the dope-loving Beatle. "For a man like McCartney to violate the law means he has no respect for Japan." Eleven hours later the tour was publicly canceled as McCartney was formally interrogated at the Drug Supervisory Center and then transferred to the Metropolitan Jail. Steve Holly recalls the confusion:

> We were already checked through customs, sitting on the bus waiting for Paul and Linda. Then someone told us there was a "minor" complication and that we were to go on to the hotel. It was, like, an eighteen-hour flight, so I checked into my room and went to sleep. At about seven-thirty that evening Linda rang. I remember her laughing nervously and saying, "Hey,

Paul's been busted." Now, because she was laughing, I assumed she was just kidding around, so I said, "Yeah, yeah, great, Linda, I'll see you for dinner," and hung up. Anyway, I went down to the bar, and there was a great many MPL staff sitting around with forlorn expressions, a lot of plainclothes police everywhere, and fans going crazy, so I suddenly realized that she must have been telling the truth. We hung out for a couple of days, hoping they would find some way around it, but after three or four shows had been missed, I realized there was no way they were ever going to save the tour.

Paul, meanwhile, was sitting in a four-by-eight cell, suddenly not quite so happy about being in Japan after all. Around midnight he was allowed his first visitor, British vice-consul Doland Warren-Knott, who, Paul assumed, had come to arrange for his release. "I'm afraid it's not going to be quite that easy, Mr. McCartney," the obviously uneasy bureaucrat began. "There's a fellow in here who had a lot less than you, and they've had him locked up for three months already. It could be eight years, you know."

"My first night was the worst," Paul recalls. "I couldn't sleep. I was frightened about the possibility of not seeing my family for years. They fed me seaweed and onion soup for breakfast, and twice a day I was handcuffed and taken to some official who kept asking questions."

McCartney quickly fell into the jailhouse routine with the seasoned aplomb of an old con. Woken at dawn, he was made to silently roll up his rush sleeping mat and sit cross-legged on the floor awaiting inspection. His jailer, Yasuji Ariga, later commented that the superstar inmate was "very polite and has made a good impression on the guards." Allowed initially neither writing implements nor a guitar, Paul passed his days singing with the other prisoners, exercising, or just plain marking time.

On the sixth day Linda was finally allowed in to visit her husband who had to bite his tongue after she nervously told him that he might be in as long as three months. "I didn't tell her it could be eight years," he later commented. One of the

most unpleasant aspects of his incarceration was being
whisked off every morning for an intensive interrogation. "I've
already told you I'm guilty," McCartney would protest, over
and over again to the stone-faced guards. "What else do you
want me to say?"

> At first I thought it was barbaric that they put handcuffs on me
> twice a day when I went to see the investigators. There seemed
> to be a different lot each time. I made a confession on the night
> I was arrested and apologized for breaking Japanese law but
> they still wanted to know everything. I had to go through my
> whole life story, school, father's name, income, even my medal
> from the Queen.

World reaction to all this was generally one of bemused indifference, with most people betting that for all Paul's massive
money and clout no one would really dare keep him too long
simply for possession of pot. A glaring exception, however,
was twenty-nine-year-old Kenneth Lambert who, a few days
into the affair, turned up at a Miami International Airport res-
ervation counter and demanded a ticket to fly to Japan to
"free Paul." He had no money and refused to leave after several polite requests to do so. A row ensued with Lambert
suddenly pulling a realistic-looking toy gun from his jacket
and waving it around wildly over his head. Police officers
called to the scene instinctively took aim and fired. The poor,
sick young man was dead before he even hit the floor.

Meanwhile, back in his cell, Paul was itching for a proper
bath. Washing with the water from his latrine was understandably getting him down. After a week of this he humbly
asked if he might be allowed a bath, a proposition passed
along through the incredible Japanese bureaucracy as if they
had been faced with a constitutional amendment. Eventually
one of the guards came rushing into his cell, asking, "Would
you take alone or with other inmates?" McCartney thought for
a moment. "With the others." After yet more high-level dis-
cussions the request was finally granted and Paul was led into
the communal bath house, much to the amazement of the

other prisoners. "Alright, lads," said McCartney, instantly "on" as he always is whenever confronted by a crowd. "How are ya?"

Stripped naked virtually in front of everyone (by now even the off-duty guards had gathered to observe the spectacle), McCartney made the most of the situation. Eyes twinkling, head cocked, and arms outstretched, the incurable showman belted out the first few lines of "Mull of Kintyre" and, instantaneously, everyone joined in. As the Japanese voices rose in pitch even the assembled fans keeping vigil outside the jail began to sing. From the little boy who started singing and playing guitar in the bathtub so many years ago back in Liverpool, McCartney had now come full circle, prompting Jo Jo Laine to quip, "Paul has played some of the classiest restrooms on the planet."

On his eighth day of captivity Linda was permitted in for a second visit, this time bringing along her brother, John Eastman. By now the whole situation had eased just a bit, enabling McCartney to receive a few "treats" from his family, including a highly prized cheese sandwich, some fresh fruit, a change of clothes, some blankets, and, wonder of wonders, several science-fiction paperbacks.

Made to turn in for the evening at 8:00 p.m., Paul whiled away the excruciatingly long evenings by tapping on the wall of his cell in an effort to communicate with his fellow colleagues in crime. "Life in jail isn't so bad," he commented, once safely back home in England. "The prison wasn't the rat-infested hole I thought it was going to be. For the first few days I was worrying all the time. For eight days I didn't see any daylight at all . . . I shared a bath with a man who was in for murder, and all because I didn't think."

Hanging about in their plush prison at the Okura Hotel, the other band members were more than a little annoyed at Paul for allowing the McCartneys' irrational love of marijuana to jeopardize the hard-won Japanese tour, not to mention their share of the profits. Although everyone was still paid their agreed-upon weekly salaries, Steve Holly says his accountants later advised him that canceling the sold-out performances personally cost him tens of thousands in lost revenues. It was Denny Laine, however, who was the most angry and hurt, still going on about it all to this day: "I felt I was entitled to an explanation," complained Laine some five years later, "but I never got one."

> I would have probably made £50,000 on the tour, not to mention the number of times we could have gone back. We were breaking new ground. Wings needed those Japanese shows to continue. I had the sense to know that without new markets the band wouldn't survive . . . [Paul] felt very sorry for himself when he came out of prison, but he didn't seem to understand he'd upset a lot of people. He and Linda knew the importance of not going to Japan carrying dope. The penalties there are heavier than anywhere else in the world, and we had already been refused entry because of drug offenses five years earlier. I think he and Linda thought that if they managed to smuggle some grass through it would be one up for them. The McCartneys are the couple who have everything, and that can get boring. What they crave now is excitement. I personally think they did it for the thrill. Of course, Paul bought himself out of jail the way he buys himself out of everything. And as long as he's got the money in his pocket he always will.

Jetting out of Japan after it seemed obvious the tour was off, Laine went directly to Paris where he joined Jo Jo on a glitzy promotional tour for her first record, the disco-inspired "Dancin' Man" at the annual MIDEM festival. While there, Laine penned a tune called "Japanese Tears" about a brokenhearted Japanese Wings fan who had patiently waited years to see her idols, only to have her hopes dashed at the very last moment by Paul's sudden and very inauspicious arrest. Recorded at Shepperton's Rock City Studios in 1980, the tune was eventually released as part of an album of the same title recorded with old friend Steve Holly and wife Jo Jo.

As for the rest of the band, Laurence Juber left for Los Angeles — he remembers that various members of the MPL hierarchy suggested that it actually might be better for Paul's situation if he and Steve Holly left Japan. He says that only recently did he ever give a second thought to the money he lost, concerned at the time only that Wings should continue as a fully working band:

> The way I understood it, Paul was made to personally sign an affidavit, stating that he no longer smoked dope, as a condition of receiving his visa. When they caught him red-handed, however, the Japanese government felt betrayed and went out of their way to try and make an example out of him. I mean, I know of several well-known artists who were also subsequently busted for drugs in Japan who walked with only a small fine. With Paul, though, they figured they'd "lost face" and so were compelled to strike back. Besides, he was, after all, a Beatle, and therefore potentially wielded such incredible influence that they were concerned he might be setting a bad example for the youth of Japan.

Holly, too, jumped ship after a few days, taking full advantage of the open-ended, unlimited-stops, one-year, first-class ticket given to all the band back in London. Flying first to Australia, meeting up with then-wife Sharon, he subsequently visited New Zealand (where he sought out and found his long-estranged dad), Hawaii, and then Canada, before returning home to England.

As for Paul, on the ninth day of his incarceration, the powers that be decided he "had been punished enough" and so cut a deal with McCartney's legal staff to release the rock star. Ever the politician, Paul insisted on touring the facility and personally greeting each of the prisoners, which he did, passing his hand through the small iron doors of their cells just to say "Sayonara."

Carted off to the airport, handcuffed, directly from jail, McCartney, surrounded by twelve burly guards, was reunited with Linda and the kids amidst dozens of frenzied photographers and reporters clawing at the waylaid Beatle and his family. "Japanese fans are so great," Paul exclaimed to those present in the special VIP departures lounge. "I want to come back again if I'm allowed." As a sweet gesture to his many disappointed fans and as a wry parting shot at his captors, McCartney then called for an acoustic guitar and did a quick tune for the TV cameras before being hustled off aboard a Japanese Airlines jet bound for London via Anchorage, Alaska, and Amsterdam. Once safely in the air, a repentant McCartney confessed to the assembled media that had joined him on the trek: "I have been a fool. What I did was incredibly dumb. I had just come from the States and still had the American attitude that marijuana isn't really too bad. I didn't appreciate how strict the Japanese are about it. I was really scared, thinking I might be in prison for so long. I've made up my mind. I've been smoking marijuana for more than eleven years now, but I'm never going to touch the stuff again." Sure, Paul.

All things considered, the whole stupid mess cost McCartney big. Japanese promoter Seijiro Udo reportedly incurred a loss in excess of £200,000 due to the canceled tour and subsequently threatened to file suit. "Paul has betrayed me," he told a Tokyo reporter. In the end, McCartney was obliged to repay Udo. In addition, the former Beatle's gaggle of high-priced London lawyers cost him another £100,000 in fees, not to mention their daily living expenses while in Japan, which have been pegged at as high as £10,000 per day.

Still, what's money to a man like Paul McCartney? He may moan about having to lay it out just like the next person, but when the chips are really down he would never hesitate to ante up to buy himself out of a jam. As he proclaimed in a mock rap recently while being interviewed on America's MTV, "Well, my name is Paul, and I got more money than y'all." Forget the tongue-in-cheek posturing for a moment, the guy wasn't kidding.

Looking at Wings' checkered past, one tends to forget just how close Paul and Denny Laine once were. As if he were some dead or ousted Communist party bureaucrat, these days Laine is never mentioned, nor does his image appear in the various *Club Sandwich* retrospectives on the band. It is as though he never existed. For Denny, Japan was definitely the last straw. Ever after, when the two men met, there was a new and poisonous edge, that, while unacknowledged in words, was nevertheless palpable. "It was very, very hard for me to forgive him for that," Laine quietly confided to me once during a late-night heart-to-heart. "I realize now it was definitely the beginning of the end."

Soon after his safe return to Britain, McCartney began preliminary work on an autobiographical treatise of his ordeal in Tokyo, titled *Japanese Jailbird*. Completed in late 1984, the manuscript for the twenty-thousand word book was rumored to have been deposited in a London bank vault in an effort to keep the highly personal contents "top secret." "The mercifully short time I spent in jail cured a block I've experienced as a writer ever since schooldays," he has commented. "It's always been my ambition to write a book . . . I wanted to write it down, just for the record, 'cause I know how I am: I forget things very easily, haven't got the world's greatest memory. Anyway, I wrote it all down. I sort of thought, 'God, this is like writing an essay for school. I can't do it, I'm frightened of the piece of paper.' But because I knew I had to write it down to remember the incident, I forced myself to write it."

In the end, Paul broke down and had one copy of the work specially printed and bound for himself. To this day not even those closest to McCartney have any idea what insights the book contains, only deepening the already dark mystery surrounding the whole uneasy affair. "We've all heard a lot of very wicked tales about who and what were actually behind the bust," says a close friend. "The only thing anyone knows for sure, however, is that so far the real story has yet to be told."

By far the most insidious suggestion bandied about back then hinted that Yoko Ono herself was the culprit. Furious that Paul and Linda were about to "invade" her homeland the always jealous and competitive Mrs. Lennon, it was alleged, saw to it that the couple's arrival in Japan was made less than pleasant. A year after the incident, Yoko's former psychic,

John Green, told a mutual friend: "She claimed to have made the arrangements by telephone, telling undisclosed Japanese authorities that McCartney had a low opinion of the Japanese." Another Lennon/Ono insider, Sam Green, backed up the naughty charge later, commenting, "She had a cousin over there who runs customs. One call from Yoko and Paul was finished." Whether the spiteful Ono tipped off the authorities that the McCartneys were indeed "holding," or worse, conspired to have the stuff planted on them after their arrival, is purely speculative. Ironically, never aware of his good wife's alleged impropriety, even John Lennon was quoted as saying that the bust had to be "somebody's cheap trick," a reality the naturally protective and compassionate Lennon found intolerable. "No way do I believe Paul was carrying," he told John Green at the time. "He was set up and that's the long and unfortunate short of it . . . Just how hard do you think it is for a customs official to lay his hands on some grass? Not that hard," he continued. "He probably had it all along under the counter or something and the minute the Beatle steps up, it's presto. Headlines." As with many things in Paul McCartney's extraordinary life, the true facts of his trial by fire in Japan may well stay hidden forever between the folds of his illusive public persona.

The first musical release following Paul's Japanese sojourn was the somewhat aimless and uneven *McCartney II.* As a strictly solo effort (well, okay, Linda as usual "oohed" and "aahed" a bit), it was competent enough, but somehow never really managed to leave the ground. Issued in Britain on May 16, 1980, it aroused sufficient public curiosity as the great one's first post-prison release to propel it all the way to number one. In the U.S., apparently, folks weren't quite as inquisitive, sending the admittedly beautifully packaged gatefold album to a very respectable number three. Despite the trio of minor-league hits — "Coming Up," "Waterfalls," and "Temporary Secretary," the rest of the LP sank like a stone, offering up such unpolished musical doodles as the abysmal "Front Parlour," "Nobody Knows," "Summer's Day Song,"

"Darkroom," and "On the Way." Two additional compositions worthy of mention are "One of These Days" and the potentially offensive "Frozen Jap." The first, a straightforward plea for spiritual understanding, takes its inspiration from McCartney's longtime relationship with Hare Krishna devotee Mahasya Dasa whom he first met in London during the mid-seventies: "[The song] happened when a Krishna bloke came round to see me. He was a nice fellow, very gentle. After he left, I went to the studio and the vibe carried through a bit. I started writing something a bit more gentle. The tune seemed right as a very simple thing, and it basically just says: 'One of these days I'll do what I've been meaning to do the rest of my life.' I think it's something a lot of people can identify with." "Frozen Jap," meanwhile, is a spunky little instrumental best remembered for its ironic title more than any great worth as a piece of music. "What happened, originally," recalls McCartney, "was I was playing around on the synths, experimenting, and I suddenly got something which sounded very oriental."

> When the track was finished I tried to think of a suitable title and things came to mind like the ice-capped Mount Fuji, or a snow scene from the Orient. But all the names sounded clumsy. Then I thought of "Frozen Jap," *frozen* being the ice bit from the snow scene idea, and *Jap* meaning oriental. Anyway, the title just stuck. It was done in the summer of 1979, but I'm sure people will think it was recorded after the incident in Japan. We decided to change the title to "Frozen Japanese" for the album over there since we didn't particularly want to offend anyone.

After the roller coaster breakup of the Beatles in 1970 the relationship between John Lennon and Paul McCartney was never really the same. They talked, they met, they still occasionally hung out together, but something had definitely changed. For years people have tried to pin at least part of the blame on their wives, but to do so ignores the complicated, tightly wound interactions between the two. When they fought, they fought like brothers, still maintaining a delicate web of care and concern amid the bitter recriminations of two screaming egos caught in a tug of war for pre-eminence. "With John coming out against me like that, it was no good for me at all," says McCartney.

> He really slagged me off, a lot of which he really didn't mean! Yoko tells me lots of it was just John, he just wanted to put me down. It's all jokes, taking the piss out of me. That was John. But I think it has probably made my image worse than it is. As I say, the truth is he didn't really think that was all my character. He knew there were all sorts of other bits. . . . I sometimes do catch myself and think, "God, do I look like that?" or, "Is that how I come over to people." And the funny thing is, I'm just struggling, trying to get through okay, trying to do well. Basically, I've never had a different philosophy than that. You get up in the morning and do your gig.

Despite Paul's "just kiddin'" philosophy, however, for a while there things did get pretty rough. After all the childish name calling back and forth on record and in the media, one of the most personally hurtful episodes to Paul was the time he and Linda turned up unannounced to see John in New York, only to be royally snubbed by his old pal. "Do you mind calling before you come round from now on," Lennon chided. "This isn't Liverpool, ya' know. In New York, you don't just drop in on people like this without warning."

"Sorry, man," McCartney intoned meekly. "We only wanted to stop by for a bit and say hello."

"Yeah, I know, man, but see, I've had a fuckin' long day today with Sean. It's bloody hard work lookin' after a kid this age, you know."

"Well, so . . . we'll shove off then. See ya."

The two lifelong friends would never see each other again.

The great abiding problem, of course, still had to do with money. With much of the Beatle millions still largely up for grabs the stakes were high. So high in fact that Lennon went berserk at the mere mention of anything remotely concerned with the group's longstanding financial maelstrom. "At the very end we suddenly realized that all we had to do was not mention Apple if we phoned each other," says Paul. "We could talk about the kids, talk about his cats, talk about writing songs; the one paramount thing was not to mention Apple . . . I remember once he said to me, 'Do they play me against you like they play you against me?' Because there were always people in the background pitting us against each other. And I said 'Yeah, they do. They sure do!'"

For all the apparently unrepented rancor that passed between them over the years, when John was killed Paul was reportedly devastated: "He was always a very warm guy, John. His bluff was all on the surface. He used to take his glasses down — those granny glasses — take 'em down and say, 'It's only me.' They were like a wall, you know? A shield. Those are the moments I treasure."

As for McCartney's 1980s relationships with the other Beatles, Paul remained really close only to Ringo, contributing the tunes "Private Property" and "Attention" to Starr's disastrous 1981 album, *Stop and Smell the Roses*. Thereafter Ringo worked on several MPL-produced projects including *The Cooler,* an eleven-minute video fantasy starring Paul, Linda, Ringo, and his glamorous wife, Barbara Bach. Intended as a vehicle to help promote Ringo's *Roses* LP, the clever, well-conceived short was seldom run on television, or anywhere else for that matter. In a surprise move, however, *The Cooler* was subsequently picked as the official British entry in the short film category at the 1982 Cannes Film Festival.

Of course the most well-known (and panned) collaboration between the two old Beatles was McCartney's unwatchable 1984 flick, *Give My Regards to Broad Street.* Stuck in an uneventful, embarrassing non-script, Starr did his best to help realize Paul's pointless vision of a kind of one-man *Hard Day's Night*, but drew the line when it came to joining his pal in re-recording some well-loved Beatles classics. "I've done them once already, remember?" he wryly observed.

George Harrison's feelings towards Paul McCartney, of course, are a vastly different matter. For all his Hare Krishna/ Peace & Love veneer, Harrison is often quite a cynical, cold, unforgiving character. McCartney had, after all, consistently given old George quite a hard time during the Beatle years, something the dour lead guitarist was not about to forgive or forget. "I think the only barrier between us is our astrological signs," observed Harrison in February of 1988. "Some of the time we get on pretty well, but I find I really don't have anything in common with him . . . I think if you have a relationship with somebody else, you have to be able to trust each other, and to do that you have to be able to talk to each other straight. The thing with Paul is one minute he says one thing and he's really charming and the next minute, you know, he's all uptight."

Denny Laine has commented publicly that, as least as far as he's concerned, McCartney has always felt somewhat superior to Harrison, even going so far as barging in on the baby Beatle's recording sessions and throwing his musical weight around. "The last time I was at George's [in 1981, to work with the surviving Beatles on "All Those Years Ago"] Paul and Linda were also there. Paul has a way of coming in and taking over and making everything a bit edgy. Everyone was uptight. When he and Linda left, the atmosphere suddenly changed and became more relaxed. Everybody seemed to physically go 'phew' and start enjoying themselves. Paul thinks he's easygoing but there is a mistrust about him. He doesn't trust people and it shows."

When at last the curtain finally came down on Wings, Paul McCartney felt both vindicated and relieved: vindicated because he had indeed proved to the world that there was life after the Beatles, and relieved that he could now truly strike out on his own without a prop band.

Denny and Jo Jo, however, see it all differently. From their perspective, Paul and Linda had their wicked way with the group and then callously moved on. In our conversations Jo Jo stated on several occasions that she felt Paul was directly responsible for "ninety percent" of Denny's disillusionment with being part of a band. According to her, Laine left Wings after what he felt was a treacherous breach of trust on the part of the McCartneys.

Few people know it, but *Tug of War* was originally intended as a Wings project rather than a McCartney solo album. Heading out for recording sessions at AIR Studios in Montserrat with Paul and Linda, Denny discovered through a loud-mouthed bartender that Jo Jo had only just been there with her young lover, EMI singer John Townley, a few days previously:

> Alan Crowder called me up and told me off, saying, "You naughty girl, your husband's devastated. He didn't even know you were with this guy let alone in Montserrat with him." So I said, "I don't care what any of you think: I wasn't allowed to go to Montserrat with you guys, and I got invited by John who right now I'm very much in love with. It's got nothing to do with you, Paul, Linda or anybody." Because I had that attitude, Denny realized our marriage was finished. I'd always denied any affairs I'd had, but this one I was open about. He blamed it on Paul and Linda. If they had only let me go with them I guess I might not have turned to somebody else.

All in all, Denny seems to confirm his former wife's theory that the McCartneys were intent on breaking up not only the band, but while they were at it, his marriage as well:

> I left Wings for two reasons: one was for money and the other was my missus. . . . They made her feel like an outsider. . . . Paul used to have his little digs at her. "I can't work with people around," he was always saying when she was there. . . . Linda is a lot older than Jo Jo and that was one of the main problems. Jo is also the extrovert Linda wishes she could be. That's where the jealousy lies. . . . Paul certainly tried to get rid of her and probably thought he was doing me a favor. Paul and Linda's refusal to allow Jo Jo on Montserrat went a long way towards destroying my marriage . . . I thought by leaving Wings Jo and I could spend more time together and work out our problems, but unfortunately it didn't happen that way.

On that fateful day, when Denny at last decided he'd had enough of what he saw as the McCartneys' perpetual psychological bullying he mentally closed up shop, stubbornly throwing away not only his future with Wings but also any last thread of friendship he had left with Paul. "He was supposed to be in the studio that afternoon," recalls Jo.

> First Trevor called and then John Hammel, but Denny said, "I'm not speaking to anybody." Eventually, of course, Paul called, asking, "Is Denny there?" So I said, "Well, he doesn't want to speak to anyone right now, Paul." I was real nice when I said it, but I secretly loved being able to tell Paul McCartney to sod off. "He's asked me to give you and everyone else the message because he finally realizes now that he's lost his family and all the damage that's been done. As far as I'm concerned he can go to the studio with my blessings, but he doesn't care to."
>
> "You fucking cow, Jo Jo!" he screamed into the receiver. "No. Sorry, luv," I said calmly, just before gently hanging up the phone. "This time it's your fault." That was the last time Denny and Paul ever had any real contact right up until 1990, ten years later.

The information the media received from the two men's PR people, however, didn't accurately reflect the true sequence of events. Brian Adams, Denny's manager at the time, told the press, "There is no row. But Denny likes to tour and Paul has decided Wings will not make any tour plans for the future." Paul's office, meanwhile, tersely denied an accusation leveled in London's *New Standard* that McCartney had halted any public appearances after receiving several death threats following John's murder. "There is no truth whatsoever to that report," said an unnamed spokesperson. "There were no plans to tour long before John Lennon died. Paul is doing other things, that's all." He also went on to say that Laine's departure didn't necessarily mean Wings would cease to exist. "Wings are Paul and Linda and whoever they wish to record with."

Asked in 1982 about the Laine/McCartney rift and the unhappy end of the band, Paul had this to say: "I hate the pressure of a group . . . Anyway, I got bored with the whole idea and I thought, 'Christ! I'm coming up to forty now. I don't really have to stay in a group. There's no rule anywhere that says I have to do it that way.' At the time Denny and I were writing together. He was going to stay on, but we had a bit of a falling out. It was nothing madly serious, but he did decide to go his own way, saying that he wanted to tour. He hasn't been on tour since."

Steve and Laurence, meanwhile, each got a phone call from Paul, saying that George Martin felt it might work out better if *Tug of War* wasn't completed as a group project. While Juber admits to having been bitterly disappointed, Holly was quite simply angry. Using Martin as an excuse, after all, was a pretty shoddy trick, even worse that McCartney actually lowered the boom himself. Around MPL the news that Paul had once and for all clipped his Wings met with only vague disinterest. (It's not as if the staff had a lot to do. Once, when they were all fed up at simply hanging out week after week and threatened to quit, McCartney quelled the unrest, not by ensuring they were a little more actively involved, but by doubling their salaries!) Other than a three-picture tribute to Denny in *Club Sandwich*, number 24, there wasn't really much word on the whys and wherefores of the group's final dissolution, save for one microscopic note in fan club executive Sue Cavanau's regular monthly column. "As I'm sure most of you know," she began, with all the warmth and sincerity of a flight attendant reciting her airline's safety procedures, "Denny, Steve and Laurence have left Wings to concentrate on their solo careers, and I know you'll join me in wishing them well."

Upon its release *Tug of War* did extremely well. *Rolling Stone*, long impatient with Paul's often uneven post-Beatles work, titled it "McCartney's Gem" and went on to give it their coveted five-star rating. Thought by many to be McCartney's *Imagine*, *Tug of War* neatly strung together the talents of not only George Martin and Denny Laine, but also drummers Steve Gadd and Ringo Starr, guitarist Eric Stewart, bassman Stanley Clarke, as well as guest artists Stevie Wonder and country gentleman Carl Perkins.

Among the twelve tunes on the album several stand out as being miles ahead of anything McCartney ever did with Wings, giving added credence to Paul's decision to go it alone. Among them, perhaps the majestic "Wanderlust" most clearly defines the composer's lifelong lyrical quest for freedom and release from the loneliness and isolation so often a biting theme of his work. Ostensibly concerning a falling-out between McCartney and the captain of his and Linda's private yacht during sessions for *London Town*, the song is one of unguarded surrender to the powers of heaven and earth.

"The Pound Is Sinking" mocks the stuffy indifference of the unreasonably rich to the needs of a world turned upside down by the uncertain finances of an economy based on the extravagant exploitation of the planet's dwindling resources. McCartney explains what was behind its creation:

> For me, it's just the funny thing about the pundits day-to-day giving us an update so that the people who've got money can gauge it all, like the weather. There is something which amuses me about this constant update of something that is always going to be different. You are never going to be able to put your finger on it, but it just might help knowing if there is snow on the M6. But generally they make more mistakes than correct predictions, it seems to me. You know, the pound is sinking, panic, and then the pound's all right now, and everyone gets back into it. It's a funny idea; I like the idea of all the ants doing what the lead ant tells them, you know, the oracle.

"Dress Me Up as a Robber" suggests the futility of our endless role-playing and the irrelevance of extraneous labels and outward designations. Recording with Steve Gadd who laid down a Latinesque beat, McCartney wails away in a convincing falsetto. "You can do whatever you like to me," says Paul, explaining the song's origin. "You can tell me what you like, but I'll still be what I am; you can dress me up as a sailor, a robber, a soldier, but it really won't matter, I will still be me. If you dress me up as a soldier I will be the little fellow who goes off to Northern Ireland and writes a book about the horrors of it all; I won't be a soldier really . . . "

Perhaps the most poignant song on the album is "Here To-day," Paul McCartney's tender, if somewhat sentimental, ballad to his lost friend, John Lennon. "Songwriting is like psychiatry," McCartney reflects. "You sit down and dredge up something that's deep inside and bring it out front. And I just had to be real and say, 'John, I love you.' I think being able to say things like that in songs can keep you sane."

Despite its seriousness of purpose, *Tug of War* thankfully lets down its guard at least some of the time, allowing the humor of its creator to shine through. On "Get It," Paul's funky down-home duet with childhood hero Carl Perkins, the listener gets the distinct impression that here at least is a Paul at ease with himself and his role as the bubbly boyish Beatle who made good. "We had a really great time," Perkins recalls. "We ate together. It was a very, very close thing. I had to tell him and Linda, 'I'm so proud to see you people in touch with reality, to see your little boy lay his head on your knee when we're singing, to know that you can do and be whatever you want and act any way, but you haven't thrown love away.' And they haven't. I mean they've got it. Paul made the statement to me 'We tried the jet set, Carl, and it's plastic. We love people.' And they do. He acts exactly like you would want the fella next door to act."

Among the rockers on the album only "Take It Away" and the loosely autobiographical "Ballroom Dancing" deserve high marks. As for longtime McCartney favorite Stevie Wonder (Paul and Linda had "WE LOVE YOU STEVIE" emblazoned in braille across the bottom back cover of *Red Rose Speedway*), his soulful duet with Paul on "Ebony and Ivory" though a tad smaltzy, turned out an effective, tuneful plea for racial harmony at a time when musical expressions of such brotherly sentiments were few and far between.

Eloquent, sincere, and humble, *Tug of War* (including the LP's spiritually oriented title track) mirrors an inner depth and clarity of vision decidedly lacking in many of Paul's other solo recordings.

Over the years quite a lot has been made of Paul's seemingly bottomless wealth. Based on his ever-blossoming Beatle millions, McCartney's fortunes have been enhanced and solidified through a lifetime of well-thought-out, carefully executed investments. Heralded in the November 1983 issue of *People* as "The Richest Man in Show Business," McCartney purposely keeps a low profile, preferring to think of himself as only reasonably well off as opposed to being the landed Beatle billionaire that he is today.

In a good year taking in more than, say, British Airways, McCartney can play country boy all he likes; the fact is that of all four Beatles he is by far the most wealthy and powerful. MPL is today the largest independent music publisher in the world holding the copyrights to a mind-boggling array of compositions, including such standards as "On Wisconsin," "Stormy Weather," "Autumn Leaves," "Sentimental Journey," "Ramblin' Wreck from Georgia Tech," "Chopsticks," "Bugle Call Rag," "Happy Birthday," "One for My Baby," "Ghostriders in the Sky," "The Theme from the Dinah Shore TV Show," "It's Tight Like That," "Sweetheart of Sigma Chi," and "Basin Street Blues," to name only a very few.

In addition, Paul and company control such mainstream musicals as *Mame*, *La Cage aux Folles*, *Peter Pan*, *A Chorus Line*, *Bye Bye Birdie*, *Annie*, *High Society*, *Grease*, *Hello Dolly*, and *Guys and Dolls*, not to mention his interests in the songwriting catalogs of composers Scott Joplin and Ira Gershwin. Thrown in for good measure McCartney also owns a good bit of former partner Denny Laine's publishing as well as the bulk of material written by Buddy Holly.

Paul and Linda also have a great eye and love for art, as reflected in their now multi-million-dollar collection of classic works by Magritte, Rauschenberg, Picasso, Eduardo Paolozzi, and longtime buddy, Willem de Kooning. According to George Harrison, the surreal Magrittes were an especially good deal; he claims that his former partner picked them up in the mid-sixties at bargain basement prices before they were "fashionable."

The McCartneys are also particularly fond of both Art Deco and Art Nouveau as evidenced by this author who once, while visiting old friend Su Gold at MPL, actually carried a large, standing antique stained glass screen into Paul's roomy third-floor office from the street below.

Swank offices notwithstanding, McCartney's home is a suprisingly humble abode. "We may have to build a third bedroom now because our youngest is a boy," Paul poor-mouthed to the press in 1981.

> But we have deliberately kept them in one room because I want a close family, just as I had when growing up in Liverpool. I don't want a mansion where I have to telephone from the east wing to make an appointment to see my kids in the west wing. Of course they are going to get a lot of money one day, but Linda and I are trying to make their growing up an ordinary one. We don't have a chauffeur; I drive the youngest kids to the local primary school. When people come and visit us in the country, they tend to drive past our cottage the first time because they are looking for a bigger house.

Although a great deal of the McCartneys' worldly success certainly stems from Paul's formidable talent as a composer and performer, many thanks are also due Linda's father, Lee, a fact that sometimes concerns the sensible, down-to-earth Mrs. McCartney. "It worries me 190 percent," she says. "I'd rather not do it that way, but that's the way we have always done it. I think [mixing] business and pleasure is poison. But what can you do?"

Following the release of *Wings' Greatest* in 1978, a none-too-clever compilation that didn't exactly set the record-buying world on its ear, McCartney's contract with Capitol Records expired, leaving him a free and very desirable agent. Hotly pursued by several top labels throughout the U.S., the former Beatle eventually signed on the dotted line with CBS for a purported $15 million plus a windfall of lucrative incentives.

To industry insiders it was clear CBS president Walter Yentnikoff wasn't so much buying a new artist as he was leasing a little prestige. Like Linda Eastman so many years earlier, Walt too had now bagged himself a Beatle, and it felt great! At Black Rock, the company's opulent American head-quarters, Paul's visit to press a little executive flesh was more akin to the Second Coming. "People were coming out of their offices just shaking," says a former top official. "To most of us there the opportunity to personally schmooze with a real live Beatle was why we got into the business in the first place. The ultimate rock and roll perk."

While personally gratifying to a precious few in the record company boardrooms of L.A. and New York, the signing of the new, Wingless Paul McCartney to CBS ultimately turned out to be an unqualified financial disaster. Receiving a record-high royalty of $1.80 per album (irrespective of any discounts), Paul must have surely been laughing all the way to the bank. According to one source, the eight-figure deal almost literally ruined the company, which only landed on its feet at the last minute thanks to the phenomenal success of Australia's answer to the Fab Four, Men at Work.

"I'm like Mr. Rich in the press these days," McCartney moaned to the media in 1984. "I'm supposed to be worth $500 million, but I'm not. It's a pity because young kids will tend to look at me as that, 'Mr. Rich.' It's a pity because your reputation walks ahead of you."

No matter what anyone says, however, if merely making money were Paul McCartney's prime motivation, he could have comfortably called it quits years ago. Though the numbers are by now out of sight, the principle for Paul is basically the same as it ever was. Looking at him now, one tends to see the former superstar Beatle in softer terms. Now undeniably middle aged, he likes a drink, loves his wife and children, watches the telly, and gets on with his job. Seeing him sit back, as I did, a few years ago in Linda's Covent Garden photo studio, with a glass of port in his hand and a couple of swirling kids tumbling around his feet, one couldn't help thinking that with a little less hair and a few more craggy lines on the brow it just might be old Jim McCartney himself, all those years ago, back in Allerton.

Paul's an amazing guy. He just smokes his joints and whistles his way through life.
                    —Harry Nilsson, 1984—

Sometimes I just have to remember that this isn't a record retail store I'm running: this is supposed to be some kind of art.
                    —Paul McCartney, 1979—

It's difficult being Mrs. Paul McCartney.
                    —Linda McCartney, 1989—

9

Musical Chairs

Failure and Hope in the Eighties

After Paul's 1980 arrest and imprisonment in Japan and his subsequent vow to never again touch his lips to another smoldering joint, the news out of Barbados on January 14, 1984, that the McCartneys were once again caught in possession of their favorite intoxicant understandably caused quite a stir. On holiday with children Stella and James, the couple were allegedly approached on the beach by a local dealer, inquiring if they might care to get down with a little bit of the old ganga.

Following the clandestine transaction, this dreadlocked Judas of the jungle immediately ran to the nearest police station and cashed in his chips, insisting that the famous Beatle was holding some "dynamite shit." The call then went out, summoning the isle's top cops for a Saturday afternoon pow-wow to decide how best to approach this potentially explosive situation. Hours later a full-scale raid was mounted, with several carloads of enthusiastic peace officers racing up the long, winding drive of McCartney's rented nineteenth-century villa. The moment Paul and Linda saw them coming, of course, they knew what was up. Teeth clenched in a stone-faced smile, McCartney threw open the large, teak double doors before the police even had a chance to knock.

"Come in," he said in a clipped, business-like timbre. "I suppose you'll want this, won't you?" Reaching deep into his pockets, the forlorn ex-Beatle matter-of-factly produced a solitary ten-gram bag of dope, and summarily dropped it into the outstretched palm of the head man, who noted that an inspection of the premises was in order.

After a rudimentary search an additional seven grams was uncovered in Linda's purse. Escorted to HQ in Bridgetown, Paul and Linda were questioned for a couple of hours, relieved of their passports, and then allowed to bail themselves out for £1400. All things considered, quite a pricey smoke.

Appearing in Holetown Magistrate's Court a couple of days later, the beleaguered pair were formally charged and without further ado solemnly pleaded guilty. Their counsel, high-powered local attorney David Simonds, assured the court that Mr. and Mrs. McCartney were definitely not "retailers" but only occasional users intent on securing the grass for their own personal consumption: "The male accused is of considerable international standing. He is a very talented and creative person. People who have this talent sometimes need inspiration. I'm instructed that Mr. McCartney and his wife obtained the vegetable matter from someone on Holetown Beach. They are certainly not pushers."

On the prosecution's side, Inspector Allan Long remarked that the McCartneys were setting a very poor example for the island's youth through their behavior. Keith Walker, the assistant police commissioner, commented: "The law is for everybody on the island — and that includes McCartney. We are treating this as a very serious case. I don't know if he'd be welcome here again."

Despite the inflammatory rhetoric, however, the judge

elected to extend to the naughty pair a mere slap on the wrists, fining them a total of just £70.

Thinking themselves out of the woods, the McCartney's packed up and boarded a flight home, breathing a sigh of relief as they landed at London's Heathrow Airport. Unfortunately, after a not totally unexpected search through their luggage, customs officers discovered yet more pot in a plastic film canister belonging to Linda. Due to the small amount of the offending substance found, however, she was not held but merely issued a ticket to appear at Uxbridge Court in West London on January 24.

Prior to leaving the airport an obviously angry Paul berated reporters, saying, "This substance is a whole lot less harmful than rum punch, whisky, nicotine and glue — all of which are perfectly legal. I'd like to see it decriminalized. I don't think that in the privacy of my own room I am doing any harm whatsoever. . . . Let's get this straight. I'm not interested in setting an example for anyone. I'm just being my own self in my own time."

Slowly making their way through the mob of reporters lying in wait for them outside the court on Linda's trial date, the McCartneys declined comment. Inside the packed courtroom, though, Linda's attorney, Edwin Glasgow, immediately shifted into high gear, attacking all those who would pre-judge the two famous dopeaholics: "The suggestion that Paul McCartney's wife ought to grow up and set an example is pretty puerile, ill-informed and a prejudiced judgement from people who have not met her. My client is a thoroughly decent lady who has done a great deal more for others than those who sneer at her now have ever done."

Eventually fined £75, Linda clung close to Paul as they once again fought their way through the offending paparazzi, pausing only long enough for her to comment: "It's much ado about nothing. It's a pity we have had to go through all this. It's horrible to feel like a criminal when you are not. They never seem to get the heroin pushers, the Mafia, and the murderers."

Although Paul McCartney has always been a little too self-conscious to ever attempt becoming a "serious" actor, he has nonetheless long been interested in working on film. There was of course his filmic dabbling in the sixties. And, if his numberless videos and three Beatle movies over the years count, he's also managed to rack up quite an impressive list of credits as well. Still, running around mugging to the camera, miming songs, hardly qualifies him to write and star in his own feature-length motion picture. "In this business," says a Hollywood insider, "what you can do is limited to only what you can afford to do. And with McCartney, that's just about anything."

Paul's idea to create a vehicle for himself in the pictures came out of the same kind of mundane circumstance from which he seems to draw so much of his creative inspiration; this time he was sitting in London's horrendous morning traffic. Working first with writer Tom Stoppard on a proposed anti-war film based on *Tug of War*, he began interviewing prospective directors for the project, finally settling on a young, relatively unknown director of television commercials, Peter Webb. Still reasonably wet behind the ears when it came to the movies, Webb was, for McCartney, the perfect choice: hungry enough to be the kind of accommodating yes-man Paul expected, and just smart enough never to tell the king when he had no clothes on.

Eventually, the admittedly tired anti-war theme was dropped in favor of a kind of pseudo-documentary featuring the now-Beatleless solo incarnation of Paul, entitled *Give My Regards to Broad Street*. "It's kind of a parody of me now," says Macca.

> When I was faced with making it, it was like, "Well, should we go into this kind of space blockbuster, ridiculous music on the moon thing? That's Spielberg, that's Lucas, that's those guys. They do it so well, there's no point tryin' to compete with them." The other thing was "National Lampoon," "Saturday Night Live," "Monty Python" . . . But I'll look second class to

any of them if I try and do their thing. So this was just more my thing. And it comes off a bit more English, a bit lighter on the comedy, 'cause I'm not any great, stunning comedian. Ringo's the funny one.

In all fairness the original premise of the film did have potential. A world-famous superstar rocker's master tapes go missing with an ex-con assistant the primary suspect. The remainder of the movie centers around the intensive search for said masters along with an array of million-dollar fantasy sequences thrown in for good measure. Put into such singularly dry terms, of course, it doesn't really sound all that exciting, but remember that *Raiders of the Lost Ark* was just a story about a guy trying to find an ancient relic. The problem was the producers (who were edged in later) allowing the inexperienced McCartney so much creative control. This penchant for always having to "do it all" has certainly brought the former Beatle a terrifically long way over the years, but has caused him a lifetime of grief as well. The other three Beatles certainly didn't appreciate it, nor, by and large, did the various configurations of Wings. As Denny Laine has said: "If only he could relax a bit, and let somebody else occasionally take the wheel . . ." Still, Paul is Paul and loved the world over for it. It's hard enough sometimes to remember that, despite his overwhelming accomplishments, McCartney is every bit as human, frail, and afraid as any one of us. Maybe even more so. It is, after all, his unique ability to successfully mirror so much of what we as his audience think and feel that has placed him squarely on top. "Anyway," Denny once reflected, regarding his ex-partner's stellar flop, "you can't hit the friggin' bull's-eye all the time, can ya?" True enough. But perhaps this dart missed the board entirely.

"The public will be the judge," McCartney proclaimed to reporters during his October 1984 cross-country promotional tour of America to help sell the film. And they were, staying away in record numbers, causing the $9-million fiasco to close literally everywhere within just two short weeks. Of course the critics too had a say in all this, despite McCartney's warbling about how only the "people's" opinion matters. The Sacramento *Bee* called it "slow freight, overloaded with blandness" and gave it a "B" for "boring." The Orange County *Register* (also a California paper) printed a bold headline, declaring "Don't Give Much Regard to Paul McCartney's Film," and went on to trash the movie piteously, commenting, that "the only good thing to say about the climax of *Broad Street* is it's safer than sleeping pills and cheaper than a lobotomy." The paper's film critic, Jim Washburn, was something less than kind, stating: "GMRTBS is touted as depicting 'a day in the mind of a pop star.' Let's hope not, because any mind as empty as the one behind *Broad Street* could be rented out as a racquetball court. . . . The problem seems to be Paul McCartney. The minute he appears up there on the screen, his mouth set in its permanent oval of mild surprise, it's as if a monstrous vacuum begins sucking up every minute of razzle-dazzle. He's so enervating nothing can help." Finally, the Tucson *Weekly* may have summed it up best in saying that " . . . all Paul needs is someone willing to criticize and add to his ideas, who he is willing to recognize. John Lennon played that role once, and the partnership was brilliant. It's not that McCartney isn't a genius — he is — or that he's run out of good ideas. But, left on his own, Paul McCartney just doesn't explore the potential of his material."

After its disastrous term in movie theaters *Broad Street* found a temporary home on various cable TV channels and was even molded into a commercially unsuccessful video game. For McCartney, making his very own motion picture was the culmination of a lifelong dream. In the cold light of day, however, it turned out the artist's dreams required just a little more editing than he perhaps cared to admit. "I'm too human for all this [criticism]," he explained to American TV critic Gene Siskel at the time. "I don't like sitting around with someone telling me they don't like my picture. I'm just a real little person inside this box."

Trying to come to terms with that "little person" in a meaningful way is another important (though almost never talked
about) feature of McCartney the man. Paul and Linda both
have a strong covenant with at least the concept of inner
truth and, while not overtly religious, cling to a kind of convoluted hippie philosophy that rules out nothing. Denny Laine
insists that Paul, especially, is quite the closet mystic, vora-
ciously plowing through book after book on reincarnation,
pyramids, karma and the like:

> We were all involved in that. Right back from the early Moody
> Blues days we were into the mysteries of life, not to the point
> where we would do anything more than have the odd seance
> though . . . I was frankly a little bit surprised that Paul was into
> it all as much as he was . . . He was always open minded, he . . .
> didn't slag things off without knowing more about them: he's
> an intellectual in that way . . . He came to me once with this
> book on the pyramids and I was amazed he knew as much as
> he did, but there again, he obviously spends a lot of time
> composing songs and looking for material to write about. From
> that day on I saw a different side to him; he'd shown me the
> depths he was capable of.

Ever since the Beatles' introspective Maharishi days, McCartney has been very much the silent supporter of many similar
spirit-centered pursuits. Located, as he is at MPL, just steps
away from the London Radha Krishna Temple and their top-
drawer vegetarian restaurant, Govinda's, the ex-Beatle has
become a kind of devotee from afar, often yelling out "Hare
Krishna" to the gentle saffron-robed yogis as they scoot
across Soho Square. On his birthday each year the local
Krishna kids generally drop off an inscribed cake at his office.
"It's just a neighborly, good-natured relationship," says senior devotee Dhananjaya Dasa. "Paul understands the philosophy of our movement and appreciates the teachings of our
spiritual master, Srila Prabphupada. Both he and Linda are
especially interested and knowledgeable on the doctrines of

vegetarianism, meditation, and what we call "ahimsa," or non-violence to all creatures — all tenets every aspiring devotee holds dear."

Musically, too, McCartney has made note of his interest in Krishnaism on several recordings both past and present, including a rare Beatle demo of the "Hare Krishna Mantra" done in 1969 as part of the group's marathon *Let It Be* sessions, as well as the masterful "Man Who Found God on the Moon" on the 1973 collaboration album, with brother Mike, entitled *McGear*. "Paul was going into the studio on the day of the session and had no idea what we were going to do," Mike told me in 1984.

> But I had these two or three stories I had to link together somehow. Mainly it was about this little Krishna girl who came into Island Sound while I was sitting there waiting for a taxi. Just an ordinary little girl in a tartan skirt and flowers in her hair. She said, "Do you want to know about Krishna?" So the doorman said, "No, no, get out of here." "Do you want to buy a book for Krishna? Do you want to buy a flower or something for Krishna?" He said, "Get on your way." He was going to kick her out, but I said, "It's all right." I might have bought a flower off her. As she was leaving, she turned around, looked at both of us, and very quietly, very innocently, said, "Hare Krishna," and walked out the bloody door. That's the way to get out aggression in this life: disarm with complete honesty.

Perhaps McCartney's most direct nod to his secret admiration for this playful, rain-cloud-colored incarnation of the great god Vishnu was the picture cover for his "This One" single culled from the 1989 *Flowers in the Dirt* album. Right there, in blazing Hindu blue, a blissfully smiling baby Krishna (known officially as "Gopal") is seen flying over a deeply calm ocean, riding a giant white swan. After McCartney had hundreds of billboard-sized posters of the eye-popping artwork plastered all over London, even the most die-hard Krishna haters were forced to take notice. Sad to say, the single was still only a hit in heaven.

Perhaps McCartney's most enduring connection with something beyond his own life's drama is through Mother Nature. For years now, just walking through the countryside on his own, or riding his favorite horse along the beach up in Scotland, has helped ground the singer spiritually. "Things mystical rule his life, I can tell you," says Laine. Once again, each time you think you've pegged him, McCartney eludes detection with yet another quick change of personality that leaves observers scratching their heads.

Paul's second post-Wings musical adventure (after *Tug of War*) was the flaccid and unfulfilling *Pipes of Peace* released in Britain on October 31, 1983. A haphazard collection of eleven painfully trite and uninteresting compositions, it couldn't be salvaged even by such superstar contributors as Ringo Starr, Andy McKay, Stanley Clarke, Steve Gadd, and the androgynous Michael Jackson. Both Laurence Juber and Steve Holly recall rehearsing much of the material included on the album during the final days of Wings, giving credence to the suggestion that the record was basically a throwaway mix of leftovers McCartney had lying around.

Masterfully produced by George Martin, perhaps the biggest break for the album came when Michael Jackson (then impossibly popular) rang up McCartney out of the blue and asked if they might consider working together. "He just said, 'I wanna make some hits,'" remembers Paul. "I said, 'Sounds good.' So he came over. We sat around upstairs on the top floor of our office in London and I just grabbed a guitar and "Say Say Say" came out of it. He helped with a lot of the words on that actually. It's not a very wordy song, but it was good fun working with him because he's enthusiastic. But again, it's nothing like working with John." Another McCartney/Jackson collaboration, "The Man," was just plain silly, sounding more like the theme song to the "Care Bears" than anything resembling a proper piece of music.

From there things begin to disintegrate so badly, to say any more would be pointless and cruel, like torturing a defenseless animal, or deliberately tripping an old man. Nevertheless, McCartney seems to have a hard-core audience ready to purchase every last piece of vinyl issued under his name, no matter how vacuous or obscure. Heading the list of *Billboard* magazine's most unexpectedly disappointing albums of the year, *Pipes of Peace* also held the rare distinction of being the only McCartney studio LP ever to miss making America's Top 10. Finally, it should also be noted that this was the last McCartney record on which Denny Laine appears. It is possible to see the dissolution of their partnership as the beginning of the end of Paul's amazingly prolific and successful recording life. The post-Lennon-and-Laine musical liaisons can't honestly be said to have maintained the magic. Despite his still enormous popularity both as an outstanding performer and larger-than-life celebrity, McCartney's best work as a recording artist may well be behind him. One always hopes, of course, but judging from the only sporadically interesting *Press to Play* and disappointing *Flowers in the Dirt* it doesn't really look too promising.

Life in the passing lane has not always been easy, and in 1983 this unhappy truth was brought all too close to home with the uncovering of a deadly serious plot to kidnap Linda from the McCartneys' Sussex home and hold her for $12.5 million ransom. It was masterminded by former Brit soldier Allan Gallop, who, along with two additional unnamed co-conspirators, planned to snatch Paul's unsuspecting missus in a Rambo-style military raid on the McCartney compound. Said to have spent the better part of a week stalking the famous pair, Gallop had intended, after the abduction, to hold Linda at a remote farmhouse until the always tricky transfer of funds could be accomplished. "I could have done it easily," he later bragged to London's *Sun*, "despite McCartney's state-of-the-art security measures." Fortunately, the would-be kidnappers never got the chance, foiled by local cops before they could make their big move. A McCartney spokesman would say only that too much was being made of the affair, noting that by the time the story reached the attention of the media, the incident was already more than a year old.

On July 13, 1985, Paul joined with the *crème de la crème* of the pop world to perform live for the first time in eight years at Live Aid, Irish rocker Bob Geldof's all-star bid to help feed the starving masses of Ethiopia. Although McCartney's name was not included on the first bill issued to the press, Geldof eventually managed to convince him that his participation in the event would ensure expanded TV coverage around the globe. The more people who saw the high-energy concerts, of course, the more money would be raised, thus helping to save thousands more innocent lives in Africa. The logic was unarguable.

Slipping out onto the darkened stage, Paul felt a thin tingle of electricity racing up his spine as he sat down at the all-white grand piano to perform the day's grand finale, a full ensemble rendition of "Let It Be." Just prior to McCartney's set, Freddie Mercury and Brian May had performed, and one of their road crew accidentally pulled out Paul's mike jack, thinking the cable was theirs. As a result, although the crowd picked up on the first plaintive chords of the sentimental favorite, McCartney's vocal was inaudible, something the incurable perfectionist probably couldn't have envisioned in his worst nightmare. "My mind was saying, 'Well, we haven't got the monitors, but I bet the sound's great on the telly,'" McCartney recalls in his 1989/90 tour program.

> Suddenly the terrible moment came, after the first verse, when the monitors came in, voices going, "You've got the wrong plug; that's not your plug!" "Oh dear," I thought, "I wonder if that's coming over on the BBC." Meanwhile, this other half of me is singing "Let It Be," trying to remember the words. And I went, "There will be an answer" and I heard the crowd go "Yey!!" I thought, "It's OK, we're cool." The speakers had come on for a moment. Then it started to feed back. Another nightmare. And I had this sudden thought I should sing "There will be some feedback, let it be." Then I thought, "No, you can't do

that, this is Ethiopia. Don't be so facetious . . . " The truth of it was that this guy Geldof has set out to raise a lot of money for people who were dying, and it didn't really matter if my mike went out.

Paul McCartney's search for a friendly collaborator after his falling-out with both Lennon and Laine says a lot about his need to work closely with someone whose musical instincts mesh cohesively with his own. His great love for Linda aside, his so-called songwriting partnership with her was a bad joke, more a cagey business maneuver than any sort of artist-to-artist *simpatico*.

Far more interesting and productive was his spell as one half of the creative consortium of "Mac and Jac" (or McCartney and Jackson respectively). Meeting Michael first at a Wings party aboard the *Queen Mary*, and then later at yet another hip Hollywood soiree, Paul told the wiry singer/dancer that he had only recently composed what he thought would be the perfect song for Jackson to record, entitled, simply, "Girlfriend." When Jackson teamed up with fabled producer Quincey Jones to record his first solo album, *Off the Wall*, for Epic, the idea of including the sultry "sand through silk" number came up, which led to a flurry of transatlantic calls between the two artists. The connection was now solidly made.

By the time Jackson's landmark *Thriller* came around Michael had written a number called "The Girl Is Mine" which he, in turn, felt would be a perfect McCartney/Jackson duet. Recorded in L.A. between sessions for *Tug of War*, the tangled love song was issued as a single in both the U.S.A. and Britain, reaching the top five in both countries. Publishing on the tune was split between the two as McCartney had helped with a few finishing touches upon his arrival in the States.

In 1983, this roving black-and-white minstrel show got together once again, of course, to work on *Pipes of Peace*. Two years later, Jackson cast the successful bid of $50 million in an on-going war of numbers to purchase the rights to ATV Music, which included the Northern Songs catalog of Beatles classics. McCartney reflects:

Michael's the kind of guy who picks brains . . . I don't think he'd even had the cosmetics then . . . He's had a lot of facial surgery since then, as I think most people on the planet know. He actually told me he was going to a religious retreat — and I believed him. But he came out of that religious retreat with a smashing new nose. The power of prayer, I guess . . . I gave him a lot of advice, and you know, a fish gets caught by opening its mouth. I advised him to go into publishing. And, as a joke, he looked at me and he said, "I'm going to buy your songs one day." And I just said, "Great, good joke." I really treated it as a joke . . . Then someone rang me up one day and said, "Michael's bought your . . . " "What?!?" . . . I haven't spoken to him since. I think he thinks it's just business. But I think it's slightly dodgy to do things like that — to be someone's friend and then to buy the rug they're standing on.

Without question Brian Epstein's greatest folly as a manager was allowing his young charges to sign away their publishing in the first place. In those days the Beatles left literally all their business affairs to him, trusting in his ability to do the right thing. It was a near-fatal mistake.

As the Beatles were busy tuning into their inner voices high in the hills of Rishikesh with the Maharishi in 1968, Dick James, the group's first music publisher, sold Northern, in a surprise move, to Sir Lew Grade and his ATV Corporation. Paul attempted to buy back the tunes in 1969 but eventually lost out to Australian magnate Robert Holmes à Court.

When the publishing came up for sale again, some sixteen years later, both Paul and Yoko were seemingly anxious to "bring home" the many Lennon/McCartney compositions, if only to keep them from being "cheapened" by their potential commercial exploitation as background music to sell everything from maxi-pads to dog food. "Paul and Yoko want to keep the songs in the family," Linda commented at the time. "Morally, it is madness that Paul does not own any of the songs he wrote with John. To Paul they are a part of him just as his children are."

Banding together for the first time ever, Paul and Yoko discussed making a wide range of offers for the portfolio, but Ono always drew back, trying to convince McCartney that the songs could be had at bargain basement prices if only they hung together and bided their time. McCartney and Ono, however, weren't the only players interested in acquiring the valuable property: big leaguers CBS, Warner Communications, Paramount, EMI, and the powerful Entertainment Company were all circling the waters, sizing up the competition. When Jackson secretly entered, and actually scored the prize on August 10, 1985, McCartney was left with a lot of egg on his face and more than a few suspicions.

According to industry sources, Paul later became aware of the little-known provision in American copyright law which stated that if a composer passes away during the first twenty-eight-year phase of a copyright, his or her heir can claim an additional term of the same duration, regardless of any pre-existing publishing agreements. As a result, McCartney may have some right to feel that Ono intentionally short-circuited his bid to control the tunes, knowing that the copyrights would eventually revert back to the Lennon estate without her having to lay out a penny. Paul explains: "In publishing in America, you have renewals; we don't have them here. After twenty-eight years — and, believe it or not, twenty-eight years for some of the Beatles songs is imminent — you, as a composer, get the chance either to go with this publisher again or not. And so, John's renewals will all be coming up, and Yoko can get the rights back. But my renewals don't come up, because I'm still alive, and we signed our renewal rights away for life. So, pretty soon, I think Yoko will own more of 'Yesterday' than I will."

To add insult to injury, the suggestion has even been made that Ms Ono may have actually assisted Jackson in putting the deal together, if true, a very nasty trick to have played upon her late husband's former partner. Sam Havadtoy, meanwhile, Yoko's on-call spokesperson and almost instantaneous stand-in for Lennon following his murder in 1980 (Havadtoy moved

in with the supposedly grieving widow just weeks afterwards), told the New York *Post*: "Paul and Yoko may have had
a phone conversation about the catalog, at which time she
said she wasn't interested, but if McCartney wanted the publishing rights he could have bought them himself. Yoko does
not control Paul McCartney."

In the end McCartney just had to grin and bear it, knowing
that his one real chance at truly holding onto the Beatles'
great songwriting legacy was probably gone forever. The unhappy episode, though, certainly nixed any chance of Paul
and Yoko's remaining anything more than quasi-congenial
adversaries. And even in that, a bitter enmity lies perpetually
bubbling just below the surface.

By the early summer of 1986 McCartney was once again itchy
to get back up on stage before a live audience, a pastime always particularly close to his heart. Issued an invitation to
appear at the Prince's Trust Birthday Party at Wembley Arena
on June 20, Macca graciously accepted, performing alongside
Tina Turner (in a wild rendition of "Get Back") as well as in a
grand slam superstar jam of "I Saw Her Standing There" and
the inevitable "Long Tall Sally." Featuring such regal rockers
as Eric Clapton, Elton John, Phil Collins, Mark Knopfler, Howard Jones, Bryan Adams, Ray Cooper, and Midge Ure, the
show was a great success. It was first transmitted over the
BBC a week later. "The audience was great, it was an incredible back-up band, and I enjoyed every minute," McCartney
later remarked.

Paul's next album release, *Press to Play*, was a definite departure for the singer, in many ways more like a far-out Pink
Floyd LP than the usual bubbly McCartney fare. Not exactly a
barnburner commercially, artistically it was just unusual and
oblique enough to challenge the listener a bit more than his
previous few offerings. Well constructed and flawlessly produced by the team of Hugh Padgham and Paul McCartney, the
ten-track opus contained the mature fruit of what appeared to
be a lot of creatively intensive soul searching by the artist.

Tunes such as the mystically inclined "Good Times Coming/ Feel the Sun," the otherworldly "Talk More Talk," and the majestic "Only Love Remains" work well alongside such instantly likeable numbers as "Press" and the lyrically surreal "Pretty Little Head."

Issued in England on September 1, 1986, *Press to Play* also boasts cameo appearances by a who's who of celebrated rock 'n' roll greats including Pete Townshend, guitar wizard Carlos Alomar, Phil Collins, Eric Stewart, and old standby Ray Cooper, among others. Of his relationship with ex-Mindbender and 10CC member Stewart (who along with McCartney co-wrote six of the cuts on the album), Paul had this to say: "It didn't really work out as well as I wanted it to, although we did a couple of nice things. But it wasn't a very successful album. It all got a little bit sticky because he thought I'd wanted him to co-produce the album with me and I must have led him to believe that . . . Then I said, 'Oh, we're getting so and so to produce it,' and he went into shock. So that fell through mainly because of that production misunderstanding."

Of Apple's many Beatle and post-Beatle employees over the years Alistair Taylor was one of the very few to become close friends with Paul. Let go by strongman Allen Klein during an almost all-inclusive house cleaning at the classy Savile Row address, Taylor soon lost touch with his former boss, moving on to an only moderately successful career managing local pop groups and doing freelance PR out of his suburban London home. In the early eighties, while clearing out some old books from his library, Taylor accidently came upon Paul's original design sketch for the famous 1968 Apple want ad depicting Taylor as a perfectly bizarre one-man band performing under the legend "This Man Has Talent!" And below: "One day he sang his songs into a tape recorder (borrowed from the man next door). In his neatest handwriting, he wrote an explanatory note (giving his name and address) and, remembering to enclose a picture of himself, sent the tape, letter and photograph to Apple Music, 94 Baker Street, London, W.1. If you were thinking of doing the same thing yourself — do it now! This man owns a Bentley!"

Realizing that such a supremely historic Beatle document would be worth a lot of money, Taylor decided to try to sell it back to his old mate after hearing that Paul was then into collecting Beatles memorabilia in a big way. "I thought, 'Shit, this is priceless!'" Taylor told me at a New York Beatles convention in September of 1984:

> I was unemployed and I had this pop group I was trying to manage [the Actors], and I wrote and said, "Hey, I found this old sketch you did. Do you remember being in my flat? We were drinking coffee until two in the morning." We must have thrown dozens of these away . . . It literally dropped out of a book after fourteen years. The next thing, his manager rang to say Paul wasn't interested. So I said, "Fine." The next thing, Paul himself rang and just dived straight in by saying, "It's not yours to sell and you've no right, you know." I haven't spoken to the guy for fifteen years and we were once so close that I was taken aback. So anyway, I ended up by saying, "It *is* mine, it was in my house and I need the money, so I'm going to go ahead and put it into Sotheby's." So he said, "You go ahead if you want to. It's up to you. I don't want to know." So I put it into Sotheby's, and the next thing there was an injunction from McCartney's lawyers, so I had to settle out of court. I sold it back to Paul at an agreed figure which was about a tenth of what it was worth.

It is truly incredible just how many people once close to McCartney tend to walk away with a bitter taste in their mouths. Why is it? Surely not everyone is lying. There's just too much smoke for there not to be at least a spark of truth somewhere. Almost all of these horror stories in one way or another revolve around money. I asked Taylor why he thought that was. "I don't know. I think he's just rather selfish and resents anyone making anything, however little, from him. He believes we milked him during the Beatle years, but he forgets what we did for him."

Occasionally, though, McCartney does try to spread things

around a bit by engaging in projects designed primarily to help others. A good example of his late-blooming philanthropy was his involvement in the all-star remake of *Let It Be* in aid of the 1987 Zeebrugge ferry disaster in Belgium, as well as his on-going support of various environmental and vegetarian causes around the globe.

Perhaps his most generous (and astute) move of late was his 1988 foray into the Russian music market with the release of a rock-solid collection of fifties oldies such as "Kansas City" and "Ain't That a Shame." The germ of the idea was planted in the summer of 1987 when Paul approached his manager, Richard Ogden, with a plan to issue a batch of recently recorded rock standards in England as if they had been smuggled in from Russia on the underground market. The idea of Paul McCartney bootlegging his own record, however, didn't really appeal to the straightforward businessman who quashed the concept but went ahead on his own and had a couple of dozen copies of the sessions pressed and packaged in Russian-looking jackets as a Christmas present to his famous employer.

After the cold war began to thaw out a bit with the first warm glow of Mikhail Gorbachev's ground-breaking *perestroika* and *glasnost*, MPL sent Ogden packing off to Moscow for a heavyweight meeting with officials from the state-run Melodya record label. Following a fair bit of wrangling, a licensing deal was struck, allowing the Soviets to press an initial 400,000 copies of the record, aptly titled *Back in the U.S.S.R.*

The plan was never to release it anywhere in the West, making the disc a special present from Paul to his many loyal Eastern Bloc fans. Immediately after its release, though, the thirteen-track album started turning up for sale in both England and America fetching upwards of two hundred dollars a copy among collectors. Bootleg versions (issued not only on record but also on CD and cassette as well) were far better value at a mere ten- to twenty-dollars apiece. Everyone back at Soho Square, of course was astounded. "We're trying to decide how to deal with this," Ogden commented to reporters at the inception of the controversy.

> We still have absolutely no plans to release the record elsewhere, but we're not happy about Paul's fans having to pay so much if they want a copy. We are mailing members of our fan club a letter telling them not to pay those prices because if we can find a way of sorting it out with the Russians, we'll make the record available to them ourselves . . . From our point of view, this was never meant to be a commercial venture. We're earning virtually nothing from it, and we are donating part of what we earn to the Armenian earthquake appeal. The record is something Paul made for fun . . .

Back in Russia, meanwhile, rock fans from Georgia to Siberia were lining up to score a copy of the hot new release which reportedly sold out completely within forty-eight hours of first hitting the streets on October 1. In yet another sweeping gesture McCartney agreed to promote the album not by train-stomping in the Soviet Union but rather by sitting down for a live transcontinental satellite give-and-take with the Russian people via the BBC World Service in London that January. For fifty-five minutes, callers chatted with McCartney about not only the new album but his long-dead original group as well. "We [the Beatles] always heard the young people were buying our records and were interested in the music we made, so that always made me very optimistic about the relations between our countries. It didn't put us off Russians. We love you — madly." Paul's amazing power to PR, it seems, has now become truly global.

The kids are always saying, "Mum, Dad, we're supposed to be the hippies. You're supposed to be the straight parents. It's the wrong way around." We joke about it but there is an element of truth to it. How many people have fathers who play electric guitar and scream, "Lucille"?

—Paul McCartney, 1990—

10
Fond Farewells
Busking in the Brave New World

E ver since the final note of the Wings Over America tour of 1976 people have been badgering McCartney to get back up on the boards for another high-profile world tour. In almost every interview since, poor Paul has had to endure not only questions concerning a possible Beatles reunion but also the ever-present performance issue. After John died, of course, the overriding concern was security. Although it was never actually said in so many words (Paul in fact continually denied that he was afraid) the billionaire family man had no wish to expose himself to unnecessary danger.

Still, it's not that he didn't want to perform. As early as 1977 McCartney discussed the daft idea of converting MPL's Replica Studios into a quasi-Cavern Club with Wings jamming free at lunchtimes for Soho's wandering business trade. Having had to endure both the aborted 1980 Japanese concerts (which Steve Holly and Laurence Juber claim was planned as the initial leg of a much larger tour), as well as John's murder, was just too much. It would be a full nine years before Mc-Cartney again summoned up the nerve to actually go back out on the road.

"It scares me and it doesn't scare me," said McCartney, commenting on the unhappy possibility of being blown away by some loony Beatle fan out to get his name in the paper. "When the time for me to leave this mortal world comes, that'll be the time. And I don't know when or how that will be. So, yeah, it kind of scares me, but not enough for me to really do anything. I mean, I probably stand a worse chance of getting killed coming to work, or going on holiday."

Getting his chops together first in a sold-out series of gigs in Europe commencing in Oslo, Norway, on September 26, 1989, McCartney and his new band — Chris Whitten (drums and percussion), Linda McCartney (back-up vocals and Roland synthesizer), Robbie McIntosh (lead guitar), Paul "Wix" Wickens (keyboards), and Hamish Stuart (guitar, bass, and vocals) — soon made their way to the United States where they met with predictable enthusiasm. Despite a very few negative criticisms (the hands-down best was a headline reading "Bland on the Run"), the tour was an unqualified success, allowing fans young and old the once-in-a-lifetime chance to see McCartney perform such classics as "Hey Jude," "Got to Get You into My Life," "Let It Be," "Get Back," "Sgt. Pepper's Lonely Hearts Club Band," "Eleanor Rigby," "The Long and Winding Road," "Live and Let Die," "Band on the Run," "Jet," "Let 'em In," "Silly Love Songs," and at least a dozen more equally special tunes.

That's not to imply, however, that the often-riveting two-hour-plus show was nothing more than a live jukebox of McCartney's greatest. Fitted in nicely among the more august material were quite a number of new tunes from his *Flowers in the Dirt* LP. Unlike the music of many other big acts, McCartney's catchy, hummable melodies can be quickly as-similated by the listener thus making it easier for him to include unfamiliar songs in a show's repertoire. "In the end," says Paul, "you pay attention to your fans."

> Most of them will only see the show once, so they want from me what I wanted when I saw Bill Haley . . . The danger with all of us pterodactyls on the road is that you don't want to become a sixties package show. Or if you aren't careful with some of the songs, you can get a little lounge-pianoish . . . I find now that I want to do my songs as close to the originals as possible . . . I've heard that with Bob Dylan, if a song gets too recognizable he throws it out. That's great for him, but it's not for me.

For both the McCartneys a major benefit of the fifteen-country tour was the extensive publicity the shows would give to the vegetarian and environmental causes so close to their hearts. Despite a few catty Jo Jo Laine remarks to the contrary, Paul appears to be every bit as strict concerning his much-written-about vegetarian lifestyle as he pretends, reportedly even going so far as sneaking out with Linda occasionally to seafood restaurants and markets to purchase live lobsters which they then set free in the ocean.

The McCartneys' formal alliance with the across-the-board environmental watchdog group Friends of the Earth also got a big boost from the tour, both publicity-wise and financially. On November 27, 1989, Michael S. Clark, president of the U.S. chapter of the privately funded organization sat down with Paul at a press conference to discuss some of the problems we all now face due to man's willful abuse of the planet. "Paul McCartney has embraced Friends of the Earth and is spreading the word to audiences throughout the world that by joining us they can help save the planet," explained Clark. "And that is a public service of significant value to the environment and our movement to protect it. Today we know only too well how badly the Earth is hurting — and that it needs every friend it can get. Mr. McCartney has become one of the Earth's best friends."

As for Paul's part in this international mutual admiration

society, he personally contributed heavily to the more-than-worthy cause and actively encouraged his many fans to do the same, even going so far as to include a coupon in the tour program for them to fill out and mail in with their offerings: "When I was a boy, I would never have believed it if someone had told me that one day we'd have a hole in the sky — in the ozone layer — that there would be acid in our rain, that the seas wouldn't be clean enough to swim in and the air not clean enough to breathe. All I am trying to do on this tour is hopefully make people think about how we're wrecking this world and ask them to challenge their politicians to act."

For all the good will, however, the tour also spawned its share of controversy with McCartney's acceptance of a $3 million contract to allow the concerts to be promoted under the banner of the Visa credit card company. The concept of corporate sponsorship of rock 'n' roll, although here to stay, is distasteful to many who resent the implications of Madison Avenue meddling with this, America's purest, most native, and most uninhibited art form. McCartney, of course, dished out the usual propaganda about big tours being so incredibly expensive these days that without such support the fans would be forced to take up some of the slack at the ticket counter. Most observers though saw such rhetoric as more of the same old McCartney fast talk. Robert Christgau, senior music critic of the *Village Voice,* hit the nail squarely on the head with a biting assessment of McCartney's latest world-class deal: "I don't think Paul is anything but a businessman, and I'm not surprised he made this decision . . . the credit card sponsorship is especially odious. It's a financial institution. There's something funny about it, and what I regard as typical of a very shrewd, very wealthy entrepreneur, which is what McCartney basically is."

Rushing to the aid of their newest public mascot, representatives of Visa's own ad agency, BBDO in New York, only succeeded in making matters worse with managing director G. Gary de Paolo telling the *Wall Street Journal,* "What we've determined is he [Mr. McCartney] is very establishment. There isn't anybody more establishment than Paul McCartney. He's got a family of four, he jets home at every available moment, he's a twenty-year vegetarian . . . It could almost get boring." One imagines that, for all his evangelical familial commitment, Paul couldn't have been too thrilled with de Paolo's double-edged defense. However squeaky clean his image these days it must still irk him somewhat to be thought of as such a musical milquetoast. He is, after all, a get-down, goodtime rock 'n' roller, once part of the most ground-breaking, experimental, revolutionary group of its day. In the final analysis it's difficult to imagine, say, John Lennon ever soliciting, or accepting such an offer. "I don't feel I have to apologize," McCartney later commented from the eye of the hurricane. "It seems to me that we're in a fairly obvious capitalist society . . . We all accept money for what we do and if you ever go in to your boss for the best deal you can get, you don't say, 'Give me the lowest wage you can think of.' I'm the same." His perpetual whining about how he's really no different from you or me (and therefore should be cut some slack) grows only more pathetic and unbelievable with each escalating royalty rate and multi-million-pound advance. The simple truth remains that as the single richest performer in all of show business he is a one-man walking monetary system with more assets than several mid-sized third world countries combined.

The recording that first inspired Paul's second great world tour was the only occasionally absorbing *Flowers in the Dirt.* Hyped by McCartney's minions as the best thing since *Band on the Run*, the thirteen-track work offered little of real import, serving up instead much of the same old McCartney musical mumbo jumbo or what one critic called, "pop for potheads." "I really took more care with the songs than anything," says Paul. "I wanted an album I could go out on tour with, an album people could relate to. I just didn't want some crummy album dogging the tour."

In all honesty *Flowers in the Dirt* is about a fifty-fifty proposition. That is, half of the tunes work admirably while the other half simply slog by, weighed down by their own over-blown sense of self. Tunes in the first category include the Paul McCartney/Elvis Costello number "My Brave Face," as well as the funky "Rough Ride," exuberant "We Got Married," "Où est le Soleil," and "Figure of Eight." The touching "Put It There" also gets high marks, not only for its folksy "Black-bird"-like guitar work, but for the honest, captivating way it seeks to delineate the often-mercurial ups and downs of the timeless and tricky father/son relationship. Among the stink-ers on the meticulously packaged LP are the Paul/Elvis duet "You Want Her Too" (a kind of tired, backstreet "The Girl Is Mine") and the faceless "Don't Be Careless, Love," "That Day Is Done," "How Many People," and "Motor of Love."

Costello remembers the day-to-day buzz of the extended (almost two-year) recording sessions for the album: "Paul has a clever way of sidestepping confrontation by making jokes like, 'Well, you can never trust anything he says because he hates effects!' So rather than disagreeing with you, your argu-ment's devalued before it's started. After a while that made the production kind of redundant."

Surprisingly, one of the few people to spring to McCartney's defense regarding his questionable work on *Flowers* was old pal Denny Laine:

> I like *Flowers in the Dirt* because it's a band again and to me there's some good songs there. A couple of them I don't like, you know, because of the performance really. But some of them I really like, and the rest are of good quality . . . I think Elvis Costello was a fine writing companion for him. Paul needed to have other people of the same stature giving him ideas. As for the band he put together, he was looking for people he admired and it took him that long to find a good combination of people who weren't so much in awe of him. When that came together he felt right to go on the road. I wish Paul would go on tour more often. After all, he's in a position to because everybody wants to see him and he's always bringing out albums. He's good enough to go out once a year.

Despite his prodigious output as an artist, Paul McCartney's off-hours still remain all-important to him. His twenty-three-year relationship with Linda is as stable as ever, although both parties claim the union is definitely a "real" marriage with all the attendant highs and lows. Paul has never strayed, a fact remarkable to many who see the dashing, witty, powerful ex-Beatle as the perfect over-forty candidate for a clandestine affair.

Although the McCartneys do row, it is never, ever in public. On the single occasion that Linda took flight after a fight with Paul, showing up at Denny and Jo Jo's, she was home again within a couple of hours. Above all, it is an intensely private and personal relationship. "There have been plenty of difficulties, but I'm not a very public person about those kinds of things," says Paul. "I'm not an easy person to live with, and I think sometimes she's not easy. . . ." Although it was suggested to me by several people once close to the McCartneys that Paul and Linda's relationship is more mother/son than husband/wife the remark, it seems to me, is based on jealousy rather than on fact. Their marriage seems a union of equals, a bond of mutual respect and love of family and home.

"Having seen them since before they got married," remembers George Martin, "I think the most impressive thing has been their determination to make it work . . . They were determined to build loyalty into their marriage and family, because it's not just a marriage, it's a family. They've gone out of their way to raise their family in a natural environment, and I think they've handled it extraordinarily well."

Perhaps the sweetest story ever told about the fairy tale McCartney marriage concerns an incident in September of 1982 when Linda exhibited her photographs in a London gallery only to discover that the high-priced prints weren't exactly setting any sales records. In the end, Paul secretly shelled out the $23,630 necessary to buy the unsold thirty-seven shots, managing to keep the transaction confidential to all but the nosey *Sun* who predictably splashed the romantic gesture all over their front page. "He didn't want to see her hurt," says a friend. "Deep down he's as soft as anyone. When Linda found out, she was so touched I was told she actually cried."

Having long ago outgrown the claustrophobic intimacy of their circular first home down south, in 1978 the McCartneys purchased adjacent East Gate Farm from local businessman Jim Higgs for a reported £100,000. In 1982 the old farmhouse on the property was razed and a luxury five-bedroom home of Paul's own design built on the site. Complemented by a full stable and a paddock for their several impossibly expensive thoroughbred horses, it includes a swimming pool as well an imposing sixty-five-foot watchtower McCartney insists was constructed for the sole purpose of allowing the family the pleasure of viewing the lush, green countryside. Just to be safe, a sturdy six-foot fence was also constructed at the request of local officials who feared for the family's safety after the murderous attack on John Lennon and reports of out-of-town cranks showing up in nearby Peasmarsh, trying to gain entry to the former Fab's retreat.

Inside the grounds of the stately country home are ducks, geese, chickens, and even peacocks which, when not roaming freely, reside in coops built by McCartney's own hands. Both homebodies in the extreme, Paul and Linda draw a definite line between family and business, with absolutely no gold records, awards, or other memorabilia anywhere to be seen. In fact, if it weren't for the baby Steinway grand piano and a small collection of Paul's favorite Martin guitars scattered around, one might think the tidy, well-organized household was that of some local solicitor or old-money blueblood.

Unfortunately, as is so often the case with Paul McCartney, at some point the ugly specter of pounds, shillings, and pence raises its head, interrupting even the pastoral quietude of his homey lifestyle in the grassy belly of England's upper-crust heartland. In the summer of 1990, one of McCartney's neighbors, single parent Pauline Jeal, who resides in a rustic cottage in Peasmarsh, received a notice that not only had Paul

Summer '90 Peasmarsh
future development

purchased the house she had been renting for the previous four years but also intended to renovate and then rent it out for big bucks, thus forcing her out. "When I asked Paul why he was so determined to kick us out of the cottage that's in the middle of a marsh, he wouldn't answer me. I only found out later that he's planning a big development in the area. They're thinking of putting up condos and shopping malls. This area is full of all kinds of wildlife. I couldn't imagine someone like Paul not caring about any of that and worried only about the almighty dollar. . . . I'm glad John Lennon isn't here to see this." Fruitless as it probably is, Mrs. Jeal plans to try to stave off McCartney's advances to her little home for as long as she can before moving on.

Meanwhile, back at Chez McCartney, one of the big attractions for country squire Paul is that most exalted of all twentieth century art forms, the TV game show. "They just love 'The Price Is Right,'" says a friend. "It's true!" Other big favorites for Paul, Mary, Stella, and James include the now-defunct American series "Fame" as well as, what seems as if it would be very small potatoes for the McCartney clan, "The $20,000 Pyramid." (Just about the amount Paul rakes in on his various publishing royalties while he's watching.) Linda, on the other hand, apparently just adored "Dallas" and that raunchy lowdown cow poke JR Ewing. Jo Jo Laine, too, counted the long-winded soap as her fave rave, an ironic similarity of taste between two women who have precious little else in common.

Another high priority for Paul at home is his middle-class insistence that women pay attention to their prescribed duties, like housework. "I'm from your northern stock where women didn't get jobs. I was used to women who did the laundry on their knees, scrubbing the front step. I never thought that was degrading, but wonderful of them to do it." From all accounts, Linda, being as she is from such an upwardly mobile Jewish household, never even had to make her own bed as a child let alone engage in the kind of elbow-grease activities her working-class husband had in mind.

At first I thought Paul was so old-fashioned, with all this tidi-
ness, and doing your own laundry and ironing . . . Well, when
you read the little story books, it was the mother and the father and the kids . . . It wasn't "And the cleaning lady came and
. . . " Paul was saying that there's a lovely pleasure in launder-
ing something and smelling it, or ironing something. He remembers the smell in his house, of his mother, his auntie. His
mum died when he was so young. So to have a wife who is intelligent, independent, artistic — but who also fulfills that role
— was important. He thought I was missing something; I
thought, "Come on, I want to be outdoors with my horse . . ." If
I were working, believe me, I wouldn't take this "You're the
wife, this is your role." Oh, no, thank you!

McCartney explains his obviously outdated thinking by saying, "I mean my class likes to polish. But I suppose you
couldn't tell a modern woman she should like to polish."

To his eternal credit Paul McCartney is definitely a man
who loves his children. So much does he revere his own un-
complicated childhood he is determined that his kids too enjoy a similarly free and simple youth. So much available
money one would think might tend to make such an ideal difficult to attain. It is a problem both Paul and Linda struggle
with almost daily. Paul McCartney's head may indeed be in
his business, but his heart is with his family. In that, he is un-
movable.

I don't want them looking down on ordinary people. I see that
as the main danger when you get money, especially inherited
wealth. You start to think, "Well, I'm better than him, anyway,
I've got more than him," and you tend to look down on him . . .
So my kids go to ordinary schools in order for them to learn
how it is first. Then if you want to be terrific and privileged afterwards, you can handle it. You've got some humanity and
compassion with it. So I'm trying to bring them up to have values, to have heart, more than anything . . . I want them to actually care, you know, if someone gets hurt. And they do.
They're very good kids like that.

It is not easy to get McCartney to talk about his offspring. Knowing full well that his exalted situation could instantly rocket them into the media, forcing them to grow up in public like, say, young John Kennedy, or maybe Tatum O'Neal, he keeps that part of his life very close to home. These days his two oldest, Heather and Mary, live together in a house in St. John's Wood, though not the family home (which is still owned by the McCartneys) on Cavendish Avenue. By all accounts the two young women both work and play with equal enthusiasm, just like their famous parents. Heather is a potter and Mary an assistant at MPL. Stella and James, of course, still live at home, something their admittedly possessive father is in no hurry to change. "I get strict when I think I have to," says Paul. "We don't swear around the house — usually it's me who does — and then I have to go around and apologize to everybody."

Another big concern of the former swinging London bachelor is the possible hidden agenda of his daughter's suitors. He's been there himself, he says, and knows the score.

> It's very weird when you were man-the-hunter and you know what visiting boyfriends are after. . . . I try to get on with them, which is not always successful. I know what it was like for me to talk to fathers of girlfriends when no one was famous, and it was terrifying . . . It's very difficult as a parent to smell out dishonorable motives. . . . If I tell Mary her boyfriend's not that great, that's the one she'll have. I tell them, "When I was a kid you could mess around a bit, experiment, before you got engaged . . . When the pill arrived, me dad was jealous. I said, 'Didn't you?' And he said, 'No, there was VD in my day.' I was lucky."

One of the most impressive aspects of Paul and Linda's life these days is their philosophical commitment to ethical vegetarianism. Linda remembers their reasons for kicking the meat habit:

> During the course of a Sunday lunch we happened to look out the kitchen window at our young lambs racing happily in the

fields. Glancing down at our plates, we suddenly realized we were eating the leg of an animal that had until recently been gambolling in a field itself. We looked at each other and said, "Wait a minute, we love these sheep — they're such gentle creatures — so why are we eating them?" It was the last time we ever did.

So identified is Linda with the protection of wildlife that in Sussex the local RSPCA rings her regularly when they've run out of options in finding a home for a helpless creature. Unless these animals are predators the McCartneys generally take them in. "Linda is a crazy animal lover," says Paul. "We have lots of pets, and as a kid I used to run around with my *Observer* book of birds in my pocket. So from then on we stuck to eating things where nothing had to lose a life. One Christmas, Linda even managed to make a kind of macaroni turkey: you could cut it into slices just like the real thing. I know it sounds a bit corny, but we really value being vegetarians, and it doesn't seem too daft because our place is a nuthouse anyway!"

As time passed and the issue of animal protection became even more volatile and imperative, Paul and Linda both significantly stepped up their efforts on behalf of not only edible livestock but research animals as well. At the risk of being called "radical," late in 1990 they even went so far as to record a series of messages on behalf of PETA (People for the Ethical Treatment of Animals) which were played to callers on a special eight-hundred number throughout North America. An excerpt follows:

PAUL: "Wheel of Fortune" is the only big-name game show that still gives away fur coats as prizes. Help us get them to drop fur by calling Merv Griffin, the show's executive producer . . .

LINDA: Come on, Merv, you don't like fur coats. Give me a break. Thumbs up for Estée Lauder, Clinique, Avon, and Revlon for ending animal tests. Thumbs down to L'Oréal and Gillette for refusing to stop poisoning and killing animals . . .

PAUL: The Sill Spring monkeys are survivors of a lab closed down by police nine years ago. They've been kept in tiny cages by the National Institute of Health ever since the research was arrested. Please call President Bush . . . and ask him to give the word for those poor monkeys to be moved to a sanctuary.

To some, however, the McCartneys' unbridled love of animals seems occasionally at cross purposes with even the call of the wild they so revere. Denny explains:

You can't change the course of nature to my mind, but Paul and Linda tried. They kept their car outside at their home in St. John's Wood because their garage was full of rare livestock they planned to release into the Scottish hills to breed. Linda can't bear to see anything killed so she was heartbroken when the dogs got into the garage one night and killed some of her chickens. The survivors were taken up to Scotland and freed. But they wouldn't leave. They just sat around in the front garden waiting to be fed. Eventually the dogs killed the lot. I thought it was a stupid exercise.

As Kahlil Gibran once observed of people: "I saw them eating and I knew who they were." The McCartneys' commitment of more than twenty years to refusing to support the violent and bloody meat industry is cause for celebration. They are very influential role models. "For the forest to be green each tree must be green." So said the mirthful Maharishi. His indisputable logic places the responsibility to act clearly where it has always belonged. It is a challenge the McCartneys have graciously accepted. In this life it makes sense to try to be as nonviolent as possible. For the McCartneys, anyway, refusing to eat dead animals seems a good place to start.

Twenty years after Paul and the other Beatles officially called it a day, the group's complex karma was still coming back to

haunt them. Following years of spiteful infighting, circumstances eventually forced the three surviving Beatles to re-
group (if only for the sake of ongoing business) to proceed
against Capitol, their old record company, in an effort to
collect substantial monies allegedly owed the band. It would
prove a long, painful, and arduous process for everyone involved. Although by 1990 most of the group's business hassles
were resolved, there were, sadly, still a lot of jagged emotions
among them. Despite Paul's tedious posturing that they were
all the best of friends, his real feelings about his former colleagues were (and are) quite different. In fact, during the final
days of the Beatles' much-publicized Apple/Capitol suit, he
was overheard referring to his former colleagues as "arrogant,
big-headed dopes" who should be grateful for the deal that
was being offered them and join with him in "blowing up
Apple" once and for all.

Perhaps the most shocking revelation of all is McCartney's
devastating attitude towards Beatle peacemaker, Ringo. "They
really think they're something," he complained to business
associates, "especially someone like Ringo!" Incredibly, the
congenial drummer was apparently so broke at one point during the late eighties that he considered selling off a portion of
his holdings in the Beatles' vast multi-million-pound business
empire to an unidentified Arab investor. As a last-ditch effort
to maintain the status quo, Starr turned to McCartney for a
little help from his friend. "Okay," Paul told him, "I'll give you
one more set of promotion fees . . . I hate to see you begging
me." In return for the hand-out, however, McCartney demanded that Ringo side with him in any ensuing negotiations
relating to the permanent dissolution of Apple, "a far more
reasonable reality" quips a former Beatle aide, "than the Fab
Four suddenly becoming, say, 'John, Paul, George, and
Abdul.'" In the cold light of day, it seems even the great
Beatles themselves are as petty and sorrowful as the rest of
us, something John and George, in particular, had been saying
publicly for years.

1990 Beatles Lwues

Denny Laine's departure from Wings was the unfortunate precursor of several years of unrelenting hard luck. Only just now slowly climbing back towards the top, Laine has successfully moved on, but in many ways is still seen as one-half of something as opposed to an artist whole and independent. Disturbing as it is, it's not really all that unusual in the business. Being part of any popular, well-loved team brings with it a public identification with one's partners that's often tough to shake; witness Simon and Garfunkel, Jagger and Richards, even Lennon and McCartney. Although the world doesn't yet seem to recognize it, the writing and performing team of McCartney/Laine was very special indeed. Bringing out the bottom-line best in each other, their unique talents intertwined, bringing to Wings' music both a sensitivity and a rough edge it would otherwise never have had. After over eight years of not speaking a word to each other (and both feeling pretty miserable about it into the bargain), Paul attempted to make contact again in February of 1990, ringing a number one of his road crew had dug up while the whirlwind McCartney tour was steaming through Boston. Denny, unfortunately, wasn't in, with Jo Jo, of all people, answering the early evening call. "Hello," said a voice she instinctively and immediately recognized to be McCartney's. "Is Denny in, please?"

"No, sorry," said Jo Jo. "He just left a little while ago with his girlfriend and the baby. They've gone to his house in New Hampshire. Who's this?" "This is a friend of his, Paul." Taking the bull by the horns, Jo Jo, as usual, dove straight in with both feet. "Is this Paul McCartney?" she asked, barely able to hide both her excitement and nervousness at once again speaking to her old arch-nemesis. "Yeah, who's this?" replied Paul, seeming at last to catch on that this was no ordinary answering service. "Why it's your old friend Jo Jo!" she chirped, rendering McCartney literally speechless for the longest time. "Jo Jo?" he finally continued, surprisingly much warmer than she ever had any right to expect. "You know, Paul," she continued, seizing the precious moment in an effort to try to say something positive that might help bring the two ex-mates back in line once again, "those articles in the *Sun* that Denny did on you and Linda weren't really his words. It was all so twisted. I know he feels terrible about it." "I realize that, Jo," said Paul, suddenly even warmer and more sincere. "Look, just tell him I called, okay? I'll have someone ring tomorrow to try and connect up with him so we can get together. It was great to talk to you again. I'm just about to go on stage in a minute so I'll ring off. See you."

Like clockwork, the next afternoon John Hammel did indeed ring, making arrangements for Denny to come out to Worcester that evening to see the gig and drop backstage afterwards. By the time Denny got to the stadium the show had already started. A stranger to the area, he and an associate had gotten lost, turning off at the wrong ramp and then having to backtrack at least two or three times. It's difficult to imagine what was rushing through Laine's head as he stood there, down near the front of the stage, watching someone else play guitar alongside his old mate up there under the blinding lights. Hearing the first strains of "Band on the Run" ring out, and feeling the crowd swell under the plaintive, rising rhythms must have been very strange. It was he and Paul, after all, who had created those chords, on a similar evening, once many years ago in faraway Nigeria.

Stamping out the last of at least ten cigarettes he had smoked over the last hour and a half, Denny pulled on his coat after the last encore and walked backstage. Happily, among the sea of darting, unfamiliar faces he soon picked out old Wings-minder, Mike Walley. He threw his arms around the burly roadie in the kind of spontaneous arms-around reserved for those on the inside of rock 'n' roll.

"How ya doin', Den?" asked the obviously surprised and pleased assistant. "God, it's great to see you, man. Do Paul and Linda know you're here?"

"I think so," said Laine quietly.

"Well Christ, man," replied Walley, anticipating the long-awaited reunion he was about to witness, "let me take you back, then." Leading Laine and his friend down a long, heavily guarded corridor, the good-natured Brit paused just outside a large, well-secured hallway leading to the band's strictly off-limits dressing rooms. "I'll just go in and see what's up, mate," he said, darting off inside. "Hang on a sec."

Leaning up against the cold, concrete wall, Laine began to feel a bit sick to his stomach. After about ten minutes Mike emerged from inside, saying that he could go in just as soon as they cleaned up a bit and finished one quick interview. "You know how it is, mate," said the roadie, shrugging his shoulders in resignation. "It'll just be a minute."

Denny waited around another twenty minutes or so and then nodded to his partner that they should cut out. Walking unrecognized through the parking lot, back to the car, he paused only to zip up his jacket against the suddenly chilly late-night air. On the way home, says Jo Jo, neither of the men said a word.

Back at the stadium, the limo drivers too were getting restless waiting for the McCartneys to emerge with their entourage on their way back to the hotel. It had been a long night.

To me, Paul's the guy who drank milk out of the bottle and blew cigarette smoke in front of the TV so I couldn't see the cartoons. I wondered what all the girls saw in him. He even left his socks at the foot of the bed.

—Ruth McCartney—

11
Time Is Tappin' on My Forehead
McCartney in Motion

In the same ongoing pattern since John Lennon's death, once again it took an outside force to seriously challenge McCartney's musical evolution. This time it was a most unlikely catalyst: the Royal Liverpool Philharmonic commissioned McCartney to compose an original work to mark its 150th anniversary. In 1991 McCartney unveiled the eagerly awaited composition, some two years in the making, his *Liverpool Oratorio*. The ambitious 95-minute choral work debuted within the cavernous Liverpool Anglican Church (the second largest in Europe), ironically on the very spot its esteemed composer once failed a childhood audition.

"My dad sent me to try for a scholarship because several free books came with it," Paul remembered. "But I didn't manage it. So it was kind of strange to see all these kids in the chorus the night of the premiere, because they *had* gotten the gig."

Billed as a simple tale of one man's search for love and faith, the piece, in eight extended movements, focuses on the life and times of a fellow named Shanty. The work's centerpiece—the complex relationship between father and child—highlights its strikingly autobiographical overtones. McCartney, however, downplayed that angle, stressing his composition is ultimately about "giving peace a chance."

In truth, the *Liverpool Oratorio* was Paul's uneven attempt at reclaiming his working-class roots. "I have met prime ministers, including Harold Wilson and Margaret Thatcher, and the mayors of most American cities," he pointed out, "but I have never met anyone whose common sense and values can match those of your ordinary Liverpool working man."

During its worldwide tour of select cities the *Oratorio* played to decidedly mixed reviews. While the *Orange County Register* praised select passages as bearing "great charm and melodic inventiveness," *Time* magazine rendered it "strangely flat." *The Guardian*'s Paul Fisher prodded old wounds by writing, "McCartney's literary self is far more uncertain than his musical self and the sugary libretto needed an editor with even a fraction of Lennon's cynicism."

In light of the generally less-than-glowing reviews McCartney said: "In some sort of innocent, ignorant way I'd forgotten I'd be putting it out there for every Cambridge matriculation exam on the planet. Of course, I was foolish not to expect the critics to go after it but I suppose it was just a safety valve in me, something that says 'Don't worry about it.'"

As the buzz swelled about the cool new "classical" Beatle, McCartney quietly celebrated his fiftieth birthday on June 18, 1992. Slight jowls now tugged at the once youthful, impish face, crow's feet etched the corners of his eyes, while tasteful silver flecks dusted his well-kempt hair. He even joked about plastic surgery. "A little makeup here and there is fine. It's show biz. But actually cutting and snipping? I live

► Paul's distinctive autograph, circa 1964.

Woolton Parish Church

Garden Fete

and

Crowning of Rose Queen

Saturday, July 6th, 1957

To be opened at 3 p.m. by Dr. Thelwall Jones

PROCESSION AT 2 p.m.

LIVERPOOL POLICE DOGS DISPLAY
FANCY DRESS PARADE
SIDESHOWS   REFRESHMENTS
BAND OF THE CHESHIRE YEOMANRY
THE QUARRY MEN SKIFFLE GROUP

ADULTS 6d.. CHILDREN 3d.   OR BY PROGRAMME

GRAND DANCE

at 8 p.m. in the Church Hall

GEORGE EDWARDS' BAND
THE QUARRY MEN SKIFFLE GROUP
Tickets 2/-

▲ The rare original poster advertising the legendary Quarrymen gig in Woolton at which Paul first met John.

The Beatles on the road around Liverpool in the early days. ▼ ▼ ►

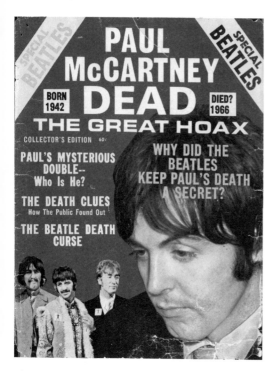

▲ A 1969 magazine cashing in on the alleged "death" of Paul McCartney.

▼ A vintage game piece, circa 1964.

▶ The ridiculous notion that Paul was killed in a car crash in the mid-sixties and replaced with double "William Campbell" is taken to extremes in this 1969 article.

▼ Jim and Paul, circa 1965.

◄ The charming "Mrs. McCartney" that never was, Jane Asher. London, 1967.

▼ Paul carries the new Mrs. McCartney across the threshold to their life together in St. John's Wood, 1969.

▲ A rare shot of Lennon at the press launch for *Sgt. Pepper*, Belgravia, London, 1967.

▶ Twiggy's face adorns her 1967 line of pantyhose for the "now" people. The diminutive supermodel became Linda's best friend.

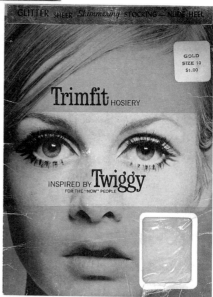

▲ Lennon alone in the early seventies.

▲ John Lennon working on his *Mind Games* album at the Record Plant in New York City, April 1972.

▼ Brian Hines (Denny Laine) aged three.

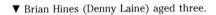

▼ Denny as a lonely teen in Birmingham.

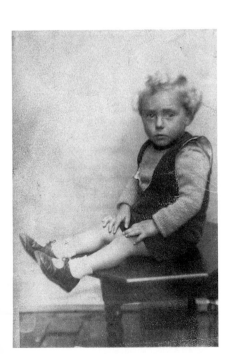

▲ Jo Jo and Denny in their busy home office, 1976.

▲ Pop star Denny at home at Yew Corner.

▼ A man with several skeletons in his closet.

▼ St. John's Wood, 1983. A period when Denny was particularly unpopular and broke.

Macca wailing away on the drums.

▲ James and Paul during session for *Tug of War*.

◄ Arriving at New York's Kennedy airport, September 1976.

▼ In the winner's circle. Jim McCartney enjoying a rare day at the races, 1967.

◄ A happy family. Ruth and Jim McCartney on vacation in Paris in the early sixties.

▼ Chatty Ruth poses for photographers inside Rembrandt.

► Showing off outside Rembrandt.

WINGS Tour Publicity Schedule

Date	City	Media	Participants	Timing
September 10th	Bristol	nothing scheduled		
September 11th	Cardiff	Harlech TV	whole group	2p.m. hotel
		BBC Wales TV		
		Swansea Sound	whole group	after sound check at theatre
September 12th	Manchester	Chris Welch coach ride interviews	whole group	coach ride from Cardiff to Manchester
		Piccadilly Radio & Granada TV	whole group	after sound check at theatre
		Manchester Evening News	whole group	15 minutes in dressing room after show
September 13th	Birmingham	German TV film	whole group	
		local radio	Denny Laine and group if they want	after show in dressing room
September 14th	Day off	nothing scheduled		
September 15th	Liverpool	Rolling Stone	whole group	after show dressing room
		Paul Drew RKO Radio	whole group	
		local radio	Paul & Linda McCartney and group if they wish	after show in dressing room 15 minutes
September 16th	Newcastle	nothing scheduled		
September 17th	London	BBC radio	whole group	after show in dressing room
		Capitol Radio	whole group	after show in dressing room
September 18th	London	nothing scheduled		
September 19th	Day off	nothing scheduled		
September 20th	Edinburgh	local radio	whole group	after sound check at theatre
September 21st	Glasgow	local radio	Jimmy McCullough and group if they wish	after show in dressing room 15 minutes

▲ A rare Wings publicity schedule.

◀ Wings on the road.

MIDLAND HOTEL.

PAUL McCARTNEY & WINGS ROOMING LIST

BAND		Room No.	CREW BAND		Room No.
Paul & Linda McCartney - 1	dbl. suite	221/9	Trevor Jones - twin		216
			John Hammill		
McCartney children (three)	1 triple	257	Peter Morley	twin	218
			Thomas Sellen		
Rose Martin	single	247	Derek Unwin - Twin		222
			Andy Collins		
Gary Foskett	single	257	Ray Watouski	twin	230
			Ian Peacock		
Mr. & Mrs. Laine	double	240	Craig Schertz	twin	156
			Maurice Lyda		
Mr. & Mrs. Dorsey and child	Double & extra bd.	351/3	Kirby Wyatt	twin	160
			Alan Owen		
Jimmy McCulloch	single	215	Jack Maxson - single		164/162
Joe English	Single	238	Pamela Keats - single		242
Stephen Howard	single	149	Steve Mately - single		130
Thaddeus Richard	single	263	Ian Knight - single		132
Howie Casey	single	209	Coach driver - single		274
Brian Brolly	single	273	Truck driver - twin		152
			Truck driver		
Alan Crowder	single	275	Clint Jones - single		224
Barry Humphries	single	277			
Bob Ellis	single	226			
Tony Brainsbury	single	168			
Brian Hunt	single	158			
Ann Bush	single	146			
Steve Coton	single	136			
Patrick Barthropp Co.	single	120			
(chauffeurs) " "	single	126			
Coach driver	single	281			
Ann Gillham	single	268			

M. BUSH. 241

GEE WIZARD SINGLE 249

GEE WIZARD TWIN 261.

▲ Gentleman Pete Best, Liverpool, 1983.

▲ The obviously lovely, talented, and keenly intelligent Ruth McCartney. Today Ruth is the head of a successful multi-media firm in L.A.

► Apple girl Mary Hopkin back in the mid-eighties at her sprawling home in Shiplake, Oxfordshire.

▲ McCartney's famous revolving glass meditation room behind his London townhouse. The Beatles were photographed here on several occasions in the late sixties.

▼ The author and company, Covent Garden, London, 1982.

▲ The author and Steve Holly at a recording session in New York, 1992.

▲ George Harrison meditating in Vrndavana, India, April 1996, just prior to the celebrated Beatles reunion. These days Harrison has recommitted himself to his practice of Bhakti Yoga.

► The McCartneys during their jolly World Tour in the early nineties.

▲ The charismatic McCartney in concert, 1990.

on a farm in rural England. Nobody buys new noses where I'm from!"

If the ever-steady Paul lapsed into a mid-life crisis, it certainly wasn't apparent. McCartney retreated quite happily to the family's 160-acre Peasmarsh estate, where reindeer roam casually in the front yard. Paul proudly tells visitors how he designed the mock Tudor home with its octagon windows and wildfowl pond, and how he and Linda established their own sanctuary on Exmoor to protect the deer.

Paul spent his leisure time sailing a Sunfish or in his studio painting, an avocation he took up at forty. In a short time McCartney created, in both oils and watercolor, some two hundred canvases, consisting of landscapes, abstracts, and several awkward likenesses of his wife. They hang side by side with the family's collection of old masters, which now reportedly includes a Rembrandt and a Renoir. It is rumored that Paul even quietly accepts commissions.

Just twenty minutes down the road McCartney continued to compose and record in his private 48-track, state-of-the-art Hog Hill Studios, a renovated mill dating back to the 1700s. Standing beside the latest technical wizardry was the Mellotron used in "Strawberry Fields Forever" and Elvis Presley's stand-up bass from "Heartbreak Hotel."

In 1992, Linda published yet another coffee table book, *Linda McCartney's Sixties*, a compilation of her insightful photographs of that decade's most famous personalities, including Janis Joplin, Jimi Hendrix, and the Rolling Stones. The collection, which also traveled throughout the United States, sparked some talk of Paul having squelched her career by turning her into a reluctant band member. "Paul jokes he ruined my career," she responded, "but I never really thought of myself as having a 'career' in photography."

To the press McCartney paints a Currier & Ives portrait of life at the edge of the Romney Marshes: the down-home boy repairing the cow shed or lovingly feeding the chickens. According to Linda, "The house is always full. The kids come by; we have friends over." It has been widely observed, however, that except for a handful of celebrity chums like Brian Clarke, Elvis Costello, and Keith Richards few outsiders have ever set foot inside McCartneyland.

Conversely, Peasmarsh natives haven't exactly embraced their celebrated neighbors, dubbing the property's looming watchtower "Paulditz," after Colditz, the notorious World War II P.O.W. compound. Paul, it seems, has placed an informal gag order on the entire village; even brother Mike will no longer speak publicly about the family. Stephen Jempson, proprietor of Jempson's Family Food Centre, which occasionally delivers groceries to the famous residents, acknowledged, "The consensus here is that no information should be given to journalists as is the McCartneys' express wish. Therefore, I'm not prepared to comment."

The town's reward for its collective silence was a hundred weight of potatoes to each and every pensioner at Christmas! As one resident wisecracked, "Goodness knows what the old dears will do with them, but I'm sure they send their grateful thanks."

One newcomer, obviously not yet indoctrinated into the way of Mr. McCartney's neighborhood, recently commented, "The McCartneys live in the wilds beyond the village. As the crow flies, they're neighbors, but socially a million miles away. Paul had a couple of perfectly good cottages knocked down because they spoiled the view. . . . They're really soppy about animals. *Over* sentimental, some say. . . . On Valentine's Day we had three blokes called Cosmotheka doing a music hall act, but McCartney didn't come. I'm sure he likes to think of himself as a man of the people; it's just that so few of us have ever actually seen him!"

The local observations, though, aren't entirely negative. As one villager noted, "I did see him in a shop once telling his children not to jump the queue like any other responsible parent. His children went to the Church of England school here and he attended parents' evenings. Linda served up vegetables at the weekly jumble sales. When the children went to the state secondary school, Linda was always taking photographs. They seem like very devoted parents and have made a real effort to avoid their children being spoiled. . . . It's impossible to go for a walk round these country lanes without being asked where Paul McCartney lives. You can't really blame them for hiding."

To their credit Paul and Linda educated their children at the local Thomas Peacocke Community in Rye. The McCartneys then sent Mary and Stella to Barrow Hill State Junior School. Paul personally picked them up every weekday afternoon.

"The nannies used to go mad," said one student. "Here was the most famous pop star in the world and he was one of the only parents to show up when it was time to go home."

Brenda Loydell, a teacher at Peacocke, noted, "I very much admire their decision to send the children to comprehensive. The girls still have close friends who went to this school."

Paul simply wasn't comfortable with the idea of boarding school: "I considered sending James to Eton, but I couldn't bear the thought of him coming home talking all posh saying, 'Hello, Pater.'"

The McCartney kids definitely grew up learning the value of a pound. One time on vacation in Barbados then ten-year-old Stella was shopping with the family and spied a ring in a store window. Although the price was a mere $1.60, she tentatively asked her father if it was too much. A smiling Paul, knowing he'd done his job, replied that it was indeed reasonable and bought the ring.

"You see," Paul once remarked, "if my kids are going to inherit money, and they will, it's important they have their feet on the ground. That's what Linda and I have tried to teach. In fact, we wanted to give them only one thing really; we wanted them to have big hearts."

Shielding the children from the limelight was also a top priority. Paul and Linda always made sure a trusted friend or family member, never a celebrity, escorted the girls.

Friends of the McCartney children attest they still generally shun the London nightlife for more sedate evenings at the movies or casual weekends at home.

Observed one friend, "Stella and Mary could easily do the Browns and Harry's Bar scene if they wanted, but they're more eclectic than that. You're more likely to find them in Notting Hill, in less glamorous, more funky places. They certainly like having fun, but they do it away from the paparazzi."

Incredibly, it seems as if the McCartney brood hardly realizes they're the progeny of a lauded former Beatle. One evening Mary, wearing thigh-high boots, a paisley waistcoat, and mini skirt, made a rare public appearance at the *Sirens* premiere when a photographer asked to take her picture. Hastily covering her face with a fan, she protested, "Why are you taking my picture? I'm nobody!"

When a reporter asked Stella what it was like to be the daughter of a Beatle, she replied, "It's just so naff. So uncool. You never even have to introduce yourself. You're famous before you even do anything."

Spending time at East Gate with the family, Paul continued his unfettered lifestyle, beginning the day with a simple fare of tea and toast, and perhaps on Sundays vegetarian sausage and eggs. "I remember when the Beatles first went to Hamburg, our bedrooms were just behind the toilet in this cinema and we were earning the huge fee of fifteen pounds a week; all we seemed to eat was egg and chips. We didn't know what German food was, so it was always egg and chips. And being Continental, they'd always serve it with a gherkin. As a Liverpool lad I'd never seen a gherkin before. The only pickled thing I'd seen was an onion in the chippie."

Inevitably, their simple veggie fare is culled from one of Linda's two successful cookbooks. She has called herself a "peasant cook" who believes the key to tasty dishes is in the flavoring (lemon and oregano, in particular) and light sauteing of the vegetables in oil before cooking. "I grew up in a family that loved good food, but I was the only one who really liked to cook," she remembered. "When I was growing up in Scarsdale, we had a cook. Maybe because of my insecurity I used to hang around the kitchen and watch her."

As for her husband, Paul's favorite meal these days seems to be quiche and tomato soup. Like Lennon before him, Macca is apparently quite a fair breadmaker, according to Linda, who said he made it everyday during England's bread strike. "My best dish is mashed potatoes," he has acknowledged. "A little milk, some chopped onions, that's the Liverpool version."

The McCartneys' zeal for strictly meatless fare extends to their professional life as well. During Paul's last tour the ever-frugal entertainer decided it would be economically savvy to serve a veggie banquet. "The food was so good," claimed McCartney, "most people didn't miss meat at all. We even had a few converts by the time it was over."

According to Paul's kid sister Ruth, however, during a 1991 show in Munich the roadies were locked inside the arena to prevent them from going to the Pizza Hut across the street in violation of Paul's strict "veggies only" mandate. No one knows who gave the order for the surprise lock-up. There were also rumors of a top-secret "meat room," where the roadies could eat what they liked, as well as a private air-conditioned glass "meditation box" Paul takes on tour with him and uses faithfully before every show.

Even with the mighty McCartneys leading the way, not everyone blissfully jumped on the bandwagon. *The Guardian*, ever a thorn in the McCartneys' side, went on the attack in a searing article entitled, "The Unbearable Smugness of Being Vegetarian": "Vegetarianism has never just been about not eating meat. It has almost always involved lifestyle choices, moral poses, and ascetic habits. That all-or-nothing attitude to vegetables runs all the way from Pythagoras, who believed animals had souls, to Tolstoy, who liked to think vegetarianism might help establish God's kingdom on earth."

Unphased, Linda continued to refer to meat as "flesh" or the more provocative "slab of fear." Her first cookbook has sold over 250,000 copies, and her *Linda McCartney's Home-style Cooking* (a top-flight line of tasty frozen entrees, whose eighteen items include lasagna, pot pies, and even goulash) reportedly nets a staggering 55 million dollars annually.

"Humans have won the species battle on this planet," Paul has said. "Perhaps in victory we could be noble, but we're not. We still continue to mash every little thing that moves."

The health-conscious McCartney, though, still confesses to a fondness for Johnnie Walker Red and Coke Classic, but he now imposes strict limits: "Four is my max. Four and I'm anybody's. It all began with the Beatles. It started as bourbon and 7-Up, which I think Ringo drank, being the sophisticate among us. If there was anything American like Lark cigarettes, Ringo knew about it. To us Ringo was older. Besides, he'd worked at Butlin's, grown a beard, and wore a suit. That was all very sophisticated to us, especially drinking bourbon, which I'd never heard of. But bourbon and 7-Up was the drink, which turned into Scotch and Coke somewhere along the line, probably when we couldn't find any bourbon."

As 1993 approached, McCartney was planning an eight-month world tour that would include his first televised concert from Charlotte, North Carolina to support his 23rd album, *Off the Ground.* The album's release was tied, of course, to McCartney's $100-million recording deal with Capitol/EMI, signed in December—virtually a lifetime contract.

At 51, Paul declared it was all about a continuing need to prove himself: "I'm not desperate for people to think of me as a rock star, but it's true that once you get on tour you start hearing them say, 'Hey, you can sing. You're not really bad, are you? I didn't realize you wrote that!' When you hear that, you think, 'Where have they been for the past twenty years? It kind of surprises you how soon people forget what it is you do. . . . So I pack my bags, pick up the Hoffner, and get out on the road again, aiming to give people a party they can remember the rest of their lives.

"People say to me 'Paul, what is there left to work for?' But the point is I don't do this for the money anymore, or even the honor or applause. I do it for *myself*. That's what's left to work for. Always."

A May appearance at the Hollywood Bowl for Earth Day, sponsored by Concerts for the Environment, found the musician propelled into the activist role by contemporaries like Sting, Pete Townshend, and Peter Gabriel. Unlike his unusually well-versed colleagues, McCartney's approach was less subtle as he illustrated with his earnest, painfully polemical, unintentionally humorous lyrics for "Looking for Changes": "I saw a monkey that was learning to choke/A guy beside him gave him cigarettes to smoke/And every time that monkey started to cough/The bastard laughed his head off." Real stirring stuff indeed!

Paul told the Los Angeles press, "Enjoy Earth Day. In this universe this is the planet we live on. We must be aware of it and take care of it." When pressed for further wisdom, he admitted, "Generally, I'm not a guy with a lot of messages. . . . I say, 'Hang in there and let's hope things get straightened out and we're going into a good phase.'" With that, he politely begged off, saying he had a show to do.

The L. A. gig was most notable for an impromptu appearance by Ringo Starr for a celebrity chorus of "Hey Jude." Once again, the incident ignited rumors of a Fab reunion, which Paul was quick to dismiss: "If you could bring back Charlie Chaplin and Buster Keaton and have them do a funny little routine, wouldn't we love it? We always want what we can't have. We want summer, *that first summer*, those golden days when we all had nothing to do except look for girls." Little did he know just how soon he would swallow those words.

With the tour came the inevitable press junket, an obligation which Paul admitted he was never really comfortable with: "I'm not a great believer in the public me. When John and I were having our ding dongs, and he was getting at me in the press, I thought, 'This isn't me'. I don't like to give anyone the whole deal. I think it's stupid. I haven't seen Madonna's book [*Sex*], but I presume she gives it all away. People are doing too much of that for their own good."

He then candidly admitted, "I'm a smoke-screen expert since John got shot. I lie all the time. It's the price of fame."

One could scarcely blame the aging rock star for his stellar distrust of the press. In 1991 a bootleg tape of Linda's backing vocals—a particularly indictful and off-key snippet—leaked to the press, which broadcast it worldwide. "It was a horror," grimaced McCartney. "I had to remind her the Stones also have tapes out like that. It's easy to isolate harmonies. You just take it out and it sounds horrible on the radio. She had to be very strong because it's not easy to be made fun of."

"I really don't give a damn what people think," retorted Linda. "I've always wanted to meet [the people responsible] and stick my fingers in their eyes."

The image-conscious McCartney was savvy enough, however, to use it to promote the "sensitive" Paul, the one who takes his entire family on the road, whose kids show up for rehearsals to cheer on their rockin' dad. His party line promotes the image of a clean-living, ever-faithful husband and stalwart father who never misses a chance to remind the public he's still just a man of the people.

"I'm an ordinary bloke," he has said. "Not because I'm famous, but ordinary in the sense I was brought up in Liverpool by very ordinary people. They were earthy people who taught me straight values: honesty, respect, and politeness. I've stuck with those and tried to pass them on to my kids. When certain people get rich, they sometimes wear fur coats and big diamond watches. I've gone the other way. I'd rather be remembered as a musician than a celebrity."

As a teenager Paul used to wait outside Liverpool theaters hoping to snag a celebrity autograph. "Some just didn't want to know and walked by this scruffy kid with his bit of paper and a pencil. But one American band stopped, signed the autographs, and their leader said, 'Hey kid, you can walk with me to the car.' That made me feel so good that when I got my bit of fame, I thought, 'If you can help make someone's day by signing your name for them, why not do it?'"

But then there is that *other* Paul, the one who manipulates interviews when he isn't being deliberately curt with the media. One journalist complained, "Seldom did McCartney offer more than short, monosyllabic answers. He couldn't conceal his boredom." According to one British reporter, the appearance of the gracious, accommodating, more mellow Paul hinges on whether he's smoked his "herbal jazzed cigarettes" as he calls them. The reporter recalled a one-on-one chat in St. Paul, Minnesota during the mid-seventies: "I remember him as friendly and charming. His answers to questions were thoughtful and he spoke in paragraphs, not sentences. It was not unlike many other interviews with big stars I've conducted over the years. With one exception. McCartney smoked a joint during the interview. And being a nice guy, he passed it around to the others in the room."

A writer from the *Star Tribune* described a less-easygoing encounter: "McCartney and his people can be very demanding. For every happy 'My Encounter with a Beatle' story ('we talked about our sandals,' said a staffer), there was a tale from hell. For instance, on one occasion there was a frantic scramble to remove several Cornish hens from the backstage catering area as the McCartneys didn't approve of such food."

While such actions might be forgiven on a public level, it's not so easy to absolve the McCartneys for transgressions that involve their own family. The meticulously run, multi-million-dollar McCartney PR machine paints a portrait of a loving family man who treasures home, hearth, and Mother Earth above fame. Few, however, have peered behind the massive, impenetrable wall that guards his private life. In an extended series of taped interviews recorded in 1994 with Paul's stepmother Angie McCartney and his adopted sister Ruth, they bared their souls about their entire fourteen-year experience with Paul and Linda. According to Angie and Ruth, when deemed necessary, McCartney has turned his money and status into a weapon of intimidation to silence all naysayers. Then why did they dare to step forward after so many years?

"Because we've been written out of history," Angie affirmed, "and because Paul has chosen not to even recognize our existence. After the many fine years I shared with his father it is the final insult."

Indeed, only a few years ago, a German reporter asked McCartney to comment on sister Ruth's show-biz success. "I don't have a sister," he answered and walked steadily past.

Conversely, Angie and Ruth vividly recalled visiting the Bahamas during the filming of *Help!*, and happily swapping stories with John Lennon and actor Victor Spinetti by night. In the middle of a press conference, before a packed room of reporters, Paul spotted his family and coldly snapped, "What are *you* doing here!" Fortunately, John defused the mortifying moment by congratulating Jim and Angie on their recent marriage and making plans to get together later in the day.

Back home with Jim in Liverpool, Angie quickly became the target of the clannish, gossipy McCartneys, led by the acerbic matriarch Auntie Jin and the kind-but-sheepish Millie (who basically raised Paul following the death of his mum). "Don't get any ideas above your station," they constantly reminded Angie. "Never forget, you're only a married-in!"

Intent on keeping her an outsider, they accused Angie of a sordid past as well as of having countless torrid affairs with everyone from the gardener to family friend Michael Barratt, a popular British television presenter.

Throughout their marriage Angie was regularly traumatized by Paul's nearly constant manipulation. The first great shock occurred when suddenly—without reason—Jim approached his young wife and declared, "Angie, it's just not working out. I don't think we should be married anymore. I know Paul will see you and Ruth alright." This horrifying vignette was repeated only a few years later when the Great Beatle, in a rage over Angie attending a concert without being specifically invited, ordered his father to "get rid of her!"

In fact, Jim McCartney was an exceptionally kind, loving man who doted on Ruth and even adopted her, making her under British law a full-fledged daughter and forever a McCartney—something that obviously irks Paul to this day. Naturally meek and ultra-conservative, Jim could never stand up to his superstar son and suffered in silence under his own roof, a victim of Paul's role as financial benefactor. Another point of contention was Paul's legendary devotion to pot.

"Don't be bringing that stuff into this house!" warned Jim.

"Whose house is it anyway?" Paul challenged.

"Well, it's in my name," the obviously mortified elder McCartney replied.

"I paid for it and don't you bloody forget it!"

Another time, after the sudden death of Angie's sister Mae, several close friends were invited over to give comfort and support. No one was aware that Paul and Linda were heading up to Liverpool; one of McCartney's iron-clad rules was always "no guests when we come to visit." Despite apologies from a grieving Angie, Paul reportedly exploded. "Listen, this is my house! Don't ever forget I put every fuckin' crumb of food into your mouth and your kids. If it wasn't for me, you'd be on the bloody street!"

When Aunt Millie tried to smooth things over, Paul lashed out, "Just keep out of it, Millie! This is my fuckin' house! I paid for it and I feed *all* of them!"

Paul's reputation as a miser reached an all-time low when the errant multi-millionaire forced his own family out of Rembrandt and into a modest bungalow. While his aging father was suffering from crippling arthritis and a debilitating decline in his general health, Paul allotted them a meager income of only L7,000 a year. As Jim's condition worsened, the extended McCartney clan openly challenged Angie's decision to respect Jim's wish that he not be placed in a nursing home. Angie and Ruth's unconditional devotion caused even Paul to admit, "I can't thank you enough for everything you've done for my dad. You'll never want for anything."

Never would words ring so dreadfully hollow. Following Jim's painful death in 1976, Paul shunned Angie and Ruth, severing all assistance and cold-shouldering them emotionally. No one attended the funeral; even Aunt Millie refused to come. The very day of the funeral a close relative seized the opportunity to empty out the old man's closet, while a younger relative stole a case of whisky from the house. The bitter truth then gushed out: the McCartney clan had viewed Angie as a gold digger all along. Paul even left Angie to pay for the flowers he sent on his and Linda's behalf.

Incredibly, after Jim's death Angie and Ruth were actually snipped out of family pictures as if they'd never existed. Forced to sell their home, they were soon living in an empty building and sleeping on the bare floor! Angie recalled the humiliation of applying for a meager weekly allotment from social services, and having to sell precious mementos (including a copy of Paul's birth certificate). It was an unfortunate episode that garnered international headlines and further alienated the former Beatle. Mother and daughter, however, pushed on, with Ruth working five jobs for only L92 a week. "Six years after Jim died, we were living in our car, dating boring men for a free dinner," Angie bitterly recalled.

Their final contact with Paul occurred in 1980 when they reluctantly asked for his help. McCartney's callousness was palpable: "Why can't you stay at home, bottle fruit, and be a proper widow, Ange? I could easily help you, but I think it would be far more character-building for you to go it alone. Scrub floors, if you have to!"

Then to Ruth: "You're never gonna make it in the business. This dancer/choreographer nonsense is just a phase.
You don't have anything going for you but my name. You're
not really too bad-looking. Why don't you hang around the
clubs and pick up a rich Arab boyfriend and do what women
like you are made for." The fact is, however, that Ruth
McCartney is one of the most persuasively beautiful, talented, and disciplined young women this author has had the
pleasure to have known.

During that same call Paul also railed against Ruth and
Angie for selling a family piano Paul had used extensively
throughout the turbulent Beatle years.

Angie admitted: "Yes, we were guilty. We sold the piano
for L680, along with a load of other old furniture we couldn't
use anymore because we were being evicted by the mortgage company and we were flat broke."

"It turned up later at Sotheby's and went for L14,000," explained Ruth. "Mum was trying to dig out of a mountain of
debt, much of it from Jim's medical expenses. . . . I put the
phone down on him that day. I was his sister, we'd shared
a bathroom, so I didn't see him as a god. I was one of the
very few people left who would tell him to fuck off. I actually
dared put the phone down on him. I'll never forget his last
words to me. He said, 'You can't put the phone down on me.'
'Why?' I asked. 'Because,' came the pompous reply, 'I'm Paul
McCartney!' I never heard from him again."

According to the pair, Linda was never especially charitable to them *or* Jim. Ruth said Linda thought nothing of reading Angie's private diary and deeply embarrassed her by
disclosing a particularly personal entry before the entire
family. Linda also prevented Ruth from attending a long-an-
ticipated Wings launch party, yet allowed her own daughter
Heather to go. When Linda was in Liverpool, she constantly
"borrowed" food from Jim and Angie's refrigerator and then
casually let it go to waste.

Sometimes, Angie said, flies would fall into the aging Jim's
milk and Linda would expect him to still drink it. Wood-

worms too were tolerated at Rembrandt because "every creature has a right to live."

At the 21st birthday of Carol McCartney (Jim's niece), Mike warned Angie, a competent pianist, "if they ask you to play the piano tonight, give it a miss. There's only *one* star in this family!"

"Paul was such an immense presence," Ruth recalled, "traveling the world like a colossus. He began to see everything through a prism that was Paul McCartney. Others had no reality as entities apart from him. But Paul never intimidated John. Lennon would say, 'That bridge sucks, let's try something else.' He needed that. They were brothers, partners, and serious rivals. Their terrible infighting made the material that much better. Now when Paul works with someone [like] Elvis Costello, Costello is so in awe of him it doesn't work. No one can tell him, 'No, that doesn't make it. Let's try it this way.' If they do say what they think, they're not around long.

"The Beatles were not just a milestone, they were a saga, an ongoing musical drama they created and lived. Many of us remember our lives in terms of the Beatles. People tell me they got married around the time of *Sgt. Pepper*, sacked when *Abbey Road* was released, divorced when John was murdered.

"My memories are no different. They're forever linked to my mother Angie, my father Jim, my brothers Mike and Paul, to George, Ringo, and John. I was fortunate. I got closer to the light than most. I'll cherish the privilege of those memories while I exult in the life I have now. The life *I've* chosen."

On stage, however, the public image prevails. The ageing Beatle is still an impeccable showman. For the sheer love of performing Paul McCartney is unchallenged and remains the greatest single draw on the concert circuit. What distinguished the '93 tour (which played to 1.3 million fans in America alone) was McCartney's decision to perform Beatles tunes the Fabs had never played live, including "Paperback Writer," "Penny Lane," and "Lady Madonna." McCartney explained that the timing was finally right. "When the Beatles broke up, we all independently agreed we wouldn't do Beatles songs. We didn't talk to each other. Now there's so much water under the bridge it's time again. Either we completely turn our backs on that period forever and say, 'No, I didn't have a youth,' or we say, 'Jesus Christ, it was great!' I love singing those old songs, or rather rediscovering them."

But this was still very much a tour to support McCartney's latest album, *Off the Ground*, and considering the disappointing sales of past endeavors, his new material took center stage. This was a much-improved effort, with Paul recapturing the feel of his early Beatles roots. *The Washington Post* wrote: "McCartney's *Off the Ground* impresses with its unmistakable tunefulness and pop craft, beginning with the typically buoyant title cut. The entire album fairly resonates with echoes of things past, some as obvious as the 'All You Need Is Love' sentiment expressed on 'Hope of Deliverance,' others as subtle as the 'Penny Lane'-ish trumpet on 'Mistress and Maid.'"

For the project Paul again teamed up with his *Flowers in the Dirt* cohort, Elvis Costello, whose coauthorship on "The Lovers That Never Were" reined in the familiar McCartney chirpiness. Paul even drew shock waves for his first-ever use of profanity on "Big Boys Bickering." The publicity generated by the tour paid off, with sales for *Off the Ground* reaching three million dollars worldwide in just five months.

Coming off the triumphant American and Australian legs of his tour in September, McCartney was back on English soil in the middle of a wildly successful three-night date at the Earl's Court Olympia in London. On the 12th of that month he and Linda received a harrowing call from the Coast Guard: James McCartney was reported missing at sea. The boy, along with a party of four friends, had gone bodyboarding off Camber Sands near Rye to celebrate his sixteenth birthday. When the others surfed back to shore,

James was nowhere to be found and in a panic they called for help. As twilight approached, the Coast Guard mounted a helicopter-and-lifeboat search while a distraught Paul and Linda, along with daughter Stella, rushed to the site. The family could only watch helplessly as gusty twenty-m.p.h. winds coupled with a fierce rainstorm to unleash terrorizing swells over the dark ocean waters.

One official told them grimly, "Anyone in distress at sea at dusk is in serious trouble."

For several hours the search continued, the McCartneys in tears. At last, young James—shaken and exhausted but otherwise safe—drifted into shore. The storm had blown him a mile and a half out to sea, but thanks to a wet suit and his considerable experience as a swimmer he managed to keep his wits about him.

The album and tour behind him, Paul kept a relatively low profile over the next two years. He reportedly spent a lot of time in his immaculate Regency-style MPL Soho offices, a company so clandestine not even a telephone listing exists and the number of employees (believed to be about twenty) is top secret. These days, however, the company is prominent on the internet with at least two first-class sites hawking its vast publishing concerns as well as Paul's new *Flaming Pie* album.

As Derek Taylor recalled: "When Paul first set up MPL, I went to see what he'd made of it. It was on three or four floors and was exactly what he'd wanted Apple to be. It was beautiful, orderly, nice carpets, plenty of hush, nice modern paintings on the walls. Paul likes to keep his office as orderly as possible, a quality he shares with George. They are tidy people. Apple was messy. All sorts of people wandered in and out.

"Paul pays enormous attention to detail. All perfectionists can be exacting at times and Paul doesn't like short cuts. He puts in a strict five-day week. This is a man who could be sitting on an island in the sun, but he loves hard work."

McCartney has been also keeping close tabs on the renovation of his old family home at 20 Forthlin Road. Purchased by the National Trust in 1995 for $50,000, the Allerton home of Liverpool's most famous son, heralded as the "Birthplace of the Beatles," is being readied for its slated opening in 1998. Heading the project is Julian Gibbs, Historic Buildings Representative for the Trust. His zeal for the property has often placed him at odds with elitist officials who declared this public shrine an unworthy piece of pop culture. In Gibbs's view: "The Trust looks after the houses of Churchill, Kipling, Hardy, why not McCartney? The Beatles are certainly twentieth-century icons."

Gibbs faces a formidable and exciting challenge. The home's last owner, one Mrs. Jones, did a complete overhaul, coating the walls with a heavy-duty plaster called Artex. The kindly woman often acted as an unofficial tour guide, inviting in fans and giving them souvenirs like tiny pieces of the old net curtains.

Most of the budget, however, will be reserved for the exterior, preserving the original front door, timber sash windows, and wooden gate, along with the privet hedge. Inside there will be prominent displays of photographs by Mike McCartney (who is acting as an advisor on the project) and Jim's old piano. Gibbs hopes the Hard Rock Cafe will donate Paul's bedroom door. "Everyone expects it to become a popular attraction, fun and evocative, not precious or sentimental. Forthlin Road is the stuff of dreams: a legend was created in this ordinary house, which looks exactly like thousands of others."

McCartney himself is more than pleased. "My mum would have been dead chuffed to think our little council house would end up with the National Trust. It's a fantastic honor for me and my family. This house was the scene of many formative Beatles years such as leaving for Hamburg, rehearsing our act, and writing songs. Sometimes we made a bit of a row. I hope it will be quieter now that the National Trust has got it."

One time, when he and Linda pulled up outside in their sleek black Mercedes, Paul recalled a young boy knocking on the car window. "You know, Paul McCartney used to live there," he smartly informed the pair.

"Have you ever seen him?" Paul grinned.

"No, but me dad has."

"Well, now you can tell your dad you've met Paul McCartney as well and he's come back to look at his old digs." With that he drove off, leaving the youngster staring back in awe.

This was one example, noted Derek Taylor, of McCartney's inherent benevolence. "What is obvious is his enormous personal charm. Behind, where nobody sees, he's also extremely generous. He can be quite sensitive to criticism like anyone. We had some very bad rows over a book I wrote, but he bore no malice because it was not a disloyal book. He's nice with the little people."

Another project that kept McCartney busy over 1994 and 1995 was a new cinematographic adventure, one of the former Beatle's little-known passions. It all started when the musician began perusing contact sheets Linda had shot of the Grateful Dead over 1967–1968. Not only had she photographed the band performing in New York's Central Park, but she'd also captured rare private moments of the Dead at home in San Francisco. Studying the shots reminded McCartney of an experience he'd had as a kid while trying to amuse himself when bedridden with an illness: "By concentrating on a photograph in a newspaper I seemed to be able to make it move. Looking at these images, I got that feeling again and thought maybe I could make these four rolls more interesting by making a film of the Dead at a time of which not much footage exists."

McCartney then filmed the prints in a variety of styles on a rostrum camera and loaded the resulting film into a computer and began to edit. The final product, *The Grateful Dead, A Photofilm*, a nine-minute presentation, featured a soundtrack compiled from excerpts of three Dead tracks: "Now Potato Caboose," "That's It for the Other One" and "Alligator." McCartney's coproducer, Robert "Robbie" Montgomery, said it was definitely Paul's baby from start to finish. "It became a film that examines a time and a feeling that no longer exists."

The film debuted at the London Film Festival in November 1995 and was subsequently shown at major festivals worldwide over the next year, culminating with its triumphant run at the prestigious New York Film Festival in October 1996.

That modest coup notwithstanding, it was greatly overshadowed that November by the eagerly anticipated airing of the ABC-television series *The Beatles Anthology*, along with the accompanying three-volume, six-CD set of the same name. The six-hour documentary, produced under the working title *The Long and Winding Road*, had long been on McCartney's agenda. The timing among the three surviving Beatles, however, hadn't really yet been right.

As Paul explained: "The fact is we were arguing for so many years over business, we couldn't have done it. Once we started to resolve our differences—now we're chatty and mates again—we began looking for the CD, the T-shirt and the cookbook!" It was widely reported that the $130-million compensation very much appealed to George Harrison and Ringo Starr, both rumored to be in need of ready cash.

Actually, the Beatles ball started rolling again in 1994 with the release of the two-CD *Live at the BBC*, which quickly sold an enticing eight million copies. The market for Beatles product was definitely still happening and simply waiting for the remaining Fabs to capitalize. For McCartney, of course, the motivation went further than mere dollars. As always, his competitiveness with John figured prominently. Writer Richard Corliss put it this way: "Paul always shivered in John's shadow. Partly it was his looks. He was cute, coquettish—almost the *girl* of the group—so how could he also be smart? He was the favorite of the girls, whose screams dominated early Beatles concerts, but he wasn't really a guy's guy. No way could he satisfy the emerging establishment of rock critics, a strictly male coterie. He just tried too hard.

Paul always wanted to be loved, which is the essence of the pop star. John didn't care. The essence of the rock star. His edginess suggested a rolling interior life; you could write a novel about what you imagined was inside John Lennon. Then he had the rock star's karma to die violently. Now he is in the Rock'n'Roll Hall of Fame as a solo artist and McCartney isn't."

Anthology video director Bob Smeaton added his own insight: "Since John's death Paul has faded into the background. It has become very much 'John Lennon and the Beatles.' And I think Paul desperately wanted to put his side of the story across."

So some twenty-five years later, the Fab Three gathered before the cameras to film their by-now-rather-Spartan reminiscences. If fans were perched on the edge of their seats hoping for some untapped nuggets of revelation, they were keenly disappointed. Of the LSD experience McCartney sheepishly recalled, "John was excited by that prospect and I was rather frightened." Of Beatlemania itself Harrison had this view: "They used us as an excuse to go mad, the world did, and then they blamed it on us." Stirring stuff indeed.

Despite the contention of most critics that the highlight of the show was Paul's primal performance of "I'm Down," it was more likely Lennon's terse, insightful quip about the band's dissolution that percolated most in viewer's minds: "It was a slow death."

Poor Paul, it seemed, couldn't win. Even from the grave Lennon lay at the heart of the project, providing the kind of Beatles reunion even the public hadn't dreamed possible. The ever-ambitious Yoko Ono had donated one of John's scratchy cassette demos he'd recorded around 1977: a wistful ballad of hope and redemption entitled "Free As a Bird." Once the track was digitally cleaned up, McCartney, Harrison, and Starr strolled into Abbey Road, prepared to make history. Under the tutelage of soppy producer Jeff Lynne, Ringo laid down his drums, Paul added bass and acoustic guitar, while George provided slide. Modern technology did the rest, at last allowing them to reunite with their slain comrade. As they put on the final touches, those distinctive Fab harmonies, the ever-ingratiating Lynne declared, "God, it sounds like the Beatles in there!"

The Beatles may have been back, but it became quickly evident they couldn't recapture the past. The resulting "Free As a Bird" sounded heavy-handed, hokey, and hopelessly dated. The only saving grace was Harrison's stirring guitar solo. The Beatles' accompanying "tragical history tour" video was even worse. Paul's added lyrics proved as limp as ever: "Whatever happened to/The life that we once knew/Can we really live without each other?" Despite Derek Taylor's repeated public predictions to the contrary, the tune peaked briefly in the lower end of Billboard's Top Forty before its inevitable crash and burn. Artistically and even culturally, the Beatles were as irretrievably lost as the late John Lennon. A fact that only a few thousand obsessive-compulsive fans and the Beatles themselves refused to acknowledge.

On the heels of the media frenzy, just when McCartney sought to kick back for some well-deserved time off, his idyllic world was shattered abruptly; in early December during a routine exam doctors found a suspicious lump in Linda's breast. A biopsy confirmed the diagnosis: the 53-year-old Linda McCartney had cancer. For Paul, the devastating news unearthed agonizing memories when his own mother Mary succumbed to the disease. For Linda, it was perhaps the cruelest of ironies. Just weeks before in a public appearance tied to one of her many vegetarian causes she proclaimed, "Doctors say you're far less likely to die of cancer and heart disease if you don't eat meat." Even a pristine lifestyle was unable to protect her from this insidious, often fatal, illness.

Ten days after the diagnosis Linda underwent a lumpectomy at London's Princess Grace Hospital, an operation Paul deemed "100 percent successful, thank God. Doctors have told her just to get some rest. We're very optimistic about the future and for the moment everything goes on as normal."

Except nothing was normal at all. While Linda recuperated uneasily in the hospital, Paul vigilantly at her side, thieves broke down the door of their Cavendish Avenue home, ransacking Stella's basement flat, nabbing an expensive camera and dozens of CDs, and causing thousands of pounds' worth of damage. "This is unfortunately a common occurrence," a weary Paul told the press. "This house has been broken into many times during the past thirty years, as this part of London is a favorite areas for burglars. Luckily, nothing of value was taken. We are improving security, but obviously this incident doesn't help at a time like this."

As soon as Paul brought Linda back to the farm, their peace was promptly invaded by hordes of photographers lying in wait to get a shot of the famous patient fresh from surgery. This time, the usually diplomatic Paul didn't mince words. "The doctors have said she will need a couple of months recuperation; she just needs peace and quiet at the moment. I have always played ball with the press, but now I ask all the reporters and photographers to please back off, as our family needs to be very positive. If they don't back off, I believe that under the circumstances they will be guilty of harassment and I promise I shall report them to the Press Complaints Commission."

With that, the McCartneys retreated behind an airtight veil of secrecy. After a few months Linda opted to follow up the surgery with chemotherapy. But no one caught so much as a glimpse of her. As one neighbor observed, "Linda used to run around in a modest cerise Ford Fiesta, but I haven't seen her out and about for a very long time."

Meanwhile, as 1996 rolled around, McCartney was busy realizing a seven-year dream. In January the doors opened to his Liverpool Institute of the Performing Arts [LIPA]. Situated on the site of his old grammar school, Paul founded the college by investing some two million dollars, helped along by a hefty donation from the Queen. The state-of-the-art facility is the first of its kind, offering 200 students a practical approach for breaking into—and surviving—the entertainment business. In the words of David Price, pop musician turned managing director for learning: "At degree level I think we are probably the only institute in the world which brings students from a number of disciplines together to study under one roof. We also have very high business and technological input into the courses."

In Paul's view: "It's all very well being able to write songs, but Lennon and McCartney were pretty neatly ripped off because they didn't know anything about business. So why not learn a little bit about business as you're writing the songs; it could save a lot of trouble in the future."

LIPA boasted a truly universal flavor, enrolling aspiring artists in the theater, music, and dance disciplines from all over the world. One aspiring recording engineer from Tokyo admitted, "I can't deny I took an interest in this place because it is Paul McCartney's school. I find what LIPA offers unique. It is very difficult to make money out of classical or modern music simply because it is not so popular."

One of the institute's greatest draws was its all-star faculty. Only a heavyweight like Paul McCartney could lure Tony award–winning theater designer John Napier, choreographer Gillian Lynne, and top rockers like Mark Knopfler and Elvis Costello into his classrooms. The institution put not only Liverpool but all of England on the map as "a very important place for pop," affirmed Price.

As the year advanced, McCartney's public appearances were noted for the conspicuous absence of Linda. In June, when he attended the official opening of LIPA by Queen Elizabeth, he would only say, "It's a bit hectic for her, but she's doing well."

Not surprisingly, by September speculation ran wild. Linda hadn't been seen since the surgery, some *nine* months earlier. Paul, seeking to quash the rumors, stated, "She is doing incredibly well and the doctors are amazingly pleased with her. Linda is the most positive person on Earth. She's fantastic. That's the thing about this, you have to be positive. No one gets away with a perfect life, and Linda and I have been luckier than most."

The McCartneys' ever-vigilant agent Geoff Baker chimed in as well. "[Linda's had] a complete recovery. She's feeling great. She's been horse riding nearly every day." He added that Linda had opted out of the public eye simply to spend more time with her family.

By October 6th, scarcely one month later, even the genial Mike McCartney, who had himself survived a frightening bout with skin cancer two years earlier, was forced to issue damage control when Paul failed to show for Abbey Road Studios' 65th birthday bash. "Everything is going fine," he stated. "Linda has more stamina than all of us and Paul is always there for her. There was a point when everyone was really concerned for her, but I think she is in the clear and we are all delighted. Thank God for modern science. Things have changed a lot since our mum died. Thank goodness we've got the facilities to arrest this thing early on."

But was the deadly cancer really arrested? A critical turning point occurred on November 23, 1996 when Linda was scheduled to attend the opening of an exhibit of her photographs (entitled *Roadworks* for her accompanying book) at the National Museum of Photography, Film, and Television in Bradford. The exhibition included shots taken over thirty years, ranging from her stint as resident photographer at the Fillmore, to life on the road with Paul, to portraits of modern-day street life featuring panhandlers and bag ladies. The exhibit's curator, Martin Harrison, praised the collection as being "like their author, natural and spontaneous."

The anticipation of Linda's appearance took center stage. Geoff Baker, as always, confidently stated, "As far as I am aware she will certainly be at the opening. It will mark her return to public life."

Yet the exhibition came and went with Mrs. McCartney a disturbing no-show. Clearly, something was very wrong. It had been nearly a year since the operation to remove "a small lump" (as Paul had categorized it) and it was apparent the "few months recuperation" had metamorphsed into something far more worrisome.

In the wake of the family's adamant silence the press was giving increasing credence to an agency report, which had been circulating, that Linda had suffered a serious recurrence of the cancer and was receiving intensive treatment for several months in Los Angeles. Friends, however, claimed the couple were merely enjoying an extended holiday in southern California.

At last, in mid-December Linda braved the cameras for a brief appearance in Los Angeles. She videotaped her acceptance of a Lifetime Achievement honor from the animal rights organization People for the Ethical Treatment of Animals [PETA]. Linda stood at the podium for a mere forty-two seconds, but it was long enough to tell a very grim tale. Her usually healthy complexion now pasty and puffy, she wore a baggy blouse and jacket, her once-blonde tresses reduced to a wispy short crop of drab brown hair.

One guest remarked, "Her face was waxy and her eyebrows heavily penciled. Her hair looked very thin and it was a uniform length all over as if it was just growing back." These were clear indications, not of the usual small dose of chemo, but of the high concentration that causes hair loss and fatigue. Linda looked as if she'd been fighting an intense, perhaps even losing, battle for some time.

Paul stood valiantly at her side, casting reassuring smiles. His hair was cut short in a display of "sympathetic suffering." According to renowned psychologist Martin Skinner: "This is an attempt to share pain through looking physically alike. It is a loving act. Couples do tend to mimic each other and in the end can look almost identical, especially in a marriage as loving and close as this."

It was clear that even so simple an endeavor as briefly attending a ceremony had exacted a severe toll. Linda thanked the hosts, actors Alec Baldwin and wife Kim Bassinger, before reading her brief speech from the teleprompter. Moving not a muscle, Linda slowly and awkwardly delivered her speech, glancing several times in Paul's direction for encouragement. The *Daily Mirror* reported, "Her eyebrows moved up and down like a cartoon character as she spoke about how much receiving the award meant to her. Paul stood behind her, supportive and proud, nodding in agreement."

Mrs. McCartney wound up the speech by saying, "You've certainly brightened up my year," with Paul chirping in, "Peace and love from me." "And from the kids," Linda added. Spontaneously they both cried, "And from the animals!" Linda then made a fist and exclaimed, "*Yes!,*" as they carefully exited the podium. All things considered, it was a highly suspect performance.

McCartney chum Carla Lane was understandably supportive. "I think Linda looks wonderful. Paul is so pleased and the rest of the family overjoyed at the progress she's making. Right from the start she's been very spiritual about everything. She decided she wasn't going to let the cancer get her. She always remained bright, got on with life, and wondered how she could help others with the disease. She's also been talking about buying a scanner for a hospital. Her award from PETA will do her a power of good and she more than deserves that. Bless her."

Those carefully chosen words of optimism, however, belied the reality. In the aftermath the London papers quoted Dr. Tony Leathem, a breast cancer expert who spoke about fatality and how the "secondary spread" of tumors claimed the most victims. The type of chemotherapy Linda appeared to be receiving was so dangerously potent five percent of recipients died from the ill effects alone. "A positive attitude and a good quality of life determine how well a patient responds to chemotherapy," Leathem noted.

Once again spin-doctor Geoff Baker did his best to put a cheery veneer on the increasingly bleak situation. "I spoke to Linda only yesterday. She's doing great. She's happy, full of life, and back to work putting together a photo film of stills she took of the Beatles and working on a new book."

Rather ominously, he added, "I can't comment on any treatment she is receiving or has received. And I can't say if she's beaten the cancer. I'm not God!" This was a clearly definite departure from the supreme confidence of the past year.

Three months later, the attention once more returned to Paul as all of London was buzzing about his imminent investiture in the Order of Knighthood. While his Beatles cohorts ribbed him about the honor, reportedly calling him "Your Holiness," this was exactly the kind of mantle McCartney coveted, one that exceeded mere pop stardom, an acknowledgment of respectability and esteem from the highest authority. After all, in pop music only George Martin and Cliff Richard had been knighted. While Lennon had returned his MBE (one step below knighthood) some thirty years earlier, Paul had not only kept his, but now, finally, he had something Lennon didn't: a "sir" before his name.

Linda, of course, was fully expected to attend the ceremony. "She wouldn't dream of missing such an important event," a close friend divulged.

Yet on March 11, 1997 it was a solo McCartney, elegantly decked out in tails, who passed through the gates of Buckingham Palace. In a centuries-old tradition he knelt on one knee before Her Majesty. Tapping each shoulder with a sword, Queen Elizabeth officially knighted him for his service to popular music. Just like that, the 54-year-old Liverpool institution and international business man was now and forever "Sir" James Paul McCartney.

Emerging from the palace to a cadre of photographers and well-wishers sporting "Arise Sir Paul" t-shirts, he said, "I'm proud to be British. It's a wonderful day. It's a long way from a little terrace house in Liverpool. My mum and dad would have been extremely proud and perhaps they are."

Yet beneath the cultured, smiling "my brave face," Paul appeared noticeably subdued. Without Linda at his side on this most auspicious occasion one could only imagine the fears that loomed beneath the facade. As always, McCartney drew on the lodestar of his family. "The McCartneys are extremely close and it is wonderful to watch their ease when they are together," says Edward Sexton, the Knightsbridge tailor who used to design for the Beatles.

Of all the McCartney children it is clearly Heather who is not only the most talented but also the most troubled, having survived a perilous stretch in her twenties. At 33 she continues to gain respect as a potter, and, interestingly, has chosen India as her second home. Her coiled pots fashioned by the same ancient methods utilized by Mexican-Indian and Japanese potters (priced between $100 and $250) have been showcased in Selfridges on Oxford Street. Her work has even gained notice in the galleries of New York.

Mary, now 27, a dark-haired, delicately featured version of her father, remains in the family business, moving up at MPL as a copyright handler and photo editor. Determined to pay her dues, she worked for six years at the West End publishing company Music Sales on a L6,000 annual salary. She began there as a photo researcher, locating shots to illustrate books about rock musicians.

"She wasn't flashy," said managing director Chris Charlesworth. "She drove an oldish car and never seemed to have much money in her pocket. She would come down to the pub with us after work and have a good chat. She was always smartly dressed, but not flamboyant. I remember thinking it was a credit to the McCartneys for bringing up their kids that way."

The brunette beauty has recently been linked with ex-Jam and Style Council front man Paul Weller. The pair was spotted holding hands and kissing at the launch of Weller's latest album. Weller was alleged to be "completely besotted" with the McCartneys' eldest. No word on Paul's reaction.

Meanwhile, the McCartney's youngest daughter Stella, now 25, a strawberry-blonde, moon-faced edition of her mother, was making quite a splash in the fiercely competitive fashion industry. A graduate of London's Central St. Martins School of

Art and Design, Stella earned a reputation as a hard worker, toiling long hours over the sewing machine.

"I was impressed she even bothers getting up in the morning, let alone sewing her own clothes," a fellow student commented. "Lots of us paid people to finish off our sewing, but not Stella."

Her initiative was admirable, but Stella wasn't foolish enough to turn down the perks that came with having an influential father. At fifteen she traveled to Paris to work under Christian Lacroix and later in the fashion department at *Vogue*. Beatles-tailor Edward Sexton then took on the fledgling designer as an apprentice. Asking her to buy him a box of black buttonholes at the store, he found her as green as they come. "She got all the way down the stairs and out the door before she realized," he recalled with a grin.

Sexton reminded his young apprentice of one very important thing she could learn from her father. "If he writes a bad song, he'll never publish it. It's the same with your garments: they have to be *perfect*. Anything else is not worth it." Sexton might be a superb tailor, but it was clear he hadn't listened to much of the McCartney catalog!

If, as Paul insists, he is still "just an ordinary bloke," one particular episode severely compromised that carefully crafted image. The incident centered around Stella's graduation fashion show in June 1995, presented by fellow students at Central St. Mary's. A heavy media blitz was to be expected; there was little even the McCartneys could do to avoid it. But once inside, their behavior had a definite air of "big star" boorishness.

First off, the famous parents reportedly delayed the start of the show by manipulating front seats while other less-connected families waited to get in. Paul also rather untactfully penned a song "Stella Mayday" to honor the occasion. The event promptly turned into a circus when Stella's pals, supermodels Kate Moss and Naomi Campbell, cruised the runway strutting her line of neo-1940s fashions.

"Stella's a friend of mine," explained Campbell. "I wanted to help her out on this."

The resulting "Stellabration" splash in the morning papers praised her talents and announced that the young McCartney had been offered a position with Ralph Lauren. The coverage left the other participants quite rightly outraged.

"The press completely forgot there were seventy other students in the show," complained one graduate. "They all left after Stella's collection."

The gold-plated McCartney name, of course, has allowed Stella more than one precious foot in the door. As one industry insider pointed out, her creations have that built-in "association with the famous" to attract potential buyers. How many couture hopefuls fresh out of college have their own studio, are photographed with Oasis' Liam Gallagher and Patsy Kensit, and win layouts in *Cosmopolitan, Harper's*, and *Vanity Fair?* Just this past April, Stella landed a prime position as designer for the elite Paris fashion house Cloe, succeeding the now legendary Karl Lagerfeld. "This is all very exciting for Stella," beamed her dad. "Her mum and I and all of her family are very proud of her."

In her personal life Stella recently ended a long-term relationship and has been known to socialize with a pair of gay male designers. After hours she can often be found at Edward Sexton's Beauchamp Place Tailors enjoying a pint of beer and a friendly gab.

As for the McCartney "baby," James Paul, now nineteen, resembles his famous father in looks and personality. He is known to be good natured and smart, displaying the same saucy sense of humor as his dad. Like Paul, James, too, shows an aptitude for painting and plays both drums and guitar, though not left-handed. Still uncertain of what he wants to do, James has reportedly expressed an interest in enrolling in the Liverpool Institute for the Performing Arts.

Today, as a shadow of uncertainty hovers over his family, McCartney, to his credit, hasn't folded up his tent. He is currently producing yet another photofilm of Linda's photographs and will soon release an album entitled *Flaming Pie*. In hopes of hyping the project, Paul licensed two cuts, "Young Boy" and "The World Tonight," to the soundtrack of Billy Crystal and Robin Williams' dubious comedy, *Father's Day*. As for *Flaming Pie* itself, the title alludes to a long-ago bio of the Beatles John Lennon wrote in which he refers to people jetting in and out of the scene aboard a flaming pie. The album includes the first-ever collaboration between Paul and Ringo. McCartney's also working on a symphonic piece to be unveiled at the 100th anniversary of EMI Records during the summer of 1997.

Paul hasn't lost the drive to perform nor forgotten his incredible history. On April 11, 1996 McCartney surprised and delighted Soho passersby with an impromptu twenty-minute concert from the rooftop of MPL. Had it really been twenty-eight years since the Beatles played their exuberant swansong atop the Apple offices?

Fans and industry insiders alike hope the new CD will be the one that will revive the old McCartney magic. Radio Merseyside disc jockey Spencer Leigh observed, "What Paul needs now is a really strong album. It's a long time since he wrote a song that had the world singing."

As always, in business McCartney remains fiercely competitive and territorial. In March he fought Lily Evans (widow of Beatles roadie, Mal) over her intent to auction off the original lyrics for "With a Little Help from My Friends." Although it was certainly part of her husband's estate, Paul claimed Evans was never supposed to sell the collectible for his own enrichment. BBC-TV's *Watchdog* quickly labeled McCartney a "widow beater." The composer, however, stood firm on his vow to get his property back. Lily Evans eventually bowed to the tidal wave of pressure and quietly withdrew the coveted item from the selling block. All vintage McCartney.

Paul waged an even bigger battle with Quarrymen pianist John "Duff" Lowe over possession of "the holy grail of all Beatles memorabilia," the demo tape of "That'll Be the Day" recorded long ago in Liverpool. A High Court eventually ruled that the tape, reportedly worth at least $100,000, was owned by McCartney.

It is precisely this tenacity that sustains and fuels the towering McCartney empire. The figures are staggering. His 25 percent of Apple and 40-percent share of Maclen are worth some $150 million alone. Beatles royalties pay him an extra $20 million a year. Sales of *The Beatles Anthology* six-CD box sets netted $8.5 million with worldwide television rights garnering millions more. His $100 million art collection and extensive properties (most recently, the $350,000 addition of farmland in the Mull of Kintyre) continue to appreciate in value. Conservative estimates put McCartney's fortune at around $450 million; the fact is he is swiftly approaching billionaire status.

Worldly fortunes aside, McCartney stubbornly stands by his priorities: honesty, loyalty, and, above all, family. In a recent interview with *Time* magazine he summed up his homespun philosophy: "I still get wounded but I've come to the point where I tell myself 'Give yourself a break. No one else will.' I *like* ballads. I *like* babies. I *like* happy endings. They say domesticity is the enemy of art, but I don't think it is. I had to make a decision: am I going to be just a family guy or should I go up to London three nights a week, hit the nightclubs, occasionally drop my trousers, and swear in public? I made my decision and I feel okay with it.

"Ballads and babies. That's what happened to me."

Life on the Back Beat
An Afterword by Steve Holly

Although Chuck Berry's "No Particular Place to Go" was the record that really whetted my juvenile appetite for rock 'n' roll, the Beatles were the first group that convinced me there was nothing in my life I wanted more than to play the drums well enough to one day enter that exuberant world myself.

Imagine, then, how I felt when, only ten years later, I somehow found myself waiting nervously for an audition with Wings in the basement of MPL's swank London offices. I first met Paul and Linda briefly at a party at Denny Laine's home in Laleham (close to my hometown) and also appeared with them, on a dare, in the promotional video for "With a Little Luck." Still, I had never really seriously considered the possibility of becoming a full-time member of the group. Those kinds of extraordinary things just don't happen. Or do they?

When the audition finally began (some two hours later than originally scheduled), I remember playing to a potpourri of swirling reggae, rockabilly, blues, as well as a smattering of classic rock, but, strange to me at the time, no Wings or Beatles tunes. Paul and Linda, however, seemed pleased, and thus began my almost three-year involvement with the group.

Working with Paul and the band, as well as many other people, in those first, incredibly heady days, was an education one could never have paid for. Or as a friend of mine once put it, "Earn while you learn!" Inevitably, of course, there was much to be learned. Paul's disdain for any absolute principles of right and wrong in music, coupled with his eagerness to experiment with so many different and difficult sounds, illustrated to all of us the man's great genius on an almost-daily basis. For pop music very often walks a treacherously thin line between the lowest common denominator and pure, unbridled brilliance, only very occasionally intermingling both. McCartney, at his best, easily defies all such labels, delivering some of the most memorable music of all time. And yet, on occasion, he chooses to walk so perilously close to the edge as to almost invite the critical disclaim that has at times dogged him throughout his now long and varied solo career. Perhaps this illustrates just a bit of the magic of Lennon and McCartney's ability to so tastefully ferret out only each other's best and deepest work.

For my part, I enjoyed three exceptional years with Wings, not discounting my final year as a time filled with much doubt and a goodly measure of deep frustration all around. If only we could have gotten round to recording at least one more album together. What would have transpired? Would the group have somehow survived? I also never realized just how immensely intertwined one's professional and private lives can become until my involvement with a group of Wings' magnitude.

Wings' legacy remains, and nothing can ever dim my great memories of Paul, the times, and the band. I will continue to savor the best forever.

Steve Holly
July 26, 1990
Temple, Arizona

Paul McCartney's Family Tree

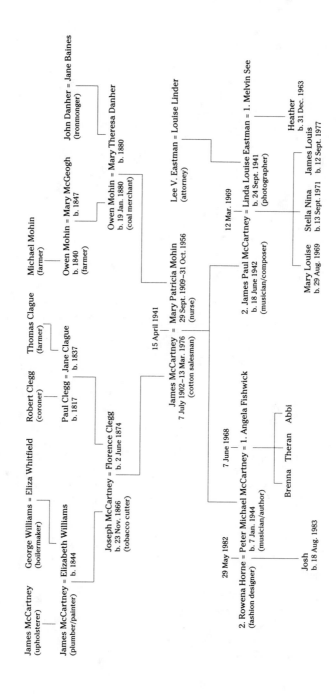

A Diary of Events

1866–1997

1866

November 23   Paul's paternal grandfather, Joe McCartney, is born in Everton. A lifelong lover of music, Joe plays brass double-bass in a band sponsored by Copes, a local firm, and in another sponsored by the local branch of the Territorial Army.

1874

June 2   Florence Clegg, Paul's maternal grandmother, is born at 131 Breck Road, Everton.

1902

July 7   Jim McCartney, Paul's father, is born at 8 Fishguard Street, Everton, Liverpool, to Joe and Florence McCartney.

1909

September 29   Mary Patricia Mohin, Paul's mother, is born at 2 Third Avenue, Tazakerley, Liverpool.

1926

Beatles' producer George Martin is born in Muswell Hill, north London.

1930s

Jim McCartney founds his own orchestra. Known as Jim Mac's Jazz Band, it becomes a popular Liverpool dancehall attraction.

1931

December 18   Allen Klein, one of the Beatles' future managers and well-known Paul McCartney nemesis, is born into a poor family in Newark, New Jersey.

1933

February 18   Yoko Ono is born into a wealthy Tokyo banking family.

1934

September 19   Beatles' manager Brian Epstein is born in a private nursing home on Rodney Street in Liverpool.

1935

Mal Evans, the Beatles' lovable and loyal chief roadie, is born in Liverpool.

1940

June 23   Future Beatles bassist Stuart Sutcliffe is born.

July 7   Richard Starkey (Ringo Starr) is born to parents Richard and Elsie just after midnight in their home at 9 Madryn Street in the Dingle section of Liverpool.

October 9   John Winston Lennon is born to Julia Stanley Lennon at the Oxford Street Maternity Hospital in Liverpool during a German air raid. His father, Alf, is away at sea.

1941

April 15   Paul McCartney's parents are married at St. Swithin's Roman Catholic Chapel, Liverpool.

September 24   Linda Louise Eastman is born in Scarsdale, New York, to parents Lee and Louise.

November 24   Future Beatles drummer Randolph Peter Best, better known as Pete, is born in Madras, India.

1942

June 18   James Paul McCartney is born at Woolton Hospital in Liverpool. He is the first of two sons born to Jim and Mary McCartney.

1943

February 25   George Harold Harrison, the youngest child of Harold and Louise Harrison, is born at 12 Arnold Grove, Wavertree, Liverpool.

July 10   Future Wings drummer Denny Seiwell is born.

July 21   Future Wings guitarist Henry McCullough is born.

1944

January 7   Peter Michael McCartney, later known professionally as Mike McGear, is born in Liverpool.

July 22   Peter Asher, brother of actress Jane Asher (Paul McCartney's future fiancee) is born. He will eventually become one-half of the popular sixties duo Peter and Gordon and then go into a high-profile position as director of A&R for the Beatles' Apple Records.

October 29   Brian Frederick Hines (Denny Laine) is born in Birmingham to Herbo and Eva Hines.

1946

April 5   Actress Jane Asher is born into the family of wealthy London physician Richard Asher.

1949

February 7   Joe English, future Wings drummer, is born in Rochester, New York.

October 8   Guitarist and vocalist extraordinaire Hamish Stuart is born in Glasgow, Scotland. He becomes the driving force behind the R&B group The Average White Band before joining Paul McCartney's band several years later.

1950

George Martin accepts a position as assistant A&R man for EMI's Parlophone label.

1952

July 13   Joanne Alice Linda Patrie (Jo Jo Laine), the future wife of
            Wings collaborator Denny Laine, is born in Salem,
            Massachusetts.

November 12   Wings' final lead guitarist, Laurence Juber, is born in London.

1953

June 4   Jimmy McCulloch, Wings' most passionate and troublesome
            lead guitarist, is born in Glasgow, Scotland.

August 24   Wings' final drummer, Steve Holly, is born in Isleworth,
            Middlesex.

September   Paul enters the Liverpool Institute.

1954–55

            Paul McCartney and schoolmate George Harrison get
            together for the first time and begin bashing out Lonnie
            Donegan material in the front room of the Harrisons' home at
            25 Upton Green.

1956

March 27   Keyboardist Paul "Wix" Wickens is born in Brentwood, Essex.
            Wix enjoys his first success working with longtime friend Paul
            Young before signing on with boyhood hero McCartney.

October 31 Mary McCartney dies unexpectedly from breast cancer.

1957

January 16 A former wine cellar on Mathew Street in Liverpool is opened
            under the name Cavern Club as a showcase for local jazz and
            skiffle groups. Rock 'n' roll is strictly forbidden by order of
            the management.

July 6   John Lennon's schoolboy group, the Quarry Men, performs at
            the St. Peter's Parish Church garden fête in Woolton village, a
            lovely Liverpool suburb. In the crowd is Paul McCartney, who
            is later introduced to Lennon by their mutual friend, Ivan
            Vaughan. A few days later McCartney is invited to join the
            group by Quarry Man Pete Shotton.

August   John Lennon's Quarry Men play Liverpool's Cavern Club for
            the first time.

October 18 At the New Clubmoor Club in Liverpool, Paul McCartney
            plays his first gig with the Quarry Men.

October 25 Guitarist Robbie McIntosh is born in Sutton, south London.
            Robbie (or "Tosh" as he is known) learns to play the guitar at
            the age of ten, giving his first concert one year later,
            performing "Thank U Very Much" for his peers at primary
            school. He later plays with the Pretenders and Tears for Fears
            before joining Paul McCartney's band in 1989.

Late 1957

            Percy Phillips, owner of a bare-bones recording studio in his

Liverpool basement, records the Quarry Men performing several high-powered skiffle numbers. He later erases the tapes in order to reuse them. It is Lennon and McCartney's first bona fide recording session.

1958
March 13
Paul McCartney introduces John Lennon to crackerjack guitarist, fourteen-year-old George Harrison.

Late 1958

John and Paul do a few gigs together as the Nurk Twins following a brief hiatus from their work with the Quarry Men. Soon, however, they are back with Lennon's renamed group, Johnny and the Moondogs.

**Late 1958 or
early 1959**

McCartney composes the instrumental tune "Hot As Sun," later released on his solo *McCartney* album in 1970.

1959

Paul, George, and John leave school, along with Stuart Sutcliffe, to begin the business of playing rock 'n' roll in earnest. By this date the songwriting team of Lennon and McCartney has written approximately one hundred songs.

February 3
Early rock legends Buddy Holly, Ritchie Valens, and J.P. "The Big Bopper" Richardson are killed in the crash of a private plane near Clear Lake, Iowa. Twenty years later, the cufflinks worn by Holly on the fatal flight will be presented to Paul McCartney by Holly's widow, Maria.

March 29
Drummer Chris Whitten is born in Wimbledon, London. After working with Julian Cope and Edie Brickell, Chris would go on to add a sharp edge to the 1989/90 Paul McCartney World Tour.

August 29
The Moondogs are invited to play the opening night party at the Casbah, a teenage coffeehouse run by Mona Best, Pete's gregarious mother.

October 18
Johnny and the Moondogs fail an audition for British television personality Carrol Levis at the Manchester Hippodrome.

Early 1960

Denny Laine forms his own group, Denny and the Diplomats, playing sporadically throughout the Birmingham area.

1960
April
Now called the Silver Beatles, John, Paul, George, and Stuart begin a tour of Scotland, backing British balladeer Johnny Gentle.

August
Paul McCartney invites Pete Best to join the newly-named Beatles as their regular drummer on their first trip to Germany.

Autumn	The Beatles record with members of their rival Liverpool group, Rory Storm and the Hurricanes, at Akustik Studios in Hamburg.
November 21	The Beatles' engagement in Germany is interrupted after George Harrison is found to be under age by German immigration officials and is unceremoniously deported. The rest of the group soon returns to Liverpool.

1961

February 21	In a lunchtime session the Beatles appear at the Cavern for the first time. Over the next two years they will play 292 gigs at the celebrated Liverpool cellar.
March 1	Allan Williams, the Beatles' manager at the time, writes a letter to the German consulate in Liverpool asking that the group be allowed to return now that Harrison has become of age.
March 24	The Beatles depart from Liverpool for their second trip to Hamburg.
May	While in Hamburg the Beatles participate in a Polydor-sponsored session with British singer Tony Sheridan, performing as the Beat Brothers. They record a Lennon-fronted version of "My Bonnie" backed by "The Saints."
June	Stuart Sutcliffe leaves the Beatles in order to marry German photographer and early Beatles supporter Astrid Kirchherr. Paul takes over duties on bass guitar.
July 2	The Beatles depart Hamburg for Liverpool.
October 1	Lennon and McCartney embark on a two-week hitchhiking trip to Paris. It is there that the celebrated Beatle haircut is born when the two young men meet up with German photographer friend Jurgen Vollmer, who had reportedly been sporting the soon-to-be-famous fringe for several months.
October 29	Raymond Jones walks into NEMS Record Store in Liverpool's Whitechapel shopping district and asks proprietor Brian Epstein for a copy of "My Bonnie."
November 9	Intrigued that a local Liverpool group has cut a record, Epstein and his personal assistant, Alistair Taylor, attend a lunchtime session at the Cavern, where they witness the Beatles in action.
December 3	Epstein meets with the Beatles at NEMS to discuss the possibility of his taking over management of the group.

1962

January 1	The Beatles travel to London for an audition at Decca Records during which McCartney handles lead vocals on several numbers. Recording manager Dick Rowe subsequently turns down the group, confiding to Epstein that groups with guitars are on the way out.

January   By means of a five-year contract Brian Epstein officially becomes the Beatles' manager.

April 10   Stuart Sutcliffe dies in Hamburg of an apparent brain hemorrhage.

April 11   The Beatles leave for Hamburg to begin a seven-week engagement at the Star Club.

April 23   "My Bonnie" is issued in the United States on the Decca label.

May 9   Brian Epstein wires the Beatles in Germany that EMI Records has agreed to audition the group at their recording facility on Abbey Road, St. John's Wood.

June 4   The Beatles are offered a Parlophone recording contract by Martin. Brian Epstein happily signs on their behalf.

June 6   The Beatles perform six songs for EMI/Parlophone staff producer George Martin in London.

August 16 Brian Epstein informs Pete Best that Ringo Starr will soon replace him as the Beatles' drummer.

August 18 Ringo Starr plays his first session with the Beatles at the Cavern.

September 4 The Beatles arrive in London to begin recording with George Martin. The group's first single, "Love Me Do" backed by "P.S., I Love You," is culled from these sessions.

October 31 The Beatles once again travel to Hamburg to begin a two-week engagement at the Star Club.

November 26 At London's EMI Studios the Beatles record the songs "How Do You Do It," "Please Please Me," and "Ask Me Why."

December 18 The Beatles begin their final engagement at the Star Club in Hamburg. Alleged McCartney love child Bettina "McCartney" Heubers is born.

1963

February 22 "Please Please Me" becomes the number-one single on the *New Musical Express* charts. Twenty-four hours later it will do the same on the *Disc* charts.

April 18   On the BBC radio special, "Swinging Sounds '63," Paul McCartney meets young British superstarlet Jane Asher.

April 26   "From Me to You" reaches number one on the British pop charts.

June 18   McCartney's twenty-first birthday celebration is held at his Auntie Jin's home on Dinas Lane, Huyton.

September 7 "She Loves You" becomes the number-one song on the *Melody Maker* singles chart, remaining there for the next five weeks.

October 13 The Beatles appear on Britain's top television show, "Sunday Night at the London Palladium."

October 17 London's normally conservative Bond Street is overrun with teenyboppers when Paul McCartney arrives to dine with the winner of the "Why I Like the Beatles" magazine contest.

November 4 The Beatles play a Royal Command Performance.

December 31 Heather See is born to Linda Eastman and her first husband, American college professor Melvin See.

1964

January 30 *Mersey Beat* magazine prints an interview with Brian Epstein in which he assures McCartney fans that the Beatle has no plans either to be engaged or married to Jane Asher or anyone else.

February 1 "I Want to Hold Your Hand" becomes the number-one record in America.

February 7 The Beatles and their entourage land at Kennedy Airport in New York, where they experience their first taste of the intensity of American Beatlemania.

February 9 The Beatles appear on the "Ed Sullivan Show" in New York. During their performance an estimated 73 million television viewers experience John, Paul, George, and Ringo for the first time.

February 22 McCartney is chauffeured to Canterbury to see Jane Asher perform in the Elizabethan drama *The Jew of Malta.*

March 20 While taping an appearance by the Beatles on the popular British television series "Ready, Steady, Go!" McCartney denies the persistent rumor that he will soon marry Jane Asher.

April 4 The Beatles hold the top four positions on the American pop charts.

May Denny Laine joins the Moody Blues.

June 2 Paul and Jane attend a performance by Cilla Black at the London Palladium.

July 10 A civic reception is held in Liverpool to honor the Beatles. Over one hundred thousand people attend.

August The Beatles make their second trek to the United States to begin a rigorous twenty-five-city tour.

November 24 Paul McCartney gains a stepmother when his father, Jim, marries thirty-four-year-old widow Angela Williams.

December 8 McCartney hints to the media that he may indeed marry Jane Asher, eventually, although he hastens to add that no specific date has been set.

1965

February 4 Paul and Jane vacation together in Hammamet, Tunisia.

April The Moody Blues' "Go Now," featuring Denny Laine on lead vocals, climbs to number ten on the U.S. *Billboard* charts.

April 13	It is announced that Paul McCartney has purchased a home on Cavendish Avenue in St. John's Wood for £40,000.
July 7	Paul and Jane, along with George and Pattie Harrison, attend a party at the Roehampton home of the Moody Blues.
August 15	Jane Asher hints to the media that her marriage to Paul is imminent.
	While in the U.S., the Beatles are visited by Bob Dylan in their suite at the Warwick Hotel.
August 22	The Minneapolis vice squad raids McCartney's room at the Lemington Motor Inn, where he is in the company of a woman who is under age. The incident receives sporadic media coverage but is effectively suppressed by Brian Epstein.
August 27	The Beatles visit Elvis Presley at his Bel Aire mansion, where they spend the evening drinking Cokes, jamming, and playing billiards with "The King."
October 26	The beatles receive MBEs from Her Majesty Queen Elizabeth II in the Great Throne Room at Buckingham Palace.
	Afterwards the group holds a press conference at the Saville Theatre, a new pet project of Brian Epstein's.
December 8	The Moody Blues, who have been touring with the Beatles, dine with the Fabs after a concert at Sheffield city hall.

1966

January 16	Martha, Paul McCartney's celebrated Old English sheepdog, is born in High Wycombe.
January 17	McCartney purchases High Park Farm near Campbeltown, Scotland.
January 26	While the Beatles are in Hamburg, Paul and a former girlfriend visit the Star Club and the Indra.
February 3	McCartney attends a performance by Stevie Wonder at the Scotch of St. James nightclub.
March	At Dolly's, a swank London nightclub, McCartney spends the evening with Bob Dylan.
August 26	McCartney denies rumors that he will wed Jane Asher during the Beatles' brief stay in Los Angeles.
August 29	At Candlestick Park in San Francisco, the Beatles give their final concert.
October 13	Denny Laine quits the Moody Blues.
November 9	It is rumored that McCartney is involved in a fatal car crash in which he was supposedly decapitated. According to the widespread "Paul Is Dead" hoax, McCartney has been replaced by mysterious double, William Campbell.
December 6	Recording sessions for *Sgt. Pepper's Lonely Hearts Club Band* begin.

December 18	*The Family Way*, starring Hayley Mills, premieres in London. McCartney wrote the incidental music for the film. Paul and Jane attend.

1967

January 13	Jane Asher leaves for America to tour with the Bristol Old Vic Repertory Theatre. Paul and Ringo attend a high-powered performance by Jimi Hendrix at the Bag O' Nails club in London.
February 7	In St. John's Wood, McCartney spends the evening with Mickey Dolenz of the Monkees.
March 30	Photographic sessions for the cover of *Sgt. Pepper's Lonely Hearts Club Band* are held in the Flood Street studios of Michael Cooper.
April 5	McCartney catches up with Jane Asher in Denver, Colorado, to celebrate her twenty-first birthday.
April 7	Denny Laine's single "Say You Don't Mind" backed by "Ask the People," is released on the Deram label.
May 15	While attending a Georgie Fame performance at the Bag O' Nails, McCartney meets his future wife, photographer Linda Eastman, for the first time.
May 26	*Sgt. Pepper's Lonely Hearts Club Band* is released.
May	Linda Eastman attends a press party at Brian Epstein's Chapel Street flat to celebrate the release of *Sgt. Pepper*.
June	McCartney confirms that he has taken the controversial drug LSD.
June 4	Paul and Jane attend a concert by the Jimi Hendrix Experience, Procol Harum, Denny Laine and His Electric String Band, and the Chiffons at the Saville Theatre.
June 21	American televangelist Billy Graham comments that he will pray for Paul following McCartney's revelation that he has experimented with LSD.
August 24	The Beatles attend an introductory lecture by the Maharishi Mahesh Yogi at the London Hilton.
August 26	Brian Epstein is found dead in his Belgravia townhouse from a suspected drug overdose.
December 25	Paul McCartney and Jane Asher announce their engagement, ending over four years of speculation by the media.

1968

February 10	The Scaffold, a comedy group featuring Paul's brother, Mike McGear, performs at the Queen Elizabeth Hall, London. Paul and Jane attend.
February 19	Paul and Jane (accompanied by Ringo and Maureen Starr) fly to New Delhi, India, to join John and George for a teachers' training course in Transcendental Meditation at the Maharishi's exclusive Rishikesh ashram.

March 26	Paul and Jane return to England, somewhat disillusioned with the Maharishi and his otherworldly philosophy.
May 15	Linda Eastman slips Paul her phone number at a New York press party held to mark the launch of the Beatles' Apple Corps Ltd. They spend the night together at business associate Nat Weiss's Manhattan apartment.
May 21	Paul and Jane dine with singer Andy Williams and later attend his concert at the Royal Albert Hall.
June 7	Paul and Jane attend his brother Mike's marriage to Angela Fishwick. Paul is best man.
June 22–24	McCartney is ensconced in a bungalow at the Beverly Hills Hotel with Linda Eastman.
July 20	Jane Asher announces on British television that her seven-month engagement to McCartney is over.
August	McCartney hanger-on Francie Schwartz moves into his St. John's Wood home and stays for three weeks.
October 12	In London's *Evening Standard* Jane Asher discusses her on-again, off-again romance with McCartney publicly for the first time.
October 31	McCartney calls Linda Eastman from London and invites Linda and her seven-year-old daughter, Heather, to move in with him. Days later Linda arrives, alone, in St. John's Wood.

1969

February 12	McCartney's personal corporation, Adagrose Ltd., is formed in London. He will later change the name to McCartney Productions Ltd. (MPL).
March 11	The Apple press office announces McCartney's intention to wed Linda Eastman the following afternoon.
March 12	Paul and Linda are married at the Marylebone Register's Office, London.
March 16	The McCartneys, along with Linda's daughter, Heather, fly to New York for a visit with Linda's family.
March 24	Reporters from *Life* magazine track down McCartney at his farm in Scotland and quash rumors that the recently reclusive Beatle was actually dead.
May 8	Allen Klein becomes the Beatles' new business manager. Paul, however, is adamantly opposed to the appointment. It is the beginning of a bitter feud between John and Paul that would never be fully resolved.
May 15	The McCartneys vacation on the island of Corfu. Publicists announce that Paul and Linda are expecting a child.
June 14	Peter Asher resigns his position as A&R director of Apple.
July	Recording sessions for *Abbey Road* begin.

August 29	Paul and Linda's first child together, Mary Louise, is born in a London nursing home.
September	Jim McCartney is hospitalized in Cheshire. Both Mike and Paul visit him frequently.

1970

January 14	McCartney purchases Low Ranadran Farm, adjacent to his own property in Scotland.
April 2	In an interview with the *Evening Standard*, McCartney hints that the Beatles may soon go their separate ways due to the rapid disintegration of their multi-million-pound Apple empire.
April 9	McCartney appears on a "London Weekend Television" segment performing the hit "Maybe I'm Amazed."
April 11	The *Daily Mirror* reports that Paul McCartney has officially left the Beatles.
April 12	The *New Music Express* reports that McCartney has purchased the film rights to the popular British cartoon character Rupert the Bear. In 1984, the animated short *Rupert and the Frog Song* will run as the opening feature for Paul's mega-flop, *Give My Regards to Broad Street*.
April 17	Paul's solo *McCartney* album is released in Great Britain.
December 31	McCartney files suit in a London court to permanently dissolve the Beatles' partnership.

1971

February 19	Hearings begin in the London High Court in *The Beatles and Company* case.
February 26	McCartney personally gives evidence in court. The other three Beatles, however, testify via sworn statement.
March 12	The court appoints a receiver to control the Beatles' collective finances until further notice.
May 12	Mick Jagger marries Bianca Perez Mora Machias in the south of France. Paul and his family fly out from London to attend.
May 21	McCartney's *Ram* album is released in Great Britain.
August 3	McCartney forms a new group, Wings.
September 13	Stella Nina McCartney is born to Paul and Linda at King's College Hospital, London.
December 7	Wings' first album, *Wild Life*, is released in Great Britain.

1972

February 9	Wings play their first gig, at Nottingham University, thus beginning the first leg of a British college tour.
February 25	"Give Ireland Back to the Irish," Wings' debut single, is banned by the BBC and IBA due to its potentially inflammatory lyrical content.

August 10	Paul and Linda are arrested by police in Göteborg, Sweden, for possession of marijuana. They are fined the Swedish equivalent of £800 and spend several hours locked in a holding cell.
September 20	The McCartneys are charged with possession of marijuana after a raid on their farm in Campbeltown, Scotland, on a tip from one of the locals. Several suspected pot plants are found in the outdoor greenhouse.

1973

March 8	The McCartneys are fined £100 plus court costs by a Campbeltown judge on their marijuana-growing charge from the previous year.
April	John, Ringo, and George terminate their contract with Allen Klein.
April 16	The "James Paul McCartney" special airs on American television.
May 3	*Red Rose Speedway* is released in Great Britain.
August 9	Prior to Wings' departure for Lagos, Nigeria, to begin recording the *Band on the Run* album, Denny Seiwell and Henry McCullough unexpectedly leave the group.
November 30	*Ahh Laine*, Denny Laine's first solo LP, is released on the Wizard label.
December 7	Wings' *Band on the Run* is released in Great Britain.

1974

April 13	Jane Asher gives birth to a baby girl at Middlesex Hospital. Under Ms Asher's instructions, no further details are released to the media.
April 26	McCartney holds auditions at London's Albery Theatre in hopes of finding a new drummer for Wings. In the end, he and Denny Laine settle upon Geoff Britton.
June	Jimmy McCulloch replaces the departed Henry McCullough on lead guitar. Wings jet off to Nashville, Tennessee, for recording sessions.
July 24	Denny Laine is quoted in the *Evening News* as saying that his relationship with Paul McCartney does not require a written contract as it is based solely on trust.
October 5	Mike McCartney's solo *McGear* album is released by Warner Brothers.
November 20	Wings appears on the popular British TV show "Top of the Pops" to promote their "Junior's Farm" single. Denny Laine's longtime live-in love, Jo Jo, meets Wings at the Odeon Cinema, Lewisham, to attend a performance by her ex-boyfriend, Rod Stewart.
December 21	Paul McCartney and Wings are awarded a platinum disc for over 500,000 British sales of the album *Band on the Run*.

1975

January 16   Wings arrives in New Orleans to begin recording sessions at Wally Heider Studios for the *Venus and Mars* album.

March 3   Linda McCartney is charged with possession of marijuana, this time in America.

March 24   Wings parties aboard the *Queen Mary* in Long Beach, California. Among the guests are George Harrison, Ryan O'Neal, Karl Malden, Dean Martin, Rod Stewart, and Cher.

September 9   Wings' first world tour commences with a show at the Gaumont, Southampton.

November 1   Linda's American drug charge is withdrawn.

1976

January   Work begins on *Wings at the Speed of Sound*.

January 5   The Beatles' former road manager and friend Mal Evans is shot dead by Los Angeles police after an incident in which Evans allegedly pointed a gun at officers responding to a domestic disturbance call.

March 13   Paul's father, James McCartney, dies at his home in Heswall, Cheshire.

May   *Wings at the Speed of Sound* is released.

May 3   In Fort Worth, Texas, Wings Over America tour begins.

May 22   At the Boston Garden for a Wings concert, Paul McCartney and Jimmy McCulloch engage in a major backstage row.

June 23   Wings Over America tour ends.

December   *Wings Over America*, a three-record set culled from the Wings Over America tour, is released.

1977

February 7   Wings enters EMI's Abbey Road Studios to begin sessions for their *London Town* album.

March 16   *Wings Over the World*, a film documentary of Wings' 1976 tour, is aired on CBS television.

May   Wings sets up shop in the Virgin Islands, recording aboard the luxury yacht *Fair Carol*, for further work on *London Town*.

September 8   Jimmy McCulloch leaves Wings.

September 12   Paul and Linda's only son, James Louis McCartney, is born at the Avenue Clinic, London.

November 11   An exhibition of photographs by Linda McCartney opens in Los Angeles.

1978

January 23   Wings puts the finishing touches on their *London Town* LP.

March 22   Wings holds a press party on a boat on the Thames to promote the release of *London Town*.

346 Blackbird

May 6	A Linda McCartney photographic exhibition opens in New York.
June 29	Wings begins sessions for what will be their last album, *Back to the Egg*, at McCartney's home studio in Campbeltown, Scotland.
September 7	The McCartneys throw a party to mark the third annual Buddy Holly Week sponsored by MPL.
October 3	Members of Wings are joined by virtually every major figure in British rock 'n' roll for an all-star session at Abbey Road Studios, laying down two songs together. They call themselves Rockestra.

1979

May 19	Ringo, Paul, and George perform an impromptu concert in the back garden of Eric Clapton's home in Ewehurst, Surrey, on the occasion of Clapton's marriage to George's ex-wife, Pattie.
June 11	A launch party for *Back to the Egg* is held at Abbey Road Studios.
September 14	Wings joins Buddy Holly's backing group, The Crickets, on stage at Hammersmith Odeon Cinema in celebration of the fourth annual Buddy Holly Week.
September 27	Jimmy McCulloch is found dead in his London apartment of a suspected overdose of narcotics.
October 24	McCartney is honored by the Guinness Book of World Records at a bash at the Les Ambassadeurs Club in London. He is presented with a valuable rhodium disc for being the most successful songwriter in the history of popular music.
November 23	Wings performs a special free concert for pupils of the Liverpool Institute, Paul's alma mater, at the Royal Court Theatre in Liverpool.
November 24	Wings begins its last-ever tour, playing three nights at the Royal Court Theatre, Liverpool.
December 29	Wings takes part in UNICEF's Concert for the People of Kampuchea at the Hammersmith Odeon Cinema.

1980

January 16	McCartney is arrested by customs officials at Narita International Airport in Tokyo when 219 grams of marijuana are found in a toilet bag inside one of his suitcases. He is detained in jail for the next nine days.
January 21	Steve Holly, Laurence Juber, and Denny Laine fly home to England after it becomes clear that the tour can no longer proceed, owing to McCartney's arrest.
January 25	McCartney is released from jail and deported from Japan. He and Linda fly home and cloister themselves on their Sussex farm for the next several days.

February 27	Wings wins a Grammy award for their "Rockestra Theme" from *Back to the Egg*.
May 9	McCartney receives an Ivor Novello Award at London's Grosvenor House Hotel.
July 7	Paul McCartney and Ringo Starr begin work on Ringo's *Stop and Smell the Roses* album at Superbear studios in France.
October 31	McCartney once again joins forces with producer George Martin, recording the tune "We All Stand together" at AIR Studios, London.
November 26	*Rockshow*, a concert film from the Wings Over America Tour of 1976, premieres in New York City.
December 8	John Ono Lennon is murdered as he returns home from a recording session with Yoko. The world mourns.

1981

February 26	Stevie Wonder joins McCartney in Montserrat. They record two tunes together, "Ebony and Ivory" and "What's That You're Doing."
April 8	Paul and Linda attend the gala British premiere of *Rockshow* at London's Dominion Theatre.
April 27	Ringo Starr marries actress Barbara Bach at Marylebone Register's Office, London. Both the McCartneys and the Harrisons are in attendance. Wings officially disbands.

1982

January 11	*The Cooler*, a cinematic short featuring Paul, Ringo, and wives, begins shooting in London.
May 29	Mike McCartney marries Rowena Horne at St. Barnabas Church, Penny Lane, in Liverpool.
June 23	McCartney tapes a video for the single "Take It Away" at Elstree Street Film Studios.
September 24	The McCartneys attend a reception to mark the opening of a photographic exhibition by Linda McCartney.
November 8	*Give My Regards to Broad Street*, begins shooting in London.
November 24	An exhibition of Linda McCartney's photographs opens in Paris.

1983

February 10	McCartney is presented with two British Phonographic Industry awards at the Grosvenor House Hotel.
July 23	Paul, Ringo, and George have a few drinks together in a London hotel.
October 4	The McCartneys, along with Michael and La Toya Jackson, begin shooting a promotional video in Los Alamos, California, for "Say, Say, Say."

| December 1 | George, Ringo, and Paul meet with Yoko Ono at the Dorchester Hotel in London to try to resolve their remaining business differences over their jointly-owned Apple Corp. Ltd. |

1984

January 16	The McCartneys are fined $200 each after being arrested for possession of marijuana in Barbados.
January 17	Upon the McCartneys' return to England, customs officials uncover a small amount of marijuana in one of Linda's bags at Heathrow Airport. She is arrested and charged by London police.
January 24	Linda McCartney receives a small fine at Uxbridge Magistrates Court stemming from her most recent drug charge.
October 18	McCartney flies to New York to promote *Give My Regards to Broad Street.*
October 22	The McCartneys attend the world premiere of *Broad Street* at New York's Gotham Theater.
November 7	Paul McCartney and Julian Lennon meet for the first time in several years during separate appearances on the American television show "Friday Night Videos."
November 28	McCartney is awarded Freedom of the City honors at the Picton Library in Liverpool. Later that evening he and Linda attend the British premiere of *Give My Regards to Broad Street* at the city's Odeon Cinema.

1985

March 30	Michael Jackson spends a few days with Paul and Linda at their Sussex home.
July 13	McCartney participates in the Live Aid concert at Wembley Stadium, performing "Let It Be."
August 10	The Northern Songs catalog of classic Beatles tunes is sold to Michael Jackson for a cool $47 million.
October 9	Dan Ackroyd, Chevy Chase, and Paul McCartney shoot a promotional video for the song "Spies Like Us" at Abbey Road studios.

1986

January 27	McCartney accepts an Award of Merit from the American Music Awards at the Hippodrome nightclub. The broadcast is beamed by satellite back to the U.S.
June 20	McCartney plays at the Prince's Trust Birthday Party with Tina Turner, Elton John, and Eric Clapton.
September 1	*Press to Play* is released.
October 16	Paul and Linda are awarded honors for the bestselling video of 1985 and for their *Rupert and the Frog Song* short at a party at the Grosvenor House Hotel, London.

November 20   While in Munich, Germany, McCartney receives the Personality of the Year Award at the annual Bambi bash.

December 16   Denny Laine declares bankruptcy in a London court.

1987

Paul McCartney's *All the Best* compilation album is released in the U.K. and goes platinum within three days. The stirring single "Once Upon a Long Ago" enters the top ten.

McCartney goes into the studio with fellow Liverpudlian Elvis Costello. Their collaborative writing/recording efforts result in nine tracks.

February 2   McCartney records at Audio International Studios in London.

February 28   An exhibition of Linda McCartney's photographs opens at the Octagon Gallery in Bath.

March 4   The McCartneys appear in the film *Eat the Rich*, playing themselves in a cameo role.

1988

Choba B CCCP (Back in the USSR), a new collection of rock classics performed by McCartney, is released in the Soviet Union.

Sussex University awards McCartney an honorary doctorate.

The Nordoff-Robbins Music Therapy Foundation in Great Britain presents McCartney with the "Silver Clef" award.

McCartney appears in the BBC-TV documentary "The Power of Music."

1989

McCartney participates in a live phone-in with the Russian people courtesy of the BBC World Service.

September 26   The Paul McCartney World Tour kicks off in Oslo, Norway.

1990

March   McCartney is presented with a Lifetime Achievement Award by the National Academy of Recording Arts and Sciences during their annual Grammy award ceremonies.

July 29   The Paul McCartney World Tour ends with a sold-out show at Chicago's Soldier Field stadium.

September 4   McCartney appears onstage at the Lone Star Roadhouse in New York City with Linda and members of The Crickets to promote *Buddy*, a Broadway musical based on the life of Buddy Holly.

November   At an auction in Houston, Texas, Paul McCartney's birth certificate, which had been sold by his stepmother, is acquired for $18,000 by an American collector.

1991

A very embarrassing vocal mix of Linda McCartney "singing" backup vocals on "Hey Jude," recorded during Paul's tour, makes the rounds of radio stations throughout America and Britain.

April 3 McCartney and his band of unknowns appear in a special hour-long segment of MTV's "Unplugged," performing acoustic renditions of numerous Beatles and solo McCartney tunes. Paul performs "I Lost My Little Girl," the first song he ever wrote, his first public performance of the song since 1960.

April 30 At a London press conference the McCartneys introduce Linda's new line of strictly beefless burgers.

1992

Linda McCartney's Sixties, a collection of Linda's vintage portraits of rock stars, is published.

June 8 Paul grants an exclusive interview to *Time* magazine in celebration of turning fifty. "I'm only interested in looking back now, because I have this misbelief about my life," he says. "Did I really get here?"

October 24 McCartney's *Liverpool Oratorio* makes its West Coast premiere at the Orange County Performing Arts Center. Paul fails to show up, explaining, "I didn't want it to have to depend on my presence. I wanted it to be able to stand on its own, so I could go on with other things I want to do."

March 12 On their 24th wedding anniversary Paul reveals he and Linda have spent just eleven days apart, separating only during his 1980 incarceration in a Japanese prison for marijuana possession.

February *Off the Ground* is released, a critically heralded upbeat album that sees McCartney returning to his Beatles roots.

April Paul embarks on an eight-month world tour, which will keep him on the road until Christmas.

May Paul calls an impromptu, five-minute press conference in Los Angeles just two hours before a performance. The mad scramble, full of technical glitches, prompts one reporter to call it a "Beatlesque comedy of errors."

June 15 Paul's first live television concert, *Live in the New World*, is broadcast on the Westwood One Network from Charlotte, North Carolina.

1994

Paul begins work on a long-awaited Beatles documentary under the working title, *The Long and Winding Road*.

Paul donates a carved wood sculpture to aid Bosnia. McCartney's Peasmarsh neighbor notes, "All he needs to do is put his name on a piece of paper and it will sell."

August Renowned chef Pierre Franey invites Linda McCartney to his Long Island home to prepare a meal from her *Linda McCartney's Homestyle Cooking.* While *The New York Times* documents the event, Paul composes on guitar.

1995

Britain's National Historic Trust purchases Paul's Forthlin Road, Allerton home for $50,000 to help rescue it from "commercial exploitation."

June Stella McCartney's graduation fashion show from Central St. Martins School of Art and Design causes a media circus. Her retro-forties lemon silk creations win rave reviews; Hilary Alexander, fashion writer for the *Daily Telegraph,* calls it "a very strong collection."

November McCartney's *Grateful Dead: A Photofilm* debuts at the London Film Festival and subsequently is shown worldwide, including the Finland, Brisbane, Krakow, and New York Film Festivals.

November 20 ABC Television airs the first of three installments of *The Beatles Anthology,* featuring the Fab's reunion single "Free As a Bird." Comments McCartney, "We just pretended John was off on holiday." The shows do not do well in the ratings.

December 8 Linda McCartney is diagnosed with breast cancer and undergoes surgery at London's Princess Grace Hospital to remove the malignancy. "Luckily," says Paul at the time, "we caught it in time." While the McCartneys are at the hospital, thieves ransack the family's St. John's Wood mansion.

1996

January The Liverpool Institute for the Performing Arts [LIPA], dubbed "Paul's *Fame* School," opens its doors to aspiring artists.

June Queen Elizabeth officially opens LIPA. Paul attends with daughter Stell, but strangely, without Linda.

September The Royal Liverpool Harmonic marks the 100th performance of Paul McCartney's *Liverpool Oratorio.*

October 6 At a 65th birthday bash for Abbey Road Studios, Paul is conspicuously absent. Rumors fly that he is in Los Angeles to support Linda as she undergoes several rounds of risky high-dose chemotherapy treatment.

November 23 Linda McCartney's *Roadworks* is published by Little Brown.

December 17   A year after her cancer surgery, Linda makes her first video-taped public appearance at the PETA awards in Los Angeles.

1997

Paul is busy directing his second photofilm, based on Linda's collection of Beatles photos, and finishing a symphonic work that will debut at the Royal Albert Hall in late summer.

March 11   Paul gains the title of "Sir" as Queen Elizabeth officially knights him in a brief ceremony at Buckingham Palace. It is reported McCartney was so nervous his hand caught in his pocket when he accepted Her Majesty's congratulations. Linda is still too ill to attend the festivities.

March 22   Bonham's Auction House conducts simultaneous sales in London and Tokyo of Beatles memorabilia, including McCartney's lyrics of "Penny Lane" and his custom-made, gold-plated Hoffner violin bass guitar.

April 11?   Paul gives a free, unannounced, twenty-minute concert atop his MPL offices in Soho to promote his upcoming album, *Flaming Pie*.

April 16   It is reported that Stella McCartney will replace lauded designer Karl Lagerfeld at the vaunted Paris fashion house Cloe.

May   McCartney is featured for a full week on VH1, the popular American music channel.

June   *Flaming Pie* is released worldwide to considerably mixed reviews.

An Interview With Paul McCartney

This interview was conducted at a pre-show press conference early in McCartney's 1989/90 world tour.

QUESTION: How does it feel to be singing the old Beatles songs again?

PAUL: It feels great. With some of the songs, like "Sgt. Pepper" and "Hey Jude," the Beatles had given up touring before they were written so I never got to play them live before until this tour and so they feel really fresh.

QUESTION: Will you be having any guest artists joining you on stage?

PAUL: It's kind of difficult to work in guests because we've got the show set now. Really the only person who's guested so far was Stevie Wonder in L.A., but that was easy because we do "Ebony and Ivory" in the set. It's just not too easy to open up the set when you get to this stage with a production.

QUESTION: What made you decide to tour again after thirteen years off the road?

PAUL: It was the fact that I'd got a good band together. I'd been recording and doing solo stuff and little guest spots, like Live Aid. But during the recording of *Flowers in the Dirt* the band felt really good; we've got a sense of humor in common and they're good musicians too. So it was either a question of saying goodbye, see you next album, or shall we stay together. And if you stay together it's like, what shall we do now? So it's like, let's go on tour. So here we are.

QUESTION: How did you approach this album mentally? Do you ever get to the point of saying, "Right, I'll shove it right down their throat?"

PAUL: Yeah. I get to that point. I was not pleased with the album before, which was *Press to Play*. I just wasn't that keen on it. So I did want to make this one better and shove it down a few people's throats. I'm quite happy with the album itself. There's some nice songs on it.

QUESTION: Has coming out on the road inspired you to go back into the studio a little bit faster than you would have in the past?

PAUL: Not really. But it's good for you to get out on the road. It's a stimulating thing, you know, to actually see your fans instead of getting letters from them. To actually see those faces really lifts you. It gives me a great buzz.

QUESTION: Many people have said that they've found your concerts to be a very moving, emotional experience — especially because you are taking so many of us back to the sixties. Why has it taken you twenty years to perform these Beatles songs again?

PAUL: When the Beatles broke up, it was a little bit difficult. It was a bit like a divorce—you really didn't want to do anything associated with the ex-wife. You didn't want to do "her" material. So all of us took that view independently. John, George and Ringo and me all stopped doing Beatles stuff — because I think it was just painful for a while. It was painful memories. But enough time's gone by now to do 'em again. And because of the last tour I did with Wings in '76 — we avoided them — it feels kind of unnatural to do them again. But it's a question of either getting back to them or ignoring them for the rest of my life — which I think would be a shame. And, as I said earlier, some of them I haven't actually done before. I found myself saying, "This feels great, 'Sgt. Pepper,' this feels really good. Why does this feel so great?" And someone reminded me, "You've never done it live before." It was like a new song to me.

QUESTION: Will there be a time when you'll get together with George and Ringo for a jam or whatever?

PAUL: Well, I don't know. It's always on the cards. But a reunion as such is out of the question because John is not with us, and the only real reunion you could have would have been with John. We might easily get together—there's a couple of projects that are possible now — now that we've actually solved our business differences.

QUESTION: Why did it take so long to resolve your business differences?

PAUL: Have you ever been in a lawsuit? I was in one for the last twenty years. It just takes forever. You get your advisors and they get theirs. I think lawyers are trained to keep those things going. It must be the first rule in law school, you know, keep it going.

QUESTION: Do you ever regret that the four ex-Beatles never got together again after the break-up?

PAUL: Oh yeah, I regret it. But it's just life you know. It just didn't happen — for a number of reasons. It would have been great. But John not dying would have been even better.

QUESTION: What do you think about what's going on in Eastern Europe?

PAUL: I think it's very exciting. To me it seems like the sixties kicking in — that's my point of view. It's all the stuff that was said in the sixties — peace, love, democracy, freedom, a better world, all that stuff. The way I look at it, people like Gorbachev grew up with the sixties, like we all did, and I don't think you can be unaffected by it. And I think it's all kicking in now; you look at the people coming across that border now and they're all wearing denim, and I think China's next.

QUESTION: Are you going to play any dates in Eastern Europe?

PAUL: I'd like to. But we've got so many dates on this tour and they don't include Eastern Europe. We tried to go to Russia but the promoter said it was too cold, so we went to Italy instead.

QUESTION: What are your plans after the tour?

PAUL: I'll be writing. I've got a lot of writing I want to do. I'm doing a very interesting thing, a sort of classical work for an orchestra and stuff which is due to be performed by the Liverpool Philharmonic Orchestra in Liverpool Cathedral in 1991. And that's a serious work so I've got a lot of writing to do.

QUESTION: What about your memoirs — why don't you write them now?

PAUL: I always thought you had to be about seventy before you do that.

QUESTION: How do you feel when you look out into the crowds and you see parents holding their children up to see you?

PAUL: It's really beautiful because I've got four kids, and the great thing about me and my kids is that there isn't this generation gap that I thought would be there.

QUESTION: Do they listen to any music that bothers you?

PAUL: No, but I know what you mean. I thought that they'd get into some odd punk music and I'd be saying, "Well, the sixties was better," but they're not. My son loves the Beach Boys. His big new turn-on album that I turned him on to is *Pet Sounds*. And he loves James Brown, Otis Redding, The Commodores—he's got some good taste.

QUESTION: Are you surprised how many young people on this tour are responding to your music?

PAUL: Well, kind of. But a couple of years ago I started to notice how kids like my nephews, who are eighteen now, but who I've known since they were two or whatever, started getting into the Grateful Dead. Now they're all Deadheads. It's incredible. I think maybe it is because modern music is a little bit synthetic and shallow that they're looking back to the sixties. And the great thing about a lot of that sixties stuff is that it does stand up still.

QUESTION: Are your children musically inclined?

PAUL: Yeah, they are, but Linda and I have always said that we'd never push them because it's a tough game, and unless they're really keen. . . . But they're all very good. They're all very interested in music and they can all carry a tune and stuff.

QUESTION: Would you ever have your children play on stage with you?

PAUL: Not really, because that's a little bit too much showbizzy for me. But if they really wanted to do it, desperately wanted to, then I'd help them. But it's got to come from them. As I said, it's a tough game.

QUESTION: How do you think your performances of the sixties compare with your performances today?

PAUL: They're strangely similar, you know. Some of the crowds have been strangely sixties. It's very good, but you can hear yourself now, with the new technology. Compared with what we started out with, we've got Cape Canaveral out there. When we started we had two guitars and a bass and one amp.

QUESTION: When you get away from this for a while is there anything that strikes you that you would like to effect, being a father and with your stature in the world?

PAUL: The thing we're doing on this tour is hooking up with the Friends of the Earth and mentioning the environmental issues a lot. I mean, I'm no expert but I've got four kids and I see this Exxon spill and how well they cleaned up. . . . I don't think anyone wants that to happen. I don't think anyone wants the hole in the ozone layer to get any bigger. But I was like anyone else. I thought, well, the government will fix it for us. But last year it became apparent that no-one was going to fix it, and we've got to address the problem ourselves. So that's what I'm doing on this tour. I'm mentioning it just to give the issues publicity, because I really think we have got to get serious on all that stuff.

QUESTION: What are you trying to do with Friends of the Earth?

PAUL: Friends of the Earth are basically just trying to clean up the planet. Instead of putting your toxic waste in your water, instead of blowing a hole in the sky, instead of having acid rain. . . . If someone had told me when I was a kid that when I grew up the land would have poisons in it, the rain would have acid in it, the sky would have a hole in it, I would not have believed them. But here we are, we're at that point now, and my hope is that going into the next century we really address that problem and get the planet straight. My point is that we are definitely the species that's won. Man has definitely beaten all other animals hands down, and what I'd like to see is us be cool dudes about that. But instead we're still blasting the hell out of everything. It's time we realized we've won an Earth that fouls its own nest. Everything else, all the birds and stuff, go over someplace else to take a dump, but we don't. We do it right here, right where we live. We put all our toxic waste in our lakes and we put all these poisons in cans and dump it under the sea, saying it'll be all right for a hundred years. But what about a hundred and one years, when it blows up?

A Conversation With
Denny Laine

This interview with Denny Laine was conducted by the author at Mark Recording Studio in Clarence, New York, in the fall of 1989.

GEOFFREY: Tell me about the first time you recall working with the Beatles after forming the Moody Blues.

DENNY: We all used to meet in a club called the AdLib which was not really a rock place. It was a very expensive club. I got friendly with George and then John. The Moodys used to have parties they [the Beatles] attended. We were invited to do the tour, and eventually we signed to Brian Epstein's company. We used to do lots of NEMS dates at different places, but we did the Beatles tour because they invited us to close the first half.

GEOFFREY: What specific memories do you have of touring with the Beatles?

DENNY: You could tell that they'd been together a few years because they just bounced off one another like it was going out of style. We would be staying at some country hotel (those were the days we used to smash a few glasses and have a good laugh). The owners would expect us all to be nice boys, but we weren't quite as nice as they expected.

GEOFFREY: Surely the squeaky clean Beatles didn't encourage that sort of reputation, did they?

DENNY: I beg to differ. I can remember a few glasses being spilt! I'm not going to go any further than that. It was pretty harmless stuff, but of course it was blown out of proportion. Years later when the Who used to smash up hotel rooms or toilets and rip things out of the wall, that was a development of something everybody was doing.

GEOFFREY: How did your relationship with McCartney first develop?

DENNY: Well, Paul was probably the most outward going of the Beatles. He was always the one that tried to sell his songs and get to know people. Deep down the others were pretty friendly when you got to know them, but he was the most "commer-cially" friendly. He tried to get me to do [the song] "Those Were the Days" and I thought, yeah, that's a good one. We didn't get round to doing it, but I became his friend on a song-writing level, I suppose.

GEOFFREY: How was your friendship with Paul during those post-Moody years before Wings?

DENNY: I didn't really have much of a relationship with Paul. He was living in London and I was living in Putney. A lot of people who lived in London didn't mix with people who bought houses out of town. John Lennon was one of the people who moved to the area near me. I suppose I developed a relationship with him before even Paul in those days.

GEOFFREY: So were you dropping acid with John?

DENNY: Not literally with him, but we were all doing it at the same time. I can remember coming down off some acid and I bumped into him. I went over to his house and we went off somewhere. I don't know whether he'd just started tripping, but he was definitely stoned. We were both stoned. We went to the Alexandria Palace and naturally were surrounded by people. It was a real happening. They were all smoking banana skins — pretty much of a laugh in those days. Looking back, even more of a laugh. Anyway, somebody spat on John and it really didn't do him any favor psychologically. He just couldn't handle it. I couldn't handle it. So we left and went home. That's when we started to realize that drugs were dangerous. You tended to read more into a situation than was actually happening.

GEOFFREY: What was it like, working with Paul?

DENNY: We didn't have any personality problems because we were friends before. Musically, though, we pushed each other to the limit. We criticized each other about the lyrics or music to the point that we would come up with something good at the end of the day. We disciplined ourselves a lot to do it. Just like everybody else goes to work every day, we were doing the same thing.

GEOFFREY: It looks like so much fun to those of us on the outside.

DENNY: It was fun, but we spent a hell of a lot more time alone working than we did in the public eye having a ball.

GEOFFREY: Ever since the Beatles, Paul's needed someone to work with. I think possibly he had his best experience though with you. Could you sense he needed someone?

DENNY: Yes, he did, as we all do. He was used to being in a situation where he wrote with someone, even though we can all write on our own (as he proved with "Yesterday" and "Blackbird"). You go off on your own solo adventures, but you eventually come back to forming a group because that's where you get the most satisfaction.

GEOFFREY: When you first joined Wings, what were you all doing —just busking to get your feet wet?

DENNY: Paul had a little studio in the barn, a four-track set-up EMI had sent up for us to use.

GEOFFREY: *Wild Life*, of course, was the album that came out of all that. I remember the record company had to put a sticker on the cover of the album saying, "Wings Wildlife" because people didn't realize who the hell it was.

DENNY: We were keeping a low profile. We were a new band. Even though the public didn't think so, we felt we were. We weren't trying to push it. We were just starting out. Even after we were called "Wings" and people knew us, they were still calling us "Paul McCartney and Wings" because it was more of an attraction.

GEOFFREY: What's ironic is that despite all the human shortcomings of your former wife, Jo Jo, she's certainly a far better singer than Linda McCartney, isn't she? She could have added a lot to Wings if only things could have been a bit looser. Certainly in terms of backup vocals anyway.

DENNY: That's true in a sense, but Jo didn't fit personality-wise. She was just too neurotic — maybe she wouldn't have been if she'd been accepted—whereas Linda was a far more together person.

GEOFFREY: She has certainly been a strong presence in Paul's life. Do you think it's fair to say she might have been a kind of mother figure to him though?

DENNY: Oh yes, I would say so, but there's nothing wrong with that. A lot of people have that relationship.

GEOFFREY: Did he generally defer to her if there was an argument? Who really wore the pants in the family, would you say?

DENNY: He did in some respects, but not in everything. In many ways her earthiness kept him grounded, I think.

GEOFFREY: So she didn't really want all the limos and all that then?

DENNY: No, not really, but there again, it was necessary. If you're going to expose yourself to that kind of an audience, you've got to live that life. You must have security. You've got to remember that Linda was from quite a wealthy family anyway and was used to all the trappings. She just wanted a little bit of a simpler life, I think.

GEOFFREY: So you think without Linda Paul would have been a bit more flash?

DENNY: Probably, yes, but Paul always wanted that simple side of life as well. So he found it with Linda, you might say.

GEOFFREY: I can't remember if it was you or Jo Jo that told me you guys were in Abbey Road, telling a dirty joke, when Linda walked into the room, and it was like, Oh, come now lads, Linda's here. You'd have to immediately curtail any so-called loose talk.

DENNY: Yes, but I mean that can happen with lots of people. It's not like she was that much of a prude. She really wasn't. It's an image that they projected and stuck to as well. Of course, there were lots of kids around too, you've got to remember that, so that was part of it as well.

GEOFFREY: So whereas Paul might be an old hippie in some ways, he's a very straight Liverpool dad too.

DENNY: Well, yes, but so am I. We all are to a point. I think because they were in the public eye they made a bit more of a point of it. In fact, in my opinion, too much of a point of it, but that's their prerogative.

GEOFFREY: You played quite a bit of bass with Wings, I've noticed.

DENNY: Some bass, a little keyboards. When I was doing harmonies though I couldn't very well be playing lead, so we would bring in a lead guitarist. Henry [McCullough] was a blues guitarist who could also turn his hand to other styles. He was very into Irish folk music. He was into show music. He was into all sorts of things. When he played the solo on "My Love," in the studio (with an orchestra), he did it live.

GEOFFREY: You mean he came up with that solo on the spot?

DENNY: Right off the top of his head. He was the kind of guy that fitted musically because he balanced out the sweet side of the band. But of course Henry was a bit of a case on the road. He liked to drink and he was never any good at time-keeping.

GEOFFREY: He wasn't too diplomatic either, was he?

DENNY: No. He was a bit of a rebel in that sense, but I don't mind that. I can remember Henry falling over one night doing a solo and not getting up for the rest of the set, which I actually thought was funny. But at the same time you rather think, Well, wait a minute, he was a bit of a loony.

GEOFFREY: How did you feel with your own background—being a pretty heavy, sort of rugged, rebel, gypsy guitarist — to be suddenly playing something like "Mary Had a Little Lamb?"

DENNY: Look, I don't take the business that seriously. If I was running the band, which I wasn't, I wouldn't have put it out as a single. I would have picked something a bit more in line with what I like in music.

GEOFFREY: The next Wings single [issued in December, 1972] was "Hi Hi Hi." What did you play on that?

DENNY: Henry and I both played lead. We had a dual guitar part. A lot of the Wings stuff was recorded like that.

GEOFFREY: Some people say that since you left, McCartney's been like a boat without an anchor, searching around for a place to hang his hat creatively.

DENNY: Well, personally I think it worked out really well with Stevie Wonder and Michael Jackson.

GEOFFREY: You were involved in the Stevie Wonder collaboration, weren't you?

DENNY: I was to begin with, but not with "Ebony and Ivory." I left just before that. When Paul was writing it though, I was saying, "I really like that." I've encouraged Paul to do several things he probably wasn't that happy with himself. "Get on the Right Thing" was one he never really thought was finished. He did it in New York during the *Ram* sessions. He never wanted to use it on anything. He didn't think the lead vocals were any good. He just laid the vocal down at the end of the day and really didn't know all of the words. I used to say, "But it's great. I love it. If you change the vocal though, it won't be as strong." And eventually he put it on *Red Rose Speedway.*

GEOFFREY: It's been said that Henry left because he got sick and tired of Paul telling him what to play.

DENNY: There's a certain amount of that involved, but then, when anybody's in a band together, you've got to decide what you're going to do. You can't have complete freedom when the rest of the band is knuckling down to another approach. I think eventually Henry called Paul or the office and said, "I'm not going to be making this next thing." Henry was a bit of a problem. He wouldn't want to do certain things because he was too into one style. It was hard work to get him to do things, but once he did them he was fine. That's where I'm a little bit more open than Henry.

GEOFFREY: You once said that being in Wings was a twenty-four-hour-a-day gig.

DENNY: It was hard work. We'd have the odd month off, but we were always trying to dream up what we'd be doing next, continually thinking up new ideas for promotion or whatever.

GEOFFREY: By the time *Band on the Run* rolled around you really were quite intimately involved in writing with Paul, weren't you?

DENNY: Actually, I only wrote one song on that album, "No Words."

GEOFFREY: Still, musically, it's really a bona fide McCartney/Laine album, isn't it? Of course it's called Wings, but it's really just the two of you, right?

DENNY: Well, yes. Then Linda would be taught her little bits and come up with her harmonies afterwards. We took the album back to London and added the clarinets and the strings. People like Bryan Ferry would often drop by the studio.

GEOFFREY: How did you feel when *Band on the Run* went through the roof the way it did?

DENNY: All it meant to me was that I made a bit more money and everybody was giving us gold albums. The fact that it got recognized as it did proved to me we didn't really need anybody else. But even so, I thought, well, now we've got to tour, we've got to go back out on the road. One thing I really did want to do in Wings was tour more, which was actually a big reason I left.

GEOFFREY: Why do you think Paul didn't want to go on tour so much?

DENNY: I don't know. Perhaps he was a bit tired of having to go to all the trouble of putting it together [or of] the pain he would get from too many people for too long of a time, always prodding him, questioning him.

GEOFFREY: Let's discuss *Venus and Mars*. What did you sing on that?

DENNY: "Spirits of Ancient Egypt," but I didn't write it.

GEOFFREY: What can you remember about recording the album?

DENNY: We did it at Sea Saint Studios in New Orleans because it was in that area where they've got that great music, that Cajun sound. We were jamming in the different clubs. I remember we had a wrap party on the river, and this young photographer we hired had all his fucking film stolen. The poor guy was devastated. Once the bed tracks were finished we went to L.A. to do some of the overdubs. I remember Tom Scott putting the clarinet part on "Listen to What the Man Said" in one live take, just leaning over the control board. José Feliciano and Mickey Dolenz were hanging out with us, and even Rod Stewart came by. Then for the launch we had this big party on board the *Queen Mary*. It seemed everyone in show business was there —Dean Martin, Carl Malden, Cher, The Jacksons, Joni Mitchell, all these people we'd brought from New Orleans, and even Dylan.

GEOFFREY: You know, it's curious — during that whole Wings period John Lennon never once came around.

DENNY: No, he didn't, but then John was like that. When Paul tried to talk to him he would say things like, "Not tonight, man, we're sleeping." You can't just come around though and knock people up in the middle of the night and expect to come in.

GEOFFREY: Tell me about the "Wings Over America" tour, because that was basically the first of the great mega tours. What was that like?

DENNY: You've got to remember that people like Zeppelin were doing it too, as were the Who. They had people make their equipment, and the Who had the lighting company, Showco, who really developed all the laser things. We had them build all our equipment — a tailor-made set-up. We paid over the top to get the best. We had our own stage built. We weren't just going to places and setting up on the stages they supplied. We took everything with us. We took seventy people on the road to build everything on the day of the gig. We certainly had the most up-to-date laser show, the most up-to-date sound, everything. We had a real cross-section of people in the audience, too. It wasn't just the heads, the dope smokers, it was all sorts — Beatles' fans, Moody Blues fans maybe, and of course the kids. I was as surprised as anyone that we actually had a whole set of fans that were never into the Beatles or the Moody Blues.

GEOFFREY: Tell me briefly how Joe English left.

DENNY: Again, the same story as Denny Seiwell. He was an American. He'd made some money, bought a house and got his Porsche. He'd had enough of whatever it is that pisses off people at that level.

GEOFFREY: Other than the unfortunate fact that Paul kept getting busted for possession of marijuana on a semi-regular basis, you guys weren't really a big doping band, were you?

DENNY: No. We never used to get stoned on gigs at all, never. We were too concerned about doing what we'd rehearsed and making it right. We didn't want to come across like a stoned-out band. After all, there were kids, grandparents and all sorts of people in our audiences. We only smoked as a social thing or in the studio to come up with new ideas. But we never got into "H" or anything like that.

GEOFFREY: Wings had a reputation of being a bubblegum band at the time. Were you all aware of it?

DENNY: Yes. We always tried to get a heavier image all the way along the line. That's one of the reasons I wasn't one hundred percent satisfied with my years in Wings, because it wasn't the more bluesy-orientated music or rock that I was influenced by. I was always trying to give it a little bit more of an edge. It actually went there for a while too.

GEOFFREY: With the "Wings Over America" tour especially.

DENNY: That just proved to me that once we had a group together long enough and we were touring, we would come across heavier than in the studio. Paul also had a raunchy side to him too. He was into lots of different things. In fact, he was into so many different things that sometimes I don't think he really knew who he was [or] what direction he was going in musically.

GEOFFREY: You've said that when McCartney composes, he writes compulsively. How did you and he actually collaborate? What went on during that process?

DENNY: Somebody would come up with an idea for a tune and then the other would say, "I like that bit, but I don't like that." Then we'd iron that out and generally there wouldn't be enough words. Or maybe the tune was a little bit too low, or perhaps it wasn't the right kind of song for an acoustic guitar. Anyway, we would come out at the end of the day with a solution, a song that we both knew, with the lyrics, guitar, and piano bits all vaguely together.

GEOFFREY: You seem to have gotten everyone in Wings the job, didn't you?

DENNY: No. I didn't get Denny Seiwell the job. Nor Joe. Steve was my neighbor. He used to write songs. He was a drummer, but really he was a writer. His mother was a terrific jazz singer and he was just a friend. I liked his music. He'd play piano and write songs. He was working with Elton John on and off and a guy called Brian Chapman. He wasn't really the kind of rock drummer I was looking for, but he knew how to play and how to do sessions. He played on a solo album for me that was partly stuff I'd done with Wings and several other songs [*Japanese Tears*]. For Steve's Wings audition we went along to Soho Square which is where our office is [MPL]. We had a theater downstairs which we had built in the basement. He and Laurence just joined in and we all had a good old play. Just prior I'd done a Dave Essex show, a weekly series he had. David was an old friend and admirer of mine. Anyway, Laurence's brother happened to be the conductor of the studio band and Laurence was the guitar player. So he came up to me and said, "The guitar solo on 'Go Now,' do you want me to do this or that? Who played it on the record anyway?" And I said, "I did." So he copied my guitar solo and played it on the show.

GEOFFREY: Tell me a bit about the creation of "Mull of Kintyre."

DENNY: Originally, Paul came to me with this verse, and I said, "I love that." And he went, "Oh really?" He hadn't got any great ideas to do anything with it. I said, "I love that and that would be fantastic with the Campbeltown Pipe Band maybe." I injected my enthusiasm and his eyebrows went up. Well, Paul's not really a big drinker, but he does like his Scotch and Coke, so we got through a bottle during the course of this one afternoon, sitting on the wall outside the cottage [in Scotland]. I threw in most of the lyrics which Paul finished off later. Then we got the pipe band in. But because we'd recorded it in a certain key they couldn't come in on the first verse, so we brought them in as a feature, which really gave the tune a lift. That was the bit of magic for that song.

GEOFFREY: Wasn't that single supposed to be what they call a "double A-side?" "Girls School," I believe, was on the flip side.

DENNY: Yes. But that was more of a rock song. You see, in England people just love nostalgic songs. They particularly adore this kind of Scottish-era, "God Save the Queen" type of thing. It became a kind of national anthem for Scotland in a sense. In actual fact people from all over the world used to visit Kintyre, thinking it was this fantastic place. The name stuck and they now call the whole area the Mull of Kintyre. Of course it never existed before, so we've made some kind of mark in history. Paul definitely wrote the chorus, which is the selling point, so you can't say I was responsible for that. But he had the idea and it was really just an idea.

GEOFFREY: What if Paul went off in a direction that you instinctively felt was wrong?

DENNY: Oh, I would rebel if it was something I didn't really like.

GEOFFREY: That's something very few people would dare do with Paul McCartney to this day, isn't it?

DENNY: I think anybody who works closely with him, George Martin as well, should say, "Look, that's all right, but don't you think this should happen?"

GEOFFREY: How does he take to that?

DENNY: He's like any artist. First he thinks, "Well, wait a minute, who are you to tell me?" But it's like life. If you've got something better to say, I'll listen. But if you haven't, shut up.

GEOFFREY: Denny, why did you leave Wings?

DENNY: I left because Paul got busted in Japan and we'd been waiting five years to get there. That was the biggest upset of the lot.

GEOFFREY: You didn't get paid for the tour?

DENNY: Not really, but then again, I would have made the money up in other ways. That wasn't the reason I left.

GEOFFREY: How do you look back on Wings?

DENNY: Well, I'm very happy I did it. I certainly made some bread and saw a lot of the world. I'm very regretful, though, that I don't have an on-going friendship with Paul and Linda anymore. That's all. But I think if I were to make the effort to go and see them, things would be different. It's down to me. But it's also down to Paul to kind of let me know. He has been in touch with me through other people, I'm told, saying that we should get together. It just hasn't come about. Maybe I'll go and see him on this tour [1990]. I don't know.

GEOFFREY: How do you think Paul will be remembered?

DENNY: Like Beethoven. Yes. He'll be remembered in that same league. And also there will be films and recordings of McCartney which there obviously aren't of Beethoven. It will be the same kind of thing. He'll be remembered as one of the biggest influences in the world for his lifetime.

GEOFFREY: Considering your songwriting relationship with Paul, did you ever feel you were in any way competing against John Lennon?

DENNY: No, not at all. That didn't ever come into it. I never thought about what the public might be thinking. We were doing something that was me and Paul. I wasn't a substitute for John to him. I was just another step in a different direction. I put a few raw edges on some of the things he was coming up with. And some of the ideas I had he would help put them into more form. For example, I would write a song and think, well, it's all right, but I'm not that keen on the melody. And he would say, "I'd like it better if we do this to it, if we change that a little bit there." I would be surprised that the song would turn out that good. So I was happy to have that influence as well. We were teaching each other, learning together, but at the same time we weren't in competition with each other or anyone else for that matter.

GEOFFREY: And you didn't leave because of Jo Jo?

DENNY: That contributed to it. You know, I was at the point where we were going through bad times as a family anyway. She was running around and I was running around—living separate lives virtually. It was a way of saving my marriage. The point was though, it had gone too far. Right? That wouldn't save the bloody marriage, leaving the band. I didn't physically leave right then. I came back. In fact, I went to France to meet him [Paul] and I started working on my own solo career. What was I going to do for two years? The band couldn't tour. It would have meant going back into the studio. One day I was really pissed off and Paul kept calling up to say, "Let's get back to work." I said, "Tell him I'm not coming in today."

GEOFFREY: That was for *Tug of War*, wasn't it?

DENNY: Then it was, "If he doesn't come in, we'll forget it." He was getting pissed off. I said, "Well, forget it, then." I didn't actually talk to him. I just didn't feel like carrying on. But by that token, I'd been there before over silly things and hadn't felt like doing anything. I know if I had called him I could have carried on. I just didn't. It's as simple as that.

GEOFFREY: You never had any words with him about it?

DENNY: We never had any words about it, but I knew from other sources that he was pissed off about certain things that had been said. Within the context of my book it wouldn't have mattered, but there you go. So as a result I haven't seen a hair on his head since.

GEOFFREY: How do you feel about Paul's music since Wings broke up?

DENNY: Well, I don't really see Paul as a solo artist. I've always seen him as a band member. I've always thought he contributes more when he's working with someone. Now that he's got a band together I think probably it's done him a lot of good. In between that time he's kept a low profile musically as well. I wasn't that wild about *Tug of War*.

GEOFFREY: How long were you and Paul together?

DENNY: Over ten years. The only reason it didn't last any longer was because of the group. We'd gone through so many different line-ups. He got busted in Japan and the band just went back into the studio. We couldn't do any big tours because you have to wait for visas. So I drifted away. We didn't fall out at that time. I haven't seen him since, but we haven't really fallen out. Unfortunately, the press got hold of some bad stuff. I was doing a book and somebody got hold of the things I said about Paul and took them out of context. It looked like I was having a go at Paul, which I wasn't. I'm sure he wasn't too pleased about that. Since then I've heard through various mutual friends that he doesn't hold any real grudge and I certainly don't have any bad feelings about it all.

GEOFFREY: Would you ever consider going back and playing with him?

DENNY: If he asked me to. I wouldn't push the idea, but if he wanted to do something I would.

GEOFFREY: Do you like his new work?

DENNY: Yes. I enjoyed the new album [*Flowers in the Dirt*]. I like the band he's got now as well.

GEOFFREY: Was Wings a real high point for you?

DENNY: Yes, but I've always had a solo thing going too. Actually, I like to do things a little bit lower key than Wings. It's because of the audience contact, playing smaller places, which I've enjoyed doing while not being with Wings. But you can't have both.

GEOFFREY: Do you think you were ever Paul McCartney's best friend?

DENNY: I don't know. I felt we were friends. Whether I was his best friend . . .

GEOFFREY: Well, there wasn't anyone else who was around anymore, was there?

DENNY: No. But I mean he had his brother, he had his family.

GEOFFREY: Was he very close with Mike?

DENNY: Yes. But in an elder brother sort of way. I mean he certainly wouldn't spoil Mike, but he'd still buy him a car once in a while or help him out. I don't think they were the best of friends all the time. There's a competition there, but then you get that in a lot of families.

GEOFFREY: Personally, I think Mike is extremely talented and his *McGear* allbum was brilliant. I always look on that LP like a Wings album.

DENNY: Yes. Well, we all played on it. Paul was very much the main man there, the producer.

GEOFFREY: I don't quite understand why it didn't do anything.

DENNY: I know. That's always upset me as well. Let's put it this way: if Paul had pushed that like he did his own albums, it would have been big, and it deserved to be. Frankly, I was a little bit disappointed that Paul didn't get behind that. I think he mainly left it to Mike. We all know that Mike hasn't got his kind of money and couldn't have promoted it properly.

GEOFFREY: It's funny how he never drew Mike into the family business.

DENNY: Mike might not have wanted to, you know. There's that brotherly rivalry there.

GEOFFREY: Did Paul ever talk to you about his attitude towards the Beatles?

DENNY: We never really discussed the Beatles, ever. Once in a while, though, he might say something like, "It's kind of hard after being in a band like I was in."

GEOFFREY: How would you sum up John Lennon as a person?

DENNY: John wasn't complicated with me. We tended to cling to each other in those days because lots of people around were frightened to talk to us and didn't know how to approach us. I was with John Lennon when Mike Pinder came around with their [The Moody Blues'] new album, *Days of Future Past.* We sat around and listened to that all day. George would come around with "Ticket to Ride," their new single, and play it just to get friends' opinions.

GEOFFREY: There's been a lot of controversy over the years (certainly in the tabloids in Great Britain) about your marriage to Jo Jo and how it didn't really mix with the business side of your life. You met Jo Jo in France, right?

DENNY: She was a Paul McCartney fan from the time she was in school. She's a friend of a guy called Phillip Constantine who worked for Decca in Paris. Anyway, she stayed with me from then on. I think Paul and Linda always resented the fact that she was initially a fan. They held that against her. I was determined, however, not to let that interfere.

GEOFFREY: In a way it sounds like they were a bit unfair to her.

DENNY: Well, maybe they were. Jo didn't get on well with them. On the other hand, she wasn't part of the group so she didn't get to spend enough time around us. That's not good for a family relationship either. We all know that music interferes with people's private lives. It always has, it always will.

Paul McCartney's Band History

Unnamed Duo
1956

Paul McCartney	Ian James
guitar/vocals	guitar/vocals

The McCartney Brothers
Summer 1957

Paul McCartney	Mike McCartney
guitar/vocals	vocals

The Nurk Twins
Late 1958

Paul McCartney	John Lennon
guitar/vocals	guitar/vocals

The Quarry Men
July 1957 to October 1958

Paul McCartney	John Lennon	Colin Hanton	Rod Davis	Eric Griffiths	Len Gary	Nigel Whalley
guitar/vocals	guitar/vocals	drums	banjo	guitar	tea chest bass	manager

Johnny and the Moondogs
October 1959 to December 1959

Paul McCartney	John Lennon	George Harrison	Stuart Sutcliffe	Various Personnel
guitar/vocals	guitar/vocals	guitar/vocals	bass	drums

The Silver Beatles
January 1960 to August 1960

Paul McCartney	John Lennon	George Harrison	Stuart Sutcliffe	Various Personnel
guitar/vocals	guitar/vocals	guitar/vocals	bass	drums

The Beatles (Phase 1)
August 1960 to May 1961

Paul McCartney	John Lennon	George Harrison	Stuart Sutcliffe	Pete Best
guitar/vocals	guitar/vocals	guitar/vocals	bass	drums/vocals

The Beatles (Phase 2)
June 1961 to August 1962

Paul McCartney	John Lennon	George Harrison	Pete Best
bass/vocals	guitar/vocals	guitar/vocals	drums/vocals

The Beatles (Phase 3)
August 1962 to April 1970

Paul McCartney	John Lennon	George Harrison	Ringo Starr
bass/vocals	guitar/vocals	guitar/vocals	drums/vocals

Wings (Phase 1)
August 1971 to August 1973

Paul McCartney bass/vocals	Linda McCartney keyboards/vocals	Denny Laine guitar/vocals	Henry McCullough guitar	Denny Seiwell drums

Wings (Phase 2)
August 1973 to April 1974

Paul McCartney vocals/various instr.	Linda McCartney keyboards/vocals	Denny Laine guitar/vocals

Wings (Phase 3)*
June 1974 to January 1975

Paul McCartney bass/vocals	Linda McCartney keyboards/vocals	Denny Laine guitar/vocals	Jimmy McCulloch guitar/vocals	Geoff Britton drums

Wings (Phase 4)
January 1975 to September 1977

Paul McCartney bass/vocals	Linda McCartney keyboards/vocals	Denny Laine guitar/vocals	Jimmy McCulloch guitar/vocals	Joe English drums

Wings (Phase 5)
September 1977 to June 1978

Paul McCartney vocals/various instr.	Linda McCartney keyboards/vocals	Denny Laine guitar/vocals

Wings (Phase 6)
June 1978 to April 1981

Paul McCartney bass/vocals	Linda McCartney keyboards/vocals	Denny Laine guitar/vocals	Laurence Juber guitar	Steve Holly drums

McCartney goes solo.
May 1981 to June 1987

Paul McCartney and His Band
July 1987 to February 1991

Paul McCartney bass/guitar/vocals	Linda McCartney keyboards/vocals	Hamish Stuart guitar/vocals	Robbie McIntosh guitar/vocals	Paul "Wix" Wickens keyboards/vocals	Chris Whitten drums/vocals

Paul McCartney and His Band
March 1991 to Present

Paul McCartney bass/guitar/vocals	Linda McCartney keyboards/vocals	Hamish Stuart guitar/vocals	Robbie McIntosh guitar/vocals	Paul "Wix" Wickens keyboards/vocals	Blair Cunningham drums/vocals

* Britton and McCulloch joined Wings in April and June, 1974, respectively.

Paul McCartney
Solo Discography

Compiled by
Geoffrey Giuliano
and
Dennis Toll

*An asterisk (*) indicates information the
author has been unable to verify.*

ALBUMS

Title	Artist	Release Date American British	Label American British (unless otherwise noted)
You've Got to Hide Your Love Away Produced by John Lennon and Paul McCartney. McCartney plays rhythm guitar on side one, cut one.	The Silkie	11/22/65 *	Fontana *
Got to Get You into Our Life Side one, cut one, written by Lennon and McCartney. Produced by McCartney.	Cliff Bennett and The Rebel Rousers	* 1/27/67	* Parlophone
Mellow Yellow McCartney contributes vocals on title track.	Donovan	1/30/67 1967	Epic Epic
The Family Way Soundtrack composed by McCartney.	The George Martin Orchestra	6/12/67 1/6/67	London Decca
England's Greatest Hits Side two, cut five, by The Silkie. Produced by Lennon and McCartney.	Various Artists	9/12/67 *	Fontana *
Smiley Smile Side one, cut two, produced by The Beach Boys and McCartney.	The Beach Boys	9/18/67 11/20/67	Brother Brother
McGough & McGear Produced by McCartney.	Roger McGough and Mike McGear	5/17/68 *	Parlophone *
James Taylor Side two, cut one, "Carolina in My Mind." McCartney plays bass guitar.	James Taylor	2/17/69 12/6/68	Apple Apple

Post Card Produced by McCartney. American release includes "Those Were the Days."	Mary Hopkin	2/21/69 3/3/69	Apple Apple
Urban Spaceman Side one, cut one, "I'm the Urban Spaceman," produced by McCartney (as Apollo C. Vermouth).	The Bonzo Dog Doo Dah Band	6/9/69 1969	Imperial Liberty
Brave New World Side two, cut five, "My Dark Hour." McCartney on bass guitar, drums, and backing vocals.	The Steve Miller Band	6/16/69 *	Capitol *
Wall's Ice Cream (EP) Mary Hopkin, "Happiness Runs" (on Pebble and the Man). Produced by McCartney.	Various Artists	No American release 7/18/69	Apple
Tadpoles Side one, cut six, produced by McCartney.	The Bonzo Dog Doo Dah Band	1969 8/1/69	Imperial Liberty
Barabajagal McCartney plays tambourine and sings backing vocals on "Atlantis."	Donovan	8/11/69 1969	Epic Epic
Through the Past, Darkly (Big Hits Vol. 2) Side one, cut six, "We Love You." Lennon and McCartney on backing vocals.	The Rolling Stones	1969 9/12/69	London Decca
Magic Christian Music Side one, cut one, "Come and Get It," written by McCartney.	Badfinger	3/16/70 1/9/70	Apple Apple
The Magic Christian Side one, cut two, and side two, cut three, written and produced by McCartney. Album produced by McCartney.	Ken Thorne and Orchestra "Come and Get It" by Badfinger	2/11/70 4/10/70	Commonwealth United Pye
Battersea Rain Dance Cut five, "Catcall," written by McCartney.	Chris Barber Band	* 3/13/70	* Polydor
Sentimental Journey "Stardust" arranged by McCartney.	Ringo Starr	4/24/70 3/27/70	Apple Apple
McCartney	Paul McCartney	4/20/70 4/17/70	Apple Apple

Progressive Heavies Side two, cut five, produced by McCartney.	Various Artists	6/15/70 1970	United Artists United Artists
The Beast of the Bonzos Side one, cut eight, produced by McCartney.	The Bonzo Dog Doo Dah Band	7/17/70 8/2/71	Liberty United Artists
Ram	Paul and Linda McCartney	5/17/71 5/21/71	Apple Apple
Wild Life	Wings	7/12/71 3/12/71	Apple Apple
20 Monster Hits Record two, side one, cut two, "Atlantis." McCartney plays tambourine and sings backing vocals.	Various Artists	8/72 *	Treasury *
Those Were the Days Side one, cuts one, two, and three, and side two, cuts three and five, produced by McCartney. Side two, cut five, written by Lennon and McCartney.	Mary Hopkin	9/25/72 11/24/72	Apple Apple
No Secrets Side two, cut four. McCartney on backing vocals.	Carly Simon	11/3/72 12/15/72	Elektra Elektra
More Hot Rocks Side two, cut six, "We Love You." Lennon and McCartney on backing vocals.	The Rolling Stones	12/20/72 1972	London Decca
Anthology Side four, cut four, "My Dark Hour." McCartney on bass guitar, drums, and backing vocals.	The Steve Miller Band	2/9/73 11/6/72	Capitol *
Red Rose Speedway	Paul McCartney and Wings	4/30/73 5/4/73	Apple Apple
Live and Let Die Side one, cut one, by Paul McCartney and Wings.	The George Martin Orchestra	7/2/73 7/6/73	United Artists United Artists
I'm the Urban Spaceman Side one, cut six, produced by McCartney.	The Bonzo Dog Doo Dah Band	9/7/73 *	Sunset *

Ringo "Six O'Clock" written by Paul and Linda. McCartney also arranged strings and played piano synthesizer. Paul and Linda perform backing vocals. McCartney plays kazoo on "You're Sixteen."	Ringo Starr	11/9/73 11/2/73	Apple Apple
History of British Rock Side two, cut five, produced by Lennon and McCartney. McCartney plays rhythm guitar.	Various Artists	3/25/74 *	Sire Sash *
Hard Goods Side four, cut five, "Vegetables," produced by The Beach Boys and Paul McCartney.	Various Artists	5/9/74 *	Warner Brothers *
Walking Man Side one, cuts two and three. McCartney on backing vocals.	James Taylor	7/2/74 6/26/74	Warner Brothers Warner Brothers
Pass on This Side Disk Side one, cut one, "God Bless California." McCartney on bass guitar and backing vocals.	Thornton, Fradkin, Unger and The Big Band	8/8/74 *	ESP *
I Survive Side two, cuts two and three. McCartney plays synthesizer. Side one, cut five. McCartney on synthesizer and backing vocals.	Adam Faith	9/2/74 9/20/74	Warner Brothers Warner Brothers
History of the Bonzos Side three, cut one, produced by McCartney.	The Bonzo Dog Doo Dah Band	9/9/74 5/24/74	United Artists United Artists
McGear Produced by McCartney. Side one, cuts two and four written by McCartney. Side one, cuts three and five, and side two, cuts two through five, written by McCartney and McGear. Side two, cut one, written by McCartney and McGough.	Mike McGear	9/27/74 10/14/74	Warner Brothers Warner Brothers
Smiler Side two, cut six, "Mine for Me," written by McCartney.	Rod Stewart	10/7/74 9/27/74	Mercury Mercury

Let's Love Produced by McCartney. Side one, cut one, and side two, cut six, written by McCartney.	Peggy Lee	10/8/74 11/8/74	Atlantic Warner Brothers
Friends/Smiley Smile Record two, cut two, produced by The Beach Boys and Paul McCartney.	The Beach Boys	10/28/74 1974	Reprise *
Deep Ear Side one, cut two, "Rock 'n' Roll Is Music Now." McCartney sings backing vocals with James Taylor.	Various Artists	11/19/74 *	Warner Brothers *
History of British Rock, Vol. 2 Side one, cut two, written by Lennon and McCartney. Side four, cut one, produced by McCartney.	Various Artists	12/2/74 *	Sire Sash *
Sold Out Side one, cut one, produced by McCartney.	The Scaffold	* 2/7/75	* Warner Brothers
The Force Side three, cut six, "Norton," written by McCartney and McGear. Produced by McCartney.	Various Artists	2/14/74 *	Warner Brothers *
Venus and Mars	Wings	5/27/75 5/30/75	Capitol EMI
History of British Rock, Vol. 3 Side four, cut six, "Those Were the Days," produced by McCartney.	Various Artists	10/27/75 *	Sire Sash *
Rolling Gold: The Very Best of the Rolling Stones Side three, cut five, "We Love You." Lennon and McCartney on backing vocals.	The Rolling Stones	* 11/14/75	* Decca
Best of Carly Simon Side two, cut three, "Night Owl." McCartney performs backing vocals.	Carly Simon	11/24/75 12/19/75	Elektra Elektra
Blast from Your Past Side one, cut one. McCartney plays kazoo.	Ringo Starr	11/20/75 12/12/75	Apple Apple
Wings at the Speed of Sound	Wings	3/25/76 3/26/76	Capitol Parlophone

Best of Rod Stewart "Mine for Me" written by McCartney.	Rod Stewart	4/29/76 6/18/77	Mercury Mercury
Ringo's Rotogravure Paul and Linda sing backing vocals on "Pure Gold." Side one, track three, written by McCartney.	Ringo Starr	9/27/76 9/17/76	Atlantic Polydor
Wings Over America	Wings	12/10/76 1976	Capitol EMI
Original Artists Hits **of the 60's** "Got to Get You into My Life" by Cliff Bennett and The Rebel Rousers produced by McCartney.	Various Artists	3/18/77 *	Music For Pleasure *
One of These Days in **England** McCartney sings backing vocals on title track.	Roy Harper	3/21/77 2/11/77	Chrysalis Harvest
Best of Steve Steve Miller **'68–'73** McCartney on bass guitar, drums, and backing vocals on "My Dark Hour."	The Steve Miller Band	3/25/77 *	Capitol *
Holly Days Produced by McCartney. McCartney also plays drums, guitar, and sang backing vocals.	Denny Laine	5/19/77 5/6/77	Capitol EMI
One of the Boys Side two, cut two, "Giddy," written by McCartney.	Roger Daltrey	6/10/77 5/13/77	MCA Polydor
The Rolling Stones' **Greatest Hits** Lennon and McCartney sing backing vocals on "We Love You."	The Rolling Stones	* 7/77	* ABKCO
The Best of Peter and **Gordon** "Woman" written by McCartney.	Peter and Gordon	* 8/5/77	* Nuts
Thrillington McCartney working under an alias on this obscure instrumental version of the *Ram* album.	Percy "Thrills" Thrillington	1977 1977	Capitol Regal Zonophone
London Town	Wings	3/31/78 1978	Capitol Parlophone

Wings' Greatest	Wings	11/22/78 1978	Capitol Parlophone
Back To The Egg	Wings	6/11/79 1979	Columbia Parlophone
McCartney II	Paul McCartney	5/21/80 1980	Columbia Parlophone
The McCartney Interview	Paul McCartney with Vic Garbarini	12/4/80 1980	Columbia Parlophone
Stop and Smell the Roses McCartney composed and produced "Private Property," on which he plays bass and piano, and sings backing vocals. McCartney plays bass, piano, and percussion on "Attention," which he also wrote and produced.	Ringo Starr	1981 1981	Boardwalk *
The Concerts for the People **of Kampuchea** McCartney performs with Wings and with Rockestra.	Various Artists	1981 1981	Atlantic Atlantic
Standard Time McCartney plays bass on "Maisie."	Laurence Juber	1982 No British release	Breaking Records
Tug of War	Paul McCartney	4/26/82 1982	Columbia Parlophone
Japanese Tears McCartney plays bass on "Send Me the Heart." Laine and McCartney co-wrote "I Would Only Smile" and "Weep for Love," both recorded by Wings.	Denny Laine	1983 1983	Takoma Scratch
Pipes of Peace McCartney performs two songs with Michael Jackson.	Paul McCartney	10/31/83 1983	Columbia Parlophone
EB '84 "On the Wings of a Nightingale" written by McCartney.	The Everly Brothers	1984 1984	Mercury Mercury
Let's Beat It "Say, Say, Say" by McCartney and Michael Jackson. Jackson also appears solo on this album.	Various Artists	1984 No British release	K-Tel
Give My Regards to Broad **Street**	Paul McCartney	10/16/84 1984	Columbia Parlophone

Press to Play	Paul McCartney	8/21/86 9/86	Capitol Parlophone
Conspiracy of Hope (For Amnesty International) "Pipes of Peace" appears on side one.	Various Artists	11/14/86 1986	Mercury Mercury
It's a Live-In World (The Anti-Heroin Project) McCartney contributes "Simple as That."	Various Artists	No American release 1986	EMI
All the Best	Paul McCartney	12/12/87 1987	Capitol Parlophone
Rock for Amnesty McCartney is featured.	Various Artists	1988 1988	* *
Prince's Trust 10th Anniversary McCartney is featured.	Various Artists	1988 1988	* *
Spike McCartney co-wrote "Veronica" and "Pads, Paws and Claws."	Elvis Costello	1988 1989	Columbia *
Choba B CCCP (Back in the USSR) Intended solely for the Russian market, it quickly surfaced as a bootleg throughout the rest of the world.	Paul McCartney	1988	Melodiya (USSR)
Flowers in the Dirt	Paul McCartney	6/89 1989	Capitol Parlophone
After the Hurricane McCartney contributes a song to this George Martin-arranged album in aid of Montserrat Hurricane Relief.	Various Artists	1990 1990	Chrysalis *
Knebworth — The Album Includes live versions of "Hey Jude" and "Coming Up."	Various Artists	1990 1990	Polydor *
Tripping the Live Fantastic	Paul McCartney	11/90 11/90	Capitol Parlophone
Tripping the Live Fantastic — Highlights!	Paul McCartney	12/90 12/90	Capitol Parlophone
Unplugged: The Official Bootleg A live acoustic set of McCartney and the band, recorded for the April 1991 MTV program.	Paul McCartney	5/91 5/91	Capitol Parlophone

Choba B CCCP **The Russian Album**	Paul McCartney	10/91	Capitol
Paul McCartney's **Liverpool Oratorio**	Paul McCartney	10/91	EMI
Off the Ground	Paul McCartney	2/93	Capitol
The Family Way **Variations Concertantes**	Paul McCartney	1995	Polygram Records
Flaming Pie	Paul McCartney	5/22/97	Capitol

SINGLES

Title	Artist	Release Date American British	Label American British (unless otherwise noted)
A It's You B I Knew Right Away McCartney plays tambourine.	Alma Cogan	10/30/64 1964	Columbia *
A It's For You B He Won't Ask Me McCartney plays piano on A-side.	Cilla Black	8/17/64 7/31/64	Capitol Parlophone
A You've Got to Hide Your Love Away B City Winds Produced by Lennon and McCartney. McCartney plays rhythm guitar on A-side.	The Silkie	9/20/65 9/20/65	Fontana Fontana
A Got to Get You Into My Life B Baby Each Day A-side written and produced by McCartney.	Cliff Bennett and The Rebel Rousers	8/29/66 8/5/66	ABC Parlophone
A From Head to Toe B Night Time Produced by McCartney. He also plays tambourine.	The Escourts	* 11/18/66	* Columbia
A Love in the Open Air B Theme from the Family Way Both sides written by McCartney.	The George Martin Orchestra	* 12/23/66	* Columbia
A The Family Way Theme B The Family Way Theme Written by McCartney.	The George Martin Orchestra The Tudor Minstrels	* 12/66	* United Artists
A Love in the Open Air B Bahama Sound McCartney wrote A-side.	The George Martin Orchestra	* 4/24/67	* United Artists
A We Love You B Dandelion Lennon and McCartney perform backing vocals on A-side.	The Rolling Stones	8/28/67 8/18/67	London Decca
A Catcall B Mercy Mercy Mercy A-side written by McCartney.	The Chris Barber Band	* 10/20/67	* Marmalade

A **And the Sun Will Shine**   Paul Jones   *   *
B **The Dog Presides**   3/8/68   Columbia
McCartney plays drums on A-side.

A **Thingumybob**   John Foster and   8/26/68   Apple
                                Sons Ltd.
B **Yellow Submarine**   The Black Dyke   9/6/68   Apple
Produced by McCartney.   Mills Band

A **Those Were the Days**   Mary Hopkin   8/26/68   Apple
B **Turn Turn Turn**   8/30/68   Apple
Produced by McCartney.

A **Quelli Grand Giorni**   Mary Hopkin   10/25/68   Apple (Italy)
B **Turn Turn Turn**
Produced by McCartney.

A **Enaquellos Dias**   Mary Hopkin .   10/25/68   Apple (Spain)
B **Turn Turn Turn**
Produced by McCartney.

A **Le Temps des Fleurs**   Mary Hopkin   10/25/68   Odeon
B **Turn Turn Turn**   (France)
Produced by McCartney.

A **An Jₑ ₙem Tag**   Mary Hopkin   10/25/68   Odeon
B **Turn Turn Turn**   (Germany)
Produced by McCartney.

A **Lontano Dagli Occhi**   Mary Hopkin   10/25/68   Apple (Italy)
B **The Game**
Produced by McCartney.

A **Atlantis**   Donovan   1968   *
B **I Love My Shirt**   11/22/68   Pye
McCartney on tambourine and
backing vocals on A-side.

A **I'm the Urban Spaceman**   The Bonzo Dog   12/18/68   Imperial
B **Canyons of Your Mind**   Doo Dah Band   10/11/68   Liberty
Produced by McCartney (as Apollo
C. Vermouth).

A **Atlantis**   Donovan   1/20/69   Epic
B **To Susan on the West**   1969   Epic
   Coast Waiting
McCartney on tambourine and
backing vocals on A-side.

A **Rosetta**   The Fourmost   2/21/69   CBS
B **Just Like Before**   *   *
Produced by McCartney.

A **Carolina in My Mind**   James Taylor   3/17/69   Apple
B **Taking It In**   1969   Apple
McCartney plays bass guitar.

| A Goodbye | Mary Hopkin | 4/7/69 | Apple |
| B Sparrow | | 3/28/69 | Apple |

Produced by McCartney.
McCartney also plays guitar on
A-side.

| A New Day | Jackie Lomax | 6/2/69 | Apple |
| B Thumbin' a Ride | | 1969 | Apple |

McCartney produced B-side.

| A My Dark Hour | The Steve Miller | 6/16/69 | Capitol |
| B Song for Our Ancestors | Band | 7/18/69 | * |

McCartney (as Paul Ramone) plays
bass guitar, drums, and sings
backing vocals on A-side.

| A Penina | Carlos Mendes | 7/18/69 | Parlophone |
| B Wings of Revenge | | | (Portugal) |

A-side written by McCartney.

| A Lontano Dagli Occhi | Mary Hopkin | 1/29/70 | Apple |
| B Temma Harbour | | 1/16/70 | Apple |

A Que Sera Sera	Mary Hopkin	6/15/70	Apple
B Fields of St. Etienne		9/19/69	Apple
			(France)

Produced by McCartney.
McCartney also plays bass guitar.

| A Come and Get It | Badfinger | 1/12/70 | Apple |
| B Rock of All Ages | | 12/5/69 | Apple |

Produced by McCartney. A-side
written by McCartney.

| A How the Web was Woven | Jackie Lomax | 2/6/70 | Apple |
| B Thumbin' a Ride | | 1970 | Apple |

B-side produced by McCartney.
McCartney also plays drums.

| A Carolina in My Mind | James Taylor | 10/26/70 | Apple |
| B Something's Wrong | | 11/6/70 | Apple |

McCartney plays bass on A-side.

| A Penina | Jotta Herre | 1970 | Phillips |
| B North | | | (Holland) |

A-side written by McCartney.

| A Another Day | Paul McCartney | 2/22/71 | Apple |
| B Oh Woman, Oh Why | | 2/19/71 | Apple |

| A I'm the Urban Spaceman | The Bonzo Dog | 7/19/71 | United Artists |
| B Canyons of Your Mind | Doo Dah Band | * | * |

A-side produced by McCartney.

A Uncle Albert/Admiral	Paul and Linda	8/2/71	Apple
Halsey	McCartney	*	*
B Too Many People			

A	The Back Seat of My Car	Paul and Linda	*	*
B	Heart of the Country	McCartney	8/13/71	Apple

A	My Dark Hour	The Steve Miller	*	*
B	The Gangster Is Back	Band	2/25/72	Capitol

McCartney plays bass guitar, drums, and sings backing vocals on A-side.

A	Give Ireland Back to the Irish	Wings	2/25/72	Apple
			2/28/72	Apple
B	Give Ireland Back to the Irish (Instrumental)			

A	Mary Had a Little Lamb	Wings	5/12/72	Apple
B	Little Woman Love		5/29/72	Apple

A	Hi, Hi, Hi	Wings	12/4/72	Apple
B	C Moon		12/1/72	Apple

A	My Love	Paul McCartney	4/9/73	Apple
B	The Mess	and Wings	3/23/73	Apple

A	Live and Let Die	Paul McCartney	6/18/73	Apple
B	I Lie Around	and Wings	6/1/73	Apple

A-side produced by George Martin. B-side produced by McCartney.

A	Helen Wheels	Paul McCartney	11/12/73	Apple
B	Country Dreamer	and Wings	10/26/73	Apple

A	You're Sixteen	Ringo Starr	12/3/73	Apple
B	Devil Woman		2/8/74	Apple

McCartney plays kazoo on A-side.

A	Jet	Paul McCartney	2/18/74	Apple
B	Let Me Roll It	and Wings	2/15/74	Apple

A	Band on the Run	Paul McCartney	4/8/74	Apple
B	Nineteen Hundred and Eighty Five	and Wings	*	*

A	Liverpool Lou	The Scaffold	7/29/74	Warner Brothers
B	Ten Years After on Strawberry Jam		5/24/74	Warner Brothers

B-side written by Paul and Linda. Produced by McCartney.

A	God Bless California	Thornton, Fradkin,	6/17/74	ESP
B	Sometimes	Unger and The Big	*	*
		Band		

McCartney plays bass guitar and sings backing vocals on A-side.

A	Band on the Run	Paul McCartney	*	*
B	Zoo Gang	and Wings	6/28/74	Apple

A **4th of July**	John Christie	7/11/74	Capitol
B **Old Enough to Know**		6/28/74	Polydor
Better, Young Enough to			
Cry			

A-side written by Paul and Linda.

A **Let It All Fall Down**	James Taylor	7/22/74	Warner
B **Daddy's Baby**			Brothers

McCartney sings backing vocals
on A-side.

A **Leave It**	Mike McGear	10/28/74	Warner
B **Sweet Baby**		9/6/74	Brothers
			Warner
			Brothers

Produced by McCartney. A-side
written by McCartney; B-side
written by McCartney and
McGear.

A **Let's Love**	Peggy Lee	10/7/74	Atlantic
B **Always**		10/25/74	Warner
			Brothers

Produced by McCartney. A-side
written by McCartney.

A **Walking in the Park With**	The Country Hams	12/2/74	EMI
Eloise		10/18/74	Apple
B **Bridge Over the River**			
Suite			

Produced by McCartney. B-side
written by Paul and Linda.
Reissued in February 1982.

A **Junior's Farm**	Paul McCartney	11/4/74	Apple
B **Sally G**	and Wings	10/25/74	Apple

A **Farewell**	Rod Stewart	11/4/74	Mercury
B **Mine for Me**		1974	Mercury

B-side written by McCartney.
McCartney also sings backing
vocals.

A **Star Song**	Adam Faith	*	*
B **Maybe**		12/6/74	Warner
			Brothers

McCartney sings backing vocals
on A-side.

A **Sea Breezes**	Mike McGear	*	*
B **Given' Grease a Ride**		2/7/75	Warner
			Brothers

Produced by McCartney. B-side
written by McCartney and
McGear.

A **Listen to What the Man**	Wings	5/23/75	Capitol
Said		5/16/75	Parlophone
B **Love in Song**			

| A **Dance the Do** | Mike McGear | 7/4/75 | Warner |
| B **Norton** | | | Brothers |

Produced by McCartney. A- and B-sides written by McCartney and McGear. * *

| A **Letting go** | Wings | 9/25/75 | Capitol |
| B **You Gave Me the Answer** | | 9/5/75 | Parlophone |

| A **Medley: Venus and Mars/Rock Show** | Wings | 10/27/75 | Capitol |
| B **Magneto and Titanium Man** | | 11/28/75 | Parlophone |

| A **I Simply Love You** | Mike McGear | * | * |
| B **What Do We Really Know?** | | 11/14/75 | Warner Brothers |

Produced by McCartney. A-side written by McCartney and McGear. B-side written by McCartney.

| A **Silly Love Songs** | Wings | 4/1/76 | Capitol |
| B **Cook of the House** | | 4/30/76 | Parlophone |

| A **Let 'em In** | Wings | 6/28/76 | Capitol |
| B **Beware My Love** | | 7/23/76 | Parlophone |

| A **Medley: It's Easy/Listen to Me** | Denny Laine | 10/4/76 | Capitol |
| B **I'm Looking for Someone to Love** | | 9/3/76 | EMI |

Produced by McCartney.

| A **One of Those Days in England** | Roy Harper | * | * |
| B **Watford Gap** | | 2/4/77 | Harvest |

McCartney sings backing vocals on A-side.

| A **Maybe I'm Amazed** | Wings | 2/7/77 | Capitol |
| B **Soily** | | 2/4/77 | Parlophone |

| A **Moondreams** | Denny Laine | 5/31/77 | Capitol |
| B **Hearbeat** | | 4/15/77 | EMI |

Produced by McCartney.

| A **Seaside Woman** | Suzy and the Red | 5/31/77 | Epic |
| B **B-Side to Seaside** | Stripes | 1977 | Epic |

Linda McCartney and Wings working under an alias. Both sides written by McCartney. Also on 12" single. Re-released July 1980 by A&M in 7" and 12" formats, and in July 1986 by EMI in both formats.

A Uncle Albert/Admiral Halsey	Percy "Thrills"	1977	Zonophone
B Eat at Home	Thrillington	1977	EMI

McCartney working under an alias.

A Mull of Kintyre	Wings	11/14/77	Capitol
B Girls School		1977	Parlophone

A With a Little Luck	Wings	3/20/78	Capitol
B Backwards Traveller/ Cuff Link		1978	Parlophone

A I've Had Enough	Wings	1978	Capitol
B Deliver Your Children		6/12/78	Parlophone

A London Town	Wings	8/21/78	Capitol
B I'm Carrying		1978	Parlophone

A Goodnight Tonight	Wings	3/15/79	Columbia
B Daytime Nightime Suffering		1979	Parlophone

Also on 12" single.

A Old Siam Sir	Wings	*	*
B Spin It On		1979	Parlophone

A Getting Closer	Wings	6/5/79	Columbia
B Spin It On		*	*

A Getting Closer	Wings	*	*
B Baby's Request		6/79	Parlophone

A Arrow Through Me	Wings	8/14/79	Columbia
B Old Siam Sir		*	*

A Wonderful Christmastime	Wings	11/20/79	Columbia
B Rudolph the Red Nosed Reggae		1979	Parlophone

A Coming Up	Paul McCartney	4/15/80	Columbia
B Coming Up (Live at Glasgow)/Lunch Box-Odd Sox		4/80	Parlophone

A Waterfalls	Paul McCartney	7/22/80	Columbia
B Check My Machine		6/80	Parlophone

A Temporary Secretary	Paul McCartney	No Amercian release	
B Secret Friend		9/80	Parlophone

Issued as 12" single.

A Getting Closer	Wings	12/4/80	Columbia
B Goodnight Tonight		*	*

A My Love B Maybe I'm Amazed	Wings	12/4/80 *	Columbia *
A Uncle Albert/Admiral Halsey B Jet	Wings	12/4/80 *	Columbia *
A Band on the Run B Helen Wheels	Wings	12/4/80 *	Columbia *
A All Those Years Ago B Writing's on the Wall Paul and Linda, and Denny Laine sing backing vocals on A-side.	George Harrison	5/11/81 5/15/81	Dark Horse Dark Horse
A Ebony and Ivory B Rainclouds A-side with Stevie Wonder. Also on 12″ single.	Paul McCartney	4/2/82 3/82	Columbia Parlophone
A Take It Away B I'll Give You a Ring Also on 12″ single.	Paul McCartney	7/10/82 6/82	Columbia Parlophone
A Tug of War B Get It B-side with Carl Perkins.	Paul McCartney	10/2/82 9/82	Columbia Parlophone
A The Girl Is Mine B Can't Get Outta the Rain A-side duet with Michael Jackson.	Michael Jackson	10/2/82 10/82	Epic Epic
A Say Say Say B Ode to a Koala Bear Also released as 12″ single.	Paul McCartney	10/4/83 10/83	Columbia Parlophone
A Pipes of Peace B So Bad A- and B-sides reversed for U.S. release.	Paul McCartney	12/13/83 12/83	Columbia Parlophone
A On the Wings of a Nightingale B Asleep A-side written by Paul.	The Everly Brothers	1984 1984	Mercury Mercury
A No More Lonely Nights B Silly Love Songs Also released in 12″ single, picture disc, and dance mix versions.	Paul McCartney	10/2/84 1984	Columbia Parlophone
A No More Lonely Nights B No More Lonely Nights	Paul McCartney	10/2/84 *	Columbia *

A Do They Know It's Christmas?	Band Aid	10/84	*	
B *		1984	*	

McCartney is featured.

A We All Stand Together	Paul McCartney and	*	*	
B We All Stand Together (Humming Version)	the Frog Chorus	12/84	Parlophone	

Also on picture disc. Re-released in December 1985 in both formats.

A Spies Like Us	Paul McCartney	1985	Columbia
B My Carnival		11/13/85	Parlophone

Also released in 12" version with party mix and alternate mixes of "Spies Like Us." Also on picture disc.

A Press/It's Not True	Paul McCartney	7/6/86	Capitol
B Hanglide Press		1986	Parlophone

12" single.

A Stranglehold	Paul McCartney	10/29/86	Capitol
B Angry		*	*

A Press	Paul McCartney	7/6/86	Capitol
B It's Not True		7/86	Parlophone

"Press" and "Hanglide Press" also released in video versions.

A Pretty Little Head	Paul McCartney	*	*
B Write Away		10/86	Parlophone

Also issued as a 12" single with "Angry" added to B-side, and as a cassette single.

A Only Love Remains	Paul McCartney	1/6/87	Capitol
B Tough on a Tightrope		12/86	Parlophone

Also released in 12" version with "Talk More Talk" on the B-side.

A Once Upon a Long Ago	Paul McCartney	No American release	
B Back on My Feet		1987	Parlophone

B-side co-written with Declan MacManus (Evis Costello).

A My Brave Face	Paul McCartney	5/89	Capitol
B Flying to My Home		5/89	Parlophone

Also on 12" single. To date, this is the last McCartney single released in the U.S. on 7" vinyl. All subsequent releases are released only in cassette single and CD single formats.

A This One **B The First Stone** Also on 12" single.	Paul McCartney	7/89 7/89	Capitol Parlophone
A Figure of Eight **B Où Est Le Soleil** "Figure of Eight" released in the U.K. on 12" single in several different configurations. "Où Est le Soleil" released on 12" single with alternate mixes.	Paul McCartney	1989 1989	Capitol Parlophone
A Put It There **B Momma's Little Girl**	Paul McCartney	1990 1990	Capitol Parlophone
A Birthday **B Good Day Sunshine** Concert performances taken from the *Tripping the Live Fantastic* album. Released only as a cassette single in the U.S. Released in various formats in the U.K.	Paul McCartney	10/9/90 10/9/90	Capitol Parlophone
A All My Trials **B *** Released in the U.K. in various formats.	Paul McCartney	No American release 12/90	Parlophone

(CD single) **1. My Brave Face** **2. Flying to My Home** **3. I'm Gonna Be A Wheel** **One Day** **4. Ain't That A Shame**	Paul McCartney	5/89 * * *	Capitol * * *
A This One **B The First Stone** *(Also on 12-inch Single)*	Paul McCartney	7/89 *	Capitol Parlophone
(CD Single) **1. This One** **2. The First Stone** **3. I Wanna Cry** **4. I'm In Love Again**	Paul McCartney	7/89 * * *	Capitol * * *
(12-inch Single) **A This One** **The First Stone** **B Good Sign**	Paul McCartney	7/89 * *	Capitol * *
A Figure of Eight **B Où Est Le Soleil**	Paul McCartney	11/89 *	Capitol *
A Birthday **B Good Day Sunshine**	Paul McCartney	10/9/90 10/9/90	Capitol Parlophone

Concert performances taken
from "*Tripping the Live Fantasy*"
album. Released only as a cassette
single in the U.S. and in various
formats in the U.K.

(*CD Single*)
1. **Save the Child**   Paul McCartney   9/91   Capitol
2. **The Drinking Song**   *   *

(*CD Single*)
A **Hope of Deliverance**   Paul McCartney   1/93   Capitol
B **Long Leather Coat**   *   *

(*CD Single*)
1. **Hope of Deliverance** Paul McCartney   3/93   Capitol
2. **Big Boys Bickering**   *   *
3. **Long Leather Coat**   *   *
4. **Kicked Around No More**   *   *

(*CD Single*)
1. **Off the Ground**   Paul McCartney   3/93   Capitol
2. **Cosmically Conscious**   *   *
3. **Style Style**   *   *
4. **Sweet Sweet Memories**   *   *
5. **Soggy Noodle**   *   *

(*CD Single*)
1. **Biker Like an Icon**   Paul McCartney   9/93   Capitol
2. **Midnight Special**   *   *
3. **Things We Said Today**   *   *
4. **Biker Live**   *   *

A **Biker Like an Icon**   Paul McCartney   9/93   Capitol
B **Biker Live**   *   *

Promotional Releases

Many of Paul McCartney's works have been issued strictly as promotional releases. Most of these have had the same song on both the A- and B-sides.

Title	Date	Label
Give Ireland Back to the Irish	1972	Apple
Country Dreamer	1973	Apple
Helen Wheels	1973	Apple
Jet	1974	Apple
Junior's Farm	1974	Apple
Sally G	1974	Apple
Walking in the Park with Eloise	1974	EMI
Venus and Mars	1975	Capitol
Letting Go	1975	Capitol
Silly Love Songs	1975	Capitol
Maybe I'm Amazed	1975	Capitol
Seaside Woman	1977	EPIC
I've Had Enough	1978	Capitol
London Town	1978	Capitol
With a Little Luck	1978	Capitol
Getting Closer	1979	Columbia
Wonderful Christmastime	1979	Columbia
Goodnight Tonight	1980	Columbia
Waterfalls	1980	Columbia
Ebony and Ivory	1982	Columbia
Take It Away	1982	Columbia
The Girl Is Mine	1982	EPIC
Tug of War	1982	Columbia
Say Say Say	1983	Columbia
So Bad	1983	Columbia
Spies Like Us	1985	Capitol
Angry	1986	Capitol
Press	1986	Capitol
Pretty Little Head	1986	Capitol
Stranglehold	1986	Capitol
Let It Be	1987	Profile
Only Love Remains	1987	Capitol
Band on the Run	(release date unknown)	Apple
Let 'em In	(release date unknown)	Capitol

Paul McCartney Bootlegs

Title	Label
An Afternoon With Paul McCartney 1979 NBC Radio interview.	Ram
Band on the Run—Open End Interview with Wings to promote LP.	CO
Brung to Ewe By Copy of the *Ram* promotional disc.	Tobe Mile
Brung to Ewe By Yet another boot of the *Ram* promo.	SPRO
Can You Please Crawl Out Your Window All songs by Jimi Hendrix. Side one, cut six: Paul McCartney interview.	Jimi 1
Cold Cuts Wings oddities originally intended for "official" release by McCartney.	Club Sandwich
"Coming Up" to No. 1 1980 radio show.	Ram
Complaint to the Queen Material from *Back to the Egg* as well as other Wings-era cuts.	Maisie
Did We Meet Somewhere Before? Single from the film *Rock and Roll High School*.	Ram
Eggs Up More *Back to the Egg* fare.	Cage
Goodnight America 1976 ABC-TV broadcast with Geraldo Rivera.	Ram
Hot Hits and Cold Cuts Similar to the 1986 *Cold Cuts* bootleg.	*
James Paul McCartney From the TV special, 1973.	Berkeley
Jet 1980 radio show.	Ram
John Lennon/Paul McCartney—Ann Arbour & Now Hear This Cut five from the *Ram* promotion.	CBM/King Kong

Long Tall Sally Single; A-side by Paul McCartney and Wings.	Heavy
Love Is Strange Single.	Original Rock
Maybe I'm Amazed/Hi Hi Hi Single—original recording with comments by recording engineer Alan Parsons.	Ram
McCartney Cold Cuts Presumed to be originals.	KO
McCartney Hit Again Packaged to look like a "greatest hits" LP.	Capitol STAX
McCartney London Town 1978 BBC broadcast.	Ram
McCartney Show 1979 radio show single.	Ram
My Dark Hour/God Bless California Single—Paul plays on both sides.	Ram
My Love From the 1973 TV special "James Paul McCartney."	Berkeley
Nashville Diary EP—outtakes from the 1975 Nashville sessions.	Pro
Open-Ended Interview	CO
Oriental Nightfish Various live performances, TV special cuts, etc.	HAR
Oriental Nightfish, Part 2 Cuts from Germany, 1972.	PARX 2
Plastic Macs Coming Up Single from the promotional film for "Coming Up."	Ram
Raving On Outtakes from *McCartney II*.	Club Sandwich
Rupert the Bear Soundtrack Soundtrack for the animated film short.	*
Sunshine Superman/The Melvyn Bragg Interview An interview with Paul McCartney and Donovan.	CX
20/20 Eyesight 1979 TV interview with Geraldo Rivera.	Ram

Walking in the Park With Eloise/Bridge on the River Suite	S45

1974 picture disc of the record by The Country Hams.

War and Peace	Instant Analysis

Obscure gems from the *Tug of War* and *Pipes of Peace* sessions.

Wing' Greatest Hits	Ram

Single; sixty-second TV and radio commercial for *Wings' Greatest*.

Wings—I've Had Enough	Ram

Single; sixty-second commercial for "I've Had Enough."

Wings Over the World	WOW

From the TV special.

Wings Wild Life	Unknown

Same as original.

Wonderful Christmastime	Ryde 5226

1979 single recorded live in Brighton, England.

Yesterday and Tomorrow	Ram

1979 NBC-TV "Tomorrow" show with Tom Snyder.

There are, of course, numerous additional bootlegs chronicling McCartney's many live perfomances with Wings from 1972–79 (most of them taken from the 1975–76 Wings Over America tour) as well as a host of newer releases currently surfacing from the 1989–90 Paul McCartney World Tour. Due to space limitations, they have not been listed here.

Paul McCartney
Bootleg CDs of the Nineties

Title	Catalogue Number
Music Master	FSC007
Live Rarities	SL87042
This One	PPL514
Imagine in Liverpool	RPCD1025
Still Off the Ground	FR10
The Magical US Tour	DP002/003
The Elstree Tapes	RSCD15
Cottonfields	GEMA2325
Highlights Frankfurt	GEMA2325
Magical Mystery Tokio	PLRCD9406
Get Back to Glasgow	MCA1001-1/2
Venus and Mars Outtakes Are Alright Tonight	NP1906-1/2
All the Rest	1963-88JC
Hot Hits Cold Cuts	SP-12
Hot Hits Cold Cuts (Second Mix)	LP2337
Buddies on Holly Days	LP2323 2
Back in the USSR	RT787-2
Deliverance Now	RS9318
Merci Bercy!	GC001/2
Mamunia	001 Perth 1975
Paul Is Vision	PIV 002/003
Wings: Welcome-Canceled	*
What a Mean Fiddler	MIK014/15
By Invitation Only	IU9301
Junior's Farm	RSCCD023
Little Woman Love	RSCCD093
Live Tonight	CC340-41
Working Holiday	PMC-01
Over Seattle	XXCD15
Sayonara Mr. Paul	LSCD51550
Hey Tokyo!	KTS250
Wings Over America II	DS94J056/7
Liverpool Live!	ARC-011-50CD
Live in Venezia	FU205/2
Paul McCartney Destroys Anaheim	SLICK-O 100-200
The Lost McCartney Album	GTF-222CD-A/B
DeLIVErance	*
The Animated Film Soundtracks	ML9634
A Dream Apart	BIG028
Out in the Crowd	NK005/006
Eggs Up	*
Rock and Roll	CD043

Deleted Gems and Live Treasures	CD010
Rude Studio Demos	CD080
It's Now or Never (The Complete Russian Sessions)	CD3013
The Lost McCartney Album	KSK-7120
I Am Your Singer	LLRCD087
Condor 1963: Hot Hits-Cold Cuts	*
Live in Paris 1989 (Vol. 1 & 2)	DP002/003
Goodbye America 1993	PSCD1272
The Soundcheck 1993	SCR001
Good-Bye America 1993	LSCD51272

MASTER OF ORANGE RECORDS
(Japanese label)

McCartney-Venus & Mars Unknown Mixes	MOO-00003
McCartney-Great Lost Takal Master (2CD)	MOO-10004
McCartney-Venus and Mars-Paul's Rough Sketch	MOO-10008
Various-Paul's Work on Apple Singles	MOO-10009

MISTRAL MUSIC

London Town Roughs and Demos	MM9105
Wings Over Switzerland	MM9110/11
A Toot and a Snore 1974	MM9225
The Piano Tape	MM9231
Plugged and Unplugged	MM0234

PRESS CONFERENCES

The 1993 Docklands Press Conference	*
Press Conference Madrid and Los Angeles	*
Press Conferences Rome and London 1989	*
Interview Picture Disc Limited Edition	BAK2003

ISSUED IN AUSTRALIA[1]

Paul McCartney Back in the USA (Vol. 1)	BAN-029-A
Paul McCartney Back in the USA (Vol. 2)	BAN-029-B
Paul McCartney Back in the USA (Vol. 3)	BAN-029-C
Paul McCartney-Greatest Hits Live	CHER-073-A
Live Vol. 1	JOK-038-A
Paul McCartney-Live (Vol. 1)	JOK-0430-A
Paul McCartney Live "Unapproved"	MOJO032
Macca Does Melbourne	RH006/7
Paul McCartney Live (Vol. 1)	SW4
Paul McCartney Live (Vol. 2)	SW88

[1]These Australian issues were apparently quite legitimate releases when first manufactured and are included here only for the sake of completeness.

A Note on Sources

Throughout the long process of researching and then writing this book I have been fortunate in enlisting the participation of many of the people closest to Paul McCartney over the last forty-odd years. Among them several asked not to be identified by name for reasons best known to themselves, a request which I have honored without exception. For the most part, however, there was no such intrepidation and I therefore acknowledge their kindness in having confided in me their memories of not only Paul and Linda McCartney, but also the Beatles and Wings and the marvelously heady, bygone days that spawned them.

In Liverpool: Julia Baird, Mona Best, Norman Birch, Paddy Delaney, Clive Epstein, Joe Flannery, Leila Harvey, Sam Leach, Charlie Lennon, Gerry Marsden, Mike McCartney, Rowena McCartney, "Father" Tom McKenzie, Eddie Porter, Allan Williams, Bob Wooler, Georgie Wood.

In London: Dahanjaya Dasa, Su Gold, Helen Grant, Mary Hopkin, Denny Laine, Herbo Laine, Hayley Mills, Chrissie Hynde, Peter O'Donaghue, Earl Okin, "Legs" Larry Smith, Krissy Wood.

In North America: Pete Bennett, Peter Brown, Donovan, Horst Fasher, Richie Havens, Heidi Jo Hines, Laine Hines, Jennifer Holly, Steve Holly, Laurence Juber, Jo Jo Laine, Julian Lennon, Sean Lennon, Yoko Ono, Charles F. Rosenay!!!, Alistair Taylor, Derek Taylor.

And also Paul McCartney, himself responding to an extensive list of my questions at MPL in London, 1986.

Photo Credits

Frontispiece photo: Jasmine and Peach Archive

Photo Section One

Page 1   top: Deliberate Alchemy Archives
center: Skyboot Productions Ltd.
bottom: Deliberate Alchemy Archives

Page 2:   Pink Shoes Café

Page 3:   top left: Pink Shoes Café
right: My Perna Productions Inc.
center: Deliberate Alchemy Archives
botton: Deliberate Alchemy Archives

Page 4:   top: Deliberate Alchemy Archives
bottom left: Pink Shoes Café
bottom right: Pink Shoes Café

Page 5   top left: Jasmine and Peach Archives
top right: Deliberate Alchemy Archives
bottom left: Pink Shoes Café
bottom right: Pink Shoes Café

Page 6   Deliberate Alchemy Archives

Page 7   Deliberate Alchemy Archives

Page 8   top: Deliberate Alchemy Archives
bottom: Jasmine and Peach Archives

Page 9   top: Deliberate Alchemy Archives
bottom: Deliberate Alchemy Archives

Page 10   top left: Geoffrey Giuliano Collection
top right: Pink Shoes Café
bottom: Lunatic Fringe Images

Page 11   top: Pink Shoes Café
bottom: Pink Shoes Café

Page 12   Butter Thief Productions Ltd.

Page 13   Pink Shoes Café

Page 14   top: Pink Shoes Café
center: Pink Shoes Café
bottom: Pink Shoes Café

Page 15   top: Deliberate Alchemy Archives
center left: Deliberate Alchemy Archives
center right: Deliberate Alchemy Archives
bottom: Deliberate Alchemy Archives

Page 16   top: Pink Shoes Café
bottom: Skyboot Productions Ltd.

Photo Section Two

Page 1   top: Deliberate Alchemy Archives
bottom: Deliberate Alchemy Archives

Page 2   top: Top of the Pops
bottom: Pink Shoes Café

Page 3   top left: Cinnamon Pussy Productions Ltd.
top right: Cinnamon Pussy Productions Ltd.
center: Cinnamon Pussy Productions Ltd.
bottom left: Cinnamon Pussy Productions Ltd.
bottom right: Cinnamon Pussy Productions Ltd.

Page 4   top: Jasmine and Peach Archives
bottom: Cinnamon Pussy Productions Ltd.

Page 5   top: Deliberate Alchemy Archives
bottom: Deliberate Alchemy Archives

Page 6   top left: Jasmine and Peach Archives
top right: Jasmine and Peach Archives
center: Cinnamon Pussy Productions Ltd.
bottom left: Cinnamon Pussy Productions Ltd.
bottom right: Cinnamon Pussy Productions Ltd.

Page 7   Cinnamon Pussy Productions Ltd.

Page 8   top: Cinnamon Pussy Productions Ltd.
center: Cinnamon Pussy Productions Ltd.
center right: Deliberate Alchemy Archives
bottom left: Skyboot Productions Ltd.

Page 9   top: Deliberate Alchemy Archives
center: Deliberate Alchemy Archives
bottom: Cinnamon Pussy Productions Ltd.

Page 10   top left: Cinnamon Pussy Productions Ltd.
top right: Cinnamon Pussy Productions Ltd.
bottom left: Cinnamon Pussy Productions Ltd.
bottom right: Cinnamon Pussy Productions Ltd.

Page 11   top: Cinnamon Pussy Productions Ltd.
center: Pink Shoes Café
bottom: Skyboot Productions Ltd.

Page 12   Square Circle Productions

Page 13   top left: Pink Shoes Café
top right: Cinnamon Pussy Productions Ltd.
bottom: Jasmine and Peach Archives

Page 14   top: Deliberate Alchemy Archives
center: Cinnamon Pussy Productions Ltd.
bottom: Cinnamon Pussy Productions Ltd.

Page 15   top left: Cinnamon Pussy Productions Ltd.
top right: Steve Holly
bottom left: Geoffrey Giuliano Collection
bottom right: Dennis C. Enser

Page 16   top: Charles F. Rosenay!!!
bottom: Charles F. Rosenay!!!

Photo Section Three

Page 1   all photos: Tulsi Devi Archives
Page 2   all photos: Tiny Avatar Photos
Page 3   all photos: Tiny Avatar Photos
Page 4   all photos: Shrinking Planet Press
Page 5   all photos: Shrinking Planet Press
Page 6   all photos: Deliberate Alchemy Archives
Page 7   all photos: Deliberate Alchemy Archives
Page 8   all photos: Possibly An Armchair Productions
Page 9   all photos: Possibly An Armchair Productions
Page 10   all photos: Geoffrey Giuliano Collection
Page 11   top left: Cool Pope Productions
               top right: Sesa Giuliano
               bottom right: Reichadelic Images
Page 12   all photos: Guilded Cage Archives
Page 13   top: Guilded Cage Archives
               bottom: Sesa Giuliano
Page 14   all photos: Sesa Giuliano
Page 15   top left: Sesa Giuliano
               top right: Reichadelic Images
               bottom right: Good Day Sunshine
Page 16   Tulsi Devi Archieves

Bibliography

Baird, Julia, and Geoffrey Giuliano. *John Lennon, My Brother.* New York: Henry Holt and Company, 1988.

Barnes, Richard. *The Who: Maximum R&B.* New York: St. Martin's Press, 1982.

Bedford, Carol. *Waiting for the Beatles.* London: Blandford Press, 1984.

Best, Pete, and Patrick Doncaster. *Beatle! The Pete Best Story.* London: Plexus Publisher, 1985.

Blake, John. *All You Needed Was Love.* New York: G.P. Putnam's Sons (Perigee Books), 1981.

Brown, Peter, and Steven Gaines. *The Love You Make: An Insider's Story of the Beatles.* New York: McGraw-Hill Book Company, 1983.

Castleman, Harry, and Walter J. Podrazik. *All Together Now.* New York: Ballantine Books, 1975.

Coleman, Ray. *Lennon.* New York: McGraw-Hill Book Company, 1984.

———. *The Man Who Made the Beatles.* New York: McGraw-Hill Book Company, 1989.

Davies, Hunter. *The Beatles: The Authorized Biography.* New York: McGraw-Hill Book Company, 1968.

DiLello, Richard. *The Longest Cocktail Party.* Chicago: Playboy Press, 1972.

Friede, Goldie, Robin Titone, and Sue Weiner. *The Beatles A to Z.* New York: Methuen, 1980.

Fulpen, H. V. *The Beatles: An Illustrated Diary.* London: Plexus Publisher, 1982.

Gambaccini, Paul. *Paul McCartney: In His Own Words.* New York and London: Flash Books, 1976.

Gelly, David. *The Facts About a Pop Group, Featuring Wings.* London: G. Whizzard Andre Deutsch, 1976.

Giuliano, Geoffrey. *The Beatles: A Celebration.* New York: St. Martin's Press, 1986.

———. Dark Horse: *The Private Life of George Harrison.* New York: Dutton, 1990.

Goldman, Albert. *The Lives of John Lennon*. New York: William Morrow and Company, 1988.

Harry, Bill. *The Beatles Who's Who*. New York: Delilah Books, 1982.

_____. *The McCartney File*. London: Virgin Books, 1986.

Jasper, Tony. *Paul McCartney and Wings*. New Jersey: Chartwell Books, 1977.

Leigh, Spencer, and Pete Frame. *Let's Go Down to the Cavern*. London: Vermilion & Co., 1984.

Lennon, Cynthia. *A Twist of Lennon*. London: W. H. Allen & Co. (Star Books), 1978.

Lewisohn, Mark. *The Beatles Live!* New York: Henry Holt and Company, 1986.

_____. *The Beatles Recording Sessions*. New York: Harmony Books, 1988.

_____. *The Beatles: 25 Years in the Life*. London: Sidgwick & Jackson, 1987.

Logan, Nick, and Bob Woffinden. *The Illustrated Encyclopedia of Rock*. New York: Harmony Books, 1977.

McCartney, Linda, and Peter Cox. *Linda McCartney's Home Cooking*. London: Bloomsbury, 1989.

McCartney, Mike. *Mike Mac's White and Blacks*. London: Aurum Press, 1986.

_____. *Thank U Very Much: Mike McCartney's Family Album*. Liverpool: Here and Now Publishing, 1984.

McCartney, Paul. *Give My Regards to Broadstreet*. MPL Communications, 1984.

Miles. *Beatles: In Their Own Words*. New York/London: Omnibus Press, 1978.

_____. *John Lennon: In His Own Words*. New York/London: Quick Fox, 1981.

Norman, Philip. *Shout! The True Story of the Beatles*. London: Hamish Hamilton (Elm Tree Books), 1981.

Pascall, Jeremy. *Paul McCartney & Wings*. London: Phoebus Publishing Company and BPC Publishing, 1977.

Russell, J. P. *The Beatles on Record*. New York: Charles Scribner's Sons, 1982.

Schultheiss, Tom. *The Beatles: A Day in the Life*. New York: Quick Fox, 1981.

Sheff, David. *The Playboy Interviews with John Lennon & Yoko Ono*. New York: Playboy Press, 1980–1.

Shotton, Pete, and Nicholas Schaffner. *John Lennon in My Life*. New York: Stein and Day, 1983.

Southall, Brian. *Abbey Road*. Wellingborough, U.K.: Patrick Stephens, 1982.

Taylor, Derek. *As Time Goes By*. San Francisco: Straight Arrow Books, 1973.

———. *It Was Twenty Years Ago Today*. New York: Simon & Schuster (Fireside Books), 1987.

Wenner, Jann. *Lennon Remembers*. San Francisco: Straight Arrow Books 1971.

Williams, Allan, and William Marshall. *The Man Who Gave the Beatles Away*. New York: Macmillan Publishing Co. 1975.

Woffinden, Bob. *The Beatles Apart*. London and New York: Proteus Books, 1981.

Index